中华地域文化关键词 丛书

冀东文化关键词

KEY CONCEPTS IN JIDONG CULTURE

汉英对照

秦学武
褚嘉君 等 著
译

外语教学与研究出版社
FOREIGN LANGUAGE TEACHING AND RESEARCH PRESS
北京 BEIJING

图书在版编目 (CIP) 数据

冀东文化关键词：汉英对照 / 秦学武等著；褚嘉君译. —— 北京：外语教学与研究出版社，2022.12
（"中华地域文化关键词"丛书）
ISBN 978-7-5213-4169-0

Ⅰ. ①冀… Ⅱ. ①秦… ②褚… Ⅲ. ①地方文化－河北－通俗读物－汉、英 Ⅳ. ①G127.22-49

中国版本图书馆 CIP 数据核字 (2022) 第 253967 号

地图审图号：冀 S【2020】030 号，冀 S（2021）009 号

出 版 人	王　芳
项目策划	徐晓丹
责任编辑	赵璞玉
责任校对	王　琳
封面设计	彩奇风
版式设计	姚雅雯
出版发行	外语教学与研究出版社
社　　址	北京市西三环北路 19 号（100089）
网　　址	https://www.fltrp.com
印　　刷	北京捷迅佳彩印刷有限公司
开　　本	710×1000　1/16
印　　张	33.5
版　　次	2023 年 6 月第 1 版　2023 年 6 月第 1 次印刷
书　　号	ISBN 978-7-5213-4169-0
定　　价	108.00 元

如有图书采购需求，图书内容或印刷装订等问题，侵权、盗版书籍等线索，请拨打以下电话或关注官方服务号：
客服电话：400 898 7008
官方服务号：微信搜索并关注公众号"外研社官方服务号"
外研社购书网址：https://fltrp.tmall.com

物料号：341690001

河北省高等学校人文社会科学重点研究基地立项资助

河北省高等学校人文社会科学重点研究基地
冀东文化研究中心学术委员会

一、主任委员

李金善（教授，博士生导师，原河北大学副校长）

二、委员

郑振峰（教授，博士生导师，河北师范大学副校长）

孙继民（教授，博士生导师，原河北省社会科学院副院长）

郭宝亮（教授，博士生导师，河北省作家协会副主席）

薛顺平（主任记者，硕士生导师，中国孤竹文化研究中心主任）

《冀东文化关键词》编委会

主　任：秦学武

成　员：吴子国　王杰彦　李文钢　赵桂华　王芳　王姝娟
　　　　罗学锋　王海军　齐甲子

序 Preface

地域文化作为中华优秀传统文化的重要组成部分，由一定地域环境下的人类活动而产生，具有独特的生态环境、浓郁的生活气息、真挚的思想感情和深厚的人文底蕴，是我国宝贵的文化遗产。地域文化研究在当今社会具有重大意义，既传承和弘扬了传统文化，又有利于扩大中国文化的国际影响力。

地处燕山—长城文化带的冀东地区，包括河北省东北部的唐山、承德、秦皇岛三市，既是中原农耕文化与草原游牧文化的折冲交流带，也是关内汉族与东北少数民族的融合发展带。在这里，孕育了生动、多元的民族文化。

从历史的角度来说，冀东地区自商周时期商汤分封孤竹国至今，已有3600余年的区域发展史。冀东文化随着时代的变迁有所衍变，最终又在历史传统的凝聚力下趋于稳定。作为农耕文明向着游牧文明的过渡地区，冀东地区及其周边活动着大量的游牧民族，他们在悠久的历史中与汉民族交往、融合、相互学习，形成了慷慨悲歌、好气任侠的地域个性，留下了满是岁月沧桑的历史遗迹，也创作出了丰富的文学作品。从文化底蕴的角度来说，这片土地上，产生了中国传统儒家文化的重要源头孤竹文化，揭开了明清易代的历史画卷，留下了早期革命者的建党足迹，也镌刻了中华民族抗日图存的时代篇章。从文化样态的角度来说，冀东古代文化与现代文化并存，自然景观与人文景观共生，各种文化交互共融，丰富多彩，可谓是一块宝地。

秦学武教授领衔的冀东文化研究团队聚焦冀东文化的研究和传播，他们看到了冀东文化研究的重要意义，也发现学界对此的系统研究和深入挖掘尚且不足，故产生了撰写该书之念，其创获及成就主要表现在三个方面。

其一，中英对照，图文并茂，促进冀东文化当代化、国际化发展。

为促进中外文化交流互鉴、对外推广中国文化，该书采用了图文并茂、中英文对照的形式，如此既可以让读者在阅读文字的同时，增加更加真实直观的视觉体验，也使该书兼具不同语言的魅力，拓宽传播范围。但同时，为了精确、生动地传达书中之意，要将《冀东文化关键词》中的语句，尤其是涉及中国传统文化部分的内容准确地翻译传递给读者，对于译者来说，无疑是一大挑战。

所幸，该书很好地完成了这一应对。书中有着大量的名称，为方便读者理解，都采取了音译和意译相结合的方式，而非简单的直接音译。如在美食方面，"水豆腐"翻译成 soft bean curd，"缸炉烧饼"翻译成 vat-baked flatbread，"饹馇"翻译成 Gezha pancake，既形容出了口感，又用生动易懂的方式表明了食物种类；在传统民俗方面，"抡花"翻译成 Lunhua (spark swinging)，"背杆"翻译成 pole carrying，"布糊画"翻译成 cloth painting，形象直观，活灵活现。这样的翻译，最大限度地保留了中文名字的特殊含义，突显了中国传统文化的意象。

书中还有诸多文言文、诗词语句的英文翻译。在关于"潘家口"这一文化景观的介绍中，中文引用了戎昱《塞下曲》："自有卢龙塞，烟尘飞至今。"英文部分进行了准确而不失优美的翻译："Ever since the erection of Lulong Pass, smoke and dust have been rising high."。全书引经据典，多运用文言文、诗词、俚语进行中文写作，此类翻译还有很多。译者没有死板地逐字对译，但足以在中英文转换的过程中，令读者体悟到诗句中所希望表达出来的意蕴与内涵，传达出中国传统文化的情怀之美。

其二，由点及面，宏微观相结合，聚焦经典事项。

冀东文化源远流长，内容广博，在此之前，学界从未有人对冀东文化进行过系统化的整理。要将如此丰富的内容清晰全面地呈现出来并非易事，也不是一时之功。因此，该书别开生面地采用"关键词"体例，采用由点及面、宏微观相结合的方式，对研究对象进行了划分。这在学界尚属首次，具有开拓意义。

在宏观上，该书将冀东文化研究对象划分为古史文化、长城文化、旅游文化、民俗文化、饮食文化、冀东文学、产业文化、时代文化和生态文明9个领域。从大空间、系统化的角度，把握住了冀东文化"厚、雅、资、趣、美"的特征。

厚，所指的就是深厚的历史积淀。该书牢牢把握住冀东文化的这一特征，并围绕其进行深入发掘。如第一章"古史文化"，细致地以9个关键词介绍了冀东地区的古国及各国历史，又以7个关键词阐述了冀东地区的重要考古发现；第二章"长城文化"则以长城为中心，从长城的各处景观、长城保护以及有关长城的故事传说三个角度向读者介绍了长城一带的深厚历史底蕴；第三章"旅游文化"中所介绍的承德避暑山庄、卢龙永平古城等名胜古迹，是在历代的历史文化积淀之下造就而成的；甚至看似与历史无关的第九章"生态文明"中所提到的水利工程、生态修复和地质公园，都从侧面凸显出了冀东历史发展的痕迹。

雅，代表着冀东一带的文学底蕴。在该书的第六章"冀东文学"中，分时代介绍了冀东地区的作家和诗人，并且十分详尽地介绍了每一位人物的生平和代表作品，这些杰出的历史文化名人以及他们的作品，都是冀东地区闪耀的文化星光，灼照在中华优秀传统文化的历史星空。

资，所指的则是冀东地区的资源储备及经济发展状况，该书第七章"产业文化"中所介绍的工业文化、农业文化和商业文化以及第九章"生态文明"中提到的水利工程，都足以体现出冀东地区资源相济，基础雄厚，是发展要素资源富集、发展潜力巨大的地区。如书中提到的秦皇岛港、唐山曹妃甸港、沧州黄骅港三个港区的发展格局，制造出中国第一座钢桥滦河大桥的中铁山桥,以及被誉为"中国玻璃工业的摇篮"的中国耀华玻璃集团等,都创造出了令人瞩目的经济效益,也引领着冀东的经济发展方向。

趣,代表着冀东地区的风土人情。在第三章"旅游文化"、第四章"民俗文化"、第五章"饮食文化"中,41个关键词全面介绍了在冀东游览、观景、寻味的各处胜地,并配以图片,妙趣横生,更加提高了读者阅读的兴趣和实地游览体验的兴趣。

美,则指这片土地所独有的灵秀景观。第三章"旅游文化"中介绍的名胜古迹与自然风光,冀东文人才子的文学作品中对于美景的歌颂,都展现出了一幅幅当地的美丽画卷。

该书从宏观上把握住了"厚、雅、资、趣、美"的五大特征,又从微观上具体到每一处景观、每一家产业、每一名人物,由点及面,结丝成网,共同交织成了全面、立体的冀东文化特色。

其三,学海钩沉,实地走访,对冀东文化进行深入挖掘与客观认识。

该书涉及范围广泛,内容丰富,具体到每一个关键词,冀东文化团队都以专业的视角,严谨的态度进行对待,做好冀东文化的挖掘、整理和推广工作。对写作过程中的难点和分歧点,或学海钩沉、追根究底,或踏查走访、寻找一手资料,不懈进行攻克,通过对探查结果的比较、勘正,努力克服地域文化研究中地方保护的偏狭,力求得出公允、持平的判断。兹略举几点表现:

首先,团队对该书所涉及的134个关键词都进行了细致的考察和调研,全面列举出其中涉及的各种观点。

对于有争议的部分,书中往往在正文里介绍一种观点,又在注释部分将其他的说法补充完整,以供读者参考。如书中正文里提到蓟镇东起山海关、西到居庸关南的镇边城,下面的注释又补充另一说,指出蓟镇长城又或是东起山海关,西到黄花镇。介绍山海关著名的"天下第一关"匾额时,正文中所写的匾额书写人是明成化八年的进士萧显,注释中补充了另外一种可能性,即此匾为明嘉靖年间武英阁大学士严嵩所题。

其次,宣扬民俗文化,把握地方特色。

民俗文化具有社会性,经常通过人与人的交流和接触,在时间上传承,在空间中播布。它们既与生活贴近,又能给人一种新奇感,是令人对一个地域产生兴趣的最直观因素。部分民俗文化不容易通过书籍、网络等工具进行传导,且易有讹误之处,往往需要实地探访才能获得最准确的第一手资料。

该书专门在第四章中从传统音乐、传统舞蹈、传统戏曲、传统体育、传统美术、节庆民俗6个方面以16个关键词介绍了冀东各处的民俗,并且在介绍过程中充分保留了原有的传统特色。介绍冀东民歌时,对其独有的"润腔""老呔话"的发音方法、声调音调都有所形容;猴打棒、布糊画、珍珠球等小范围传播的民俗文化,作者也找到了相关资料。这对非物质文化遗产的传承起到了重要作用。

最后,融合专业知识,全面关联各个学科。

该书涉及历史、地理、经济、文学、政治等各个方面的知识内容,是一部综合性著作。团队一方面将各个学科知识融会贯通,另一方面以专业的眼光完成各部分内容,体现出了认真严谨的创作态度。

如在对兴隆雾灵山的介绍中,书中提到雾灵山属暖温带湿润大陆季风区,地处华北、东北和内蒙古三大植被区系交汇区,属暖温带落叶阔叶林向温带针阔混交林的过渡地带,其天然植被和野生物种资源都十分丰富,就属于地理学科方面的知识;提到祖籍为河北丰润的曹雪芹时,也涉及其作品《红楼梦》的大致内容和艺术特色,又是文学方面的内容;在介绍平泉特产的御膳糖饼时,甚至提到了糖饼的具体制作工艺是需按1斤面粉加5两白油的比例和成油面,再按1斤面粉加6两温水的比例和成水面。可谓面面俱到,丰富详尽。

总而言之,《冀东文化关键词》一书详尽而严谨地对冀东地区的各类文化特征进行了介绍,并采用了学界少有之新方法,具有十分重要的创新意义。该书图文并茂，中英对照，文辞优美，生动具体，读来令人获益匪浅，是全面了解冀东文化的一部难得的重要著作。

是为序。

李金善

2022 年 12 月 10 日

Regional cultures, as an important part of traditional Chinese culture, are created out of people's activities in certain geographic regions. As a valuable cultural heritage, each regional culture features its own unique ecological environment, strong flavor of life, sincere thoughts and sentiments, and profound cultural foundation. The study of regional cultures is of great significance in today's society. It not only inherits and carries forward the traditional culture, but also helps expand China's influence in the world.

Located in the Yan Mountains-Great Wall cultural belt, the Jidong region includes Tangshan, Chengde and Qinhuangdao in the northeast of Hebei Province. It is the place where the farming culture of the Central Plains and the nomadic culture of the grasslands meet, and where the Han people in the inner territories (south of the Great Wall) and the ethnic minority groups in the Northeast merge. The place has given rise to lively and diverse ethnic cultures.

From the perspective of history, the Jidong region has existed for more than 3,600 years since King Tang of Shang's enfeoffment of Guzhu. The culture in this region evolved in history and eventually stabilized over time. As a transitional area from agricultural civilization to nomadic civilization, Jidong and its surrounding areas had a vast amount of nomadic people. For a long time, they had been communicating, integrating and exchanging with the Han people, thus gradually forming their traits of gallantry and generousness, leaving behind many historical monuments, and creating a vast quantity of literary works. Jidong has profound cultural foundation. From the perspective of cultural deposits, the land was the cradle of Guzhu culture, from which the traditional Confucian culture originated. The place saw the dynasty change from Ming to Qing, the early revolutionaries' founding of the Communist Party of China, and the war to defend the nation against Japanese aggressors. From the perspective of cultural diversity, in Jidong, ancient and modern cultures merge, and natural and cultural landscapes coexist. Various cultures interact with each other, creating a rich cultural treasure.

Led by Professor Qin Xuewu, the Jidong Culture Team devote major efforts to studying and spreading Jidong culture. They realize that what they have been pursuing is significant, and recognize that the academic research on this topic is inadequate, so they came up with the idea of writing a book. The virtues and achievements of this book are mainly manifested in three aspects.

First, the Chinese texts are accompanied by vivid photos and translated into English, helping to modernize and internationalize Jidong culture.

In an effort to enhance cultural exchanges and promote Chinese culture, the book features abundant photos and bilingual texts, offering readers a visual, real-life experience, which is attractive to people both in China and abroad. For readers to have a precise, vivid understanding of the book, however, the ideas are supposed to be communicated precisely. *Key Concepts in Jidong Culture* includes a range of topics on traditional Chinese culture, and it is a big challenge for the translator to achieve accuracy, so that foreign readers can make sense of those topics.

Fortunately, the problems are solved successfully. The book includes a lot of names of things. For the convenience of understanding, the strategy is to combine homophonic translation with sense-for-sense translation, rather than solely rely on homophonic translation. Take the foods for example, *shuidoufu* (水豆腐) has been translated into soft bean curd, *ganglu shaobing* (缸炉烧饼) has been translated into vat-baked flatbread, and *gezha* (饹馇) has been translated into Gezha pancake. This strategy expresses the characteristics of those foods in a neat and accessible manner. The translation of traditional folk customs also has much to commend it. *Lunhua* (抡花), *beigan* (背杆) and *buhu hua* (布糊画) have been translated into Lunhua (spark swinging), pole carrying and cloth painting. The names depict the folk customs so lifelike that they actually stand before our eyes. The translator manages to capture the spirit of the terms, successfully establishing the conceptions of traditional Chinese culture.

The book also features a lot of classical Chinese writings and poems, and the translation is faithful and elegant. In the introduction of Panjiakou, "Frontier Song", a poem by Rong Yu, is quoted: "自有卢龙塞,烟尘飞至今." The translation is accurate without sacrificing elegance. It runs thus: "Ever since the erection of Lulong Pass, smoke and dust have been rising high." Literary allusions, classical Chinese writings, poems and idioms appear many times in the book, and the translation conveys their meanings successfully. The translator doesn't take the words literally; instead, he manages to help readers understand their connotations and appreciate the beauty of traditional Chinese culture.

Second, the examples cited in the book represent in microcosm the history of the place.

The brilliant Jidong culture has a long and extensive history. Before this book, however, the academic circle hadn't made any systematic study of it. Presenting the whole picture of Jidong is not an easy task, but a gradual process which cannot be accomplished in one move. Given this, the author adopts the novel style of "key concepts". By ingeniously delivering the macro narrative from a micro perspective, and putting the objects of study in different categories, the book has made a groundbreaking achievement first seen in the academic circle.

The book broadly divides the study of Jidong culture into nine categories: history and culture, the Great Wall culture, tourism culture, folk culture, food culture, Jidong literature, industrial culture, culture of the times, and ecological civilization. It reflects the five characteristics of Jidong culture—"*hou, ya, zi, qu, mei*"—in a wide scope and from a scientific point of view.

Hou, or profoundness, refers to the profound history of Jidong. The book is designed around the profoundness of Jidong culture and explores it in detail. Chapter I History and Culture presents 9 key concepts about the ancient states and 7 key concepts about the major archaeological findings in Jidong. Chapter II The Great Wall Culture gives readers an account of the profound history of the Great Wall and its surrounding areas, covering its scenic spots, preservation, and stories and legends. Chapter III Tourism Culture introduces Chengde Mountain Resort, Yongping Ancient City in Lulong and other places of interest, reflecting the historical and cultural accumulation of the past dynasties. Chapter IX Ecological Civilization includes water conservancy projects, ecological restoration and geopark, and the seemingly disparate topics actually highlight the historical development of Jidong.

Ya, or elegance, stands for the literary foundation of Jidong and its surrounding areas. In Chapter VI Jidong Literature, writers and poets at different times are introduced with a detailed account of their lives and masterpieces. Like the brilliant sun in the sky, these outstanding cultural figures are brightening up the traditional Chinese culture.

Zi, or resource, means the resource reserves and economic development of Jidong. Chapter VII Industrial Culture introduces its industry, agriculture and commerce, and Chapter IX Ecological Civilization gives an account of the various water conservancy projects, both showing that Jidong is endowed with rich natural resources and has enormous development potential. For example, we can read about the development pattern of Qinhuangdao Port, Tangshan Caofeidian Port and Cangzhou Huanghua Port; China Railway Shanhaiguan Bridge Group Co., Ltd.—the manufacturer of China's first steel bridge across the Luan River; and China Yaohua Glass Group Co., Ltd., which is reputed to be the "Cradle of China's Glass Industry". They have created remarkable economic benefits and fueled the economic development of Jidong.

Qu, or interest, characterizes the local customs of Jidong. Chapter III Tourism Culture, Chapter IV Folk Culture and Chapter V Food Culture include 41 key concepts. They give a comprehensive overview of the tourist attractions in Jidong for sightseeing and tasting delicacies. The photos possess some degree of interest and add a vivid charm to the book, offering readers an immersive experience.

Mei, or beauty, refers to the unique scenic beauty of this region. In Chapter III Tourism Culture, which introduces many places of interest and natural sceneries, and the literary works of local men of letters, a beautiful landscape painting is unfolded.

The book characterizes Jidong culture as "*hou, ya, zi, qu, mei*" from a macro perspective, and each scenic spot, company, individual, etc. represents in microcosm these characteristics as a whole. In this way, readers may get a comprehensive picture of Jidong culture.

Third, the authors are noted for their meticulous scholarship. They personally visited the places to investigate and learn more about Jidong culture.

The book is of wide scope and touches on many questions, and the Jidong Culture Team tended to every concept with a professional and rigorous attitude. They spared no effort to collect data, organize materials and promote Jidong culture. When they got stuck in the process of writing, the team members would strive to get it straight by visiting the places or obtaining the first-hand information. To tackle the problems, they compared and corrected the exploratory results, trying to get rid of the parochial narrowness in regional culture research and remain neutral when reaching a judgement. I'd like to mention a few instances.

First, the team carried out a close examination and investigation of the 134 key concepts in the book, and dealt fully with the viewpoints involved.

The book deals with the controversial issues by presenting a viewpoint in the text and adding other statements in the notes for the reference of readers. For example, while it says that the Garrison of Jizhou ranges from the Shanhai Pass in the east to the Zhenbian Town in the south of the Juyong Pass in the west, the note proposes another theory that the Jizhou section of the Great Wall ranges from the Shanhai Pass in the east to the Huanghua County in the west; while it says that the characters "Tian Xia Di Yi Guan" on the inscribed board of the Shanhai Pass were written by Xiao Xian, a *jinshi* scholar in the 8th year of Chenghua, the note proposes another theory that the characters were written by Yan Song, Grand Scholar of Wuying Hall in the years of Jiajing of Ming.

Second, the book aims to promote folk culture while preserving local characteristics.

Folk cultures possess a social nature, so they are often spread among communities and passed down over time through people-to-people exchanges. Close to real life while retaining a sense of novelty, they are the most direct instrument for arousing people's interest in a certain region. Some folk cultures are not easy to be spread through books or the Internet, and these means are liable to error. To obtain accurate, first-hand information, field visits are often required.

Chapter IV Folk Culture is dedicated to the folk culture of Jidong with 16 key concepts in six respects: traditional music, traditional dances, traditional opera, traditional sports, traditional arts, and festivals and folk customs. In introducing these concepts, it retains most of the traditional features, such as "*run qiang*" skills and the "Laotai dialect" unique to Jidong folk songs. We can also read about folk customs restricted to a small area, such as monkey dance, cloth painting and pearl ball. These efforts play an important role in keeping these intangible cultural heritages alive.

Last, the book integrates professional knowledge and links different disciplines comprehensively.

As a comprehensive work, the book covers a range of topics, such as history, geography, economy, literature and politics. It focuses on the universal relevance of various disciplines and offers professional opinions. The articles are compact and well organized.

When introducing Xinglong Wuling Mountain, the book mentions three important geographical features concerning its abundance of natural vegetation and wild species: 1) it lies in the humid warm temperate continental monsoon climate zone; 2) it is situated at the confluence of North China, Northeast China and Inner Mongolian vegetation regions; and 3) it is a transitional zone from warm temperate broadleaved deciduous forests to temperate mixed forests. When introducing Cao Xueqin, whose ancestral home was in Fengrun, Hebei, *Dream of the Red Chamber* and its artistic features are expounded from the perspective of literature. When introducing the Pingquan imperial sugar cake, the book says: "First, mix

500 grams of flour and 250 grams of white oil together to make an oiled dough. Then, add 300 grams of warm water to 500 grams of flour to make a watered dough." Such multifaceted and enriched contents are abundant in the book.

To sum up, *Key Concepts in Jidong Culture* has given a detailed and rigorous account of various cultural characteristics of the Jidong region. For originality, the book goes off the beaten path. Presented in a bilingual Chinese-English format, accompanied by abundant photos, and written in beautiful and vivid language, the book is a rare and important work to give readers a comprehensive understanding of Jidong culture.

The above is my preface to the book.

Li Jinshan
December 10, 2022

目录 Contents

第一章 古史文化
Chapter I History and Culture

一、地理坐标 I. Geographic Coordinates ·· 2
  1. 唐山 Tangshan ·· 2
  2. 秦皇岛 Qinhuangdao ··· 5
  3. 承德 Chengde ·· 8
  4. 渤海 Bohai Sea ·· 11
  5. 燕山 Yan Mountains ··· 13
  6. 滦河 Luan River ·· 15
  7. 青龙河 Qinglong River ··· 18
  8. 碣石山 Jieshi Mountain ·· 21
  9. 永平府 Yongping Prefecture ·· 24

二、古国古史 II. History of Ancient States ······································ 26
  10. 商汤封孤竹 King Tang of Shang's Enfeoffment of Guzhu ·········· 26
  11. 周武王封召公于燕 King Wu of Zhou Enfeoffing Duke Shao with Yan ·········· 28
  12. 齐桓公伐戎救燕 Duke Huan of Qi Attacking Shanrong to Save Yan ·········· 31

13. 燕昭王筑黄金台 King Zhao of Yan Building the Gold Terrace ······33
14. 肥子奔燕 King of Fei Fleeing to Yan with His Tribe ······36
15. 曹操北征乌桓 Cao Cao Marching North Against Wuhuan ······37
16. 唐太宗东征高丽 The Eastern Expedition Against Goryeo by Emperor Taizong of Tang ······40
17. 皇太极己巳之变 Ji Si Incident by Huang Taiji ······43
18. 清军入关 The Qing Army Crossing the Shanhai Pass ······46

三、重要考古发现 III. Major Archaeological Findings ······50
19. 四方洞遗址 Sifangdong Site ······50
20. 孟家泉遗址 Mengjiaquan Site ······52
21. 爪村遗址 Zhaocun Village Site ······54
22. 化子洞遗址 Huazidong Site ······56
23. 西寨遗址 Xizhai Site ······57
24. 北戴河秦行宫遗址 Qin Palace Ruins in Beidaihe ······59
25. 金代烧酒锅 Liquor Pot of the Jin Dynasty ······63

第二章 长城文化
Chapter II The Great Wall Culture

一、长城精华 I. Highlights of the Great Wall ············ 68
  1. 长城 The Great Wall ············ 68
  2. 蓟镇长城 Jizhou Great Wall ············ 71
  3. 山海关 Shanhai Pass ············ 76
  4. 老龙头 Laolongtou Great Wall ············ 82
  5. 角山长城 Jiaoshan Great Wall ············ 87
  6. 九门口 Jiumenkou ············ 89
  7. 喜峰口 Xifengkou ············ 92
  8. 潘家口（卢龙塞）Panjiakou (Lulong Pass) ············ 96
  9. 金山岭长城 Jinshanling Great Wall ············ 100

二、长城保护 II. Preservation of the Great Wall ············ 104
  10. 山海关长城博物馆 Shanhaiguan Great Wall Museum ···· 104
  11. 板厂峪窑址群遗址 Heritage Site of Banchangyu Kilns ·· 107

三、长城故事 III. Stories of the Great Wall ············ 110
  12. 戚继光戍守蓟镇 Qi Jiguang Standing Guard in Jizhou ····· 110

13. 孟姜女传说 Legend of Meng Jiangnü ……………… 115

第三章 旅游文化
Chapter III Tourism Culture

一、名胜古迹 I. Places of Interest ……………………… 120
  1. 承德避暑山庄 Chengde Mountain Resort ……………… 120
  2. 承德外八庙 Eight Outlying Temples of Chengde ……… 125
  3. 遵化清东陵 Eastern Qing Tombs in Zunhua …………… 131
  4. 卢龙永平古城 Yongping Ancient City in Lulong ……… 135
  5. 北戴河近代建筑群 Beidaihe Modern Architectural Complex ……………………………………………… 139

二、自然风景 II. Natural Scenery ……………………… 144
  6. 北戴河鸽子窝公园 Beidaihe Dovecote Park …………… 144
  7. 昌黎黄金海岸 Changli Gold Coast ……………………… 147
  8. 青龙祖山 Qinglong Zushan Mountain …………………… 150
  9. 兴隆雾灵山 Xinglong Wuling Mountain ………………… 156
  10. 木兰围场 Mulan Enclosure ……………………………… 160

第四章 民俗文化
Chapter IV Folk Culture

一、传统音乐 I. Traditional Music ·············· 166
  1. 冀东民歌 Jidong Folk Song ·············· 166
  2. 冀东吹歌 Jidong Trumpeting Song ·············· 170

二、传统舞蹈 II. Traditional Dances ·············· 176
  3. 冀东秧歌 Jidong Yangko ·············· 176
  4. 满族二贵摔跤 Manchu Ergui Wrestling ·············· 183
  5. 青龙猴打棒 Qinglong Monkey Dance ·············· 186

三、传统戏曲 III. Traditional Opera ·············· 189
  6. 滦州皮影戏 Luanzhou Shadow Play ·············· 189
  7. 评剧 Pingju Opera ·············· 199
  8. 乐亭大鼓 Laoting Drum Ballad ·············· 206

四、传统体育 IV. Traditional Sports ·············· 212
  9. 珍珠球 Pearl Ball ·············· 212
  10. 陀螺 Top ·············· 214

五、传统美术 V. Traditional Arts ············217
  11. 丰宁满族剪纸 Fengning Manchu Paper-cutting ············217
  12. 玉田泥塑 Yutian Clay Sculpture ············223
  13. 丰宁布糊画 Fengning Cloth Painting ············226

六、节庆民俗 VI. Festivals and Folk Customs ············230
  14. 春节 Spring Festival ············230
  15. 滦平抡花 Luanping Lunhua (Spark Swinging) ············240
  16. 宽城背杆 Kuancheng Pole Carrying ············242

第五章 饮食文化
Chapter V Food Culture

一、塞外风味 I. Savory Foods Beyond the Great Wall ············248
  1. 平泉"五奎园"改刀肉 Pingquan "Wukuiyuan" Gaidao Meat ············248
  2. 平泉御膳糖饼 Pingquan Imperial Sugar Cake ············249
  3. 隆化一百家子拨御面 Longhua One Hundred Households Royal Pushed Noodles ············252
  4. 承德满族八大碗 Chengde Manchu Eight Bowls ············254

5. 平泉羊汤 Pingquan Sheep Entrails Soup ·················· 256
6. 青龙（宽城）水豆腐 Qinglong (Kuancheng) Soft Bean Curd ·················· 258
7. 满族黏饽饽 Manchu Sticky Cake ·················· 262
8. 柞栎叶饼 Quercus Leaf Cake ·················· 265

二、沿海美食 II. Coastal Foods ·················· 267
9. 抚宁白腐乳 Funing White Fermented Bean Curd ·················· 267
10. 刘美烧鸡 Liumei Roast Chicken ·················· 269
11. 吊桥缸炉烧饼 Diaoqiao Vat-baked Flatbread ·················· 272
12. 唐山蜂蜜麻糖 Tangshan Honey Sesame Candy ·················· 275
13. 饹馇 Gezha Pancake ·················· 278
14. 赵家馆饺子 Zhaojiaguan Dumpling ·················· 282
15. 应季海鲜 Seasonal Seafoods ·················· 284

第六章 冀东文学
Chapter VI Jidong Literature

一、明清文苑 I. Literary World of the Ming and Qing Dynasties ···· 290
1. 谷应泰 Gu Yingtai ·················· 290

  2. 曹雪芹 Cao Xueqin ·················· 292
  3. 史梦兰 Shi Menglan ················ 296
  4. 张佩纶 Zhang Peilun ··············· 299

二、现当代作家 II. Contemporary Writers ········ 301
  5. 李尔重 Li Erchong ················· 301
  6. 宋之的 Song Zhidi ················· 304
  7. 张爱玲 Eileen Chang ··············· 306
  8. 管桦 Guan Hua ···················· 309
  9. 葛翠琳 Ge Cuilin ·················· 312
  10. 浩然 Hao Ran ···················· 314
  11. 从维熙 Cong Weixi ················ 317
  12. 何申 He Shen ···················· 320
  13. 关仁山 Guan Renshan ············· 322
  14. 张楚 Zhang Chu ·················· 325

三、当代诗人 III. Contemporary Poets ·········· 328
  15. 郭小川 Guo Xiaochuan ············· 328
  16. 李瑛 Li Ying ····················· 330
  17. 刘章 Liu Zhang ·················· 333

18. 张学梦 Zhang Xuemeng ········· 336
19. 大解 Da Xie ········· 338

第七章 产业文化
Chapter VII Industrial Culture

一、工业文化 I. Industry ········· 342
  1. 秦皇岛港 Qinhuangdao Port ········· 342
  2. 中铁山桥集团有限公司 China Railway Shanhaiguan Bridge Group Co., Ltd. ········· 346
  3. 中国耀华玻璃集团有限公司 China Yaohua Glass Group Co., Ltd. ········· 350
  4. 山海关船舶重工有限责任公司 Shanhaiguan Shipbuilding Industry Co., Ltd. ········· 355
  5. 唐山陶瓷 Tangshan Ceramics ········· 357
  6. 开滦煤矿 Kailuan Coal Mine ········· 363
  7. 启新水泥 Chee Hsin Cement ········· 369
  8. 唐胥铁路 Tangshan–Xugezhuang Railway ········· 374
  9. 唐钢集团 Tangsteel Company ········· 377

27

10. 唐山机车车辆厂 Tangshan Locomotive and Rolling Stock Works⋯⋯⋯⋯380
　　11. 唐山港 Tangshan Port⋯⋯⋯⋯385

二、农业文化 II. Agriculture⋯⋯⋯⋯387
　　12. 京东板栗 Jingdong Chestnut⋯⋯⋯⋯387
　　13. 山海关大樱桃 Shanhaiguan Cherry⋯⋯⋯⋯393
　　14. 卢龙甘薯 Lulong Sweet Potato⋯⋯⋯⋯396
　　15. 昌黎葡萄酒 Changli Wine⋯⋯⋯⋯402

三、商业文化 III. Commerce⋯⋯⋯⋯408
　　16. 呔商 Tai Merchant⋯⋯⋯⋯408

第八章 时代文化
Chapter VIII Culture of the Times

一、民主革命 I. Democratic Revolutions⋯⋯⋯⋯414
　　1. 辛亥滦州起义 Luanzhou Uprising of 1911⋯⋯⋯⋯414

二、先驱足迹 II. Footprints of the Pioneers ········ 417
   2. 李大钊在五峰山 Li Dazhao in the Wufeng Mountain ···· 417
   3. 王尽美在山海关铁工厂 Wang Jinmei in Shanhaiguan Ironworks ········ 429

三、救亡图存 III. Saving the Nation from Destruction ········ 431
   4. 长城抗战 Battles Against Japanese Aggression Along the Great Wall ········ 431
   5. 冀东抗战 Battles Against Japanese Aggression in Jidong ·· 436

四、设施遗址 IV. Memorial Facilities and Sites ········ 440
   6. 山海关八国联军营盘旧址 Barracks of the Eight-Power Allied Forces in Shanhaiguan ········ 440
   7. 热河革命烈士纪念馆 Jehol Revolutionary Martyrs' Memorial Hall ········ 444
   8. 冀东烈士陵园 Jidong Martyrs' Cemetery ········ 449

五、时代精神 V. Spirits of the Times ········ 453
   9. 唐山抗震精神 Tangshan Earthquake Relief Spirit ········ 453
   10. 塞罕坝精神 Saihanba Spirit ········ 457

第九章 生态文明
Chapter IX Ecological Civilization

一、水利工程 I. Water Conservancy Projects ……463
  1. 引滦工程 Luan River Diversion Project ……463
  2. 引滦枢纽工程 Luan River Diversion Multipurpose Project ·465
  3. 引滦入津工程 Luan–Tianjin Water Diversion Project ……469
  4. 引滦入唐工程 Luan–Tangshan Water Diversion Project ·473
  5. 引青济秦工程 Qinglong–Qinhuangdao Water Diversion Project ……475
  6. 桃林口水库 Taolinkou Reservoir ……478
  7. "一渠百库"工程 "One Channel and One Hundred Reservoirs" Project ……481

二、生态修复 II. Ecological Restoration ……484
  8. 开滦国家矿山公园 Kailuan National Mine Park ……484
  9. 唐山南湖公园 Tangshan South Lake Park ……487

三、地质公园 III. Geopark ……490
  10. 柳江国家地质公园 Liujiang National Geopark ……490

后记 Postscript ……494

第一章

古史文化

Chapter I History and Culture

一、地理坐标 I. Geographic Coordinates

1. 唐山 Tangshan

唐山位于河北省东部，东与秦皇岛相接，南临渤海，西与京津毗邻，北依燕山与承德接壤，地处环渤海中心地带。

唐山，因唐山(山名)而得名[1]。1877年建乔屯镇，清末改称唐山镇。这是唐山作为行政建制的开始。为区别地名与山名，20世纪30年代唐山（山名）改称大城山。1983年，唐山地区与唐山市合并，实行市管县体制。现辖7个区、3个县级市、4个县、4个开发区。总面积13,472平方千米。

唐山文化底蕴深厚，是评剧和滦州皮影的发祥地。现有全国重点文物保护单位13处。评剧、唐山皮影戏、乐（lào）亭皮影戏、乐亭大鼓、乐亭地秧歌、滦州地秧歌、唐山花吹、玉田泥塑入选国家级非物质文化遗产代表性项目名录。

唐山是中国工业重镇，近现代工业的摇篮。建于1881年的唐山机车车辆厂，是中国第一家轨道交通装备制造企业。建于1881年的唐胥铁路，是中国第一条标准轨铁路。建于1889年的启新水泥，是中国第一家水泥厂。肇始于1877年的开平（开滦）矿务局托起了唐秦两市的发展，其开滦煤矿2018年入选中国首批工业遗产保护名录。如今，河钢（唐钢）集团、中车（北车）集团、开滦煤矿、唐山陶瓷等已成为享誉世界的工业名片。

（作者：秦学武）

Located in the east of Hebei Province and in the central area of the Bohai Rim, Tangshan borders Qinhuangdao to the east, the Bohai Sea to the south, Beijing and Tianjin to the west, and Chengde along the Yan Mountains to the north.

---

1 一说为唐山因唐太宗东征高丽驻跸而得名。

唐山市地图

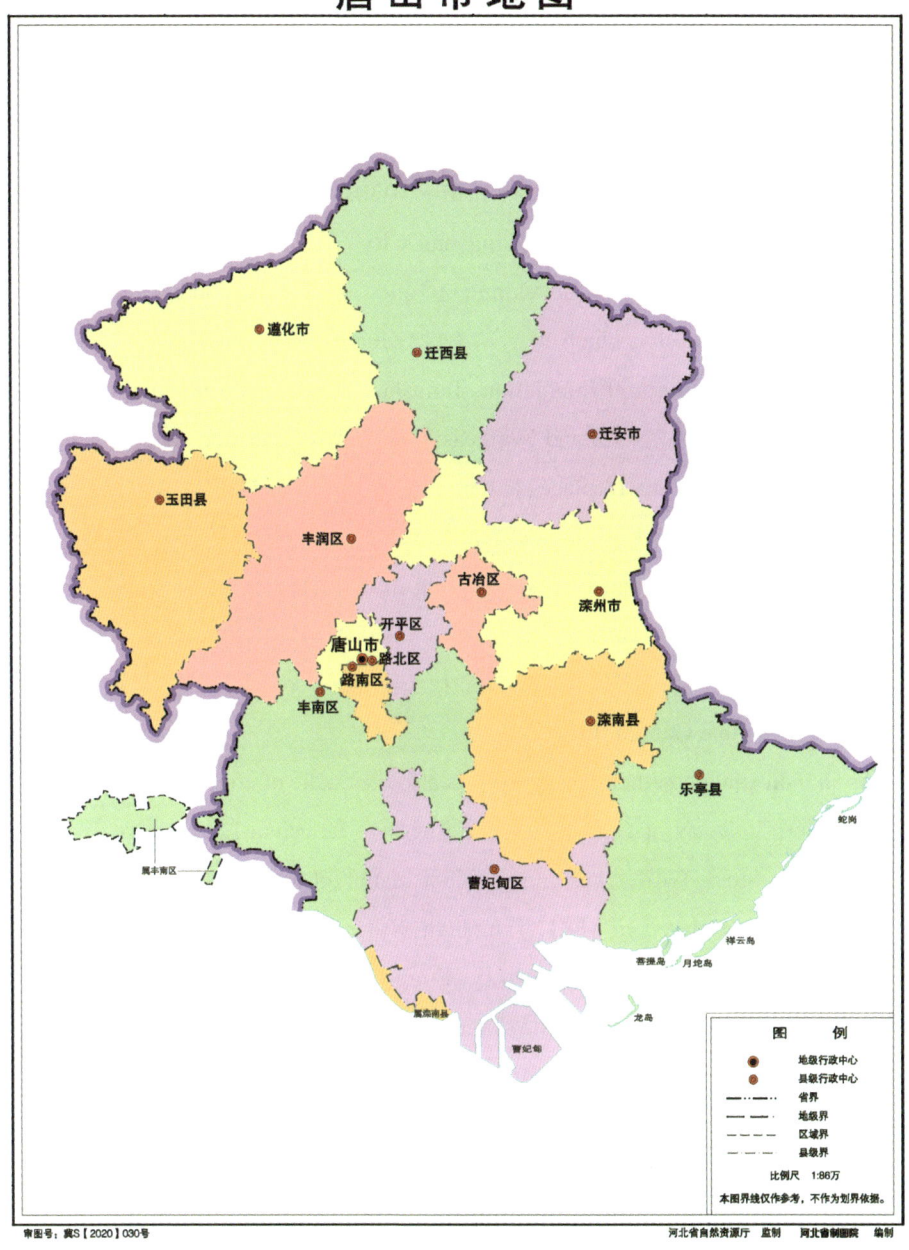

唐山市地图（编制：河北省制图院）
Map of Tangshan City (Compiled by Hebei Mapping Institute)

第一章　古史文化　　Chapter I History and Culture

The city is home to the Tangshan Mountain, hence its name[1]. In 1877, Qiaotun Town was set up here. In the late Qing Dynasty, its name was changed to Tangshan Town, which marked the beginning of Tangshan as an administrative area. To distinguish the place with the mountain, Tangshan (mountain) was renamed Dacheng in the 1930s. In 1983, Tangshan Prefecture was incorporated into Tangshan City. 7 districts, 3 county-level cities, 4 counties and 4 development zones are currently under the administration of the city, which covers 13,472 square kilometers.

With a profound cultural foundation, Tangshan is the cradle of Pingju opera (a local opera of North and Northeast China) and Luanzhou shadow play. Currently, there are 13 places among the list of Major Historical and Cultural Sites Protected at the National Level. Pingju opera, Tangshan shadow play, Laoting shadow play, Laoting drum ballad, Laoting field Yangko, Luanzhou field Yangko, Tangshan acrobatic trumpeting and Yutian clay sculpture have been included in the List of Representative Items of National Intangible Cultural Heritage.

As an industrial powerhouse, Tangshan is also the cradle of contemporary and modern industry of China. Founded in 1881, Tangshan Locomotive and Rolling Stock Works was China's first manufacturer of rail transit equipment. Completed in 1881, Tangshan–Xugezhuang Railway was China's first standard-gauge railway. Founded in 1889, Chee Hsin Cement was China's first cement plant. Established in 1877, Kaiping (Kailuan) Mining Bureau had promoted the development of Tangshan and Qinhuangdao. In 2018, Kailuan Coal Mine affiliated with the bureau was selected into the first batch of China's Industrial Heritage Protection List. Today, HBIS Group Tangsteel Company, CRRC Tangshan Co., Ltd.,

---

1　One theory is that Tangshan got its name because of the stopover of Li Shiming, Emperor Taizong of the Tang Dynasty, when he marched east against Goryeo.

Kailuan Coal Mine and Tangshan ceramics, as industrial icons of the city, are known the world over.

(By: Qin Xuewu)

2. 秦皇岛 Qinhuangdao

秦皇岛位于河北省东北部，北依燕山与承德接壤，南临渤海，东接辽宁，西靠唐山，邻近京津，地处华北、东北的结合部，战略位置重要。

公元前215年，秦始皇东巡驻跸于此。秦皇岛成为中国唯一因帝王尊号而得名的城市。1983年5月，秦皇岛从唐山分立升为地级市，原属唐山的卢龙、昌黎、抚宁三县划归秦皇岛；1984年1月，原属承德的青龙县划归秦皇岛。现辖4个区、2个县、1个自治县，以及秦皇岛经济技术开发区和北戴河新区。陆地面积7802平方千米，海域面积1805平方千米。

秦皇岛是国家历史文化名城，现有全国重点文物保护单位11处。有秦行宫遗址、秦皇求仙入海处、九门口长城、近代别墅群、老龙头等名胜古迹，留下了不食周粟、伐戎救燕、秦皇求仙、汉武巡幸、魏武挥鞭、唐宗驻跸等历史典故。抚宁鼓吹乐、昌黎地秧歌、孟姜女传说、昌黎民歌、昌黎皮影戏入选国家级非物质文化遗产代表性项目名录。

秦皇岛是国际滨海旅游名城，山、海、林、河、湖、沙、关、城、港等旅游资源富集，万里长城、山海关、北戴河驰名中外，素有中国夏都、京津后花园之称。

秦皇岛是中国首批沿海开放城市，是中国最大铝制品生产加工基地和世界级汽车轮毂制造基地，还是中国北方最大粮油加工基地。秦皇岛港是世界最大能源输出港。

秦皇岛是唯一协办过亚运会和奥运会的地级市，先后入选国家园林城市、国家森林城市，2017年被授予全国文明城市称号。

（作者：秦学武）

秦皇岛市地图

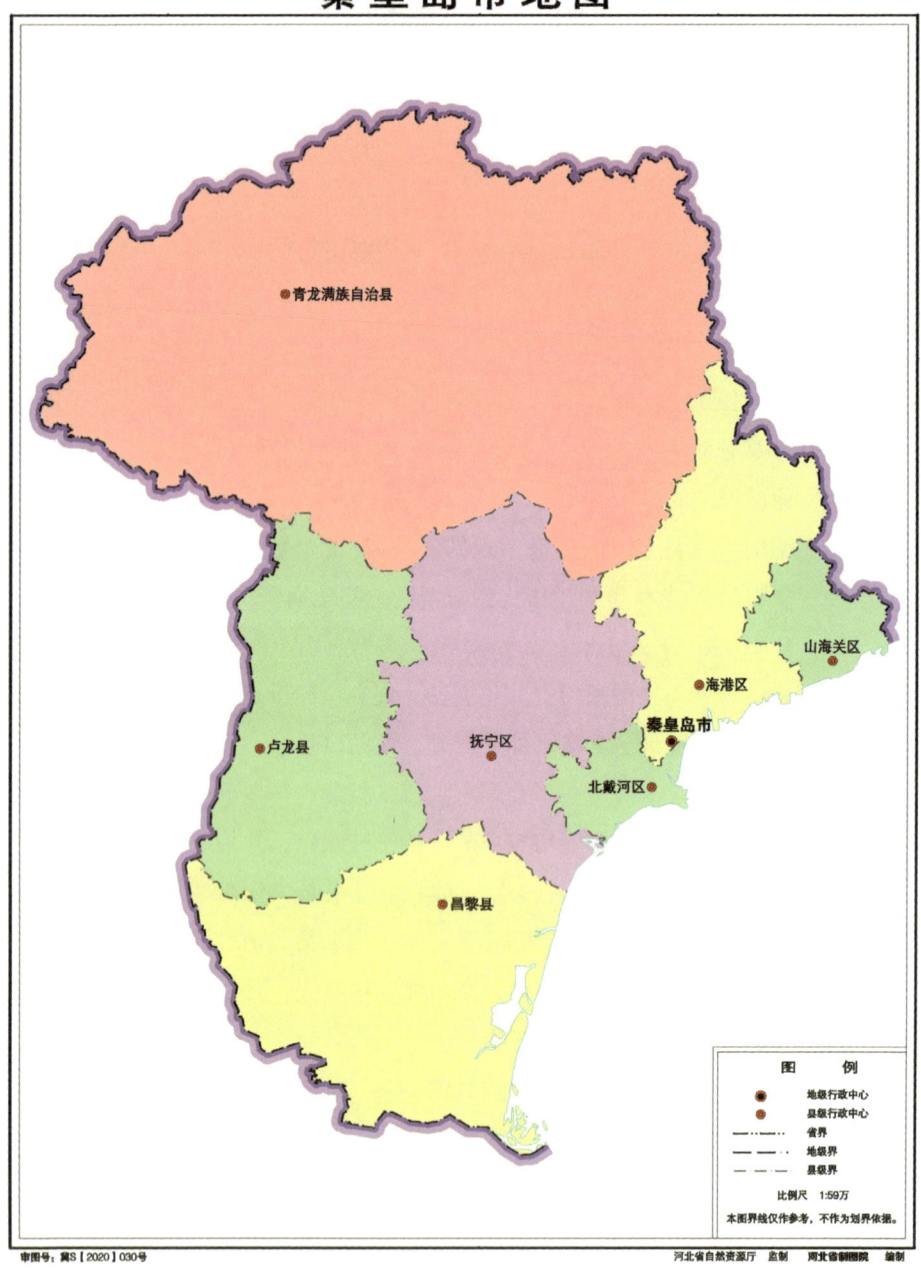

秦皇岛市地图（编制：河北省制图院）
Map of Qinhuangdao City (Compiled by Hebei Mapping Institute)

Located in the northeast of Hebei Province, Qinhuangdao borders Chengde along the Yan Mountains to the north, the Bohai Sea to the south, Liaoning to the east, and Tangshan to the west. In the vicinity of Beijing and Tianjin and at the junction of North China and Northeast China, it is of great strategic significance.

In 215 BC, the First Emperor of Qin travelled east and had a stopover here. Qinhuangdao thus became China's only city named after an emperor. In May 1983, it was separated from Tangshan to become a prefecture-level city. Lulong, Changli and Funing counties, originally under Tangshan, were put under Qinhuangdao. In January 1984, Qinglong County, originally under Chengde, was put under Qinhuangdao. The city currently administers 4 districts, 2 counties, 1 autonomous county, the Qinhuangdao Economic and Technological Development Zone, and the Beidaihe New District. The land area and the sea area of the city cover 7,802 and 1,805 square kilometers respectively.

Qinhuangdao is among the National Famous Historical and Cultural Cities. There are 11 Major Historical and Cultural Sites Protected at the National Level, and its places of interest include Qin Palace Ruins, Emperor of Qin's Starting Point to Immortality, Jiumenkou Great Wall, Modern Villas and Laolongtou Great Wall. Historical tales of the city include Refusing to Touch the Grain of Zhou, Attacking Shanrong to Save Yan, First Emperor of Qin Seeking the Elixir of Immortality, Emperor Wu of the Western Han Dynasty on a Tour, Emperor Wu of the Wei Dynasty Cracking His Whip, and Emperor Taizong of the Tang Dynasty Stopping Over. Funing percussion and wind music, Changli Yangko, the legend of Meng Jiangnü, Changli folk songs and Changli shadow play have been included in the List of Representative Items of National Intangible Cultural Heritage.

Qinhuangdao is an international coastal tourism city with abundant tourism resources such as mountains, sea, forests, rivers, lakes, deserts, passes, towns and ports. The Great Wall, the Shanhai Pass and Beidaihe District are prominent attractions in China and abroad. The city enjoys a reputation for being the "Summer Capital of China" and the "Back Garden of Beijing and Tianjin".

Qinhuangdao is one of the first Coastal Open Cities of China, China's largest manufacturing and processing base of aluminum products, a world-class car hub manufacturing base, and the largest grain and oil processing base in northern China. Qinhuangdao Port is the world's largest energy transportation port.

Qinhuangdao is the only prefecture-level city to co-organize both the Asian Games and the Olympic Games. It has been named a National Garden City and National Forest City. In 2017, Qinhuangdao was recognized as a National Civilized City.

(By: Qin Xuewu)

3. 承德 Chengde

承德位于河北省东北部，北靠赤峰和锡林郭勒，南邻京津，东和东南与朝阳、秦皇岛、唐山接壤，西与张家口相邻，具有"一市连五省"的区位优势。现辖3个区、1个县级市、4个县、3个自治县。面积39,519平方千米。

1703年，康熙修建热河行宫，避暑山庄成为清朝的夏都和第二个政治中心，见证了"康乾盛世"的百年辉煌。1733年，雍正取"承受先祖德泽"之义，设承德直隶州，始称"承德"。这造就了承德先有皇家园林和皇家寺庙群，后有城市发展的独特轨迹。1929年，建热河省，承德成为省会。1955年，热河省撤销，承德划归河北省。

承德是国家历史文化名城。五千年的红山文化、三百年的山庄文化纵贯古今。数位清代君王曾在此处理政务，见证了六世班禅和英使马葛尔尼觐见、土尔扈特部回归等重大历史事件。丰宁满族剪纸、丰宁满族吵子会、满族二贵摔跤、宽城背杆、契丹始祖传说、布糊画、抡花入选国家级非物质文化遗产代表性项目名录。

承德是文物大市。现有全国重点文物保护单位19处，地上地下文物文化遗存1300多处。隆化县头道营后街遗址，处于旧石器时代中期，距今约20万年，是滦河文化的肇始。1985年，避暑山庄入选"中国十大风景名胜"。1994年，承德避暑山庄及其周围寺庙被联合国教科文组织列入世界文化遗产名录。

承德市滦平县是中国普通话标准音采集地，被称为普通话之乡。

（作者：秦学武）

Located in the northeast of Hebei Province, Chengde borders Chifeng and Xilingol to the north, Beijing and Tianjin to the south, Chaoyang, Qinhuangdao and Tangshan to the east and southeast, and Zhangjiakou to the west. As a thoroughfare to five provinces, it currently administers 3 districts, 1 county-level city, 4 counties and 3 autonomous counties. The city covers an area of 39,519 square kilometers.

In 1703, the Mountain Resort was built by Emperor Kangxi in Jehol as a temporary imperial palace to spend summer. Chengde Mountain Resort, as the summer capital and the second political center of the Qing Dynasty, attested to the glory of the High Qing Period. In 1733, Emperor Yongzheng, to deliver the message of "blessing of the ancestors", founded a municipality here and gave it the name Chengde. All these resulted in the peculiar trajectory of the imperial gardens and temples predating the city development. In 1929, Jehol Province was established, with Chengde as its capital city. In 1955, Jehol Province ceased to exist, and Chengde was put under the administration of Hebei Province.

Chengde is a National Famous Historical and Cultural City. Hongshan culture, which goes back 5,000 years, and Summer Resort culture, which

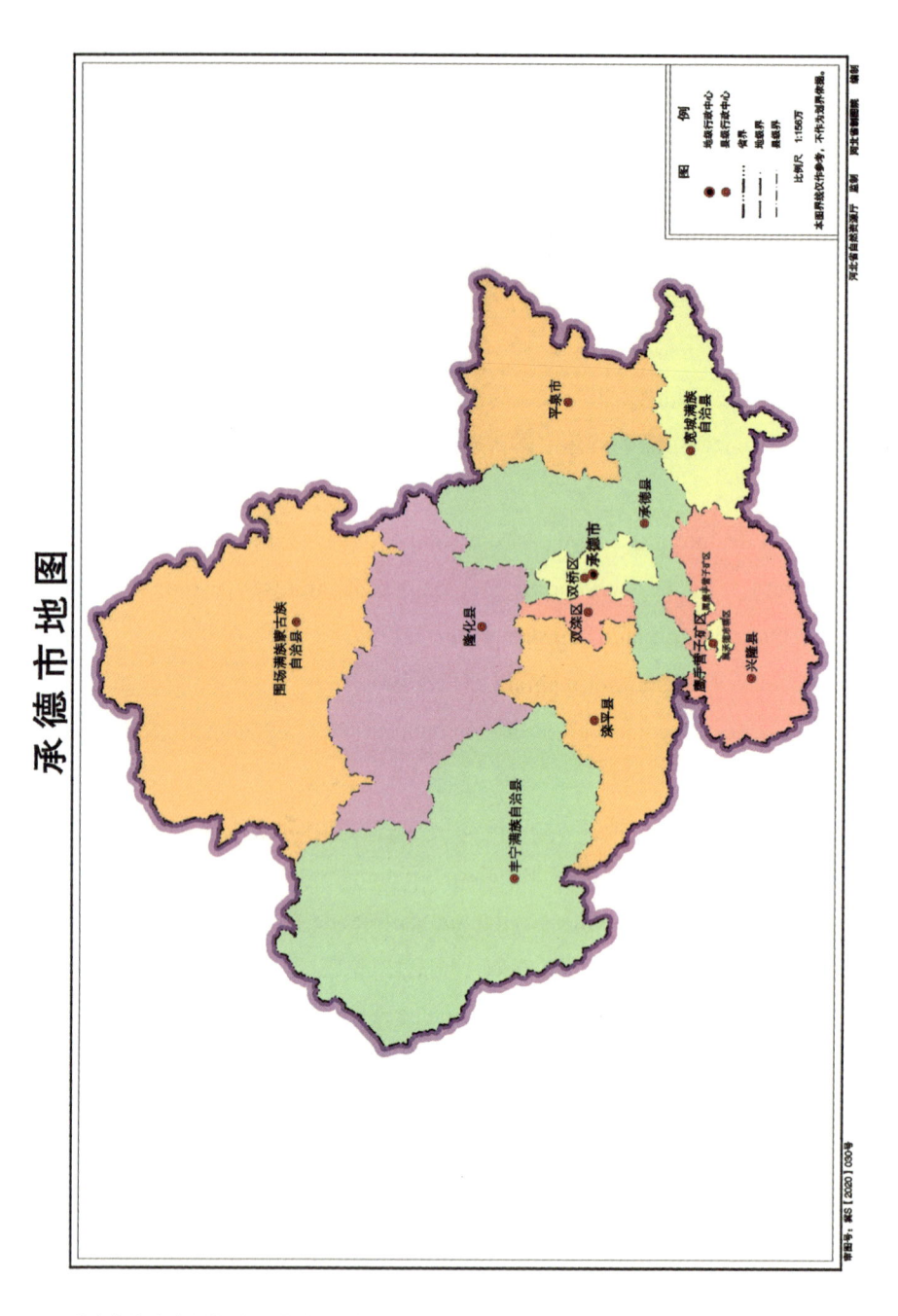

承德市地图（编制：河北省制图院）
Map of Chengde City (Compiled by Hebei Mapping Institute)

goes back 300 years, have a timeless charm. Several emperors of the Qing Dynasty attended to state affairs in Chengde, and many major events in the annals of Qing had taken place here, such as the 6th Panchen Lama and the British envoy George Macartney being received in audience, and the return of the Torghuts. Fengning Manchu paper-cutting, Fengning Manchu Chaozi music, Manchu Ergui wrestling, Kuancheng pole carrying, legend of the ancient ancestor of Khitan, cloth painting and Lunhua (spark swinging) have been included in the List of Representative Items of National Intangible Cultural Heritage.

Chengde is rich in cultural relics. There are 19 Major Historical and Cultural Sites Protected at the National Level, and more than 1,300 cultural relics and remnants above and under the ground. The relics of Toudaoying Back Street in Longhua County dates back to the Middle Paleolithic period. The 200,000-year-old site marked the beginning of the Luan River Culture. In 1985, Chengde Mountain Resort was listed among the "Top Ten Tourist Spots in China". In 1994, Chengde Mountain Resort and its Outlying Temples were designated by the UNESCO among the World Heritage List.

As the home of mandarin, Luanping County of Chengde is the collecting site of standard mandarin.

(By: Qin Xuewu)

4. 渤海 Bohai Sea

渤海,《左传》称之"北海",《韩非子》称之"少海",《史记》《汉书》称之"勃海",《战国策》《淮南子》称之"渤海"。元朝以后,"渤海"沿用至今。

渤海是西太平洋的一部分,为中国北部内海。渤海三面环陆,在辽宁、河北、天津、山东四省市之间,东面经渤海海峡与黄海相通。旅顺老铁山与蓬莱田横山之间的连线是渤海与黄海的天然分界线。海域面积 77,284 平方千米。

海盐、港口、渔业、石油、旅游是渤海五大优势资源。渤海是我国最大的盐产地，有中国最大的海上油田——渤海油田。这里盛产对虾、蟹、黄花鱼、带鱼及贝类。品尝应季海鲜是当地居民的饮食习惯和外地游客来此地的首选体验之一。

渤海湾海陆旅游资源富集，旅游业发达。北戴河景区是中国近代旅游业的发祥地。北戴河湿地是国际著名的观鸟胜地，被誉为"观鸟的麦加"。昌黎黄金海岸是国家级自然保护区，有中国唯一的天然海岸沙漠和滑沙胜地，还有华北第一大潟湖七里海。秦皇岛已成为享誉世界的滨海休闲度假地。

渤海湾大型港口众多，秦皇岛港、唐山港（包括京唐港区和曹妃甸港区）、天津港和黄骅港形成沿岸港口群，是我国北方对外贸易的重要海上通道。历史上，这里曾是古辽西地区侯国南下朝贡和徐福东渡的海上通道。

（作者：秦学武）

The Bohai Sea is called "Beihai Sea" in *Zuo's Commentary on The Spring and Autumn Annals*, "Shaohai Sea" in *Hanfeizi*, "Bóhai Sea" in *Records of the Historian* and *The History of the Han Dynasty*, and "Bohai Sea" in *Strategies of the Warring States* and *Huainanzi*. Since the Yuan Dynasty, it has been called "Bohai Sea".

The Bohai Sea is part of the western Pacific Ocean and a continental sea in northern China. With land on three sides, it is hemmed in between Liaoning, Hebei, Tianjin and Shandong, and joins the Yellow Sea through the Bohai Strait in the east. The line between the Laotieshan Mountain in Lüshun and the Tianhengshan Mountain in Penglai forms a natural divider between the Bohai Sea and the Yellow Sea. The sea covers an area of 77,284 square kilometers.

Sea salt, ports, fishery, oil and tourism are five economic pillars of the Bohai Sea, which is home to China's largest salt producing area and largest offshore oil field—Bohai Oil Field. Prawns, crabs, yellow croakers, cutlass fish and shellfish are plentiful in Bohai. Seafoods are on the seasonal menu of local residents, and they are one of the first choices of tourists.

Abundant tourism resources both on land and at sea have endowed the Bohai Bay with a prosperous tourism industry. Beidaihe Scenic Area is the birthplace of modern Chinese tourism. Beidaihe National Wetland Park, as a prominent international attraction, is recognized as the "Mecca of Birdwatching Sites". Changli Gold Coast, as a sand surfing resort and a national nature reserve, is home to China's only coastal desert. Qilihai is the largest lagoon in North China. Qinhuangdao has become a world-renowned coastal leisure resort.

Around the Bohai Bay, there are lots of large-scale ports, such as Qinhuangdao Port, Tangshan Port (including Jingtang Port Area and Caofeidian Port Area), Tianjin Port and Huanghua Port, which collectively make up an important maritime passageway for foreign trade in northern China. Historically, the Bohai Bay was the waterway through which the vassal states in ancient Liaoxi went down south to present tributes. When Xu Fu headed east for Japan, he also set off from the bay.

(By: Qin Xuewu)

5. 燕山 Yan Mountains

燕山是中国北方的重要山脉，古称幽都山。燕山西起白河谷地，东至山海关，是京津冀的重要生态屏障。雾灵山为燕山主峰，被誉为"京东第一峰"，是国家级自然保护区。祖山国家森林公园是国家风景名胜区、国家地质公园，被誉为"塞北小黄山"。

燕山既盛产板栗、核桃、苹果、梨、山楂、葡萄、杏等干鲜果，也有"如席的雪花"[1]。洋河、潮白河、滦河是流经燕山山脉的重要河流。

燕山自古就是战略要地。喜峰口、古北口、冷口、山海关等燕山长城关隘是沟通东北与华北乃至中原的重要通道。齐桓公伐戎救燕、曹操北征乌桓、唐太宗东征高丽、皇太极己巳之变、戚继光戍守长城、清军入关、长城抗战等重要历史事件就发生在这里。

燕山南北长城地带，是中国南北民族的迁徙带，也是北方游牧文化与中原农耕文化的融会带。"以燕山南北长城地带为重心的北方"是六大考古学文化区系之一，著名考古学家苏秉琦指出："中国统一多民族国家形成的一连串问题，似乎最集中地反映在这里。"从北魏鲜卑族越长城南迁，到辽金时期契丹、女真入关后的汉化，再到清代的汉满融合，燕山南北长城地带见证了多民族文化上升、整合为中华民族"多元一体"文化的历史进程。

（作者：秦学武）

The Yan Mountains, known historically as Youdu Mountains, are an important mountain range in northern China. It runs from the Baihe Valley in the west to the Shanhai Pass (Shanhaiguan) in the east as a significant ecological protective screen for Beijing, Tianjin and Hebei. As a national nature reserve, its main peak Wuling Mountain is reputed to be the "First Peak to the East of the Capital". The Zushan National Forest Park, as a National Park and National Geopark of China, is considered to be the "Equivalent of Huangshan Beyond the Great Wall".

Nuts and fruits, such as chestnuts, walnuts, apples, pears, hawthorns, grapes and apricots, are rich in the Yan Mountains. In winter, the ground "is blanketed with snow"[2]. Yang, Chaobai and Luan are important rivers flowing through the mountains.

1　出自唐代诗人李白《北风行》："燕山雪花大如席，片片吹落轩辕台。"

2　As "Song of the North Wind" by Li Bai, a poet of the Tang Dynasty, says, "The ground in Yan is blanketed with snow, / And flakes fall on the Xuanyuan Platform."

The Yan Mountains had since ancient times been a strategic area. Xifengkou, Gubeikou, Lengkou and Shanhaiguan, barriers of the Great Wall, were key corridors connecting Northeast China, North China and even the Central Plains. Yan saw major historical events such as Duke Huan of Qi Attacking Shanrong to Save Yan, Cao Cao Marching North against Wuhuan, Emperor Taizong of the Tang Dynasty Marching East against Goryeo, the Ji Si Incident in 1629 by Huang Taiji, Qi Jiguang Guarding the Great Wall, the Qing Army Crossing the Shanhai Pass, and the Battles against Japanese Aggression along the Great Wall.

The region around the Yan Mountains and the Great Wall was the migration corridor for ethnic groups in northern and southern China, and the place where the nomadic culture in the north and the farming culture in the Central Plains merged. "Northern China around the Yan Mountains and the Great Wall" is among the six archaeological cultural regions, as Su Bingqi, a famous archaeologist, noted, "In China's evolution into a unitary, multi-ethnic state, innumerable issues had come to pass. They seemed to be concentrated into this region." From Xianbei's moving south across the Great Wall in the Northern Wei Dynasty, to the sinicization of Khitan and Jurchen people in the Liao and Jin dynasties, and to the merging of Han and Manchu people in the Qing Dynasty, the region saw the evolution and integration of multiple ethnic groups and China's becoming a "unitary and diversified" state.

(By: Qin Xuewu)

6. 滦河 Luan River

滦河，古称溴（nuán）水，俗称濡水[1]。发源于河北省丰宁县小梁山南麓大古道沟，向北经河北省沽源县，内蒙古自治区正蓝旗、多伦

---

[1]《说文通训定声》载：“《水经》：'濡水从塞外来。'溴，误作濡，按即今北方滦河也。”北易水，古称濡（rú）水，注入白洋淀。

县，后向东南经河北省隆化县、滦平县、承德县、宽城满族自治县，经潘家口入塞，向东南流经河北省迁西县、迁安市、卢龙县、滦州市、昌黎县，在乐亭县兜网铺注入渤海。

滦河是河北第一大河、华北第二大河，干流由闪电河、大滦河、滦河组成，全长888千米。滦河水系主要分布在坝上高原、燕山山地与河北平原，流经河北、内蒙古、辽宁三省（自治区），流域面积44,750平方千米。主要支流有小滦河、兴洲河、伊逊河、武烈河、老牛河、柳河、瀑河、潵河、青龙河、长河、清河等。

滦河是冀东人民的母亲河，多民族文化在此交流融汇。夏商以后的华夏、先商、孤竹、令支、山戎、东胡、肃慎、屠何、匈奴、乌桓、鲜卑、契丹、奚、高丽、女真等部族，元明以后的汉、蒙古、满、回、朝鲜等民族，都曾在滦河流域繁衍生息。

滦河是河北省东北部的主要水源。全流域修建大中小型水库218座。1979年，潘家口水库、大黑汀水库建成蓄水。1983年建成的"引滦入津工程"和1984年建成的"引滦入唐工程"，通过跨区域调滦河水，解决了天津、唐山的城市用水问题。2005年建成的迁安黄台湖，成为河北省首家城市河湖型水利风景区，被水利部评为国家级水利风景区。滦河成为造福天津、河北的幸福河。

（作者：秦学武）

The Luan River is known historically as Nuanshui and colloquially as Nuánshui[1]. From its source in the Dagudao Ravine at the southern foot of the Xiaoliang Mountain in Fengning County of Hebei Province, it flows north through Guyuan County of Hebei Province, and Plain Blue Banner and Duolun County of Inner Mongolia Autonomous Region. Then, it bends southeast and flows through Longhua County, Luanping County, Chengde

---

1 As recorded in *Rhyming Version of Analytical Dictionary of Characters*, "*Waterways Classic* says, 'The water of Rushui comes from beyond the border.' Nuan（灓）was mistaken as Ru（濡），so Rushui here should be the Luan River in the north." North Yishui, historically known as Rushui, drained into the Baiyang Lake.

塞罕坝滦河源头（摄影：王怀强）
Source region of Luan River in Saihanba (Photographed by Wang Huaiqiang)

County and Kuancheng Manchu Autonomous County and across the Great Wall in Panjiakou. There, it flows southeastward through Qianxi County, Qian'an City, Lulong County, Luanzhou City and Changli County, before draining into the Bohai Sea in Douwangpu of Laoting County.

The Luan River is the largest river in Hebei and the second largest river in North China. The river, its main stream comprising Shandian River, Large Luan River and Luan River, stretches for 888 kilometers. Distributed mainly in the Bashang Plateau, the Yan Mountains and the Hebei Plain, the Luan River flows through Hebei Province, Inner Mongolia Autonomous Region and Liaoning Province, covering a basin area of 44,750 square kilometers. Its main tributaries include Small Luan River, Xingzhou River, Yixun River, Wulie River, Laoniu River, Liuhe River, Baohe River, Sahe River, Qinglong River, Changhe River and Qinghe River.

The Luan River, as the "Mother River" of Jidong, was where multi-ethnic cultures blended with each other. Since the Xia and Shang dynasties, tribes such as Huaxia, Pre-Shang, Guzhu, Lingzhi, Shanrong, Donghu, Sushen, Tuhe, Xiongnu, Wuhuan, Xianbei, Khitan, Xi, Goryeo and Jurchen had been living in the Luan River basin. Since the Yuan and Ming dynasties, the land was occupied by the Han, Mongolian, Manchu, Hui and Korean people, among others.

The Luan River is the main water source in the northeast of Hebei Province. 218 reservoirs, large and small, are distributed along the river. In 1979, the Panjiakou Reservoir and the Daheiting Reservoir were completed. In 1983 and 1984, the Luan–Tianjin Water Diversion Project and the Luan–Tangshan Water Diversion Project were completed, which have started to provide sustainable water supplies to Tianjin and Tangshan since then. The Huangtai Lake in Qian'an, built in 2005 as the first Urban River-and-Lake-Type Water Park in Hebei Province, has been recognized as a National Water Park by the Ministry of Water Resources of the People's Republic of China. The Luan River has promoted the wellbeing of people in Tianjin and Hebei.

(By: Qin Xuewu)

7. 青龙河 Qinglong River

青龙河，古称玄水、漆水，发源于河北省平泉市田耳山，流经河北、辽宁两省的承德、朝阳、唐山、秦皇岛四市，在卢龙县城附近汇入滦河，东入渤海。青龙满族自治县因青龙河得名。

青龙河是滦河最大的支流，干流总长246千米，沿燕山谷地百川汇聚，经卢龙塞由燕北入燕南。青龙河谷自古是孤竹族的繁衍生息之地，也是辽西诸族往来燕山南北的重要通道。

古玄水是先商和孤竹的发祥地。《诗经·商颂》曰："天命玄鸟，降而生商。"毛公传曰："春分，玄鸟降，汤之先祖有娀氏女简狄配高辛氏帝，帝率与之祈于郊禖而生契。""玄鸟生商的历史传说"广为传颂，入选河北省级非物质文化遗产名录。"虎头唤渡"[1] "漆流玉带"[2] 入列古"卢龙八景"。

1998年建成的桃林口水库，是"引青济秦"西线工程的源头，是秦、唐两市生产生活用水的重要水源地。2002年，桃林口景区被水利部评为国家级水利风景区。2018年，国家林业局批准设立河北青龙湖国家湿地公园。

（作者：秦学武）

The Qinglong River was known historically as Xuanshui and Qishui. From its source in the Tian'er Mountain, Pingquan City of Hebei Province, it flows through Chengde, Chaoyang, Tangshan and Qinhuangdao in Hebei and Liaoning provinces. In Lulong County, it merges with the Luan River and drains into the Bohai Sea in the east. Qinglong Manchu Autonomous County was named after the river.

The Qinglong River is the largest tributary of the Luan River. Its main stream is 246 kilometers long. In the valleys of the Yan Mountains, small streams merge together into the river that runs from northern Yan to southern Yan through the Lulong Pass. Historically, people of the Guzhu ethnic group had been living in the Qinglong Valley, which was an important passage for the Liaoxi tribes to cross the Yan Mountains.

Ancient Xuanshui was the birthplace of Pre-Shang and Guzhu tribes. Here's what "Eulogies of Shang" in *The Book of Songs* says: "The Divine Swallow was ordered by the Lord of Heaven to give birth to Shang." According to Mao's annotations, "On the Spring Equinox, the Divine Swallow went down into the human world. Jiandi, daughter of Yousong and ancestor of Tang, married Emperor Gaoxin. They prayed for a son, and

---

1 古玄水水流丰沛，河面开阔。虎头石，在卢龙"城南六里，状若虎踞"，附近滦河、青龙河合流，有渡口，曰"虎头唤渡"。

2 青龙河水质清澈；滦河裹挟泥沙，水质混沌。青龙河汇入滦河后却不混流，堪称古卢龙的"泾渭分明"。

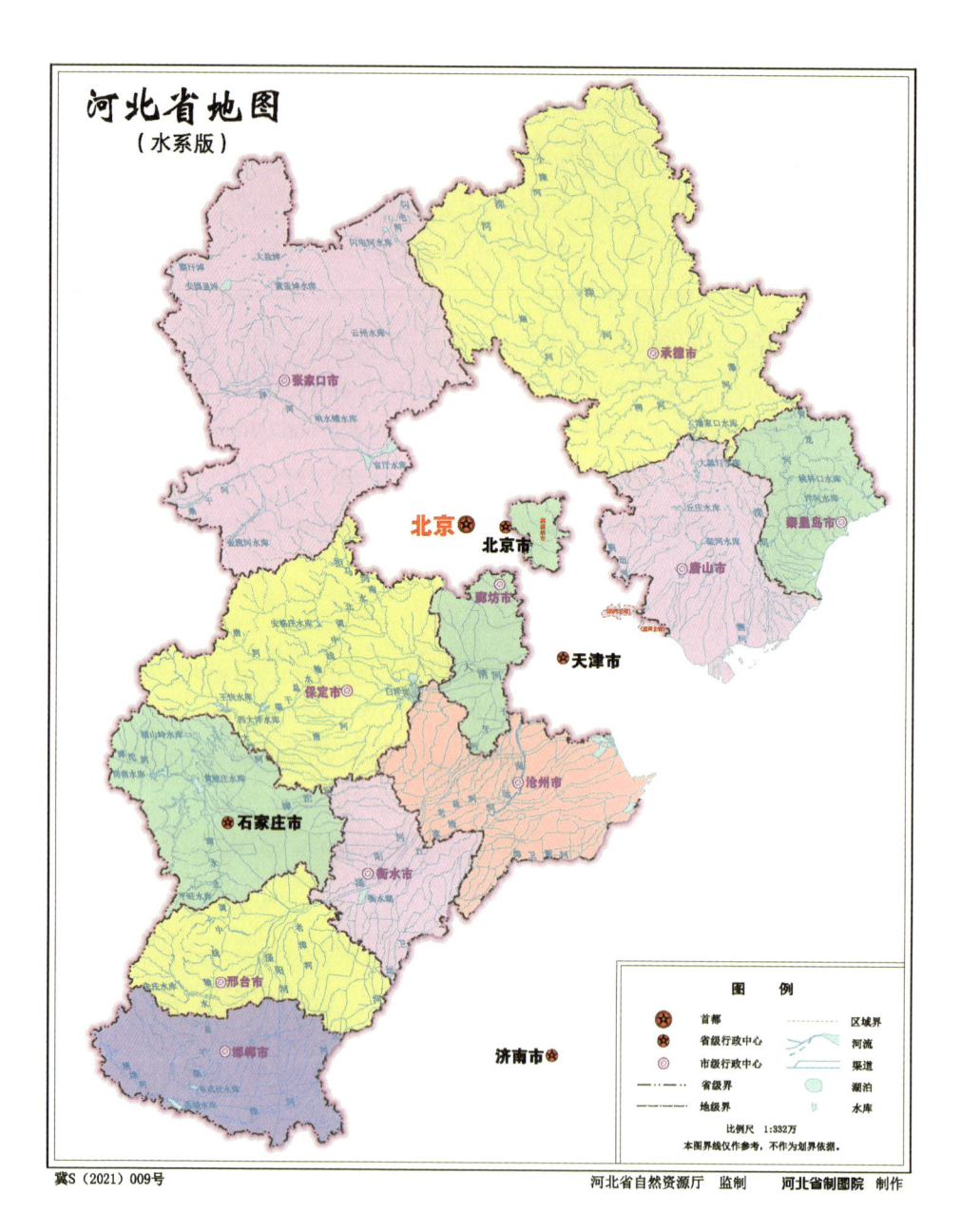

河北省地图（水系版）（编制：河北省制图院）

Map of Hebei Province (river systems included) (Compiled by Hebei Mapping Institute)

Qi was born." "The legend of the Divine Swallow giving birth to Shang" is widely circulated, and it is designated as an intangible cultural heritage of Hebei Province. The "Tiger Head Ferry"[1] and the "Jade Belt of Qishui River"[2] are among the ancient "Eight Scenic Spots of Lulong".

Built in 1998, the Taolinkou Reservoir is the source of the western route of the Qinglong–Qinhuangdao Water Diversion Project. It provides Qinhuangdao and Tangshan with sustainable water supplies for productive use and people's daily life. In 2002, the Taolinkou Scenic Spot was named a National Water Park by the Ministry of Water Resources of the People's Republic of China. In 2018, Hebei Qinglong Lake National Wetland Park was established with the approval of the National Forestry Administration of the People's Republic of China.

(By: Qin Xuewu)

8. 碣石山 Jieshi Mountain[3]

碣石山，位于河北省昌黎县城北。主峰仙台顶，又称汉武台，俗称"娘娘顶"，海拔695.1米，远望似天桥柱石，故名"碣石"。

古碣石是中国古代重要的地理坐标，《尚书·禹贡》等典籍多有记载。《尚书大传》云："东方之极，自碣石东至日出榑木之野。"《尚书·禹贡》孔颖达疏："《地理志》：'碣石山在北平骊城县西南。'是碣

1　The ancient Xuanshui was wide and had abundant water. The Tiger Head Stone, 6 *li* south from the Lulong Town, was like a crouching tiger. At the confluence of the Luan River and the Qinglong River, there was a ferry called "Tiger Head Ferry".

2　The water of the Qinglong River was crystal clear, while that of the Luan River was murky, carrying with it mud and sand. When the Qinglong River merged with the Luan River, they were not mixed with each other—arguably the equivalent of Jing and Wei in ancient Lulong.

3　传世文献以"碣石"命名者众多，或指山、或指巨石、或指地域。刘起釪《〈禹贡〉冀州地理丛考》称碣石有10处。本文取昌黎碣石说。
In the literatures that survive today, there are mountains, rocks and places bearing the name "Jieshi". According to "A Study of the Geographical Features of Jizhou Recorded in *Yu Gong*" by Liu Qiyu, the number totals 10. The theory that Jieshi is located in Changli County is accepted in this article.

石为海畔山也。"古碣石既是东方的方位起点,也是渤海湾的陆地航标。

碣石是"五岳"之外的九州名山。"南潇湘、北碣石"是古代经典意象。"碣石观海"自古就是碣石胜景。公元前 215 年,秦始皇登临,刻《碣石门辞》;前 110 年,汉武帝东巡海上,登碣石,筑汉武台;207 年,魏武帝东征乌桓回军途中登碣石,留下千古名篇《观沧海》;458 年,北魏文成帝登临,改名乐游山;553 年,北齐文宣帝破契丹回师营州,登碣石;645 年,唐太宗东征高丽登碣石,君臣唱和,刻石纪功。

碣石山名胜古迹众多。悬崖峭壁上仍留存古人镌刻的"碣石"二字。山下有千年古刹"水岩寺"。韩文公祠[1] 位于碣石山东南麓的五峰山,中国共产主义运动的先驱李大钊在此写就《我的马克思主义观》和《再论问题与主义》两篇重要文献。"碣石山传说与故事"入选河北省级非物质文化遗产名录。

(作者:秦学武)

The Jieshi Mountain is located in the north suburbs of Changli County in Hebei Province. Its main peak Fairy Platform (aka Hanwu Platform), which is commonly known as "Empress Platform", is 695.1 meters above sea level. From a distance, the mountain is like the stone pier of a skybridge, hence its name Jieshi.

The Jieshi Mountain was a significant geographical site in ancient China. We may read about it in *Yu Gong*, a section of *The Book of History*, and other classics. Here's what *Annotative Compendium of The Book of History* says, "The far ends of the East stretch across the Jieshi Mountain to where the sun rises above a large mulberry forest and rests upon the earth." According to Kong Yingda's commentaries on *Yu Gong*, "The geography section of *The History of the Han Dynasty* says, 'Located in the southwest of Licheng County, Beiping Prefecture, the Jieshi Mountain has a commanding view

---

[1] 韩文公祠,为祭祀唐朝大文学家韩愈而修筑。韩愈,郡望昌黎。

Magnificent Jieshi Mountain (Photographed by He Zhili)

of the sea." The mountain was both the starting point of the East and a navigation mark on the coast of the Bohai Bay in ancient times.

Jieshi is put alongside the "Five Sacred Mountains" as a famous mountain in China. We have a very classical saying that goes: "Due south lies Xiaoxiang, and due north lies Jieshi." The site of "Overlooking the Sea from Jieshi" had always been a famous scenic spot. In 215 BC, the First Emperor of Qin came to the mountain and had a stone carved with the "Ode to Jieshi Gate". In 110 BC, Emperor Wu of the Han Dynasty, travelled east through the coast. He crested the mountain and had the Hanwu Pavilion built. In 457, Emperor Wencheng of the Northern Wei Dynasty came to the mountain and renamed it Leyou Mountain. In 553, Emperor Wenxuan of the Northern Qi Dynasty led an army and launched the campaign to quell Khitan, an ancient ethnic minority in China. After returning to Yingzhou, the emperor went to climb the mountain. Cao Cao, Emperor Wu of Wei, launched the eastern expedition and won the war against the Wuhuan people in 207. Upon his return, he had a stopover in the mountain and improvised the immortal poem "Overlooking the Sea". After the eastern expedition against Goryeo in 645, Emperor Taizong of the Tang Dynasty had a celebratory party with the officials in the mountain. A stone was inscribed to commemorate the occasion.

Places of interests are numerous in the Jieshi Mountain. The characters "Jie Shi (碣石)" inscribed by ancient people are still preserved on the cliff. At the foot of the mountain lies the 1,000-year-old Shuiyan Temple. The Temple of Han Wengong[1] is nestled in the Wufeng Mountain on its southeastern slope. Here, Mr. Li Dazhao, a pioneer of the Chinese Communist Movement, wrote two important articles: "My Views on Marxism" and "Renewed Discussion on Problems and Doctrines". The legends and stories of Jieshi Mountain are designated as an intangible cultural heritage of Hebei Province.

(By: Qin Xuewu)

9. 永平府 Yongping Prefecture

永平府，为明清时期府级建制，府治卢龙县。1371年始称永平府，1913年中华民国裁府留县。明代至清初，永平府辖五县一州：卢龙、迁安、抚宁、昌黎、乐亭和滦州，以及永平卫和山海卫。清乾隆八年（1743）至民国，永平府辖六县一州：卢龙、迁安、抚宁、昌黎、乐亭、临榆和滦州。据《明一统志》《读史方舆纪要》所载，永平府的辖域还应包括后来分立的四县：迁西、滦南、兴隆、青龙。

明清时期，永平府是京东地区的政治、经济和文化中心。清廷曾派重兵驻守，以拱卫京师，保卫清东陵。永平府是连接京师与山海关的要冲，被誉为"京东第一府"。

1902年，"敬胜书院"改为"永平府立中学堂"，成为面向所辖州县最早招生的一所中学校。1903年，中国近代杰出地理学家白眉

---

[1] The Temple of Han Wengong was built to commemorate Han Yu, a famous litterateur of the Tang Dynasty born into the Changli branch of the Han Clan.

初[1]被聘为史地课教员。1905年，中国共产党的主要创始人之一李大钊入读该校，并于1907年顺利毕业。1914年后，学校几度迁址、易名。1928年，校址从卢龙县迁至唐山。1969年，校名更改为唐山市第一中学。原址现为卢龙县中学。

明末己巳之变、清军入关、清末辛亥滦州起义等重大事件就发生在这里。永平府城墙现为全国重点文物保护单位。

（作者：秦学武）

In the Ming and Qing dynasties, Yongping was a prefecture with Lulong County being the seat of government. The origin of the name Yongping goes back to 1371. In 1913 in the Republic of China, it was downgraded from prefecture to county in the administrative level. From Ming to early Qing, Yongping had administered five counties and one county-level prefecture: Lulong, Qian'an, Funing, Changli and Laoting counties and Luanzhou Prefecture, together with Yongping Garrison and Shanhai Garrison. From the 8th year of Qianlong (1743) to the years of the Republic of China, Yongping had administered six counties and one county-level prefecture: Lulong, Qian'an, Funing, Changli, Laoting and Linyu counties and Luanzhou Prefecture. According to *National Chorography of the Ming Dynasty* and *Summary on History and Local Politics*, Qianxi, Luannan, Xinglong and Qinglong counties, which were separated from it later on, were also under the administration of Yongping.

In the Ming and Qing dynasties, Yongping was the political, economic and cultural center to the east of the Capital. To keep the Capital and the Eastern Tombs safe, it was strongly guarded by the Qing army. As an essential hub communicating the Capital and the Shanhai Pass, Yongping was reputed to be the "First Prefecture to the East of the Capital".

---

1 白眉初，卢龙人，著名爱国进步人士。在天津时，经白雅雨介绍与永平同乡李大钊结识，三人结为至交。后来，白雅雨在辛亥滦州起义时牺牲。在北洋政府的白色恐怖下，白眉初积极营救共产党人李大钊并公开为其料理后事，这反映了二人生死不渝的友情。

In 1902, Jingsheng Academy changed its name to "Yongping Prefecture Middle School". It was the first middle school aiming at the students of the prefecture. In 1903, Bai Meichu[1], an outstanding geographer in modern China, was recruited as the teacher of history and geography. In 1905, Li Dazhao, cofounder of the Communist Party of China, attended the school, and he graduated in 1907. Since 1914, the school had moved and changed its name several times. In 1928, it moved from Lulong County to Tangshan. In 1969, it changed its name to Tangshan No.1 High School. In the place where it had once stood, there is now Hebei Province Lulong County Middle School.

Yongping witnessed many historical events, such as the Ji Si Incident, the Qing army crossing the Shanhai Pass in the late Ming Dynasty, and the Luanzhou Uprising in 1911. The walls of Yongping are designated as a Major Historical and Cultural Site Protected at the National Level.

(By: Qin Xuewu)

二、古国古史 II. History of Ancient States

10. 商汤封孤竹 King Tang of Shang's Enfeoffment of Guzhu

孤竹，也作"觚竹"。据《史记索隐》记载，约公元前1600年，商汤分封孤竹。公元前663年，齐桓公"斩孤竹"。孤竹是冀东最早出现的国家。

孤竹文化属于西辽河文明。青龙河—滦河交汇带是孤竹国的核心区。河北卢龙、迁安、滦州和辽宁喀左等地出土了大量商周时期的青

1　Bai Meichu, a native of Lulong County, was a renowned patriot. In Tianjin, he was introduced by Bai Yayu to Li Dazhao, his home folk from Yongping. The three people struck up a friendship. Afterwards, Bai Yayu died in the Luanzhou Uprising. The rebels were put down with appalling barbarity by the Beiyang Government. Trying in vain to rescue Li Dazhao, Bai Meichu took charge of his funeral arrangements. The incident evinced the faithful friendship of the two people.

铜器,有的铸有"孤竹"铭文。冀东和辽西的古孤竹国"恰好在考古学上的夏家店下层文化和夏家店上层文化的分布地带内"。[1]

伯夷、叔齐是商末孤竹国的两个王子。孤竹君立叔齐为继承人。孤竹君死后,叔齐让位兄长伯夷。伯夷不受,兄弟相继投奔善养老的周文王,不遇。文王死后,武王东进伐纣,夷齐叩马而谏,以为父丧而用兵,是不孝不仁。武王灭商后,他们不仕周朝,逃到首阳山(今山西永济市南),采薇而食,饥饿而死。

夷齐的道德、操行和风骨,对后世影响深远。夷齐精神是儒家思想的重要源头,孔孟极为推崇。多地首阳山[2]留有夷齐庙、夷齐墓。夷齐故事在当今仍具教育价值和廉政价值。孤竹、夷齐、首阳、采薇已成为古代文学的经典意象。

2009年,卢龙县获"中国孤竹文化之乡"称号。

(作者:秦学武)

Guzhu is also known as "Gūzhú". According to *Proofreading of Records of the Historian*, in 1600 BC, King Tang of Shang enfeoffed Guzhu to his relatives. In 663 BC, Duke Huan of Qi "marshalled his forces against Guzhu". Guzhu was the first state to appear in Jidong.

Guzhu culture is part of the West Liao River culture, with its center located in the area where the Qinglong River and the Luan River merged. Vast amounts of bronzewares of the Shang and Zhou dynasties were unearthed in Lulong, Qian'an and Luanzhou of Hebei Province, and Kazuo of Liaoning Province, and some of them were inscribed with characters "Gu Zhu (孤竹)". From an archaeological perspective, the ancient Guzhu in Jidong and Liaoxi (Western Liaoning) "happened to be sandwiched between the lower and upper Xiajiadian cultural layers".[3]

---

1 李学勤:《试论孤竹》,《社会科学战线》1983年第2期。
2 首阳山因夷齐而闻名。山西永济、陕西岐山、甘肃渭源、河南偃师和河北卢龙等都有首阳山。
3 Li Xueqin: "A Research on Guzhu", *Social Sciences Front*, 1983, Issue 2.

Bo Yi and Shu Qi were princes of Guzhu living in the declining years of the Shang Dynasty. Shu Qi was named by the King of Guzhu as his heir. After the death of the King, he gave the throne to his elder brother Bo Yi, but the latter wouldn't accept. The brothers went to seek King Wen of the Zhou Dynasty who venerated the elderly for asylum. By the time they arrived, the King had died. Later, King Wu planned to march east against Zhou. Bo Yi and Shu Qi endeavored to persuade him against this idea. They thought it an unfilial act to fight a battle when the King's father was just buried. When Shang was extinguished by King Wu, they refused to serve the Zhou Dynasty and escaped to the Shouyang Mountain (south of today's Yongji City of Shanxi Province). They fed themselves on vetch and were starved to death.

Bo Yi and Shu Qi, with the highest-minded fortitude, had blazed a trail for people of later ages to follow. The Yi-Qi Spirit, from which Confucianism originated, was revered by Confucius and Mencius. The Yi-Qi Temple and the Yi-Qi Tomb are seen in the Shouyang Mountain of many places[1]. Their story has significance for education and clean governance even today. Guzhu, Yi-Qi, Shouyang and Feeding on Vetch are all classic images conveying deep thoughts in ancient literature.

In 2009, Lulong County was named the "Home of Chinese Guzhu Culture".

(By: Qin Xuewu)

11. 周武王封召公于燕 King Wu of Zhou Enfeoffing Duke Shao with Yan[2]

《史记·燕召公世家》载："召公奭（shì），与周同姓，姓姬氏。周

1　The Shouyang Mountain is known for the story of Bo Yi and Shu Qi. There are mountains named Shouyang in Yongji of Shanxi, Qishan of Shaanxi, Weiyuan of Gansu, Yanshi of Henan and Lulong of Hebei.

2　传世文献对召公封燕始于武王还是成王，众说不一。本文采用"始于武王说"。

Opinions in historical documents are divided over whether Duke Shao was enfeoffed with Yan by Emperor Wu or Emperor Cheng. The former opinion is adopted in this article.

武王之灭纣，封召公于北燕。"召（shào）公，名奭，当为"邵公"，有的作"劭公"，《尚书·周书》称之为"太保奭"。召公奭为周文王庶子。保是召公的官位，公是召公的爵位，尊称太保或太公。

燕，金文称"匽"或"郾"，是在北方拱卫周室的同姓侯国，封于公元前1046年。周初，势力未及北燕。召公以太保之职，在周都镐京辅佐王室，主政"自陕（今河南陕县）而西"。北燕为召公长子[1]及其后人署理。公元前222年，燕国为秦国所灭。燕城为燕国都城，在今北京房山。武阳城为燕下都，在今河北易县。

召公奭历经文王、武王、成王、康王四世，在讨伐商纣王，周公东征、营建洛邑等重大事件中都起了重要作用。他还去江汉流域，为周朝开拓南疆。

春秋、战国之际，燕国最弱。齐桓公讨伐山戎救燕后，燕国从京津保定一带东拓到冀东，进而越过燕山，扩展至燕北、辽东。燕昭王筑黄金台，广招天下贤士，燕国复兴，跻身战国七雄。

燕文化带有草原游牧文化特征。《汉书·地理志》称之为"悲歌慷慨""不事农桑"。

（作者：秦学武）

According to *Clan of Duke Shao of Yan*, a section of *Records of the Historian*, "Shì, Duke Shao, had the same surname as King Wu of the Zhou Dynasty—Ji. When the King defeated Zhou, he enfeoffed Duke Shao with north Yan." The title of Shì was got to be "Duke Shao" or "Duke Shào". *The Book of History* referred to him as "Grand Protector Shì". Shì was the son of King Wen's concubine. He was accorded the courtesy title of Grand Protector (official position) and Grand Duke (rank of nobility).

Yan (燕), being 《匽" or "郾" in inscriptions on ancient bronze objects, was a feudal princedom established in 1046 BC to keep the Zhou Dynasty

---

[1] 有学者认为召公长子旨封匽侯，镇燕；次子宪留周继太保之职。有学者认为召公长子为克。

safe in the north. In the early Zhou Dynasty, the power of Duke Shao had not expanded to north Yan. The duke, reigning but not governing, assisted the imperial family as the Grand Protector in Haojing, capital of the Zhou Dynasty, administering the area "from Shaan (Shaan County of Henan Province) westward", and north Yan was ruled by the eldest son of Duke Shao[1] and his descendants. In 222 BC, Yan was eliminated by Qin. Yan City, the capital of Yan, was located in today's Fangshan of Beijing. Wuyang City, the lower capital of Yan, was in today's Yi County of Hebei Province.

Shì had served four kings during his tenure: King Wen, King Wu, King Cheng, and King Kang. He played a crucial role in big events such as marshalling against King Zhou of Shang, Duke of Zhou marching east, and the building of Luoyi City. He also went to the Jianghan Basin to expand the south boundaries of the Zhou Dynasty.

In the Spring and Autumn and Warring States periods, the State of Yan was the weakest of all. Since Duke Huan of Qi attacked Shanrong to save Yan, Yan had pushed the boundaries east from the Jing-jin-Baoding area to Jidong, and, by extension, to Northern Yan and Eastern Liao (Liaodong) across the Yan Mountains. King Zhao of Yan built the Gold Terrace and enlisted intellectuals across the state. This led to the renaissance of the state and placed it among the Seven Powerful States in the Warring States Period.

Yan culture had the salient features of nomads living on the grassland. Here's what the geography section of *The History of the Han Dynasty* says: "They intoned tragic songs with fervor, and never took up ploughs."

(By: Qin Xuewu)

---

1 Some scholars think that the eldest son of Duke Shao was appointed Duke of Yan to guard the state, and his second son Xian stayed in Zhou to succeed him as the Grand Protector. But others believe that the eldest son of Duke Shao was Ke.

12. 齐桓公伐戎救燕 Duke Huan of Qi Attacking Shanrong to Save Yan

齐桓公伐戎救燕，是春秋时期的重大历史事件，见于《春秋》《管子》《史记》《韩非子》等史籍。

公元前664年冬，齐桓公与鲁庄公在鲁国一侧的济水边相见。此时，山戎袭扰北燕，致其无法向周室朝贡。燕向齐求救，齐国谋划攻打山戎。公元前663年春，齐桓公从临淄千里北伐，先后"伐山戎，刺令支，斩孤竹"，"破屠何"。公元前663年冬，燕庄公送齐桓公入齐境。齐桓公割地与燕处，即今河北沧县燕留城。

齐桓公征伐孤竹途中，将到卑耳之溪（今滦河），看到了一个人，而别人看不到。齐桓公以为此事不祥。管仲认为齐桓公看到了山神俞儿，预示霸王之君即将出现。齐桓公路遇俞儿，意在烘托齐桓公成就春秋霸业乃天意。

管仲、隰朋随齐桓公攻打孤竹，回军途中迷路。管仲放老马在前面走，就找到了道路。此后，齐军山地行军，口渴难耐。隰朋说："蚂蚁窝口的土封高一寸，蚁窝下面七八尺处就有水。"士卒寻找蚁窝掘地，果然得水。这是成语"老马识途""寻蚁求水"的来历。

齐桓公伐戎救燕，直接影响燕山南北侯国的命运。孤竹、令支、屠何湮灭于历史长河。齐桓公驱赶山戎、为燕辟地后，燕国势力更为强大。

管仲辅佐齐桓公伐戎救燕，继而成就春秋霸业。这是春秋战国时期贤能治国的开端，是时代的重大转变。

（作者：秦学武）

Duke Huan of Qi attacking Shanrong to save Yan was a major historical event in the Spring and Autumn Period. It was set down in *The Spring and Autumn Annals*, *Guanzi*, *Records of the Historian*, *Hanfeizi*, etc.

In the winter of 664 BC, Duke Huan of Qi and Duke Zhuang of Lu met at the Jishui River on the edge of the State of Lu. At the time, north Yan was intruded by Shanrong, so that it failed to deliver the articles of tribute to King of Zhou. Yan turned to Qi for help, and the latter planned an attack against Shanrong. In the spring of 663 BC, the troops of Duke Huan of Qi set out from Linzi. They marched a long way north against Shanrong, Lingzhi, Guzhu and Tuhe. In the winter of 663 BC, Duke Zhuang of Yan escorted Duke Huan of Qi back to the State of Qi. The latter ceded to Yan the territory in what is today's Yanliu Town, Cangxian County of Hebei Province.

On his way to attack Guzhu, Duke Huan of Qi saw a figure by the Beier Stream (today's Luan River), who was not seen by anyone else. The duke considered it an inauspicious sign, but Guan Zhong thought otherwise. He believed that the figure was Yu Er, the mountain deity indicating the arrival of a hegemon king. The legend was meant to carry a foreshadowing of the duke's hegemony in the Spring and Autumn Period.

Duke Huan of Qi was followed by Guan Zhong and Xi Peng on his way back from attacking Guzhu. During their return, they had gone lost. The three people and the army were led by Guan Zhong's horse until they found their way. Afterwards, the Qi army was distressed by thirst on the march. Xi Peng said to the soldiers: "If the mound at the hole of an ants' nest is one *cun* high, there must be water just 7 or 8 *chi* underneath the nest." His prediction was confirmed. The anecdotes were the origins of idioms "An old horse knows the way" and "Looking for water from ants".

Duke Huan of Qi attacking Shanrong to save Yan had completely changed the fate of princedoms on the south and north sides of the Yan Mountains. Guzhu, Lingzhi and Tuhe had gone down in history, while Yan had grown more powerful.

Duke Huan of Qi was ably assisted by Guan Zhong. By attacking

Shanrong to save Yan, he became a hegemon king in the Spring and Autumn Period. This marked the beginning of meritocracy in the Spring and Autumn and the Warring States periods, representing a major shift in society.

(By: Qin Xuewu)

13. 燕昭王筑黄金台 King Zhao of Yan Building the Gold Terrace

黄金台，又称金台、燕台，为燕昭王在北易水河畔为招揽贤士而筑。遗址在河北省定兴县高里乡北章村。

燕昭王，战国时燕国国君。姓姬，名平（一说名职），与周室同姓。公元前314年，燕国发生内乱，齐国乘机侵占了燕国的土地。公元前311年，姬平被燕人拥立为君。[1] 他励精图治，欲重振燕国，夺回失去的土地，于是问计郭隗。

郭隗，燕国谋士。他认为帝王之臣，实同师友；应以揖让之礼，求得人臣之材。他愿为天下贤士开先路。燕昭王采纳其建议并敬以为师，同时筑招贤台，黄金叠垛，以广揽天下人才。赵国乐毅、齐国邹衍、赵国剧辛、周国苏子、楚国屈景相继来到燕国。燕昭王为他们修建馆舍，如邹衍之碣石宫。君臣经过二十多年努力，终使国力富强。公元前284年，燕国以乐毅为上将军，联合秦、楚、韩、赵、魏五国攻打齐国，直捣都城临淄，夺回失去的土地。

燕昭王筑黄金台，成就了燕国中兴，并使燕国跻身战国七雄。黄金台成为君王或官员延揽、重视贤才的代称，故也称贤士台。

黄金台是后世诗文的经典意象，常化用为"隗台""贤台""幽州台"等。李白、郭沫若等古今诗人都曾用此典故。陈子昂的《登幽州台歌》："前不见古人，后不见来者。念天地之悠悠，独怆然而泣下。"

---

[1] 一说由赵国护送回燕即位。

是千古传颂的名篇。

"金台夕照"为古易州十景之一。"黄金台传说"入选河北省级非物质文化遗产名录。定兴县被列为"河北省黄金台文化艺术之乡"。

(作者：秦学武)

The Gold Terrace, aka Jin Terrace or Yan Terrace, was situated near the Yishui River. It was built by King Zhao of Yan to recruit top talents. The terrace's site is in Beizhang Village, Gaoli Town, Dingxing County of Hebei Province.

King Zhao of Yan, by the name of Ji Ping (or Ji Zhi) with the same surname as the King of Zhou, was the ruler of the State of Yan in the Warring States Period. In 314 BC, Yan descended into a civil strife. Seizing the opportunity, Qi encroached on the territory of Yan. In 311 BC, Ji Ping was appointed the King of Yan.[1] To improve governance, regenerate the kingdom and recover the lost territory, he asked Guo Wei for advice.

Guo Wei was an advisor of Yan. He believed that officials should be received with civility as teachers and friends of the king, and he would like to set a precedent for all the intellectuals. King Zhao of Yan complied with his suggestion and honored him as a teacher. To enlist intellectuals, the king erected a talent-recruiting terrace laden with gold bars. Yue Yi of Zhao, Zou Yan of Qi, Ju Xin of Zhao, Su Zi of Zhou and Qu Jing of Chu were drawn over to Yan. King Zhao built mansions for them, such as the Jieshi Academy for Zou Yan. With 20 years of joint efforts of the king and the officials, Yan had grown powerful. In 284 BC, Yan joined forces with Qin, Chu, Han, Zhao and Wei. Led by Yue Yi, the army cut their way into Linzi, capital of Qi, and retook the lost territory.

King Zhao of Yan building the Gold Terrace had actualized the

---

1　One theory is that he was escorted from Zhao to Yan.

Gold Terrace (Photographed by Hao Jianli)

renaissance of Yan and made it among the Seven Powerful States in the Warring States Period. The Gold Terrace had become synonymous with kings or officials with high esteem for intellectuals, hence its name Talent-Recruiting Terrace.

The Gold Terrace was a classic image in poems and essays of later ages, and it often appeared in the names of "Wei Terrace", "Talent Terrace" or "Tower at Youzhou". The literary allusion was used by poets throughout history, such as Li Bai and Guo Moruo. Here's what "On the Tower at Youzhou" by Chen Zi'ang, an abiding literary classic, says: "Where are the great men of the past? / Where are those of future years? / The sky and earth forever last; / Here and now I alone shed tears."

"Gold Terrace at Sunset" is among the ancient Ten Sights of Yizhou. Its legend has been designated as an intangible cultural heritage of Hebei Province. Dingxing County has been designated as the "Home of Gold Terrace Culture in Hebei Province".

(By: Qin Xuewu)

14. 肥子奔燕 King of Fei Fleeing to Yan with His Tribe

公元前530年，晋国的荀吴假装会合齐军，向鲜虞国借路，乘机率军攻入肥国都城"昔阳"（今山西昔阳一带）；八月十日，灭掉肥国，虏回其君王"肥子绵皋"。此后，肥国的余众穿过太行山，东迁至今河北藁城、晋州一带，投靠同属狄族的鼓国，《汉书》《太平寰宇记》所载的"肥累城"成为其新的活动中心。

公元前520年，晋国灭掉鼓国。寄居鼓国短短10年的肥国族众被迫再次向东北逃到燕国，被燕国封在肥如，即今河北卢龙县西北。这就是历史上的"肥子奔燕"。

《明一统志》载："卢龙县……古肥子国。汉为肥如县，属辽西郡。"如，为"到""往"之意。肥如县，即"肥子所到"之县。

肥子奔燕，是冀东、辽西一带在战国燕、秦、汉时期民族迁徙的较早实例，也是齐桓公北伐山戎后，燕国利用外地来迁的异族开拓、镇守新疆域的实证。

先秦时期，各国向地广人稀之地或新占领区迁徙民众的社会开发或治理方式，称为"徕民"政策，所徙之人称为"徕民"。冀东一带的"絫"（今河北昌黎）、"无终"（今河北玉田）、"徐无"（今河北遵化）等县的史源与肥如县相类，居民主体为附属燕国的白狄族众或东夷后裔。

（作者：秦学武）

In 530 BC, Xun Wu of the State of Jin, pretending to be joining the Qi army, marched his forces to Xiyang (the area in and around today's Xiyang of Shanxi), the capital of the State of Fei, by way of the State of Xianyu. On the 10th day of the 8th month, Fei was extinguished and its king Mian Gao was captured. Afterwards, the remnants of Fei journeyed through the Taihang Mountains eastward to today's Gaocheng and Jinzhou of Hebei. They joined up with the State of Gu of the same ethnic group Di. According to *The History of the Han Dynasty* and *History of Chinese Geography*, Feilei Town became the new residential center of these people.

In 520 BC, Gu was extinguished by Jin. The Fei people, who had lived in the place for merely 10 years, were forced from their homes again. They headed northeast to Yan where they were placed in Feiru in the northwest corner of today's Lulong County of Hebei. This is the history of "The King of Fei Fleeing to Yan with His Tribe".

According to *National Chorography of the Ming Dynasty*, "Lulong County…is part of the ancient State of Fei. In the Han Dynasty, it was the Feiru County administered by Liaoxi Prefecture." "Ru" means "arrive" or "head to". Feiru County was where the king of Fei and his tribe arrived.

The king of Fei fleeing to Yan with his tribe was an early example of the migration of ethnic groups in the Warring States Period and the Qin and Han dynasties. It proved that after Duke Huan of Qi's marching north against Shanrong, immigrants had contributed to the reclaiming and guarding of new lands of Yan.

In the pre-Qin period, people might be migrated to the sparsely populated or newly-occupied lands for developing and running those regions. It was called the "recruiting people" policy, and the immigrants were known as "recruited people". The histories of "Lei" (today's Changli of Hebei), "Wuzhong" (today's Yutian of Hebei) and "Xuwu" (today's Zunhua of Hebei) in Jidong were similar to that of Feiru. The majority of people in these places were descendants of Di or Dongyi ethnic groups subject to Yan.

(By: Qin Xuewu)

15. 曹操北征乌桓 Cao Cao Marching North Against Wuhuan

东汉建安十二年（207）二月，魏武帝曹操率军北征右北平、辽西、辽东三郡乌桓；五月，至无终（今天津蓟州）；七月，时值雨季，洪水泛滥，通往辽西的碣石傍海大道不通。田畴引曹军出卢龙塞，经"卢龙—平刚"道，堑山堙谷五百余里；八月，在喀左县的白狼山下与乌桓决战，斩杀辽西乌桓的首领蹋顿，胡人、汉人投降者达二十余万。后来，这些人被放逐到松漠（今内蒙古赤峰、通辽一带），移徙到邺城（今河北临漳）、蓟（今天津蓟州）、晋阳（今山西太原西南）。

曹操北征乌桓进军的路线为：登遵化境内的徐无山，军出卢龙塞（喜峰口），经白檀（今河北宽城县东药王庙村）至平泉，历平刚（今内蒙古宁城县黑城村），登白狼山（今辽宁喀左县大阳山），到凡城（今辽宁喀左县大城子），最终抵达柳城（今辽宁朝阳县袁台子村）。

曹操回师的路线为：由柳城撤军，逆大凌河向西南至白狼山，南折到广成县（今辽宁建昌县），奔榆关（今抚宁榆关一带），沿碣石傍海大道西行。在沿北坡登上碣石山后，写就千古名篇《观沧海》："东临碣石，以观沧海。水何澹澹，山岛竦峙。树木丛生，百草丰茂。秋风萧瑟，洪波涌起。日月之行，若出其中；星汉灿烂，若出其里。幸甚至哉，歌以咏志。"

曹操平定乌桓，解除了乌桓部族对幽州、冀州地区的长期侵扰，巩固了北方的统一和边境地区汉族民众生产、生活的稳定，促进了乌桓部族与中原汉民族的融合。

（作者：秦学武）

In the 2nd month of the 12th year of Jian'an of the Eastern Han Dynasty (207), Cao Cao, Emperor Wu of Wei, marched north against the Wuhuan people in Youbeiping, Liaoxi and Liaodong prefectures. In the 5th month, the army marched to Wuzhong (today's Jizhou of Tianjin). In rainy days in the 7th month, the region was deluged with flood, and the Jieshi Waterfront Path to Liaoxi was cut off. Tian Chou took the Cao army out of Lulong Pass through the "Lulong–Pinggang" Path, which, around 500 *li* long, was made by digging up the mountain soil and filling up the holes. In a decisive battle at the foot of the Bailang Mountain, Kazuo County in the 8th month,

Tadun, leader of the Liaoxi branch of Wuhuan, was slayed, and 200,000 Wuhuan and Han people capitulated. Afterwards, these captives were exiled to Songmo (today's Chifeng and Tongliao of Inner Mongolia), from which they gradually relocated to Yecheng (today's Linzhang of Hebei), Ji (today's Jizhou of Tianjin) and Jinyang (today's southwest part of Taiyuan of Shanxi).

The route by which Cao Cao's army marched north and approached Wuhuan was: Xuwu Mountain in Zunhua–Lulong Pass (Xifengkou)–Baitan (today's Dongyaowangmiao Village, Kuancheng County of Hebei)–Pingquan–Pinggang (today's Heicheng Village, Ningcheng County of Inner Mongolia)–Bailang Mountain (today's Dayang Mountain, Kazuo County of Liaoning)–Fancheng (today's Dachengzi, Kazuo County of Liaoning)—Liucheng (today's Yuantaizi Village, Chaoyang County of Liaoning).

The route by which Cao Cao's army returned was: Liucheng–southwest upstream against the current of Daling River to Bailang Mountain–south to Guangcheng County (today's Jianchang County of Liaoning)–Yuguan Pass (roughly today's Yuguan of Funing)–westward along the Jieshi Waterfront Path. When he crested the Jieshi Mountain along the north slope, Cao Cao composed the immortal work "Overlooking the Sea". It ran thus: "I come to view the boundless ocean, / From Stony Hill on eastern shore. / Its water rolls in rhythmic motion, / And islands stand amid its roar. / Tree on tree grows from peak to peak; / Grass on grass looks lush far and high. / The autumn wind blows drear and bleak; / The monstrous billows surge up high. / The sun by day, the moon by night, / Appear to rise up from the deep. / The Milky Way with stars so bright, / sinks down into the sea in sleep. / How happy I feel at this sight! / I croon this poem in delight."

Cao Cao suppressed the reactionary forces of Wuhuan and freed Youzhou and Jizhou from the longstanding disturbance of the tribes. The move cemented the unity of northern China, secured a stable laboring and living environment for the Han people in the border areas, and promoted the integration of the Wuhuan tribes and the Han people.

(By: Qin Xuewu)

16. 唐太宗东征高丽 The Eastern Expedition Against Goryeo by Emperor Taizong of Tang

高丽，也称高句丽，是夫余[1]的一支。汉代为乐浪郡。《太平寰宇记》载："后魏、周、齐以来，高丽强盛。"据《通典》载，北魏时期，高丽占据辽东。644年至668年，唐太宗和唐高宗五次东征辽东。

642年，辽东高丽发生政变，并攻打新罗。新罗向唐朝求援，唐太宗诏谕高丽罢兵未果。644年十一月，张亮率军从莱州横跨渤海直趋平壤，李世勣绩率军走陆路攻辽东。新罗、百济、奚、契丹等部族分道进攻辽东。645年四月至六月，唐军连克盖牟、辽东、白岩等城；攻打安市城，三月未克；九月，唐军撤回。

647年三月，牛进达率军自莱州渡海攻辽东，李世勣率军与营州都督府兵自新城道攻辽东。唐军连克多城，在积利大破高丽。此战极大消耗了高丽的实力。

648年正月，薛万彻和裴行方率军再次自莱州渡海攻辽东；九月，唐军退兵。唐太宗下诏准备次年再度攻打高丽。649年，唐太宗病逝，遂罢辽东之役。668年，唐高宗平定高丽，在平壤设置安东都护府。

唐太宗645年亲征高丽时，四月二十日在卢龙赋诗《于北平作》，二十三日在秦皇岛写就《春日望海》，九月十八日班师，十月二十一日驻跸临渝宫（在今抚宁榆关），二十三日登碣石山。

唐太宗东征时，修筑了抚宁的洋河城、五花城、山西城和迁安的炼铁炉，秦皇岛因此又称秦王岛[2]；留下了"封王台的传说""亮甲山

---

[1] 也作扶余，是九夷之一。

[2] 唐高祖时，李世民曾受封秦王。

的来历""见驾坡""驷马地的传说""饮马河的由来"等故事传说。[1] 卢龙的苗官营村、陈翟坨村、滦州的王法宝村、樊各庄村、赵庄子村，都是东征留下的士卒和移民定居的村庄。

清光绪三年《抚宁县志》载："满井，在城东南二十里许。井水常满，汲取不竭，庄因以名。相传为唐太宗东征遗迹。"满井俗称"秦王井"，民间传为大将薛仁贵所凿。

（作者：秦学武）

Goryeo, aka Goguryeo, was a branch of Fuyu[2]. In the Han Dynasty, it was the Lelang Commandery. According to the *History of Chinese Geography*, "In the Northern Wei, Zhou and Qi periods, Goryeo had grown powerful." *An Encyclopedic History of Institutions* says that in the Northern Wei Dynasty, Liaodong was a dominion of Goryeo. From 644 to 668, Emperors Taizong and Gaozong of the Tang Dynasty had launched five eastern expeditions against Liaodong.

In 642, the army of Goryeo in Liaodong staged a coup and attacked Xinluo. The latter turned to the Tang Empire for help. Emperor Taizong made an effort for truce in his proclamation but failed. In the 11th month of 644, an army led by Zhang Liang set off from Laizhou. They traversed the Bohai Sea and marched to Pyongyang. The army of Li Shiji attacked Liaodong by land, while Xinluo, Baekje, Xi and Khitan split up forces to attack Liaodong. From the 4th to the 6th month of 645, the Tang army breached Gaimou, Liaodong and Baiyan. However, they had no way to breach Ansi after three months. In the 9th month, the Tang army disengaged from Liaodong.

In the 3rd month of 647, Niu Jinda's army set off from Laizhou. They

---

[1] 刘向权主编：《滦河文化研究文集》（第一卷），团结出版社2017年版。

[2] One of the Nine Wild Tribes of the East.

traversed the sea and marched against Liaodong. The troops of Li Shiji and Yingzhou Governor's Office launched an attack from Xinchengdao. The army took several cities and defeated the Goryeo troops in Jili. The battle had depleted the military strength of Goryeo.

In the 1st month of 648, the army led by Xue Wanche and Pei Xingfang set off from Laizhou again. They traversed the sea and attacked Liaodong. In the 9th month, the army disengaged. Emperor Taizong sent out a proclamation for attacking Goryeo the next year. In 649, the emperor died, and the Liaodong battle ended. After Emperor Gaozong of the Tang Dynasty suppressed Goryeo in 668, the Andong Commanding Office was set up in Pyongyang.

In 645, Emperor Taizong was on an expedition against Goryeo. On the 20th day of the 4th month, he composed in Lulong County the poem "In Beiping". On the 23rd day, he composed the poem "Overlooking the Sea in Spring" in Qinhuangdao. On the 18th day of the 9th month, he returned to the capital. On the 21st day of the 10th month, he had a stopover in Linyu Palace (in today's Yuguan of Funing). On the 23rd day, he climbed the Jieshi Mountain.

During the eastern expedition, Emperor Taizong built Yanghe Town, Wuhua Town and Shanxi Town in Funing and the steel-making furnace in Qian'an. Qinhuangdao, aka Qinwangdao[1], had many legends and stories, such as "Legend of the King Tower", "History of the Liangjia Mountain", "Emperor-meeting Slope", "Legend of Sima Ground" and "History of the Yinma River".[2] The inhabitants of Miaoguanying Village and Chenzhaituo Village in Lulong, and Wangfabao Village, Fangezhuang Village and Zhaozhuangzi Village in Luanzhou, are descendants of soldiers and emigrants of the eastern expedition.

1　In Emperor Gaozu's reign, Li Shimin was appointed as King of Qin.

2　Liu Xiangquan (ed.): *Collected Works on Luan River Culture* (Vol. 1), Unity Press, 2017.

According to *Local Records of Funing County* compiled in the 3rd year of Guangxu of the Qing Dynasty, "The Full Well is some 20 *li* in the southeast of the town. The water in the well is inexhaustible, and the village is named after the well. It is said that the well is a heritage site of the eastern expedition of Emperor Taizong." The Full Well, colloquially known as the "Well of King of Qin", was rumored to be dug by general Xue Rengui.

(By: Qin Xuewu)

17. 皇太极己巳之变 Ji Si Incident by Huang Taiji

己巳之变，是明崇祯二年（1629，农历己巳年）十月至崇祯三年（1630）五月，后金大汗皇太极借口求款不成，率军突袭北京城以及明军阻击后金军和蒙古军的历史事件。明人称之"己巳虏变"[1]，后金人则称之"己巳之役"。

1629 年十月一日，十万后金军从沈阳启行，避开袁崇焕在宁锦一线的重兵，绕道蒙古地区，多支蒙古军队汇入；二十五日至二十九日，突破明长城喜峰口及其以西的脆弱隘口龙井关（皇太极、多尔衮在此入关）、潘家口、大安口、洪山口，破墙进入明境；二十九日，围困遵化。

十一月初一，京师戒严。初三，后金兵入遵化，巡抚王元雅兵败自杀。初四，山海关总兵赵率教及四千骑兵战死遵化。皇太极潜越蓟州，绕过通州，穿越袁崇焕的防线，直扑北京，与明京城守军和袁崇焕统领的各路援军激战北京城下。

二十日，德胜门之战，宣府总兵侯世禄溃退，大同总兵满桂独战，被守城明军误伤；广渠门之战，袁崇焕、祖大寿力战多尔衮，后金军移至南海子。二十七日，左安门之战，皇太极施"反间计"，中伤袁崇焕。十二月初一，袁崇焕下狱，辽东援军军心动摇。初四，祖大寿引兵回宁远（今辽宁兴城）。初五，孙承宗移驻山海关。十六日，

1　1616 年，建州女真的努尔哈赤建立"大金"国，史称后金。明人称后金军为"建虏"。

后金军夜袭卢沟桥，七千明军战死。十七日，永定门之战，后金击败四万明军，满桂和孙祖寿战死，黑云龙、麻登云被擒。

1630年正月，后金军相继攻克永平、滦州、迁安、遵化四城并分兵驻守。初九至十四，皇太极率后金兵千人围打昌黎，知县左应选及士民登城力战，终得不破。二月二十二日，后金军主力离开永平，三月初二返回沈阳。五月初三，明军入滦州。十二日，后金兵余部从冷口关东归，永平、迁安、遵化相继复归明朝。袭扰京师及京东二十余州县七月之久的己巳战事结束。

八月十六日，督师袁崇焕被崇祯帝酷刑处死。

己巳之变，是后金军第一次入关对京师发动突袭，也是影响后来明朝命运的重大事件。崇祯帝误杀袁崇焕，替后金皇太极铲除了南下犯明的最大敌手。《明史》评价："自崇焕死，边事益无人，明亡征决矣。"

（作者：秦学武）

The historical event of Ji Si Incident lasted from the 10th month of the 2nd year (1629, Ji Si year in the traditional Chinese calendar) to the 5th month of the 3rd year (1630) of Chongzhen of the Ming Dynasty. Huang Taiji, the khan of Later Jin, after a failed attempt to ask the Ming government for money, led an army to raid Beijing. The Ming army repelled the offensive of the Later Jin army and the Mongolian army. The incident was called "Ji Si Incident of Barbarians"[1] by Ming people and "Ji Si Campaign" by Later Jin people.

On the 1st day of the 10th month of the 2nd year of Chongzhen (1629), the 100,000-strong Later Jin army set off from Shenyang. Bypassing the troops of Yuan Chonghuan standing guard on the Ning-Jin Line, they went by way of Mongolia and joined with Mongolian forces. From the 25th day to the 29th day, the army breached Xifengkou, Longjing Pass (a fragile pass

---

1　In 1616, Nurhachi, a chieftain of the Jianzhou Jurchens, founded the "Dajin" Dynasty, which was historically know as Later Jin. The Later Jin army was referred by Ming people as "Jian Barbarians".

through which Huang Taiji and Dorgon crossed the Great Wall), Panjiakou, Da'ankou and Hongshankou of the Great Wall, and marched into the Ming territory. On the 29th day, they besieged Zunhua.

On the 1st day of the 11th month, the martial law was declared throughout the capital Beijing. On the 3rd day, the Later Jin army moved to strike Zunhua. Governor Wang Yuanya committed suicide. On the 4th day, Commander Zhao Shuaijiao and a cavalry regiment of 4,000 people were killed in Zunhua. Sneaking around Jizhou and Tongzhou and bypassing the line of defense of Yuan Chonghuan, the troops of Huang Taiji drove straight to Beijing. There, they were engaged in a fierce battle with the local defending troops and the reinforcements led by Yuan Chonghuan.

In the Deshengmen Battle on the 20th day, the troops of Hou Shilu, Commander of Xuanfu, retreated in disorder. Man Gui, Commander of Datong, fought alone, and his troops were mistakenly hurt by the Ming army. In the Guangqumen Battle, Yuan Chonghuan and Zu Dashou were engaged in a full-on fight with Dorgon, and the Later Jin army retreated to Nanhaizi. In the Zuoanmen Battle on the 27th day, Huang Taiji made a counterplot against Yuan Chonghuan. On the 1st day of the 12th month, the latter was put in prison, and the reinforcements from Liaodong lost their morale. On the 4th day, Zu Dashou led his troops back to Ningyuan (today's Xingcheng of Liaoning). On the 5th day, Sun Chengzong's troops went to the Shanhai Pass and stationed there. On the 16th day, the Later Jin army launched an assault on the Lugou Bridge under the cloak of darkness, and 7,000 Ming soldiers were killed. In the Yongdingmen Battle on the 17th day, 40,000 Ming soldiers were defeated by Later Jin. Man Gui and Sun Zushou were killed, and Hei Yunlong and Ma Dengyun were captured.

In the 1st month of 1630, the Later Jin army took Yongping, Luanzhou, Qian'an and Zunhua. Soldiers were sent to station there. From the 9th to the 14th day, Huang Taiji marched a 1,000-strong Later Jin army against Changli. Under the command of County Magistrate Zuo Yingxuan, the militias warded off the assailants. On the 22nd day of the 2nd month, the main part of the Later Jin army disengaged from Yongping. They returned to Shenyang on the 2nd day of the 3rd month. On the 3rd day of the 5th month, the Ming army entered Luanzhou. On the 12th day, the remains of Later Jin army retreated east from the Lengkou Pass. Yongping, Qian'an and Zunhua were retaken by the Ming Dynasty. Beijing and over twenty prefectures and counties to its east were involved in the Ji Si Campaign, which went on for seven months.

On the 16th day of the 8th month, General Yuan Chonghuan was condemned to death by Emperor Chongzhen with cruelest punishments.

The Ji Si Incident was the first time the Later Jin army raided the Ming capital. It was a major event influencing the fate of the empire. Yuan Chonghuan's death eliminated the obstacle to Huang Taiji's going down south and attacking the Ming Dynasty. Here's what *The History of the Ming Dynasty* says: "Since the death of Yuan Chonghuan, no one ever could direct the troops in the border region. It sowed the seed for the fall of the Ming Dynasty."

(By: Qin Xuewu)

18. 清军入关 The Qing Army Crossing the Shanhai Pass

清军入关，是指大顺永昌元年（1644）[1]明将吴三桂引清军进入山海关，睿亲王多尔衮率清军击败李自成的农民起义军并攻占北京，大清开始成为中央政权的历史事件。

---

[1] 1644 年，为农历甲申年。1944 年 3 月，重庆《新华日报》连载郭沫若的《甲申三百年祭》，引起社会极大震动。1949 年 3 月 23 日，中共中央从西柏坡前往北平，毛泽东主席称之为"进京赶考"，并誓言："我们决不当李自成，我们都希望考个好成绩。"

明崇祯十七年（1644）春，李自成在西安建立大顺政权。三月十九日，崇祯在景山上吊自尽，明朝灭亡。得知北京已陷落，进京救驾的吴三桂回师山海关。

李自成攻占北京后，控制吴三桂在京家眷并令其父写信劝降，还派唐通到山海关犒赏。吴三桂将山海关让给唐通。当得知爱妾陈圆圆被掠，他怒不可遏，遂从滦州回师，重夺山海关。[1] 四月十三日，李自成率二十万大军离京，二十日抵山海关，派两万骑兵在一片石关设防，切断吴三桂东逃路线。

1644年四月初九，多尔衮率清军南下，计划绕过山海关，由长城突入。十五日，吴三桂遣使致书多尔衮，请求合力攻打李自成。清军遂由翁后（今辽宁阜新）转向山海关。二十日，吴三桂再次致书多尔衮火速发兵。二十一日，双方在一片石关展开外围激战，农民军落败。

在正面战场，李自成率20万大军自北山至南海布阵，对山海关西、北、东三面围攻。四月二十一日，战斗先在石河展开。欢喜岭的清军蓄锐不发。二十二日，北翼城的明军向李自成投降。吴三桂到欢喜岭面拜多尔衮，引清兵入关。清军遂从南水门、北水门和关中门破阵出击，利用当日大风扬沙天气，与农民军展开近战。清军"追奔四十里"，农民军"大溃，自相践踏，死者无算，僵尸遍野，沟水尽赤"。李自成携残部仓皇回京。石河大战，以吴清联军大胜告终。

三十日，李自成弃京西逃。五月初二，多尔衮率大军抵京师。九月，清世祖福临由山海关入京，清顺治元年（1644）十月初一正式登基。

清军入关，是清史和满族史上划时代的大事，标志着清朝统一全国的开始。清朝成为中国历史上第二个少数民族建立的全国性政权。

（作者：秦学武）

---

[1] 这就是历史上著名的"冲冠一怒为红颜"。

In 1644[1], the first year of Yongchang of the Dashun Dynasty, the Qing army, with Ming general Wu Sangui leading the way, crossed the Shanhai Pass. Headed by Dorgon, the Prince Rui, they defeated the peasants' insurrectionary army led by Li Zicheng and captured Beijing. The historical event of the Qing army crossing the Shanhai Pass marked the beginning of Qing as the central regime of China.

In the spring of the 17th year of Chongzhen (1644) of the Ming Dynasty, Li Zicheng founded the Dashun Dynasty in Xi'an. On the 19th day of the 3rd month, Chongzhen hanged himself in the Jing Mountain, which marked the fall of Ming. On learning that Beijing had fallen, Wu Sangui coming to the rescue of the emperor ordered his troops to return to the Shanhai Pass.

When Li Zicheng occupied Beijing, Wu Sangui's family were controlled. Wu's father was forced to write a letter convincing his son to give up. Besides, Tang Tong was sent to the Shanhai Pass to reward Wu Sangui, who gave the pass to Tang. Later, Wu Sangui learned that Chen Yuanyuan, his beloved concubine, was abducted. Furiously annoyed, he marched his forces from Luanzhou to the Shanhai Pass and recaptured it.[2] On the 13th day of the 4th month, Li Zicheng mobilized a 200,000-strong force. They set off from Beijing and arrived at the Shanhai Pass on the 20th day. Meanwhile, a cavalry regiment of 20,000 people was sent to the Yipianshi Pass to cut off the army of Wu Sangui in his retreat to the east.

On the 9th day of the 4th month of Chongzhen (1644), Dorgon marched

---

1 1644 is the Jia Shen year in the traditional Chinese calendar. In March 1944, *Xinhua Daily* of Chongqing carried an article of Guo Moruo—"Commemorating the 300th Anniversary of Jia Shen Incident", causing a sensation in the society. On March 23, 1949, the Central Committee of the Communist Party of China left Xibaipo for Peiping (today's Beijing). Mao Zedong called it "Taking the Examination in the Capital". "We should never be Li Zicheng. We want to do well in the examination," he pledged.

2 This is the famous "a fit of rage for the beauty" in history.

the Qing army south. They had a plan to bypass the Shanhai Pass and burst through the Great Wall. On the 15th day, Wu Sangui asked an emissary to take a message to Dorgon for allying with him and attacking Li Zicheng together. The Qing army shifted from Wenghou (today's Fuxin of Liaoning) to the Shanhai Pass. On the 20th day, Wu Sangui wrote to Dorgon again requesting him to send in troops. On the 21st day, the Qing army had a fierce battle with the peasants' insurrectionary army on the periphery of the Yipianshi Pass, and the latter was defeated.

On the frontline battlefield, Li Zicheng placed a 200,000-strong army from north to south to besiege the Shanhai Pass from west, north and east. On the 21st day of the 4th month, the battle began in Shihe Village, and the Qing army stayed put in Huanxiling. On the 22nd day, the Ming army stationing in Beiyi Town of the Pass surrendered to Li Zicheng. Wu Sangui met Dorgon in Huanxiling. The Qing army, with Wu leading the way, crossed the Shanhai Pass. They attacked from the South Water Gate, North Water Gate and Middle Gate. The high wind was stirring up dust, and the army was engaged in hand-to-hand combat with the peasants. The troops "chased after the peasants for 40 *li*". The latter "fled in disorder, and a lot of them were killed in the panic-stricken stampede. The blood literally made the water turn red". Li Zicheng beat a hasty retreat to Beijing with the remnants of his force. The Shihe Battle ended in the outright victory of the Qing army.

On the 30th day, Li Zicheng abandoned the Capital and fled to the west. On the 2nd day of the 5th month, Dorgon marched his army to Beijing. In the 9th month, Fulin, Emperor Shizu of the Qing Dynasty, entered Beijing through the Shanhai Pass. On the 1st day of the 10th month of the 1st year of Shunzhi (1644), he was officially crowned emperor.

The Qing army crossing the Shanhai Pass was an epoch-making event in the history of the Qing Dynasty and the Manchu people. It marked the beginning of Qing, the second nationwide regime established by an ethnic minority in Chinese history.

(By: Qin Xuewu)

三、重要考古发现 III. Major Archaeological Findings[1]

19. 四方洞遗址 Sifangdong Site[2]

四方洞遗址，位于河北省承德市鹰手营子镇东北约 1.5 千米的柳河右岸。距今 2.8 万年，为旧石器时代晚期的较早阶段。2013 年 5 月被公布为全国重点文物保护单位。

遗址于 1980 年被兴隆县文物保护管理所发现。1984 年，小规模试掘。1988 年，中国科学院古脊椎动物与古人类研究所和河北省文物研究所正式发掘。四方洞遗址为小石器文化遗存，分上、下两种文化层，发现 2000 多件石制品和动物化石。

上文化层发掘出石锤、石核、刮削器、雕刻器、石棒，加工以锤击法为主，少量为砸击法；动物化石有中华鼢鼠、鹿等。

下文化层发掘出大量动物遗骨，如中华鼢鼠、仓鼠、野兔、鹿、牛、犀牛及大型猫科食肉类动物；石制品以刮削器为主，还有尖状器、砍砸器、端刮器和雕刻器等。

---

1 本部分词条参阅：河北省文物研究所编著：《河北考古重要发现（1949～2009）》，科学出版社 2009 年版。
For the remarks on entries in this part, see *Important Archaeological Findings in Hebei Province (1949–2009)* by Hebei Provincial Institute of Cultural Relics and Archaeology, Science Press, 2009.

2 参阅：谢飞、高星、龙凤骧：《四方洞——河北第一处旧石器时代洞穴遗址》，《文物春秋》，1992 年 S1 期；王峰：《承德市四方洞旧石器文化遗址发掘简报》，《文物春秋》，1992 年 02 期。
See: Xie Fei, Gao Xing and Long Fengxiang: "Sifangdong—The First Paleolithic Cave Site in Hebei Province", *Cultural Relics Annals*, 1992, Issue S1; Wang Feng: "A Brief Report on the Excavation of Sifangdong Paleolithic Cultural Site in Chengde", *Cultural Relics Annals*, 1992, Issue 2.

四方洞遗址具有典型的洞穴遗址特征，是河北省发现的第一处旧石器时代洞穴遗址，也是滦河上游燕山深处发现的第一处旧石器时代人类活动遗迹。四方洞遗址的发现，拉开了河北省旧石器时代考古的序幕。

（作者：秦学武）

The heritage site of Sifangdong is located on the right bank of the Liuhe River about 1.5 kilometers in the northeast of Yingshouyingzi Town, Chengde City of Hebei Province. It has been around for 28,000 years since the early stage of the late Paleolithic period. In May 2013, Sifangdong Site was designated as a Major Historical and Cultural Site Protected at the National Level.

The heritage site was discovered in 1980 by the Xinglong County Cultural Relics Preservation Office. In 1984, a small-scale trial excavation was carried out. In 1988, the Institute of Vertebrate Paleontology and Paleoanthropology (CAS) and the Hebei Provincial Institute of Cultural Relics conducted a joint excavation. The Sifangdong Site of small lithic culture was divided into upper and lower cultural layers. More than 2,000 stone articles and animal fossils were unearthed.

In the upper cultural layer, stone hammers, stone cores, scrapers, sculpting tools and stone rods processed by hammering or smashing were unearthed. The animal fossils were identified as Chinese zokors and deer, among others.

Vast amounts of animal bones had come out of the lower cultural layer, such as Chinese zokors, hamsters, hares, deer, cattle, rhinoceros and big cats. The stone articles were mainly scrapers, and there were spikes, choppers, end scrapers and sculpting tools as well.

Sifangdong, as a typical cave site, is the first cave site of the Paleolithic period discovered in Hebei Province, and the first human habitation of the Paleolithic period discovered deep in the Yan Mountains in the upper reaches of the Luan River. Its discovery marks the beginning of Paleolithic archaeology in Hebei Province.

(By: Qin Xuewu)

20. 孟家泉遗址 Mengjiaquan Site[1]

孟家泉遗址，位于河北省玉田县石庄村北 200 米处。距今约 1.7 万年，为旧石器时代晚期的较晚阶段。2013 年 5 月被公布为全国重点文物保护单位。

1986 年，中国科学院古脊椎动物与古人类研究所对遗址进行试掘，出土部分马、羊、鱼化石和智人牙一颗。1990 年 4 月至 5 月，在著名考古学家贾兰坡的倡导下，省市县联合考古队正式发掘，出土 23,000 多件石制品以及大量骨制品、脊椎动物化石，发现晚期智人化石 2 件。

石制品以燧石为主料，包括石核、石片、细石核、细石叶、石器等。石器的加工方式以正向为主，还有反向、复向、错向和转向加工。这些石器可以看到运用磨光技术的痕迹，表明当时人类已经尝试使用进步的技术。

孟家泉遗址以小石器为主，处于小石器向细石器过渡阶段。与华北地区同期、同文化传统的遗址相比，它具有鲜明的燕山南麓特征，在细石器文化的发展上占据重要位置，故命名为"孟家泉文化"。人类化石命名为"孟家泉人"。

孟家泉遗址是冀东地区最早一处有人类化石出土的旧石器时代晚期文化遗存。它的发现，不仅把唐山地区的人类历史向前推进了近万年，而且为研究东北和华北史前文化的衔接提供了极为可靠的资料。

（作者：秦学武）

---

1 参阅：谢飞，孟昭永，王子玉：《河北玉田县孟家泉旧石器遗址发掘简报》，《文物春秋》，1991 年 01 期。

See: Xie Fei, Meng Zhaoyong and Wang Ziyu: "A Brief Report on the Excavation of the Paleolithic Site in Mengjiaquan, Yutian County of Hebei Province", *Cultural Relics Annals*, 1991, Issue 1.

The Mengjiaquan Site is 200 meters in the north of Shizhuang Village, Yutian County of Hebei Province. It has been around for 17,000 years since the later stage of the late Paleolithic period. In May 2013, it was designated as a Major Historical and Cultural Site Protected at the National Level.

In 1986, the Institute of Vertebrate Paleontology and Paleoanthropology (CAS) conducted a trial excavation of the site. Fossils of horses, sheep, fish and a tooth of Homo sapiens were unearthed. On the initiative of Jia Lanpo, a famous archaeologist, a formal excavation was launched by the joint archaeological team at provincial, municipal and county levels from April to May 1990. 23,000 stone articles and a large number of bone articles and vertebrate fossils were unearthed. Two fossils of late Homo sapiens were discovered.

The stone articles, most of which were made of flint, include stone cores, stone flakes, fine stone cores, fine stone blades and stone implements. The stone articles were processed in forward, backward, multiple, intersecting and swaying directions. They show signs of being polished, which suggested that people of the time were experimenting with the improved technology.

As a transition from the small lithic period to the microlithic period, the Mengjiaquan Site featured largely small stone articles. Compared with the contemporary heritage sites in North China of similar culture, it had the distinctive feature of the region in the south of the Yan Mountains. The site was critically important in the progress of microlithic culture, hence its name "Mengjiaquan Site". The human fossils were called "Mengjiaquan Men".

The Mengjiaquan Site of the late Paleolithic Age is where human fossils were first unearthed in Jidong. Its discovery has pushed back the date of human activities in the Tangshan area by 10,000 years. Besides, it has provided authentic details for the study of the prehistoric culture in Northeast China and North China.

(By: Qin Xuewu)

21. 爪村遗址 Zhaocun Village Site[1]

爪村遗址，位于河北省迁安市南 7.5 千米滦河南岸的爪村附近。距今 4.2 万至 5 万年，处于旧石器时代晚期。2006 年 5 月被公布为全国重点文物保护单位。

爪村遗址的三处地点发现于 1958 年（5801）和 1986 年（86019、86020）。1958 年，当地农民发现哺乳动物化石，河北省文物主管部门与中国科学院古脊椎动物与古人类研究所协作完成了发掘任务，但对发掘的石制品误认为是"假石器"。[2] 1973 年、1986 年、1988 年，中国科学院古脊椎动物与古人类研究所及河北省文物研究所、唐山市文物管理处进行三次调查、复查和发掘，出土大量石制品、化石，还发现了磨制的骨器。

爪村遗址的三个地点分为两类：5801 和 86019 属于一类，石制品以燧石为主料，出土众多石器，如刮削器、尖状器、砍砸器、凹缺刮器、雕刻器、石锥等，加工以锤击法为主，属于小石器工业类型，处于旧石器时代晚期的较早阶段；86020 属于另一类，石制品包括石核、石片、细石核、细石叶、石器等，石器多用压制法，如端刮器、刮削器、尖状器、雕刻器等，属于细石器工业类型，属于旧石器时代晚期的较晚阶段。

三个地点均发现骨制品，86020 还出土有带穿孔的骨针和带有平行短线纹的骨锥。

爪村遗址，小石器与细石器共存，出土的石制品为研究华北地区

1　参阅：《唐山市全国重点文物保护单位爪村遗址》，《唐山劳动日报》，2007 年 3 月 30 日第 005 版。
See: "Zhaocun Village Site in Tangshan, A Major Historical and Cultural Site Protected at the National Level", *Tangshan Workers' Daily*, March 30, 2007, Page 005.

2　三川：《爪村调查记》，《化石》，1990 年 01 期。

石器文化的起源和发展提供了珍贵的实物资料。

（作者：秦学武）

7.5 kilometers in the south of Qian'an City of Hebei Province, the Zhaocun Village Site is near Zhaocun Village on the south bank of the Luan River. It has been around for 42,000–50,000 years since the later stage of the late Paleolithic period. In May 2006, it was designated as a Major Historical and Cultural Site Protected at the National Level.

The three spots of the Zhaocun Village Site were discovered in 1958 (5801) and 1986 (86019 & 86020). In 1958, mammalian fossils were found by the local farmers. Hebei's cultural relics authority worked with the Institute of Vertebrate Paleontology and Paleoanthropology (CAS) on the excavation. However, the stone articles unearthed were mistaken for "fake items".[1] In 1973, 1986 and 1988, the Institute of Vertebrate Paleontology and Paleoanthropology (CAS) worked with the Hebei Provincial Institute of Cultural Relics and the Tangshan Cultural Relics Management Office. Together, they conducted three investigations, reexaminations and excavations. Vast amounts of stone articles, fossils and grinded and polished bone articles were unearthed.

The three spots of the Zhaocun Village Site are classified into two types. 5801 and 86019, their stone articles mainly made of flint, are of the same type. Stone implements such as scrapers, spikes, chopping tools, emarginate scrapers, sculpting tools and stone cones were unearthed. The stone articles were processed mainly by hammering. They were small lithic products made in the early stage of the late Paleolithic period. 86020, belonging to the other type, consists of stone articles such as stone cores, stone flakes, fine stone cores, fine stone blades and stone implements. The stone implements were processed mainly by pressing, such as end scrapers,

---

[1] San Chuan: "Investigation of Zhaocun Village", *Fossils*, 1990, Issue 01.

scrapers, spikes and engravers. They were Microlithic products made in the later stage of late Paleolithic period.

Bone articles were found in all the three spots. Bone needles bearing holes and bone cones bearing parallel short lines were unearthed in 86020.

In the Zhaocun Village Site, small stone artifacts were mixed with microliths. The stone articles unearthed have supplied valuable materials for studying the origin and development of the Stone Age culture in North China.

(By: Qin Xuewu)

22. 化子洞遗址 Huazidong Site

化子洞遗址，位于河北省平泉市党坝镇瀑（bào）河南岸的一处高台上，为旧石器时代晚期遗址，距今约1万年。2013年5月被公布为全国重点文物保护单位。

2000年，省市县三级文物部门联合对化子洞进行发掘，出土石制品、骨器和动物骨骼等遗存4000余件。石制品以细石器为主，以燧石为主料，各式刮削器占石器主体，普通石片也占很大比例；骨器有骨锥、骨针以及两面穿孔的骨珠；动物骨骼有鸟类、兽类、鼠类和鱼类等多种类型。

化子洞遗址出土的细石器，显示出长城以北旧石器文化的另一个特征。以小型船底形石核为代表的石制品与昌黎渟泗涧、抚宁茶棚等冀东同类遗存相近，可能属同一文化系统。

从大量细石核、细石叶、碎石屑及石器的出土，可推断此处曾为石器加工场所。此类遗址在承德尚属首次发掘。化子洞遗址，为研究承德及华北地区史前历史提供了新实证。

（作者：秦学武）

The Huazidong Site is located on a high terrace on the south bank of the Baohe River in Dangba Town, Pingquan City of Hebei Province. It has been around for 10,000 years since the later stage of the late Paleolithic period. In May 2013, it was designated as a Major Historical and Cultural Site Protected at the National Level.

In 2000, the excavation of Huazidong by the cultural relics authorities at provincial, municipal and county levels was launched. 4,000 pieces of stone articles, bone articles and animal skeletons were unearthed. The stone articles are mainly flint microliths, the bulk of which are scrapers and stone flakes. Bone articles include bond cones, bone needles and bone beads punctured on two sides. And there are skeletons of birds, beasts, murines and fish.

The microliths unearthed in the Huazidong Site display some other traits of the Paleolithic culture to the north of the Great Wall. The stone articles, represented by the small stone cores of hull bottom shape, are similar to those in Jidong's Tingsijian Village of Changli and Chapeng Country of Funing. They may belong to the same cultural system.

Vast amounts of fine stone cores, fine stone blades, stone chips and stone implements were unearthed, which suggest that the site had been a stone workshop. This kind of heritage site was first found in Chengde. The Huazidong Site provides new evidence for the prehistory of Chengde and North China.

(By: Qin Xuewu)

23. 西寨遗址 Xizhai Site[1]

西寨遗址，位于河北省迁西县西寨村东南滦河北岸的山坡上，为新石器时代遗址，距今 6000 至 7000 年。2001 年 6 月被公布为全国重点文物保护单位。

---

1 参阅：陈应祺，郭瑞海，翟良富，徐海：《迁西西寨遗址 1988 年发掘报告》，《文物春秋》，1992 年 S1 期。

See: Chen Yingqi, Guo Ruihai, Zhai Liangfu and Xu Hai: "A Brief Report on the Excavation of Qianxi Xizhai Site in 1988", *Cultural Relics Annals*, 1992, Issue S1.

遗址在1985年文物普查时发现。1988年8月，省市文物部门对遗址进行发掘，发现祭祀地、房址、器物堆积群等重要遗迹，出土遗物近5000件。

西寨遗址分两期文化层。一期出土文物，生产工具为石器，分琢制、磨制、打制、压削四种；生活用具以陶器为主，多为夹砂褐陶，如筒形罐、圈足罐、圈足碗、平底钵、平底碗等。二期文化遗存，发现烧土面1处，灶1个，灰坑5个；生产工具为磨制、琢制、打制、压削的石器，如斧、锛、凿、铲、刀、磨盘、磨棒、石杵、砺石、有槽石器等；用河卵石或自然石片加工成的网坠最多，说明渔业非常发达；生活用具以陶器为主，如筒形罐、圈足罐、圈足碗、尊形器、椭圆形底罐等，以筒形罐最多；夹砂陶以红褐陶居多，黄褐陶和黑陶较少，泥质陶中红顶陶居多。

西寨遗址是一处集祭祀、居住、制陶、制石、渔猎于一体的大型史前文化遗存，反映了滦河中下游新石器时代的文化特征及演化序列。特征鲜明的陶器和石器，为研究滦河中下游和燕山南北的史前文化提供了丰富的资料。

（作者：秦学武）

The Xizhai Site is located on a slope on the north bank of the Luan River in the southeast of Xizhai Village, Qianxi County of Hebei Province. It has been around for 6,000–7,000 years since the Neolithic period. In June 2001, it was designated as a Major Historical and Cultural Site Protected at the National Level.

The heritage site was discovered in a general survey of cultural relics in 1985. In August 1988, the cultural relics authorities at provincial and municipal levels carried out an excavation of the site. Sacrificial sites, house sites and accumulated utensils were found, and 5,000 relics were unearthed.

The Xizhai Site has two cultural layers. In the first layer, stone tools for production, which can be classified into carving, grinding, chipping and chopping types, were unearthed. Utensils for daily life are mainly earthenware. They mostly include reddish-brown coarse potteries, such as tube-shaped pots, ring-foot pots, ring-foot bowls, flat-bottom dishes and flat-bottom bowls. In the second layer, a burnt earth surface, a stove and 5 ash pits were found. The production tools are stone articles that are grinded, carved, chipped or chopped, such as axes, adzes, chisels, shovels, knives, grinding plates, grinding rods, stone pestles, sharpening stones and grooved stone items. Vast amounts of net pendants made of pebbles or natural stone flakes suggest that the fishery was prosperous. Utensils for daily life are mainly earthenware, such as tube-shaped pots, ring-foot pots, ring-foot bowls, *zun*-shaped bowls and oval-bottom tanks, the majority of which are tube-shaped pots. The coarse potteries are mostly reddish-brown, while a few of them are yellowish brown or black. Most of the clay potteries are red-top potteries.

Xizhai is a large prehistoric cultural site for sacrificial rites, living, pottery making, stone processing, fishing and hunting. It reflects the cultural characteristics and evolution sequence of the Neolithic Age in the middle and lower reaches of the Luan River. With distinctive features, the earthenware and stone articles have supplied the study of prehistoric culture in the middle and lower reaches of the Luan River and the south and north of the Yan Mountains with abundant data.

(By: Qin Xuewu)

24．北戴河秦行宫遗址 Qin Palace Ruins in Beidaihe[1]

北戴河秦行宫遗址，又称金山嘴古城遗址，位于秦皇岛市北戴河区金山嘴、横山及附近。1991 年被评为"七五"期间全国"十大考古发现"之一。1996 年被公布为全国重点文物保护单位。

---

1 参阅：王进勤：《秦皇岛古近代建筑》，海天出版社，2009 年版。
See: Wang Jinqin: *Ancient and Modern Architectures of Qinhuangdao*, Haitian Publishing House, 2009.

1984年8月至1986年1月，当地文史工作者及国家省市区有关部门的领导、专家，对金山嘴进行了13次考察，发现大批建筑构件，如夔纹大瓦当、双云纹瓦当、饕餮纹瓦当、菱形纹空心砖、柱础石等。

1986年，河北省文物研究所试掘，发现两座秦代夯土房屋建筑遗址。此后，省市区联合考古队正式发掘，清理出多组夯土建筑基址及灶、水井、水管道、窖穴等遗迹，发掘出板瓦、筒瓦、圆瓦当、半瓦当、柱础石、空心砖等建筑构件及盆、甑、罐、瓮、鉴、井圈等陶具，还有少量陶文。发掘工作持续到1991年。

1986年7月19日，河北省文物局、文物研究所组织专家鉴定。著名考古学家苏秉琦和俞伟超认为，金山嘴遗址是秦行宫遗址，与辽宁省绥中县墙子里村发现的秦行宫遗址同属一个大建筑体系。它是秦始皇的行宫，也是大秦帝国的"国门"。

北戴河秦行宫遗址（全景图）（摄影：王进勤）
Panorama of Qin Palace Ruins in Beidaihe (Photographed by Wang Jinqin)

北戴河秦行宫遗址，以大殿建筑区为中心，分主院、东院、南院、西院四部分。呈现"主建筑坐落中间，辅建筑拱卫周边"的建筑布局。大殿、亭、台、房屋及附属建筑和相关配套设施，或用夯土墙相隔，或用通道相连，构成了完备的宫殿建筑群体系。

1986年9月25日，《人民日报》头版刊文《秦皇岛得名传说有了确凿依据 北戴河发掘出秦始皇父子行宫遗址》。中央电视台、《河北日报》等媒体相继报道。此次考古发现与《史记》《北戴河海滨志略》等文献记载相契合。秦皇岛的得名有了实物依据。

（作者：秦学武）

The Qin Palace Ruins in Beidaihe, aka Jinshanzui Ancient City Site, is located in and around the Jinshanzui Mountain and the Hengshan Mountain in Beidaihe District of Qinhuangdao. In 1991, it was listed among the "Top Ten Archaeological Findings" in China during the Seventh Five-Year Plan period. In 1996, it was designated as a Major Historical and Cultural Site Protected at the National Level.

From August 1984 to January 1986, local scholars and historians, as well as leaders of relevant government departments at provincial and municipal levels, had carried out 13 investigations on the Jinshanzui Mountain. Vast amounts of architectural articles, such as eave tiles with monster patterns, tile ends with double cloud and Taotie patterns, hollow bricks with diamond patterns and column base stones, were discovered.

In 1986, the heritage site of two rammed-earth houses of the Qin Dynasty were found in the trial excavation by the Hebei Provincial Institute of Cultural Relics. Afterwards, the archaeological teams at provincial, municipal and district levels conducted a joint excavation. Relics of rammed-earth architectural foundations, stoves, wells, pipelines and pits were sorted out. Architectural articles such as flat tiles, round tiles, round tile ends, half tile ends, column base stones and hollow bricks, and pottery wares such as basins, steamers, pots, urns, mirrors and well rings, some of which bore characters, were found. The excavation continued through 1991.

On July 19, 1986, specialists at the Hebei Culture Relics Bureau and the Hebei Provincial Institute of Cultural Relics were organized to examine the site. Famous archaeologists Su Bingqi and Yu Weichao suggested that the Jinshanzui Mountain Site is actually the Qin Palace Ruins and considered it the same architectural system as the one discovered in Qiangzili Village, Suizhong County of Liaoning Province. As the temporary palace of the First Emperor of Qin, it was the "Door to the Qin Empire".

The Qin Palace Ruins in Beidaihe, with the main hall very much at the center, break down into four parts: the main yard, the east yard, the south yard and the west yard. Its architectural layout features "the annexes surrounding the main building". The hall, pavilion, terrace, houses and annexes were partitioned off by rammed-earth walls or connected by passageways, forming a comprehensive palace building complex.

On September 25, 1986, the article "How Qinhuangdao Got Its Name? The Temporary Palace Site of the First Emperor of Qin and His Son Unearth in Beidaihe Provides Conclusive Evidence" was carried on the front page of *People's Daily*. CCTV and *Hebei Daily* had also reported this discovery. The archaeological findings matched up with the accounts of *Records of the Historian* and *Chronicles of Beidaihe Seaside*, providing the foundation for the name of Qinhuangdao.

(By: Qin Xuewu)

25. 金代烧酒锅 Liquor Pot of the Jin Dynasty[1]

金代烧酒锅，1975 年 12 月在河北省秦皇岛市青龙满族自治县土门子镇水泉村（原为承德地区青龙县土门子公社井丈子大队）西山嘴自然村发现。现藏于承德博物馆，为国家一级文物。

西山嘴村位于青龙县城东 30 千米，村南为一处金代遗址。烧酒锅在金代文化层的一个竖式圆窖里发现，经河北省地质四队鉴定，烧酒锅为青铜铸成。同文化层还出土了北宋定窑白釉瓷片，金代白釉、黑釉瓷片，六鋬耳铁锅，曲柄铁锄，以及北宋、辽、金时期 23 种不同年号的铜钱 100 余斤。从地层和伴出器物判断，烧酒锅为金代遗物。

---

1 参阅：青龙县井丈子大队革委会、承德市避暑山庄管理处：《河北省青龙县出土金代铜烧酒锅》，《文物》，1976 年 9 期；郭长海：《中国蒸馏酒史探源》，《酿酒》，1998 年 04 期；李华瑞：《中国烧酒起始探微》，《历史研究》1993 年 05 期；林荣贵：《金代蒸馏器考略》，《考古》，1980 年 05 期。

See: Reform Committee of Jingzhangzi Team in Qinglong County and Chengde Summer Resort Management Office: "Bronze Liquor Pot of Jin Dynasty Unearthed in Qinglong County, Hebei Province", *Cultural Relics*, 1976, Issue 9; Guo Changhai: "A Probe into the History of Distilled Liquor in China", *Liquor Making*, 1998, Issue 04; Li Huarui: "On the Beginning of Chinese Liquor", *Historical Research*, 1993, Issue 05; Lin Ronggui: *On Distillers in Jin Dynasty*, *Archaeology*, 1980, Issue 05.

金代烧酒锅（供图：承德博物馆）
Liquor Pot of Jin (Provided by Chengde Museum)

烧酒锅高 41.6 厘米，由上下两个分体套合组成。下分体是一大半球形甑锅，上分体是一圆桶形冷却器，上下分体的接合部有双唇汇酒槽及酒流和排水流。按照烧酒锅的构造原理和使用方法，有关部门对其进行了两次蒸酒实验。一次蒸酒全过程约 45 分钟，出酒量约 1 斤，酒度近 10 度。实验表明，该烧酒锅是一套依然有效的小型蒸酒器。

金代烧酒锅是已发现年代最早的蒸酒器。从加温水酒法发展到蒸馏法造酒，这是中国古代酿酒技术的一次飞跃。它的发现，标志着金代已有成熟的蒸馏酿酒技术，元代已广泛使用，否定了中国烧酒为元代时从阿拉伯国家传入的说法。[1]

冀东地区白酒酿制历史悠久，以平泉"山庄老酒传统酿造技艺"、承德"板城烧锅酒传统五甑酿造技艺"为代表的蒸馏酒传统酿造技艺，入选国家级非物质文化遗产代表性项目名录。青龙的许多村庄也以烧酒锅命名，如烧锅杖子、烧锅店、上烧锅、下烧锅、烧锅岔等。

（作者：秦学武）

---

[1] 关于中国白酒（或称烧酒）起源年代，大致有四种说法：一是东汉说，二是唐代说，三是宋代说，四是元代说。

The liquor pot of the Jin Dynasty was discovered in December 1975 in Shuiquan Village, Tumenzi Town, Qinglong Manchu Autonomous County, Qinhuangdao of Hebei Province. As a First Grade Cultural Relic of China, it is kept in the Chengde Museum.

Xishanzui Village, where a Jin Dynasty heritage site was found on the southern edge, is 30 kilometers in the east of Qinglong County. The liquor pot was found in a vertical round cellar in the cultural layer of Jin. It was identified by the Fourth Geological Team of Hebei Province as a bronze pot. Many other cultural relics were unearthed from the same cultural layer, such as white glazed tiles from the Ding kilns of the Northern Song Dynasty, white and black glazed tiles, hexagon iron pots and cranked hoes of the Jin Dynasty, and over 50 kilograms of copper coins with 23 reign titles of the Northern Song, Liao and Jin dynasties. We may judge from the layer and the unearthed utensils that the liquor pot dates back to the Jin Dynasty.

The 41.6-centimeter-high liquor pot consists of the upper part—a barrel-shaped cooler, and the lower part—a hemispherical rice steamer. At the junction of the upper and lower parts, are a double-lip liquor trough, a funnel and a drainage channel. Following the structure and design of the liquor pot, relevant departments had conducted two distilling experiments. Each process went on for 45 minutes, and 0.5 kilogram of liquor reaching 10% ABV was distilled. Experiment results prove that the liquor pot was a small distiller that still functions.

The liquor pot of Jin is the earliest distiller ever found. The evolution from liquor warming to liquor distilling was a ground-breaking progress in brewing technology in ancient China. The discovery of the liquor pot suggested that the distilling technology had already existed in the Jin Dynasty and been used on a wide scale in the Yuan Dynasty. It refuted the theory that liquor was introduced from Arab countries in the Yuan Dynasty.[1]

The Jidong region has a well-established tradition of liquor making. The "Traditional Brewing Techniques of Mountain Resort Liquor" of Pingquan and the "Bancheng Traditional Steaming Techniques of Distilled Liquor" of Chengde have been included in the List of Representative Items of National Intangible Cultural Heritage. Many villages in Qinglong County were named after the liquor pot (shaoguo), such as Shaoguozhangzi, Shaoguodian, Shangshaoguo, Xiashaoguo and Shaoguocha.

(By: Qin Xuewu)

---

[1] There are four theories as to the date for the emergence of Chinese liquor (or *shaojiu*): Eastern Han, Tang, Song and Yuan.

第二章

长城文化

Chapter II The Great Wall Culture

一、长城精华 I. Highlights of the Great Wall

1. 长城 The Great Wall

长城，又称万里长城，是中国古代的中原王朝为防御北方游牧民族南下侵扰而在边界地带修筑的军事防御工事。长城是以高大、坚固、连绵的城墙为主体，同大量的关隘、城堡、敌台、烽燧等设施相结合的防御体系。1961年，长城被公布为全国重点文物保护单位。

万里长城是世界上体量最大、体系最完整的古代军事防御工程，是人类文明史上的奇迹。1987年，被联合国教科文组织列入世界文化遗产名录。

长城，有土城、石城和砖城之分。秦汉时期，土筑长城用土为紫色，故称紫塞。长城分布在中国15个省、自治区、直辖市，现存多为明长城，秦长城居其北。总长逾2.1万千米。

修筑长城的国家最早为春秋齐国。战国时，赵、齐、燕、秦、楚、魏、中山等国竞相筑城。秦朝将秦、燕、赵三国的旧长城连接，西起临洮，北依阴山，东至辽东，始称万里长城。此后，汉、北魏、北齐、隋、唐、五代、宋、金和明都曾修筑长城。

秦代和隋代都曾征发、迁徙十数万甚至上百万的男丁修筑长城。明代南兵北戍，来自浙江的"戚家军"戍守蓟镇。现在，蓟镇长城沿线的许多村落有长城兵后裔聚居，仅秦皇岛市就有158个自然村。近年，秦皇岛市、辽宁省绥中县曾组织义乌兵后裔重返故乡活动。

历经2500余年的长城就是一部中华民族的史诗。它是中原农耕文化与北方游牧文化的分界线，也是中国社会从先秦"血缘政治"向秦汉"地缘政治"转型的重要标志。它是文化交流、经济发展的纽带，更是"多元一体"的中华文化交汇、融合的生动体现。

长城是中华文化、民族智慧的象征。长城最核心的价值，在于它所承载的伟大精神，即团结统一、众志成城的爱国精神，坚韧不屈、自强不息的民族精神，守望和平、开放包容的时代精神。长城精神早已融入民族血脉，成为实现中国梦的强大力量。

（作者：秦学武，吴子国）

The Great Wall, also known as the Ten-thousand-*li* Wall, is a series of military fortifications in ancient China built by dynasties in the Central Plains in their border areas to keep out the invading nomads in the north. It was made of tall, strong and rolling walls and formed a defense system together with the passes, castles, watchtowers and beacon towers. In 1961, the Great Wall was designated as a Major Historical and Cultural Site Protected at the National Level.

As a miracle in the history of human civilization, the Great Wall is the largest and most sophisticated ancient military defense construction in the world. In 1987, it was designated by the UNESCO as a World Cultural Heritage.

The Great Wall is divided into three categories: earth wall, stone wall and brick wall. In the Qin and Han dynasties, it was built with purple soil, hence the name Purple Fortress. The walls are located in 15 provinces, autonomous regions and municipalities across China. What we see today was mostly built in the Ming Dynasty, with the wall of Qin lying to its north. The Great Wall spans over 21,000 kilometers in total.

The Great Wall had been first built in the Spring and Autumn Period by the State of Qi. In the Warring States Period, Zhao, Qi, Yan, Qin, Chu, Wei and Zhongshan had competed to build walls. In the Qin Dynasty, the walls of Qin, Yan and Zhao were linked together. Ranging from Lintao in the west, along the Yin Mountains in the north, to Liaodong in the east, it became known as the Great Wall. Afterwards, the Great Wall had been continuously built in Han, Northern Wei, Northern Qi, Sui, Tang, Five Dynasties, Song, Jin and Ming.

Banchangyu Great Wall (Photographed by Wang Huaiqiang)

In the Qin and Sui dynasties, hundreds of thousands or even a million laborers were conscripted for the construction of the Great Wall. In the Ming Dynasty, the "Qi Army" from Zhejiang marched north and stood guard in the Garrison of Jizhou. Today, many villages along the Great Wall in Jizhou are settlements for the descendants of the Great Wall soldiers. In Qinhuangdao alone, there are 158 such villages. In recent years, the authorities of Qinhuangdao City and Suizhong County, Liaoning Province have organized the descendants of Yiwu soldiers from Zhejiang to explore their roots.

Surviving for 2,500 years, the Great Wall is an epic of the Chinese nation. It is the demarcation line between farming civilization in the Central Plains and nomadic civilization in northern China, and a major symbol of evolution from blood-oriented politics in the pre-Qin period to geopolitics in the Qin and Han dynasties. As a cultural and economic bond, it vividly displays the cultural convergence and integration of the Chinese nation.

The Great Wall embodies the culture and wisdom of China. At the core of it is the spirit within: solidarity, unification, patriotism, resilience, peace-loving and openness. The Great Wall spirit is inherited like blood and genes and has become a potent force to make the Chinese Dream possible.

(By: Qin Xuewu and Wu Ziguo)

2. 蓟镇长城 Jizhou Great Wall[1]

为防御蒙古诸部和建州女真的侵扰，明洪武至万历年间在西起嘉峪关、东至山海关一带修筑长城，总长约 6700 千米，时称"边墙"。

---

[1] 参阅：郑绍宗：《论河北明代长城》，《文物春秋》1990 年 01 期。
See: Zheng Shaozong: "On the Great Wall of Hebei in the Ming Dynasty", *Cultural Relics Annals*, 1990, Issue 1.

明洪武至嘉靖年间，在东起鸭绿江、西至嘉峪关的长城沿线设九个军事重镇，俗称"九边"。九边既是军事防卫单位，也是行政区划单位。

蓟镇[1]东起山海关，西到居庸关南的镇边城[2]，东西绵延千里，北到长城，南到今河北中部、山东北部。蓟镇从北、东、南三个方向拱卫京师，是"九边"中最重要的关镇。

蓟镇长城由明将徐达于洪武年间在北齐长城基础上修建，弘治、嘉靖年间又曾整修，但大规模的修筑则为总兵戚继光完成。隆庆二年至万历十一年，他与总督谭纶、杨兆，在蓟镇、昌平镇修建敌台[3]1448座（蓟镇1194座），整饬边墙2000余里，使得北部长城连成一片。

蓟镇长城体现了"因地制宜、用险制塞"的建筑思想。山势低矮处，加高城墙；山势高峻处，修建敌楼，个别地方加修障墙、支墙、挡马墙。蓟镇长城成为设施完备、构筑牢固、布局严谨的军事防御体系。

蓟镇防区分东、中、西三协守。东路副总兵驻建昌营，设山海关、石门寨、燕河营、台头营四路；中路副总兵驻三屯营，设太平寨、喜峰口、松棚谷、马兰谷四路；西路副总兵驻石匣营，设墙子岭、曹家寨、古北口、石塘岭四路。总兵居中调遣，驻迁西三屯营。

蓟镇长城是明长城的精华段。山海关、金山岭、八达岭三处景区，均为国家级风景名胜区、国家AAAAA级旅游景区，最能体现明长城的景观特色和文化价值。

蓟镇长城自古就是兵家必经之地。卢龙塞道、蓟辽走廊，是通往东北、华北的交通要道。皇太极己巳之变、清军入关、第二次直奉大战、长城抗战等历史事件就发生在这里。

（作者：秦学武）

---

1 明嘉靖二十七年（1548），蓟州始称蓟州镇，简称蓟镇。蓟镇属下有昌镇、真保镇。

2 另一说：蓟镇长城东起山海关，西到黄花镇。

3 空心敌台为戚继光创建，也称敌楼，底层用于将士戍守和储藏物资，二层供士兵瞭望和燃烽火，进可攻退可守，大大加强了长城的防御功能。

空心敌楼（摄影：王进勤）
A watchtower (Photographed by Wang Jinqin)

To keep out the invading Mongolian troops and Jianzhou Jurchens, the Ming Great Wall was built between the reigns of Hongwu and Wanli in the Ming Dynasty. Ranging from the Jiayu Pass in the west to the Shanhai Pass in the east, it stretches for 6,700 kilometers, called the "Border Wall" at the time. Between the reigns of Hongwu and Jiajing, nine military towns were established along the Great Wall. Colloquially known as the "Nine Garrisons", they range from the Yalu River in the east to the Jiayu Pass in the west. The Nine Garrisons were both military defense areas and administrative regions.

The Garrison of Jizhou[1], ranging from the Shanhai Pass to the Zhenbian Town[2] in the south of the Juyong Pass, spans 1,000 *li* from east to west. It stretches north to the Great Wall and south to the present-day central Hebei and northern Shandong. Surrounding the Capital in the north, east and south, Jizhou was the most important garrison among the Nine Garrisons.

During the reign of Hongwu, Jizhou Great Wall was built on the

---

1 In the 27th year of Jiajing of the Ming Dynasty, Jizhou became known as the Garrison of Jizhou, administering the Garrisons of Chang and Zhenbao.

2 The other theory is that the Jizhou section of the Great Wall stretches from the Shanhai Pass in the east to the Huanghua County in the west.

Magnificent Dongjiakou Great Wall (Photographed by Wang Huaiqiang)

foundation of the walls from the Northern Qi Dynasty by General Xu Da. In the years of Hongzhi and Jiajing, it underwent some renovations. From the 2nd year of Longqing to the 11th year of Wanli, a large-scale construction of the Great Wall was carried out by Commander Qi Jiguang and Governors Tan Lun and Yang Zhao. 1,194 and 254 watchtowers[1] were built in Jizhou and Changping respectively, and more than 2,000 *li* of the walls were reinforced, thus linking the northern Great Wall together.

Jizhou Great Wall emphasized the architectural philosophy of "adapting to local condition". Where the hills were low, the walls were made higher; where the hills were high, watchtowers were built. In some parts, barrier walls, supporting walls and horse-blocking walls were built. Jizhou Great Wall was a well-equipped, solidly-built and integrated military defense system.

The Garrison of Jizhou area was strongly guarded in the east, middle and west. The Deputy Commander in the east route, who was stationed in Jianchangying, oversaw Shanhaiguan, Shimenzhai, Yanheying and

---

1 The hollow watchtower was invented by Qi Jiguang. Troops were stationed on the ground floor, which doubled as the storeroom. The second floor housed the lookout and beacon station. As a stronghold for both offense and defense, it enhanced the defense capabilities of the Great Wall.

Crenels (Provided by the Office of the People's Government of Luanping County)

Taitouying; the Deputy Commander in the middle route, who was stationed in Santunying, oversaw Taipingzhai, Xifengkou, Songpenggu and Malangu; the Deputy Commander in the west route, who was stationed in Shixiaying, oversaw Qiangziling, Caojiazhai, Gubeikou and Shitangling. The Chief Commander, who was also stationed in Santunying of Qianxi, maneuvered all the troops of the three routes.

Jizhou Great Wall, a highlight of the Ming Great Wall, features Shanhai Pass, Jinshanling and Badaling, all of which are National Parks of China and National AAAAA Level Tourist Attractions. It fully epitomizes the characteristics and culture of the Ming Great Wall.

Jizhou Great Wall had since ancient times been a place of strategic importance. The Lulong Pass Path and the Ji–Liao Corridor were thoroughfares leading to Northeast and North China. It saw major historical events such as the Ji Si Incident in 1629 by Huang Taiji, the Qing Army Crossing the Shanhai Pass, the Second Zhili–Fengtian War, and the Battles against Japanese Aggression along the Great Wall.

(By: Qin Xuewu)

3. 山海关 Shanhai Pass

山海关位于河北省秦皇岛市东北15千米，古称临渝关，又作临榆关。明洪武十四年(1381)设山海卫，大将徐达翌年十二月在此筑城建关。[1] 清顺治元年（1644），改卫撤关；乾隆二年（1737）废山海卫，置临榆县。因其北依角山，南临渤海，故名山海关。

山海关集古城、雄关、要塞、景区于一体。1961年，万里长城——山海关被国务院公布为全国重点文物保护单位。2001年，山海关区被列为国家历史文化名城。2006年，山海关被授予"中国长城文化之乡"和"中国孟姜女文化之乡"称号。

山海关古城，主要由关城、东罗城、西罗城、南翼城、北翼城以及外围哨城等组成，与云南丽江、山西平遥并称中国三大古城。现存有关城和东罗城，占地150万平方米。

关城是山海关长城防御体系中的主体，城墙长4727米，高14米，宽7米。建有四座城门，东为"镇东门"（即"天下第一关"），西为"迎恩门"，南为"望洋门"，北为"威远门"。东门为进出关的关门，保存最完整。四门的城台上均建有城门楼。城中建有钟鼓楼。四门之外均筑有瓮城。东墙为长城主线，东南角台和东北角台分别建有角楼。关城的东南、西北和西南隅各设水门一座，墙外有护城河。

山海关是明长城的重要关隘，具有"主体两翼，左辅右弼"的格局，即以关城为主体，以南北翼城为两翼，老龙头长城、角山长城与威远城从南、北、东三面拱卫山海关。在老龙头到九门口26千米的长城线上，构筑了10大关隘、6座卫城、30座敌台、62座城隘、14座烽火台，以及分布在外围的墩台、卫所、城堡等军事工程。[2] 山海关是万里长城唯一集山、海、关、城于一体的海陆军事防御体系，有

---

[1] 1381年，明将徐达奉命修永平、界岭等关，以为古渝关非控扼之要，遂东移60里建山海关。古渝关，今抚宁榆关镇，隋开皇三年（583）修建。唐为东北军事重镇，辽金元时渐废。可见，古渝关与山海关并非一地。

[2] 潘跃：《秦皇岛山海关 明代长城重隘》，《中国文化遗产》2008年03期。

"天下第一关"之美誉。

2006年,国家投资2亿元实施山海关长城保护工程,对包括关城四面城墙及东罗城三面城墙在内的5800余米古城墙进行修复,为新中国成立以来长城保护工程的典范。

山海关自古就是军事要塞,扼古碣石大道和辽西走廊的咽喉。明清两代均派大员驻守,是拱卫京城的门户,有"两京锁钥无双地[1],万里长城第一关"之称。645年,唐太宗东征高丽,从此回师。1644年,李自成与吴三桂、清军在此激战。1900年,八国联军从这里登陆侵华。1922年、1924年,两次直奉大战在这里爆发。

山海关是关内关外的分界线,也是中原与东北商旅往来的重镇。这里是清帝谒陵祭祖的必经之所,也是文人雅士登楼览胜的佳处。明清至民国时期,大量山东、直隶的百姓从这里出关谋生,俗称"闯关东"。这是中国历史上著名的人口大迁移。

山海关是闻名中外的旅游景区。它以长城为主线,形成了老龙头、孟姜女庙、角山、天下第一关、长寿山、燕塞湖六大景区,于1979年对外开放。"天下第一关"城楼,是山海关的标志性建筑。萧显所书"天下第一关"匾额[2],笔力苍劲浑厚,与城楼风格浑然一体。

1985年,山海关景区被列为"全国十大风景名胜"之首。2007年,被评为国家AAAAA级旅游景区。2019年,获准加入"金钥匙国际联盟"。

(作者:秦学武,王芳)

15 kilometers northeast of Qinhuangdao, Hebei, the Shanhai Pass (Shanhaiguan) was known historically as Linyu Pass. In the 14th year

---

1 "两京"指盛京(今沈阳)和京师(今北京),为清军入关前、后的都城。山海关居二者之间,位置险要,故称"两京锁钥"之地。

2 有关匾额的书写人,说法有二:一是明成化八年(1472)进士、山海关人萧显所题,原匾现藏于城楼;一是明嘉靖年间武英阁大学士严嵩所题,原匾被日寇劫掠到东京。

古城民居（摄影：王进勤）
Folk houses in Ancient City (Photographed by Wang Jinqin)

of Hongwu of the Ming Dynasty (1381), the Shanhai Garrison was established. In the 12th month the next year, General Xu Da built the Shanhai Pass here.[1] In the first year of Shunzhi of the Qing Dynasty (1644), the pass was opened. In the 2nd year of Qianlong (1737), the Shanhai Garrison was abolished and reestablished as Linyu County. Nestling against the Jiaoshan Mountain in the north and facing the Bohai Sea in the south, it was named Shanhai (literally mountain and sea) Pass.

The Shanhai Pass area features an ancient city, a pass, a fortress and a scenic spot. In 1961, the Shanhaiguan section of the Great Wall was designated by the State Council as a Major Historical and Cultural Site Protected at the National Level. In 2001, the Shanhaiguan District was designated as a National Famous Historical and Cultural City. In 2006, the Shanhai Pass was awarded the titles of "Home of Chinese Great Wall

---

1 In 1381, Xu Da, a general of Ming, was ordered to build the Yongping and Jieling Passes, among others. Since the ancient Yuguan Pass was not a strategic stronghold, the site of Shanhai Pass was shifted 60 *li* eastwards. Ancient Yuguan, today's Yuguan Town in Funing, was built in the 3rd year of Emperor Yang Jian of Sui (583). It was a military base in Northeast China in Tang, but had been laid waste in the Liao, Jin and Yuan dynasties. Obviously, the ancient Yuguan Pass and the later Shanhai Pass were not the same place.

Culture" and "Home of Chinese Meng Jiangnü Culture".

Shanhaiguan Ancient City is mainly composed of Pass Town, Dongluo Town, Xiluo Town, Nanyi Town, Beiyi Town, and Sentry Town in the periphery. It is juxtaposed with Lijiang of Yunnan and Pingyao of Shanxi as the Three Ancient Cities in China. The existing Pass Town and Dongluo Town cover an area of 1.5 million square meters.

The Pass Town was the main body of the defense system of the Shanhaiguan Great Wall. Its walls are 4,727 meters long, 14 meters high and 7 meters wide. The four gates are "Zhendong Gate" (First Pass Under Heaven) in the east, "Ying'en Gate" in the west, "Wangyang Gate" in the south, and "Weiyuan Gate" in the north. The east gate, which offered access to the pass, is best preserved. There is a gate tower on every one of the four gate platforms. A bell tower and a drum tower stand in the town. Outside the four gates are four barbican entrances. The east wall is the main line of the Great Wall, and there are two corner towers on the southeast and northeast platforms. In the southeast, northwest and southwest corners of the Pass Town, there is three water gates. Beyond the wall there is a moat.

The Shanhai Pass is a vital pass of the Ming Great Wall. Its spatial layout features the Pass Town at the center and the south and north wings on both sides. The pass is surrounded by Laolongtou Great Wall, Jiaoshan Great Wall and Weiyuan Town in the south, north and east sides. On the 26-kilometer-long section along the Great Wall from Laolongtou to Jiumenkou, 10 passes, 6 garrison towns, 30 watchtowers, 62 forts and 14 beacon towers were built. Distributed on the periphery were military installations such as warning stations, garrisons and castles.[1] The Shanhai Pass is the only sea-land

---

1　Pan Yue: "Qinhuangdao Shanhai Pass—A Military Stronghold of the Ming Great Wall", *China Cultural Heritage*, 2008, Issue 03.

山海关古城（复原图）（摄影：王进勤）
Original Shanhaiguan Ancient City (Photographed by Wang Jinqin)

defense system along the Great Wall combining mountains, sea, pass and towns, enjoying a reputation for being the "First Pass Under Heaven".

In 2006, the Chinese government spent 200 million yuan on the conservation of Shanhaiguan Great Wall. The four walls of the Pass Town and three walls of the Dongluo Town, with a total length of over 5,800 meters, were repaired. It is an example of Great Wall conservation after the founding of the People's Republic of China.

The Shanhai Pass had since ancient times been a military stronghold, controlling the strategic points of ancient Jieshi Path and Liaoxi Corridor. In the Ming and Qing dynasties, high-ranking officials were stationed in the place. As a gateway to Jingshi (Beijing), it was renowned as the "Key to the Two Capitals[1] and First Pass of the Great Wall". After the eastern expedition against Goryeo in 645, Emperor Taizong of the Tang Dynasty returned from here. In 1644, Li Zicheng launched a fierce battle with Wu Sangui and the Qing army here. In 1900, the Eight-Power Allied Forces

---

1　"Two Capitals" refer to Mukden (Shenyang) and Jingshi (Beijing). They were the capitals before and after the Qing army crossed the pass. Located between the two, the Shanhai Pass held the strategic points. Thus, It was dubbed the "Key to the Two Capitals".

山海关之冬（摄影：王怀强）
Shanhai Pass in winter (Photographed by Wang Huaiqiang)

landed here and invaded China. In 1922 and 1924, the First and Second Zhili–Fengtian Wars broke out here.

As the demarcation line between the inland and the outland, the Shanhai Pass was a commercial hub between the Central Plains and Northeast China. It was the essential route for the Qing emperors to honor their ancestors and an ideal spot for the intellectuals to climb high and gaze afar. During the period from the Ming and Qing dynasties to the Republic of China, many people of Shandong and Zhili went beyond the border through the Shanhai Pass and made a living away from home. Colloquially called the "Journey to the Northeast", this mass migration is famous in Chinese history.

The Shanhaiguan Scenic Area, opened to the public in 1979, is a tourist attraction prominent around the world. With the Great Wall as the main part, it features Laolongtou, Meng Jiangnü Temple, Jiaoshan Mountain, First Pass under Heaven, Changshou Mountain and Yansai Lake. The gate tower of the First Pass under Heaven is the iconic structure of the Shanhai Pass. Characters "Tian Xia Di Yi Guan" written by Xiao Xian on the inscribed board[1], with bold and vigorous strokes, is perfectly coherent with the style of the gate tower.

In 1985, the Shanhaiguan Scenic Area topped the ranking of "Top Ten Places of Interest in China". In 2007, it was named a National AAAAA Level Tourist Attraction. In 2019, it gained admission into the Golden Keys International Alliance.

(By: Qin Xuewu and Wang Fang)

4. 老龙头 Laolongtou Great Wall[2]

老龙头位于秦皇岛市山海关城南 4 千米，是明长城的东端起点。万里长城犹如一条翻山越岭的巨龙，在此喷薄入海，故名"老龙头"。

老龙头长城是山海关城防体系的一部分，长 725.1 米，包括入海石城、靖卤一号敌台、南海口长城、南海口关、宁海城、滨海城墙、王受二号敌台、澄海楼等建筑，占地 700 亩。

明洪武年间至明末，老龙头不断修缮。清军入关后，老龙头渐失军事防御作用，成为观海览胜的去处。1900 年，八国联军在这里登陆侵华，老龙头城池尽毁。1984 年，多家报纸共同发出"爱我中华，修我长城"的号召。1985 年至 1992 年，山海关区政府重修老龙头，总投资 1795.3 万元，其中社会捐款 150 余万元。[3] 老龙头得以重现于世。

澄海楼是老龙头最著名的建筑。明万历年间，兵部主事王致中在"观海亭"[4] 基础上主持修建。清康熙、乾隆年间两次重修。楼高 14.5

---

1 There are two opinions about the creator of the inscribed board. First, it was written by Xiao Xian, a native of the Shanhai Pass who became a *jinshi* scholar in the 8th year of Chenghua (1472) of the Ming Dynasty. The original board was kept in the gate tower. Second, it was written by Yan Song, Grand Scholar of Wuying Hall in the years of Jiajing of Ming. The original board was robbed by the Japanese invaders and shipped to Tokyo.

2 参阅：李冬宇等：《长城重镇军事与建筑的双料明珠》，《中国文化遗产》2009 年 05 期。
See: Li Dongyu, etc.: "The Military and Architectural Powerhouse of the Great Wall", *China Cultural Heritage*, 2009, Issue 05.

3 朱艳冰，宋柏松：《30 年前全中国捐款复建老龙头》，《河北日报》2014 年 8 月 8 日第 005 版。

4 "观海亭"为戚继光所建。澄海楼，取"碧海澄清"之意。

米，面宽 15.68 米，进深 12 米。澄海楼是老龙头的制高点，也是观海胜地。"雄襟万里"匾额为明代大学士孙承宗所题。乾隆帝御题"元气混茫"匾额，并书"日曜月华从太始，天容海色本澄清"对联。五位清代帝王登临。

澄海楼前的"天开海岳"碑，传说为唐代名将薛仁贵东征高丽时所立。字体遒劲苍郁，尽显老龙头海阔天高之势。

入海石城是长城延伸入海的尽端，长 22.4 米，宽 8.3 米，高 9.2 米，北接靖卤台，构成封锁海面的制高点。万历七年（1579），都督戚继光、行参将吴惟忠修建入海石城。它以巨型条石砌垒，条石凿有燕尾槽，两石用铁水浇筑的榫连在一起，坚不可摧。

靖卤台是明长城唯一海上敌台。嘉靖四十四年（1565），兵部主事孙应元在此修筑敌台。隆庆四年（1570），总兵戚继光改建为空心敌台，命名靖虏台[1]。康熙年间改称靖卤台。

南海口关为明长城东端的首关，滨海城墙是唯一滨海长城，均为徐达所建。

宁海城是山海关城的南部哨城，为巡抚杨嗣昌所建，是国内现存最完整、规模最宏大的明代军营，城内有龙武营、守备署、把总署、显功祠、龙王庙和关帝庙等。

（作者：秦学武，罗学锋）

Laolongtou Great Wall is located 4 kilometers south of the Shanhai Pass in Qinhuangdao, and it is the eastern beginning of the Ming Great Wall. The wall is like a rolling dragon running up to the sea, hence its name "Laolongtou" (literally great dragon's head).

As a part of the Shanhai Pass defense system, Laolongtou Great Wall is 725.1 meters long, including Coastal Stone Fort, Jinglu Watchtower No.1, Nanhaikou Great Wall, Nanhaikou Pass, Ninghai Fort, Coastal Wall, Wangshou Watchtower No.2 and Chenghai Tower. It covers an area of 700 *mu*.

---

[1] 靖虏台，平定虏患之意。明廷称蒙古、女真为"虏"。

老龙头之冬（摄影：王怀强）
Laolongtou in winter (Photographed by Wang Huaiqiang)

宁海城（摄影：王怀强）
Ninghai Fort (Photographed by Wang Huaiqiang)

From the reign of Hongwu to the final years of the Ming Dynasty, Laolongtou had been put into repairs. After the Qing army crossed the pass, Laolongtou no longer served as a military defense base. It became a place for admiring the sea. In 1900, the Eight-Power Allied Forces landed here and invaded China, destroying the wall of Laolongtou. In 1984, several newspapers launched an appeal for for "Renovating the Great Wall as a Manifestation of Patriotism". From 1985 to 1992, the Shanhaiguan District Government spent 17.953 million yuan on rebuilding Laolongtou, of which 1.50 million yuan was from social donors.[1] Laolongtou was revived.

The Chenghai Tower, built on the foundation of the Sea Viewing Pavilion[2], is the most famous building in Laolongtou. Its construction was headed by Wang Zhizhong, head of the Ministry of War, during the reign of Wanli in the Ming Dynasty. It underwent two reconstructions during the reigns of Kangxi and Qianlong in the Qing Dynasty. As the highest structure in Laolongtou overlooking the sea, the Chenghai Tower is 14.5 meters high, 15.68 meters wide and 12 meters deep. Characters "雄襟万里" (literally enterprising and ambitious) on the scribed board was written by Sun Chengzong, a Grand Scholar in the Ming Dynasty. Characters "元气混茫" (literally primordial chaos) on the scribed board was written by Emperor Qianlong. The couplet on either side reads: "The sun and the moon shine for immortality. The sky and the sea are clear and bright." Five emperors of the Qing Dynasty had ascended the tower.

In front of the Chenghai Tower stands a stone tablet inscribed with characters "天开海岳" (literally created by nature), which was said to be erected by Xue Rengui, a famous general of the Tang Dynasty, when he

---

1 Zhu Yanbing and Song Baisong: "Donations from across China for the Reconstruction of Laolongtou 30 Years Ago", *Hebei Daily*, August 8, 2014, Page 005.

2 Sea Viewing Pavilion was built by Qi Jiguang. Chenghai Tower bears the meaning of "clear, blue sea".

marched east against Goryeo. The bold and vigorous strokes show off the vastness and grandness of Laolongtou.

The Coastal Stone Fort, as the end of the Great Wall, is 22.4 meters long, 8.3 meters wide and 9.2 meters high. It joins the Jinglu Watchtower in the north to form a blockade line on the sea. The fort was built in the 7th year of Wanli (1579) with giant stone slabs by Military Governor Qi Jiguang and Garrison General Wu Weizhong. Dovetail grooves were drilled on the slabs, and the slabs were connected by mortise joints cast in iron, forming an indestructible fort in ancient times.

The Jinglu Tower was the only coastal watchtower of the Ming Great Wall. It was built in the 44th year of Jiajing (1565) by Sun Yingyuan, Director of the Ministry of War. In the 4th year of Longqing (1570), it was converted by Garrison Commander Qi Jiguang into a hollow watchtower. Originally called Jinglu Tower (靖虏台)[1], it was renamed Jinglu Tower (靖卤台) during the reign of Kangxi.

The Nanhaikou Pass was the first pass from the east end of the Ming Great Wall. The Coastal Wall was the only section of the Great Wall on the coast. They were built by Xu Da.

The Ninghai Fort, a sentry post in the south of the Shanhai Pass, was built by Governor Yang Sichang. Featuring Longwu Camp, Garrison Office, Commander's Office, Xiangong Shrine, Longwang Temple and Guandi Temple, it is the largest and best-preserved military barrack of the Ming Dynasty that survives in China.

(By: Qin Xuewu and Luo Xuefeng)

---

[1] Jinglu Tower bore the meaning of putting down the rebellion of Lu. In the Ming Dynasty, Mongolians and Jurchens were called "Lu (Barbarians)".

5. 角山长城 Jiaoshan Great Wall[1]

角山长城位于秦皇岛市山海关城北约 3 千米，主峰大平顶海拔 519 米。角山为燕山东段的余脉，因其山顶有巨石酷似龙首戴角，故名"角山"。角山是明长城从老龙头向北攀登的第一座山峰，有"万里长城第一山"之称。

角山长城是指从旱门关 10 号敌台到角山关段的长城，全长 1587 米，包括旱门关、角山月城和角山关，以及 5 座敌台、墙台、10 座烽火台，建于洪武元年（1368）。

角山长城的修筑突显防御思想。城墙随山就势，将城墙与山崖合为一体，形成深沟高垒的形势。外侧险峻，易守难攻；内侧低矮，便于登墙作战。这种因势利导、以险制塞的筑墙方法，体现了古人的高超智慧。

角山长城的城墙就地取材，根据地形地段而不同。山脚下，多为素土夹碎石夯筑；大平顶下南段城墙，为砖石混合结构；角山敌台以上，墙体为碎石填心、白灰浆灌缝。

角山长城是山海关城防体系的重要组成，设有三道关卡，依地势由低而高，层层向上，大有"一夫当关万夫莫开"之势，是扼守关城左翼的屏障。

（作者：罗学锋，秦学武）

Jiaoshan Great Wall is located some 3 kilometers north of the Shanhai Pass, Qinhuangdao. Its main peak Dapingding is 519 meters above sea level. The Jiaoshan Mountain is a branch of the east section of the Yan Mountains. On its top stands a large stone like a dragon horn, hence its name Jiaoshan (literally Horn Mountain). Jiaoshan is the first mountain

---

[1] 李冬宇等：《长城重镇 军事与建筑的双料明珠》，《中国文化遗产》2009 年 05 期。
Li Dongyu, etc.: "The Military and Architectural Powerhouse of the Great Wall", *China Cultural Heritage*, 2009, Issue 05.

Jiaoshan Great Wall (Photographed by Yu Wenjiang)

from Laolongtou northbound along the Ming Great Wall, so it is reputed as the "First Mountain of the Great Wall".

Jiaoshan Great Wall, ranging from the Watchtower No. 10, Hanmen Pass to the Jiaoshan Pass, is 1,587 meters long. Built in the 1st year of Hongwu (1368), it includes Hanmen Pass, Jiaoshan Barbican and Jiaoshan Pass, as well as 5 watchtowers and wall platforms and 10 beacon towers.

Jiaoshan Great Wall embodies the defense-oriented strategy. The high walls were built along the high mountain, so that the two were joined together to become a strong defense line. The enemy forces would by hindered by the high outer side, while the soldiers could climb up the low inner side to fight on the wall. Jiaoshan Great Wall took the natural environment to the best advantage, standing as a symbol of the genius of ancient people.

The wall was built utilizing local materials, which were different depending on the landscape. The sections at the foot of the mountain were typically tamped with plain soil and pebbles. The sections in the south of Dapingding were mostly a brick-and-stone structure. The sections above the watchtowers on the Jiaoshan Mountain were piled up with rubbles and filled with white mortar.

Jiaoshan Great Wall was an important part of the Shanhai Pass defense system. It features three barriers from bottom up to keep the enemies away, serving as a geographical defense for the left wing of the Pass Town.

(By: Luo Xuefeng and Qin Xuewu)

6. 九门口 Jiumenkou[1]

九门口是明长城蓟镇东部的重要关隘，又称"一片石关"，位于河北省秦皇岛市海港区驻操营镇九门口村[2]。明洪武十四年（1381）设关建城，素有"京东首关"之称。1996年，被公布为全国重点文物保护单位。

九门口古城初建于明洪武年间，明清时期多次修整。古城东西为砖墙，南北为石砌，有东、西、北三座卫城，设东、西、南三门，周长1千米。西门匾额曰"京东首关"。

过河城桥建在宽110米的九门河上，是万里长城中唯一的"水上长城"。桥下河床以条石铺砌，面积7000平方米，条石间用腰铁咬合，形成牢固、一体的河床，明代称"一片石"。康熙年间《抚宁县志》云："城下有堑，名九江口，为水门九道，注众山之水于塞外者也。"清代遂称"九门口"。桥两端筑有围城，中间为水门，桥上是牢固的城墙，城桥合一，既可高墙御敌，又可行水泄洪。

九门口长城[3]位于河北省秦皇岛市与辽宁省绥中县交界处，全长

---

1 邢留逮主编：《秦皇岛历史辞典》，中央文献出版社，2014年版；《秦皇岛长城》编委会：《秦皇岛长城》，方志出版社，2002年版。
Xing Liudai (ed.): *Qinhuangdao Historical Dictionary*, Central Party Literature Press, 2014; Editorial board of *Qinhuangdao Great Wall*: *Qinhuangdao Great Wall*, Local Records Publishing House, 2002.

2 九门口村原属抚宁县，与辽宁省绥中县新台子村接壤。1989年，绥中县文物部门重新修复东侧九门桥洞及部分长城主线。

3 李冬宇等：《长城重镇军事与建筑的双料明珠》，《中国文化遗产》2009年05期。

近7千米。始建于北齐时期，扩建于明洪武十四年（1381），后又多次修复。主要包括九门口、枣山区段和五道楼，是明代中叶的重点防御地段。

九门口南距山海关15千米，是连接华北与东北的又一要道。1644年，李自成派唐通率4万农民军在此扎营，被清军击败；1924年第二次直奉大战，双方在此激烈争夺；1933年，东北抗日义勇军在此与日军激战十余日，8次突入九门口关城；1945年，开国少将曾克林在此出关，率八路军挺进东北；1948年，解放军取道九门口，投入平津战役。[1]

（作者：秦学武，罗学锋）

Jiumenkou, aka "Yipianshi Pass", is an important pass of the Ming Great Wall in the east of Jizhou County. It is located in Jiumenkou Village, Zhucaoying Town, Haigang District, Qinhuangdao, Hebei Province.[2] In the 14th year of Hongwu of the Ming Dynasty (1381), the pass and a town were built here. Jiumenkou enjoys a reputation for being the "First Pass to the East of the Capital". In 1996, it was designated as a major historical and cultural site protected at the national level.

First built during the reign of Hongwu of the Ming Dynasty, Jiumenkou Ancient City underwent some renovations in the Ming and Qing dynasties. The ancient city, 1 kilometer in circumference, has brick walls in the east and west, and stone walls in the north and south. There are garrisons in the east, west and north, and gates in the east, west and south. Characters "京东首关" (literally first pass to the east of the Capital) were written on the scribed board of the west gate.

---

1 迟文斌：《风雨洗礼九门口长城》，《东北之窗》2021年11期。

2 Jiumenkou Village, originally administered by Funing County, is bounded by Xintaizi village, Suizhong County, Liaoning Province. In 1989, the cultural relics department of Suizhong County restored the arches on the east side and part of the Great Wall.

The Fort Bridge, spanning the 110-meter-wide Jiumen River, is the only "Great Wall section on water". The riverbed under the bridge, covering an area of 7,000 square meters, was paved with stone slabs. The slabs were connected by steel shanks, forming a solid and integrated riverbed and gaining the name "Yipianshi" (literally a stretch of stone) in the Ming Dynasty. *Local Records of Funing County*, compiled in the years of Kangxi, says: "There is a river beneath the fort, named Jiujiangkou. The nine arches let water flow from the mountains to the border area." In the Qing Dynasty, the bridge was called "Jiumenkou" (literally Nine Arches). Forts are built on both ends, with arches in between and a strong wall on the bridge, serving to both keep the enemies away and discharge floodwaters.

Running for nearly 7 kilometers, Jiumenkou Great Wall[1] is located on the spot where Qinhuangdao City of Hebei Province and Suizhong County of Liaoning Province meet. First built in the Northern Qi Dynasty, it underwent an expansion in the 14th year of Hongwu (1381) and some repairments later. Mainly composed of Jiumenkou, Zaoshan section and Five Towers, it was a key defence area in the mid-Ming Dynasty.

15 kilometers south of the Shanhai Pass, Jiumenkou was another thoroughfare connecting North China and Northeast China. In 1644, Li Zicheng sent Tang Tong, who led a peasant army of 40,000 people, to encamp in the place. However, they were defeated by the Qing army. In the Second Zhili–Fengtian War in 1924, the combatants were locked in a fierce battle here. In 1933, a major battle between the Northeast People's Volunteer Army against Japanese Aggression and the Japanese invaders broke out here. The battle lasted for a dozen of days and the Volunteer Army charged into the pass eight times. In 1945, Major General Zeng

---

1　Li Dongyu, etc.: "The Military and Architectural Powerhouse of the Great Wall", *China Cultural Heritage*, 2009, Issue 05.

九门口长城（摄影：王进勤）
Jiumenkou Great Wall (Photographed by Wang Jinqin)

Kelin crossed the Great Wall from here and led the Eighth Route Army to Northeast China. In 1948, the Liberation Army got off to the Beiping-Tianjin Campaign[1] by way of Jiumenkou.

(By: Qin Xuewu and Luo Xuefeng)

7. 喜峰口 Xifengkou[2]

喜峰口位于河北省迁西县滦阳镇，南距县城 40 千米。古称兰陉，元代称喜逢口[3]，明永乐初改称喜峰口。清代史学家和《永平府志》称喜峰口即古松亭关。[4]

喜峰口是重要的长城关隘，明清时曾驻兵设防。1381 年，大将徐

---

1 Chi Wenbin: "Jiumenkou Great Wall Witnessing the Hard Times", *A Window to the Northeast*, 2021, Issue 11.

2 参阅：郑绍宗：《论河北明代长城》，《文物春秋》1990 年 01 期。
See: Zheng Shaozong: "On the Great Wall of Hebei in the Ming Dynasty", *Cultural Relics Annals*, 1990, Issue 01.

3 相传古有久戍不归者，其父求之，喜逢于此，故名喜逢口。

4 松亭关是宋辽金时的蓟北名关，学界对其位置说法不一，有平泉西南说、宽城西南说、喜峰口说、潘家口说等。

冀东文化关键词

达建关。1423 年，修喜峰口水关。1452 年，在关内建新城。1541 年，建城池和来远楼。

喜峰口雄踞滦河河谷与长城相交之地，关门位于瀑河支流倒流河与滦河汇流处南岸。关城分内外两重，关城里又设巨大的卫所城。关门在北，名为来远楼，据说可容万人。[1] 从关门而入为外关城，再入为内关城，出内关城东北即入关内。关城周长约 1.5 千米，三道关门由坚固的城墙连为一体。

《永平府志》云，喜峰口关的东南有石筑喜峰城："城高二丈，周四百十八丈六尺，堑八十一丈五尺，南门有楼，荒城在北，有月城教场在城西，距关二里。"喜峰城即卫所城，北距关城 2.5 千米，坐落在群山环抱的盆地里，四周用条石砌成，非常坚固。

喜峰口自古就是军事要地。1399 年"靖难之役"后，明朝北界南移，喜峰口成为蓟北雄关。1428 年，明宣宗兵出喜峰口，大败蒙古兀良哈部。1629 年，清军由喜峰口等关隘破墙入关。1933 年，二十九军大刀队夜袭日军，取得喜峰口大捷，由此诞生著名抗战歌曲《大刀进行曲》。1948 年，东北野战军由此进关，解放平津唐。

喜峰口是中原通往大宁[2]和东北边陲的要道，也是明清时蒙古乌梁海部入贡的通道。康熙曾由此地巡视塞外，赋诗《入喜峰口》。现仍是唐山通往宽城、承德等县的交通要冲。

1979 年潘家口水库截流蓄水，喜峰口关和城堡被水淹没。喜峰口长城抗战遗址，2017 年入选全国红色旅游经典景区名录，2021 年被命名为全国爱国主义教育示范基地。

（作者：秦学武）

Located in Luanyang Town, Qianxi County, Hebei Province, Xifengkou is 40 kilometers south of the county seat. It was known as Linlan Passage

---

1 顾祖禹撰，贺次君、施和金点校：《读史方舆纪要》，中华书局 2005 年版。
2 今内蒙古宁城，为明代蒙古兀良哈三卫的中心。

in history and Xifengkou (喜逢口)¹ in the Yuan Dynasty. In the early days of Yongle's reign, its name was changed to Xifengkou (喜峰口). Historians of the Qing Dynasty and *Local Records of Yongping Prefecture* addressed Xifengkou as the ancient Songting Pass.²

Xifengkou, as a crucial pass of the Great Wall, was heavily guarded in the Ming and Qing dynasties. It was established in 1381 by General Xu Da. In 1423, a water pass was built here. In 1452, a new town was built inside the pass. In 1541, the town wall, moat and Laiyuan Tower were built.

Xifengkou dominates the place where the Luan River Valley and the Great Wall meet. The pass gate is located on the south bank of the confluence of the Daoliu River (a tributary of Baohe River) and the Luan River. The Pass Town is twofold, with a large garrison town inside. The gate tower in the north, named Laiyuan Tower, was said to be a place that could accommodate 10,000 people.³ Entering the pass through the gate, one could first find the outer Pass Town, then go into the inner Pass Town, and finally cross the pass through another gate in the northeast side. The Pass Town has a circumference of about 1.5 kilometers, and three gates are connected by solid walls.

According to *Local Records of Yongping Prefecture*, a stone town lies to the southeast of the Xifengkou Pass: "The town wall is 2 *zhang* in height and 418 *zhang* and 6 *chi* in circumference. The moat is 81 *zhang* and 5 *chi* in length. There is a tower on the south gate, a desolate town to the north,

---

1 According to legend, there was a man got called to the garrison and hadn't returned home for a long time. His father prayed for him and happened to meet him here. Thus, the place was named Xifengkou (literally Joyful Reunion).

2 The Songting Pass was a famous pass in Jibei in the Song, Liao and Jin dynasties. Many theories have been advanced as to its location, such as southwest of Pingquan, southwest of Kuancheng, Xifengkou, and Panjiakou.

3 *Summary on History and Local Politics*, written by Gu Zuyu, collated by He Cijun and Shi Hejin, Zhong Hua Book Company, 2005.

Xifengkou (Photographed by Wang Aijun)

and a training ground, which is 2 *li* away from the pass, to the west." This stone town, actually the garrison town, is 2,5 kilometers north of the Pass Town. Situated in a basin hemmed in by mountains, it is surrounded by stone slabs and extremely strong.

Xifengkou had since ancient times been a place of strategic importance. After the Jingnan Campaign in 1399, the northern boundary of the Ming Empire shifted southwards, and Xifengkou became a major pass of the Great Wall in Jibei. In 1428, Emperor Xuanzong of the Ming Dynasty sent troops across Xifengkou to defeat the Uriyangqa Tribe of Mongolia. In 1629, the Qing army breached Xifengkou, among other passes, and crossed the Great Wall. In 1933, the 29th Army's Big Sword Team launched a night attack and defeated the Japanese invaders at Xifengkou, which was the inspiration for "The Big Sword March", a famous battle song. In 1948, the Northeast Field Army crossed the pass from here and liberated Beiping, Tianjin and Tangshan.

Xifengkou was the key corridor from the Central Plains to Daning[1] and the northeastern frontier, and the passage for envoys of the Uriankhai Tribe of Mongolia rendering tribute to the emperors of the Ming and Qing dynasties. When he inspected the territory beyond the Great Wall through here, Emperor Kangxi improvised a poem "Entering Xifengkou". The place is still a significant thoroughfare connecting Kuancheng and Chengde counties.

In 1979, the Panjiakou Reservoir blocked the river to store water. The Xifengkou Pass and the town were flooded. In 2017, the War of Resistance Site along the Xifengkou Great Wall was included on the List of National Red Tourism Classic Scenic Spots. In 2021, it was designated as a National Demonstration Base for Patriotism Education.

(By: Qin Xuewu)

8. 潘家口（卢龙塞）Panjiakou (Lulong Pass)

潘家口古称卢龙塞，位于河北省迁西县北部[2]，南距县城 35 千米，东距喜峰口 5 千米[3]。潘家口是明清长城的重要关隘。滦河自北向南，由此入塞。

卢龙塞有广义、狭义之分。汉代至明清，潘家口以东滦河北岸的燕山通称卢龙山，其周边塞口称卢龙塞，此为广义的卢龙塞。狭义的卢龙塞，是指潘家口。

卢龙塞，是汉唐时的军事要塞。戎昱《塞下曲》云："自有卢龙塞，烟尘飞至今。"可见卢龙塞之险要。526 年北魏将领常景讨伐杜洛周，553 年北齐文宣帝讨伐契丹，583 年隋将阴寿攻打高保宁，1123 年辽将萧干攻破景州，均经由此地。

1　Located in today's Ningcheng, Inner Mongolia, it was the residential center of the Uriyangqa Tribe of Mongolia in the Ming Dynasty.

2　迁西县居迁安县西，原属迁安县（今迁安市），1946 年从迁安县析出。

3　《读史方舆纪要》《畿辅通志》称 12 里。

卢龙塞道，古称"长堑"，是汉唐时中原通往古辽西的要道，[1]大体分东、西两线。西线，由潘家口北行，至宽城县燕子峪东渡滦河奔向柳城（今辽宁朝阳）。207年，曹操北征乌桓时由此出塞，辟卢龙塞道。354年，东晋将领步浑重又整治卢龙塞道；东线，由潘家口渡滦河，东行经喜峰口、冷口，北折向柳城。《水经注》云："塞道自无终县东出，渡濡水，向林兰陉，东至青陉[2]。卢龙之险，峻阪萦折，故有九峥之名。"

《读史方舆纪要》载："今（永平）府西一百九里有卢龙镇，土色黑，山似龙形，即古卢龙塞云。"据《水经注》载，卢龙城，为曹操北征乌桓时修筑。王昌龄《出塞二首》云："但使龙城飞将在，不教胡马度阴山。"这里，卢龙镇与卢龙城、龙城所指为一处。

明洪武十五年（1382），在小河口建潘家口关。嘉靖四十一年（1562）[3]，在旧关南四里建新关城（在滦河西岸），并派重兵驻守。《永平府志》载，潘家口关城为土筑，高二丈二尺，城周二百十九丈六尺，西、南各有一门。

1559年，兀良哈部数万骑兵攻进潘家口，在京东劫掠，史称"潘家口之战"。1979年，潘家口水库建成后，关城尽没于水，被称为"水下长城"。

（作者：秦学武）

Historically known as Lulong Pass, Panjiakou is located in the north of Qianxi County[4], Hebei Province. It is 35 kilometers north of the county seat and 5 kilometers[5] west of Xifengkou. Panjiakou was an important pass of

---

1 不同朝代，卢龙塞道当有差异。汉唐时，为潘家口通往柳城（今辽宁朝阳）方向；明清时，为喜峰口通往大宁（今宁城）或柳城方向。

2 有文献称是今"冷口"，有文献则称是今"青山口"。

3 有两说：《四镇三关志》云，潘家口新关建于1562年；《卢龙塞略》云，1573年"六月甲寅，移潘家口旧关于新城"。

4 Located in the west of Qian'an County, Qianxi County was originally administered by the former (today's Qian'an City). In 1846, it was separated from Qian'an County.

5 12 *li*, according to *Summary on History and Local Politics* and *Local Records of the Environs of the Capital*.

Panjiakou (Photographed by Wang Aijun)

the Great Wall in the Ming and Qing dynasties. The Luan River flew from north to south and entered the frontier region through here.

The Lulong Pass comes in broad and narrow senses. From the Han Dynasty to the Ming and Qing dynasties, the part of Yan Mountains to the north of the Luan River and east of Panjiakou was known collectively as the Lulong Mountains, and the mountain passes were the Lulong Pass in broad sense. In narrow sense, the Lulong Pass referred particularly to Panjiakou.

The Lulong Pass was a military stronghold in the Han and Tang dynasties. Here's what "Frontier Song", a poem by Rong Yu, says: "Ever since the erection of Lulong Fortress, smoke and dust have been rising high." It is clear that the Lulong Pass was a place of strategic importance. In 526, 553 and 583, General Chang Jing of the Northern Wei Dynasty, Emperor Wenxuan of the Northern Qi Dynasty and General Yin Shou of the Sui Dynasty marched through the place on their way to fight the wars against Du Luozhou, Khitan people and Gao Baoning respectively. In 1123, General Xiao Gan of the Liao Dynasty marched through the place on his way to capture Jingzhou Prefecture.

Historically known as "Long Ravine", the Lulong Pass Path was a thoroughfare connecting the Central Plains and ancient Liaoxi.[1] It was broadly divided into east and west routes. The west route started from Panjiakou. Going north, it reached the Swallow Valley, Kuancheng County where it ran eastward across the Luan River to Liucheng (today's Chaoyang, Liaoning). When Cao Cao marched north against Wuhuan in 207, he opened the Lulong Pass Path. In 354, General Bu Hun of the Eastern Jin Dynasty mounted a campaign on the path. The east route ran from Panjiakou across the Luan River. Going east, it went past Xifengkou and Lengkou, before bending north to Liucheng. Here's what *Commentary on the Waterways Classic* says: "The path starts from the east of Wuzhong County. It runs across the Rushui River to the Linlan Passage, and further east to the Qing Passage[2]. Steep with twists and turns, Lulong has been dubbed 'Jiu Zheng' (literally Nine Steep Peaks)."

According to *Summary on History and Local Politics*, "Lulong County is 190 *li* in the west of today's [Yongping] Prefecture. The soil there is black, and the mountain is like a dragon. It is actually the ancient Lulong Pass." According to *Commentary on the Waterways Classic*, Lulong Town was built by Cao Cao when he marched north against Wuhuan. "On the Frontier", a poem by Wang Changling, says: "Were the winged general of Dragon Town here, the tartar steeds would not dare to cross the frontier."

---

1 The Lulong Pass Path was not the same in different dynasties. In the Han and Tang dynasties, it ran from Panjiakou to Liucheng (today's Chaoyang, Liaoning); In the Ming and Qing dynasties, it ran from Xifengkou to Daning (today's Ningcheng) or Liucheng.

2 Some literatures argue that it is today's "Lengkou", while some argue that it is today's "Qingshankou".

Here, Lulong Town, Lulong County and Dragon Town are the same place.

In the 15th year of Hongwu of the Ming Dynasty (1382), the Panjiakou Pass was built in Xiaohekou. In the 41st year of Jiajing (1562)[1], a new Pass Town was built 4 *li* to the south of the old one (on the west bank of the Luan River). The town was strongly guarded. According to *Local Records of Yongping Prefecture*, Panjiakou Pass Town was built with earth. Its wall is 2 *zhang* and 2 *chi* in height and 219 *zhang* and 6 *chi* in circumference, with two gates in the west and south respectively.

In 1559, tens of thousands of Uriyangqa soldiers breached Panjiakou. They devastated and looted the region to the east of the Capital. The incident was known historically as the "Battle of Panjiakou". In 1979, the Panjiakou Reservoir was built and the Pass Town was flooded. It has since been known as the "Underwater Great Wall".

(By: Qin Xuewu)

9. 金山岭长城 Jinshanling Great Wall[2]

金山岭长城位于河北省滦平县与北京市密云区交界处，素有"万里长城，金山独秀"之美誉。1982 年，被批准为国家级风景名胜区。1988 年，被公布为全国重点文物保护单位。2020 年，被评为 AAAAA 级旅游景区。

金山岭长城建在雾灵山与古北口卧虎岭间的大、小金山上，始建于明洪武年间，戚继光任蓟镇总兵时续建完成。它西起龙峪口，东至望京楼，全长 10.5 千米。一般高约 7 米，下宽 6 米，上宽 5 米。沿线设有关隘 5 处，楼台 158 座。望京楼为最高处，登高望远，据说可见

---

[1] There are two different records. According to *Chronicles of Four Towns and Three Passes*, the new Pass Town in Panjiakou was built in 1562; according to *Annals of Lulong Pass*, "in the 6th month of 1573, the old Pass Town in Panjiakou was moved to the new location."

[2] 参阅：http://www.jslcc.com/ 有关金山岭长城的材料。
For details of Jinshanling Great Wall, click: http://www.jslcc.com/

金山岭长城（摄影：郭中兴）
Jinshanling Great Wall (Photographed by Guo Zhongxing)

北京城廓或夜色中的北京灯火。

金山岭长城是万里长城的精华地段，是军事防御与建筑艺术的完美融合。这体现在依山造势的布局、峰回路转的构思，体现在墙体建筑的扎实稳重、坚固持久，体现在雄关要塞的精心设计、敌楼烽台的精心营造。挡马墙、障墙、文字砖被誉为金山岭长城的"三绝"。

金山岭长城是民族艺术长廊。数不清的射击孔、瞭望孔、吐水嘴上饰有桃形、箭头形、刀把形、云钩形、锯齿形、漏斗形等图案。敌楼造型精巧，富有变化：有方形楼、扁形楼、圆形楼和拐角楼；有平顶、穹隆顶、船篷顶、四角钻天顶、八角藻井顶；有的敌楼飞檐刻有花卉、兽类等图案。造型精美的敌楼配上充满诗意的名字：将军楼、仙女楼、望京楼、桃春楼、狐顶楼、棒槌楼、拐角楼、西域楼等，充满文化韵味。

金山岭长城是享誉世界的中国文化地标。它是国歌中的长城，是《义勇军进行曲》创作灵感的重要来源地[1]、央视《中华人民共和国国歌》中长城的取景地；它是国礼中的长城，人民大会堂河北厅有巨幅壁画

1　1933年长城抗战，金山岭—古北口一线战事最激烈。1934年，田汉为电影《风云儿女》主题歌作词，金山岭成为《义勇军进行曲》创作灵感的重要来源地。

挡马墙、障墙、麒麟影壁、望京楼（摄影：郭中兴）
Horse-blocking wall, barrier wall, *Qilin*-engraved screen wall, Capital-watching Tower (Photographed by Gou Zhongxing)

《金山岭晨光》[1]，金山岭长城成为国家重大外事活动的新名片；它是国语中的长城，滦平是普通话标准音采集地、普通话体验区，被誉为中国普通话之乡。

金山岭景区是京承秦黄金旅游线的重要节点。金山岭长城是摄影爱好者的天堂，被评为"中国十大摄影旅游圣地"。

（作者：秦学武，罗学锋）

Located in the place where Luanping County of Hebei Province and Miyun District of Beijing Municipality meet, Jinshanling Great Wall has a reputation for being the "best part of the Great Wall". In 1982, it was approved as a National Park of China. In 1988, it was named a Major Historical and Cultural Site Protected at the National Level. In 2020, it was named a National AAAAA Level Tourist Attraction.

Jinshanling Great Wall was first built during the reign of Hongwu of the Ming Dynasty on the Large and Small Golden Mountains between the Wuling Mountain and the Wohu Mountain at Gubeikou. In the days when Qi Jiguang served as the Commander of Jizhou, its construction was finished. The 10.5-kilometer-long wall runs from Longyukou in the west

---

[1] 人民大会堂河北厅素有"国门第一厅"之称。著名画家郝军于2001年创作《金山岭晨光》。

to the Capital-watching Tower in the east. It generally measures 7 meters in height, and 6 and 5 meters in lower and upper widths. There are 5 passes and 158 towers along the wall. With a commanding elevation, the Capital-watching Tower is said to offer views of the panorama of Beijing and its lights gleaming at night.

Jinshanling, a perfect combination of defense capabilities and architectural art, is the highlight of the Great Wall. This has been embodied in the layout along the mountain with many twists and turns, the solid walls, the well-designed passes and fortresses, and the sophisticated watchtowers and beacon towers. Horse-blocking walls, barrier walls and inscribed bricks are the "Three Wonders" of Jinshanling Great Wall.

Jinshanling Great Wall is a gallery of ethnic arts. There are numerous shooting holes, lookout holes and water spouts, which are ornamented with peach patterns, arrow patterns, knife handle patterns, cloud hook patterns, sawtooth patterns and funnel patterns. The watchtowers are ingeniously built with diverse shapes. There are square, rectangular, round and corner towers, with flat tops, domed tops, canopy tops, tetragon tops and octagon tops. The eaves of some watchtowers are decorated with engravings such as floral or animal designs. These elegant watchtowers have romantic names:

General Tower, Fairy Tower, Capital-watching Tower, Spring Tower, Fox Tower, Hammer Tower, Corner Tower and Western Tower, which add a lot of cultural flavor to them.

Jinshanling Great Wall is a cultural landmark with worldwide reputation. It is the inspiration for the national anthem "March of the Volunteers"[1] and appears in the *National Anthem of the People's Republic of China*, a program made by CCTV. It is a subject of national gifts; in the Hebei Hall of the Great Hall of the People, there is a huge mural painting—*Jinshanling in the Morning Sunshine*[2], making it a new icon of China in major diplomatic occasions. It is the "Great Wall" in Mandarin; as the home of Mandarin, Luanping is the collecting site and experience area of standard Mandarin.

The Jinshanling Scenic Spot is an important section on the Beijing-Chengde-Qinhuangdao tourist route. Jinshanling Great Wall, a photographer's paradise, is one of the Top Ten Places for Travel Photography in China.

(By: Qin Xuewu and Luo Xuefeng)

二、长城保护 II. Preservation of the Great Wall

10. 山海关长城博物馆 Shanhaiguan Great Wall Museum[3]

山海关长城博物馆位于秦皇岛市山海关区，占地 1.21 公顷，为明清式仿古建筑，1991 年 7 月落成，原国家主席李先念题写馆名。经

1　In the battles along the Great Wall in 1933, the Chinese soldiers and the Japanese invaders were locked in a fierce battle along the Jinshanling–Gubeikou line. In 1934, Tian Han wrote lyrics for the "March of the Volunteers", the theme song of the movie *Children of Troubled Times*. Jinshanling was one of his major inspirations.

2　The Hebei Hall of the Great Hall of the People has a reputation for being the "No.1 Hall of China". Hao Jun, a famous painter, created the *Jinshanling in the Morning Sunshine* in 2001.

3　参阅：http://www.scb-museum.com/about.asp
See: http://www.scb-museum.com/about.asp

2004年改陈和2007年扩建,现有建筑面积6230平方米,展陈面积3600平方米。现为河北省重点博物馆、河北省爱国主义教育基地、全国爱国主义教育示范基地。

山海关长城博物馆是展示长城风貌、传播中华长城文化的专题性博物馆,与八达岭中国长城博物馆、嘉峪关长城博物馆并称中国三大长城博物馆。

全馆设序厅、历史厅、建筑厅、军事厅、文化厅和山海关长城厅,共6个展厅8个展室。馆内陈列集中展示了长城历史渊源、形式建制、人文风物、军事烽烟,尤其是山海关长城的古代军事作用和宏伟壮观的建筑艺术。2005年,"华夏脊梁——山海关长城博物馆基本陈列"荣获第六届全国博物馆十大陈列精品评选"精品奖"。

该馆馆藏文物品类齐全,汇集了石器、陶器、瓷器、青铜器、玉器、货币、碑帖,尤以长城建筑材料、长城火器为特色,有元代高足杯、明代楼军石臼、号炮、长城石炮、安边神炮、清代牧鹅童子玉坠、三足铜鼎、大铁炮等精品和特色藏品。

(作者:秦学武,罗学锋)

明代字模印文砖(供图:山海关长城博物馆)
Character-printed bricks of Ming Dynasty (Provided by Shanhaiguan Great Wall Museum)

Located in Shanhaiguan District, Qinhuangdao, the Shanhaiguan Great Wall Museum, covering an area of 1.21 hectares, is a Ming and Qing-style building completed in July 1991. The inscription of the museum's name was written by Li Xiannian, former President of China. The museum underwent an upgrade in 2004 and an expansion in 2007, and

山海关长城博物馆（摄影：于文江）
Shanhaiguan Great Wall Museum (Photographed by Yu Wenjiang)

today its floor area and exhibition area is 6,230 square meters and 3,600 square meters respectively. It is a Key Museum of Hebei Province, a Hebei Patriotism Education Base, and a National Demonstration Base for Patriotism Education.

The Shanhaiguan Great Wall Museum is a thematic museum demonstrating the characteristics of the Great Wall and spreading the Great Wall culture. It is known as one of the Top Three Great Wall Museums, the other two being the Badaling Great Wall Museum and the Jiayuguan Great Wall Museum.

The museum is equipped with an Introductory Hall, a History Hall, an Architecture Hall, a Military Hall, a Culture Hall, and a Shanhaiguan Great Wall Hall, totalling 6 halls with 8 showrooms. The exhibits show the historical origins, architectural structures, cultural characteristics and military hardware relating to the Great Wall, and the emphasis is on the military significance and the magnificent structure of the Shanhaiguan Great Wall. In 2005, "Backbone of China—Shanhaiguan Great Wall Museum's Basic Exhibition" was awarded an Excellent Prize of the 6th National Top Ten Museum Exhibitions.

The museum features an inclusive range of cultural relics, such as stone artifacts, potteries, porcelains, bronze wares, jade articles, currencies and

军事展厅（供图：山海关长城博物馆）
Military Hall (Provided by Shanhaiguan Great Wall Museum)

inscriptions, with building materials and firearms of the Great Wall being the most characteristic. Its quintessential exhibits include a stem cup of the Yuan Dynasty; a stone mortar of watchtower-stationed troops, a signal gun, a Great Wall stone cannon and a barrel cannon of the Ming Dynasty; and a pendant portraying a boy herding geese, a bronze tripod and an iron cannon of the Qing Dynasty.

(By: Qin Xuewu and Luo Xuefeng)

11. 板厂峪窑址群遗址 Heritage Site of Banchangyu Kilns[1]

板厂峪窑址群遗址，位于秦皇岛市海港区驻操营镇板厂峪村，距长城仅500余米。2013年5月，被公布为全国重点文物保护单位。

板厂峪一带明长城建于1381年。1571年，戚继光任蓟镇总兵，在石筑长城基础上加砖修复，并增修砖质敌楼50座。1634年，板厂

---

[1] 孙漪娜:《河北秦皇岛发现长城砖窑遗址200余座》,《中国文物报》, 2008年8月1日第002版; 耿建扩、朱润胜、李永利:《长城砖窑唯一文字记载被发现——传世宗谱现身秦皇岛 披露明末民间捐资修建长城内幕》,《光明日报》, 2010年2月24日第004版。

Sun Yina: "More than 200 Great Wall Brick Kiln Sites Were Found in Qinhuangdao, Hebei", *China Cultural Relics News*, August 1, 2008, Page 002; Geng Jiankuo, Zhu Runsheng and Li Yongli: "The Only Written Record of the Great Wall Brick Kilns Was Found—Private Donations for Building the Great Wall in the Late Ming Dynasty Disclosed by a Genealogical Records in Qinhuangdao", *Guangming Daily*, February 24, 2010, Page 004.

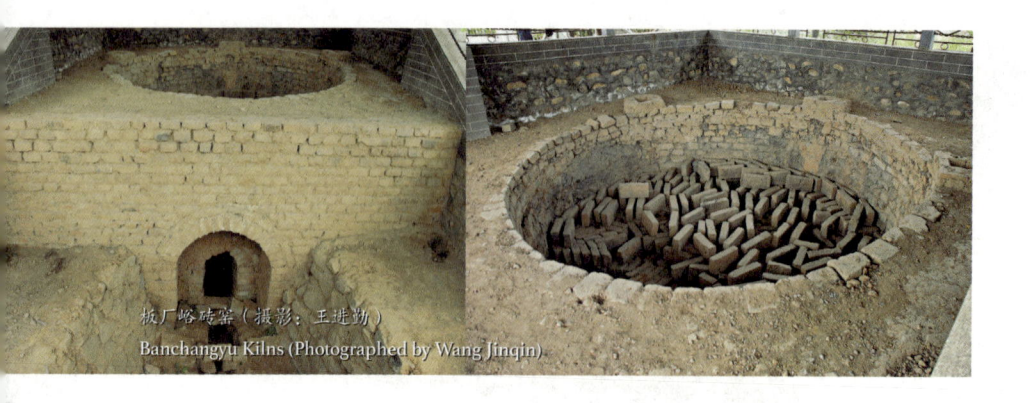

板厂峪砖窑（摄影：王进勤）
Banchangyu Kilns (Photographed by Wang Jinqin)

峪高氏先人与明长城守军进行募款，修复义院口至板厂峪一带长城。[1]

板厂峪窑址，为2002年秋长城文物调查时发现，12月试掘。2003年3月至8月，省市联合考古队进行发掘，确定66座窑址并发掘两座。目前，板厂峪长城沿线已探明窑址200余座，包括砖窑、灰窑、瓦窑、制石厂窑及炼铁炉等多种类型，还发现了石炮库、硝石库、火药库坑、陷马陶筒坑、铁蒺藜阵地等遗址，以及大量筑城工具和明代兵器。勘查发现，板厂峪80%的长城砖窑封存未用。

砖窑的形制分龙窑、马蹄窑和牛角尖窑，窑口直径为3.5米至6米不等，由窑门、窑室、工作面三部分组成。窑里大多保存烧好的长城砖，长36厘米，宽17厘米，厚9厘米，重约10.5公斤。码满砖的每座窑，码砖20层，存砖5000余块。

板厂峪窑址群，是专为修建明长城而开设的砖窑群，也是中国已发现最大的砖窑遗址群。板厂峪窑址群遗址，对研究明长城的建设史具有重要的历史和科学价值。

（作者：秦学武）

Located in Banchangyu Village, Zhucaoying Town, Haigang District, Qinhuangdao, the heritage site of Banchangyu kilns is just 500 meters away from the Great Wall. In May 2013, it was designated as a major historical

---

[1] 《临渝县志》和清代《高氏系谱》(1796年)有相关记载。

and cultural site protected at the national level.

The Great Wall near Banchangyu was built in 1381 in the Ming Dynasty. When Qi Jiguang was appointed Commander of Jizhou in 1571, he organized people to repair the original stone walls with bricks and build an addition of 50 brick watchtowers. In 1634, the ancestors of the Gao Family in Banchangyu collected donations for repairing the Great Wall section from Yiyuankou to Banchangyu, and the repair work was done by them and the troops defending the Great Wall together.[1]

The Banchangyu kilns were discovered in the autumn of 2002 during a cultural relics survey of the Great Wall. In December, a trial excavation was carried out. From March to August in 2003, the joint archaeological team at provincial and municipal levels carried out an excavation. 66 kilns were identified and two of them were excavated. At present, more than 200 kilns along the Banchangyu section of the Great Wall have been identified, including brick kilns, lime kilns, tile kilns, stone processing kilns, and ironmaking furnaces. Ballista storehouses, saltpeter storehouses, gunpowder magazine pits, horse-stopping pottery tube pits and a battle field scattered with iron caltrops were also found, along with a lot of construction tools and weapons of the Ming Dynasty. The investigation showed that the bricks in 80% of the Banchangyu kilns had not been used.

The brick kilns come in dragon, horseshoe, and horn tip shapes, with the kiln diameter measuring from 3.5 meters to 6 meters. A kiln consists of the entrance, the chamber and the working space. The Great Wall bricks preserved in these kilns had mostly been fired. They measure 36 centimeters long, 17 centimeters wide and 9 centimeters thick, and weigh

---

1 Relevant records are found in *Local Records of Linyu County* and *Genealogical Records of Gao Family* (Qing Dynasty, 1796).

about 10.5 kilograms. There was enough room in each kiln for over 5,000 bricks stacked in 20 layers.

The Banchangyu kilns, specially built for the Ming Great Wall, are the largest kiln site in China known today. It is of great historical and scientific value to study the construction of the Great Wall.

(By: Qin Xuewu)

三、长城故事 III. Stories of the Great Wall

12. 戚继光戍守蓟镇 Qi Jiguang Standing Guard in Jizhou[1]

戚继光（1528—1588），山东蓬莱人，明朝抗倭名将、军事家，创立"戚家军"。撰写兵书《纪效新书》和《练兵实纪》，被收入《四库全书》。

隆庆元年（1567），福建总兵戚继光奉诏北调。1568年五月，任蓟、昌、保定练兵总兵官。1569年正月，任蓟镇总兵，镇守蓟州、永平、山海等处。经张居正等人举荐，朝廷破例任命戚继光为蓟镇总兵兼总理练兵事务，担起蓟镇练兵与镇守的重任。

（1）组建新型军队，加强军事训练

戚继光组建新型军队"戚家军"。他引入鸟铳、佛郎机等新式火器，发明"虎蹲炮"；扩充兵源，改进军官选拔办法；创造火铳和冷兵器相配合的步兵战斗编组。1569年八月，组建车营、步兵营、骑兵营、辎重营等兵种的合成军团，综合战力有极大提高。

1571年末，他将练兵条例汇编成《练兵实纪》，在中国军事史上

---

[1] 参阅：叶玉杰:《戚继光在蓟镇》，《第十七届明史国际学术研讨会暨纪念明定陵发掘六十周年国际学术研讨会论文集》（上册），2016年。

See: Ye Yujie: "Qi Jiguang in Jizhou", *Proceedings of the 17th International Symposium on the History of the Ming Dynasty and the International Symposium Commemorating the 60th Anniversary of the Excavation of the Ming Dingling Mausoleum* (Vol.1), 2016.

产生深远影响，尤其是军队纪律训练，享誉世界军事史。1572年十月二十二日至二十八日，在蓟镇汤泉举行10万人大阅兵，开大兵团、多兵种军事演习之先河。1575年二月，完成16个营的战车、辎重车制造。他优化车营建制，军中另设辎重车营，提高军队战斗力。

（2）修筑蓟镇长城，完善城防体系

从1569年到1581年，戚继光在蓟镇、昌平镇修建敌台1448座，整修加固边墙2000余里。扩建蓟镇治所三屯营城，修建太平塞城、密云新城、潘家口关城、洪山口关城、建昌营城及喜峰口的关城、城楼和喜峰口外重楼，还修建了汤泉阅兵演练场、温泉楼馆、客兵营房、水口石桥、潮河石桥等设施。最终完成蓟镇长城防御体系。《明史》云："继光在镇十六年，边备修饬，蓟门晏然。继之者，踵其成法，数十年得无事。"

（3）依据蓟镇地形，拟定御敌方略

戚继光将蓟镇地形分为内地平原、靠近边墙的半平半山地区、边外山地，据此制定不同作战方式："平原利车，近边利骑，边外利步，三者迭用，可以制胜。"[1]

"戚家军"训练有素、纪律严明、勇猛善战，是守卫蓟镇的主力。谭纶和戚继光先后调来两万一千浙兵，其中有三千鸟铳手。戚继光发挥浙兵善用火器、善于山野步战、善于守城守台的特点，制定作战战术：一是充分利用各种火器，使"虏胡畏之，不敢近塞"；二是"蓟边天险，所贵在守"，广筑敌台，主打防御战。[2]

（4）击退蒙古鞑靼诸部，连战连捷

1568年，戚继光击退朵颜部，取得青山口大捷；1573年，先后取得桃林口捷、窟窿台捷；1575年，正月在董家口击败朵颜部，三月朵颜部请降；1578年，在马兰谷击退滚兔部万人；1579年，三月取得曹家寨、古北口大捷，十月在辽东前屯击退妙蛮部5万铁骑；1580

---

[1] 顾祖禹撰，贺次君、施和金点校：《读史方舆纪要》，中华书局2005年版。

[2] 辛德勇：《旧史舆地文录》，中华书局2013年版。

年，土蛮部 10 万之众再犯锦州、义县等地，戚继光率兵退敌。

1582 年六月，改革派重臣张居正病逝。1583 年二月，戚继光调任广东总兵。1585 年，戚继光遭罢免，后郁郁而终。

（作者：秦学武）

Qi Jiguang (1528–1588), a native of Penglai, Shandong, was an anti-wokou general, strategist and founder of the "Qi Army" of the Ming Dynasty. He composed *New Treatise on Military Efficiency* and *A Manual for Military Training*, two books on the art of war included in the *Complete Library of the Four Branches of Literature*.

In the 1st year of Longqing (1567), Qi Jiguang, Commander of Fujian, was transferred to the north. In the 5th month of 1568, he served as the Chief Training Officer of Jizhou, Changping and Baoding. In the 1st month of 1569, he served as Commander of Jizhou, defending Jizhou, Yongping and Shanhai. With Zhang Juzheng and others putting him forward, Qi Jiguang got an unprecedented promotion to Commander and Chief Training Officer of Jizhou, taking on the responsibility of training the army and guarding the frontier in Jizhou.

(1) Building a new army and strengthening military training

Qi Jiguang established the new-type "Qi Army". He introduced new firearms such as the musket and the Farangi gun, and invented the Crouching Tiger Cannon. He augmented the forces, improved the selection process of officers, and created an infantry combat formation combining muskets and cold weapons. In the 8th month of 1569, an army group consisting of carriage battalions, infantry battalions, cavalry battalions and wagon battalions was formed by him, greatly enhancing the comprehensive combat capability.

In the end of 1571, Qi Jiguang compiled his military training regulations into *A Manual for Military Training*. The book had a great influence in the military history of China, with its discipline training methods even renowned around the world. From the 22nd to the 28th day of the 10th month of 1572, a grand military parade of 100,000 people was held in Tangquan, Jizhou County. It set a precedent for large-scale and multi-branch military exercises. In the 2nd month of 1575, the manufacture of chariots and wagons for 16 battalions was completed. Qi Jiguang optimized the vehicle battalion system and set up independent wagon battalions to enhance the army's combat effectiveness.

(2) Building the Jizhou Great Wall to improve the defense system

From 1569 to 1581, Qi Jiguang had built 1,448 watchtowers in Jizhou and Changping, and repaired and reinforced 2,000 *li* of Great Wall. He expanded Santunying Town from which the Garrison of Jizhou was commanded, and built Taiping Fort Town, Miyun New Town, Panjiakou Town, Hongshankou Town and Jianchangying Town, as well as the city gate, gate tower and outside tower of Xifengkou. He also built the Tangquan Military Parade and Drill Ground, Hot Spring Tower, Nonnative Soldiers' Quarters, Shuikou Stone Bridge, Chaohe Stone Bridge, etc. At last, the Jizhou Great Wall defensive system was established. According to *The History of the Ming Dynasty*, "For the 16 years when he was in service in Jizhou, Qi Jiguang repaired the border defense facilities and kept Jizhou peaceful. His successors followed his example and the place was in peace for decades."

(3) Formulating strategies against the enemy based on the terrains of Jizhou

Qi Jiguang divided the terrains of Jizhou into three parts: inside flatlands, half-flatland and half-mountain areas near the Great Wall, and outside mountains. In light of different terrains, different modes of operation were developed: "Carriage battalions for flatlands, cavalry battalions for areas near the wall, and infantry battalions for outside mountains. A combination

Statue of Qi Jiguang in Qianxi (Photographed by Wang Jizong)

of the three may ensure victory."[1]

The "Qi Army", well-trained, highly disciplined and brave, was the main force guarding Jizhou. Tan Lun and Qi jiguang successively mobilized 21,000 soldiers from Zhejiang, among whom 3,000 were musketeers. Qi Jiguang brought the advantages of these soldiers—using firearms, fighting on foot in mountains, and guarding gates and towers—into full play and planned out a set of tactics: firstly, fully utilize the firearms to "deter the northern tribes from getting close to the border"; secondly, vigorously build watchtowers and focus on defense, since "the Jizhou border, shaped by geography, has always been easy to hold but hard to attack".[2]

(4) Deterring the Tatar tribes of Mongolia with sweeping victories

In 1568, Qi Jiguang repelled the attack of the Duoyan tribe and claimed a big victory at Qingshankou. In 1573, the Qi Army won the battles at

---

1 *Summary on History and Local Politics*, written by Gu Zuyu, collated by He Cijun and Shi Hejin, Zhong Hua Book Company, 2005.

2 Xin Deyong: *Geographic Records in History*, Zhong Hua Book Company, 2013.

Taolinkou and Kulongtai. In the 1st month of 1575, they defeated the Duoyan tribe again at Dongjiakou, who surrendered in the 3rd month. In 1578, they defeated a 10,000-strong army of the Guntu tribe in Malan Valley. In the 3rd month of 1579, they claimed a big victory at Caojiazhai and Gubeikou. In the 10th month, they repelled the attack of a 50,000-strong cavalry of the Miaoman tribe in Qiantun of Liaodong. In 1580, a 100,000-strong army of the Tuman tribe invaded Jinzhou and Yixian again, and they were repulsed by the Qi Army.

In the 6th month of 1582, Zhang Juzheng, an important reformist official, passed away. In the 2nd month of 1583, Qi jiguang were transferred to be Commander of Guangdong. In 1585, he was deposed and died of grief afterwards.

(By: Qin Xuewu)

13. 孟姜女传说 Legend of Meng Jiangnü[1]

孟姜女传说是中国四大民间传说之一，流传于山东、河北等十几个省市。秦皇岛市是孟姜女传说的五大流传区域之一。2006年至2014年，山东省淄博市、河北省秦皇岛市等五地申报的"孟姜女传说"先后入选国家级非物质文化遗产代表性项目名录。

孟姜女的故事，最早为《左传·襄公二十三年》所载史实。公元前550年，齐庄公攻打莒国，大将杞梁战死。杞梁妻不受郊吊，齐侯遂到家中祭奠。战国到唐代，《礼记》《孟子》《说苑》《列女传》《敦煌变文》《同贤记》《杞梁妻》等文献都有记载，故事逐步成型。人物：齐将杞梁→秦代范郎→燕人杞良，杞梁妻→孟仲姿→孟姜女[2]；地点：齐城→秦长城；情节主线：不受郊吊→悲歌哀哭→哭夫崩城；故

---

1 顾颉刚：《孟姜女故事的转变》，《歌谣周刊》第69号（孟姜女专号一）1924年11月。
Ku Chieh-Kang: "The Transformation of Meng Jiangnü's Story", *Popular Ballads Weekly*, Issue 69 (Special Issue 1 for Meng Jiangnü), November 1924.

2 孟姜：姜姓，行大。"孟姜"之名，始于《孟子注疏》。

望夫石（摄影：王怀强）
Husband-Gazing Rock (Photographed by Wang Huaiqiang)

贞女祠（摄影：王进勤）
Chastity Shrine (Photographed by Wang Jinqin)

孟姜女庙长联（摄影：王进勤）
Long couplet in Meng Jiangnü Temple (Photographed by Wang Jinqin)

事主题：恪守礼法→爱情绝唱→反抗暴政。明代多了"秦始皇逼婚"的情节。至此，故事情节定型。

孟姜女的故事流传已逾 2500 年。唐代以后，广泛见于变文、话本、戏曲、民歌、鼓词、民间传说等通俗文艺形式，以及庙会、祭祀等民俗活动。宋代始建贞女祠，明代中后期各地纷纷建立。各地还有姜女坟、哭泉、姜女泉、望夫石等遗迹。

山海关孟姜女庙位于山海关城东凤凰山，由贞女祠和孟姜女苑组成。明万历二十二年（1594），山海关尹张栋修建贞女祠。1956 年，被公布为河北省重点文物保护单位。2006 年，山海关被命名为"中国孟姜女文化之乡"。

（作者：秦学武，罗学锋）

The legend of Meng Jiangnü, popular in a dozen provinces and cities such as Shandong and Hebei, is one of the four most famous folk tales in China. Qinhuangdao is one of the five areas where the legend prevails. From 2006 to 2014, the Legend of Meng Jiangnü, which were applied by Zibo City of Shandong Province, Qinhuangdao City of Hebei Province and other three places, was designated as a Representative Item of National Intangible Cultural Heritage.

The story of Meng Jiangnü first appeared in *Zuo's Commentary on The Spring and Autumn Annals*. Here's what it says: In 550 BC, Duke Zhuang of Qi attacked the State of Ju, and General Qi Liang was killed in the war; since Qi Liang's wife would not hold the funeral in the countryside, Duke Zhuang came to her home. We can see the story in literatures from the Warring States Period to the Tang Dynasty, such as *The Book of Rites*, *Mencius*, *Garden of Stories, Biographies of Heroic Women*, *Dunhuang Bianwen*, *Biography of the Fellows*, and *Qi Liang's Wife*. The story gradually evolved in terms of characters, locations, scenarios, and themes:

1) Characters: General Qi Liang of Qi→ young scholar Fan of Qin→Qi

Liang of Yan, Qi Liang's wife→Meng Zhongzi→Meng Jiangnü[1];

2) Locations: Qi city→Qin Great Wall;

3) Scenarios: refusing to hold the funeral in the countryside→Wailing in deep sorrow→crying for the husband and crumbling the Great Wall;

4) Themes: following ritual practices→praising the power of love→resisting tyranny.

In the Ming Dynasty, with the scenario of "the First Emperor of Qin forcing Meng Jiangnü to get married" added, the story finally took shape.

The story of Meng Jiangnü has been handed down for over 2,500 years. Since the Tang Dynasty, it had taken different forms, such as *bianwen* (a popular form of narrative literature), *huaben* (script for story-telling), opera, folk song, drum lyrics and folklore. It was also a feature of folklore activities such as temple fairs and sacrificial ceremonies. First appeared in the Song Dynasty, Chastity Shrines sprang up in the latter half of the Ming Dynasty. Relics such as Meng Jiangnü Tomb, Wailing Spring, Meng Jiangnü Spring, and Husband-Gazing Rock can be found found across the country.

Located in the Phoenix Mountain in the east side of the Shanhai Pass, the Meng Jiangnü Temple consists of Chastity Shrine and Meng Jiangnü Garden. The Chastity Shrine was built in the 22nd year of Wanli of the Ming Dynasty (1594) by Administer Zhang Dong. In 1956, it was announced as A Major Historical and Cultural Site of Hebei. In 2006, the Shanhai Pass was designated as the "Home of Chinese Meng Jiangnü Culture".

(By: Qin Xuewu and Luo Xuefeng)

---

1 Meng Jiang, surnamed Jiang, was the eldest in her family. The name originated from *Commentaries of Mencius*.

第三章

旅游文化

Chapter III Tourism Culture

一、名胜古迹 I. Places of Interest

1. 承德避暑山庄 Chengde Mountain Resort[1]

避暑山庄位于河北省承德市中心北部，坐落于武烈河西岸的狭长谷地上，为清帝驻跸消暑、治政理国、怀柔外藩、巩固边防的夏宫，又称承德离宫。1961 年，避暑山庄被国务院公布为全国重点文物保护单位。避暑山庄及周围寺庙，是中国古代帝王宫苑与皇家寺庙完美融合的典型范例，1994 年被联合国教科文组织列入世界文化遗产名录。

避暑山庄始建于康熙四十二年（1703），历经康熙、雍正、乾隆三朝，于乾隆五十七年（1792）竣工，占地 564 公顷，是世界现存最大的古典皇家园林。1978 年，避暑山庄正式对外开放。2007 年，避暑山庄及周围寺庙景区被国家旅游局评为 AAAAA 级旅游景区。

避暑山庄的选址设计，体现了当地自然山水风貌与中国地理形貌特征的完美统一，以西北山区、东南湖区、北部平原区之地形地貌构成中国版图的缩影。避暑山庄的建造，因山就势，依水延展，不假雕饰。120 余组楼、殿、阁等建筑掩映于山水草木之间，构成融南秀北雄于一体、集全国名胜于一园的壮美景观。

避暑山庄由宫殿区和苑景区组成，呈现前宫后苑的建筑布局。宫殿区又分正宫、松鹤斋、东宫和万壑松风四组建筑。苑景区则包括湖泊区、平原区和山峦区，其间康熙和乾隆分别建有 36 景。环列避暑山庄东部和北部山路的十二座皇家寺庙占地 47.2 公顷，建筑面积 6 万多平方米。

湖泊区是苑景区的精华，康熙夸赞"天然风景胜西湖"。湖泊区州岛错落，湖面被长堤和州岛分割成多个湖，各湖以桥相通，两岸绿

---

[1] 李瑞：《承德避暑山庄及其周围寺庙：民族交往交流交融的历史见证》，《中国文物报》，2021 年 8 月 31 日第 001 版。

Li Rui: "Chengde Mountain Resort and Its Outlying Temples: Historical Testimony of Ethnic Exchanges", *China Cultural Relics News*, August 31, 2021, Page 001.

冬日金山岛（摄影：王怀强）
Golden Mountain Islet in winter (Photographed by Wang Huaiqiang)

树成荫。风景建筑散落在湖泊区四周，曲折有致，秀丽多姿。湖泊区的风景建筑大多仿江南名胜建造，如金山岛，康熙四十二年（1703）仿江苏镇江金山而建；烟雨楼，乾隆四十五年（1780）仿浙江嘉兴烟雨楼而建。"环碧""如意洲""月色江声"是湖中的三个小岛，以芝径云堤连接，从空中俯瞰，有如三座仙岛漂浮海面。"如意洲"是风景区的中心，有假山、凉亭、殿堂、庙宇、水池等，布局巧妙。"月色江声"，由一座精致的四合院和几座亭、堂组成，每当月上东山，皎洁月光洒满湖面，山庄万籁俱寂，只闻湖水轻拍堤岸。

避暑山庄是清政府的第二个政治中心，乾隆曾在此接见漠西厄鲁特蒙古杜尔伯特部首领三策凌、土尔扈特部首领渥巴锡以及六世班禅等重要人物，还接见过以马戛尔尼为首的英国访华使团。[1]1860年，英法联军进攻北京，避难于此的咸丰帝批准了丧权辱国的《中俄北京条约》。影响中国历史进程的"辛酉政变"亦发端于此。

热河泉，是避暑山庄内的一汪温泉，也是一处水源。泉侧有一石碣，上书"热河"。热河，被称为世界上最短的河流。承德，古称热河。避暑山庄，故名"热河行宫"。

（作者：秦学武）

---

[1] 我国首部沉浸式皇家园林实景体验剧《梦入避暑山庄》生动演绎了这些历史故事。

热河（摄影：王怀强）
Jehol Spring (Photographed by Wang Huaiqiang)

Located in the north of Chengde City, Hebei Province, Chengde Mountain Resort sits in a narrow valley on the west bank of the Wulie River. The summer palace, aka the Chengde Temporary Palace, was where emperors of the Qing Dynasty spent summer, attended to state affairs, claimed the allegiance of vassal states, and consolidated frontier defenses. In 1961, Chengde Mountain Resort was designated by the State Council as a Major Historical and Cultural Site Protected at the National Level. The resort and its outlying temples are a shining example of the harmonious combination of the two building types in ancient China. In 1994, it was designated by the UNESCO as a World Cultural Heritage.

The construction of Chengde Mountain Resort lasted from the 42nd year of Kangxi (1703) to the 57th year of Qianlong (1792), during which period the empire was successively ruled by Kangxi, Yongzheng and Qianlong. As the largest classical royal garden that survives in the world, the resort covers an area of 564 hectares. In 1978, it was opened to the public. In 2007, Chengde Mountain Resort and its Outlying Temples were named a National AAAAA Level Tourist Attraction by China National Tourism Administration.

The location and design of Chengde Mountain Resort managed to combine the natural landscape with the amazing variety of landforms. The hill area in the northwest, the lake area in the southeast, and the plain area in the north are a miniature of China's territory. Following the topography of natural hills and water, the resort was built without any needless decoration. The 120 towers, halls and pavilions are half-hidden in the trees and hills, integrating both the elegance of the south and the magnificence of the north and reflecting all the splendor of China.

Chengde Mountain Resort consists of the palace area in the front and the garden area in the back. The palace area comprises the Main Palace, the Pine and Crane Hall, the East Palace and the Gully and Pine Study. The garden area is further divided into the lake area, the plain area and the hill area, with 72 scenic spots designated by Kangxi and Qianlong. There are twelve royal temples distributed across the eastern and northern hills outside the resort. They cover an area of 47.2 hectares with a floor area of more than 60,000 square meters.

The lake area is the highlight of the garden area. Emperor Kangxi praised: "Its natural scenery is more beautiful than the West Lake." Islets sprinkle on the lake area, which is divided by the dike and islets into many parts joined by bridges. The tree-shaded shores, with scenic spots and architectures all round, have a natural beauty. The scenic spots and architectures are mostly replications of the famous sights south of the Yangtze River. For instance, the Golden Mountain Islet, built in the 42nd year of Kangxi (1703), was modelled after the Golden Mountain in Zhenjiang, Jiangsu; the Pavilion of Mist and Rain, built in the 45th year of Qianlong (1780), was modelled after the Pavilion of Mist and Rain in Jiaxing, Zhejiang. "Swirling Jade", "Ruyi Sandbar" and "Moon River", three islets in the lake, are connected by the Zigzag Causeway. Viewed from above, they look like three fairy

Mid-lake Pavilions (Photographed by Yu Lei)

islets floating on the lake. As the center of the scenic area, the Ruyi Sandbar has an ingenious layout, featuring rockeries, pavilions, halls, pools and a temple. The Moon River consists of an elegant quadrangle dwelling, pavilions and halls. When the moon rises in the east, it shines on the lake with extraordinary brightness. In the silence of night, little waves of the lake clap against the bank.

Chengde Mountain Resort is the second political center of the Qing government. Here, Qianlong received Three Celings of the Dorbot Tribe of Olot Mongolia, Ubashi Khan of the Torghut Tribe, the 6th Panchen Lama, and the British mission led by George Macartney.[1] In 1860, the Anglo-French Allied Forces launched an offensive on Beijing. Emperor Xianfeng taking refuge here approved the humiliating Sino-Russian Treaty of Peking.

---

1 *A Dream of the Summer Resort*, China's first immersive live drama of the royal garden, is a vivid interpretation of these historical tales.

芝径云堤（摄影：于磊）
Zigzag Causeway (Photographed by Yu Lei)

The 1861 Coup affecting the history of China also started here.

The Jehol Spring is a hot spring and water source in Chengde Mountain Resort. Beside the spring is a stone tablet bearing Chinese characters "热河". The Jehol River is said to be the shortest river in the world. Chengde was known historically as Jehol, and Chengde Mountain Resort was also called "Jehol Temporary Palace".

(By: Qin Xuewu)

2. 承德外八庙 Eight Outlying Temples of Chengde[1]

外八庙，指承德避暑山庄周边的八座皇家寺庙，是世界现存最大的皇家寺庙群，占地 40 余公顷。1982 年，承德避暑山庄外八庙风景

---

1 徐鑫:《承德外八庙的文化价值与保护策略探析》,《知音励志》2016 年 8 期。
Xu Xin: "On the Cultural Values and Protection Strategy of the Eight Outlying Temples of Chengde", *Appreciative Friend*, 2016, Issue 8.

名胜区被国务院批准为国家级风景名胜区。

外八庙始建于康熙五十二年（1713），乾隆四十五年（1780）建成。避暑山庄周围边的十二座寺庙中，溥仁寺、溥善寺建于康熙年间，其余十座建于乾隆年间。其中普宁寺、溥仁寺、溥善寺、殊像寺、广缘寺、安远庙、普陀宗乘之庙以及须弥福寿之庙等八座寺庙由清政府直接管理，故称"外八庙"。溥善寺现已不存。

溥仁寺、溥善寺，建成于清康熙五十二年(1713)，为外八庙中最早建成的庙宇。是年，康熙六十大寿，蒙古各部王公贵族朝觐贺寿，奏请建立寺庙以示祝贺。康熙允准在武烈河东岸建造两座寺庙，供蒙古诸部在热河大聚会使用。溥仁寺和溥善寺的形制、布局基本相同，仅一墙相隔，故称溥仁寺为前寺，溥善寺为后寺。2001年，溥仁寺被国务院公布为全国重点文物保护单位。

普宁寺位于避暑山庄北部的武烈河畔，建成于乾隆二十四年(1759)，占地3.3万平方米，为外八庙中最为完整的寺庙。因寺内有一尊金漆木雕大佛，又称大佛寺。1755年，清政府平定准噶尔部蒙古台吉达瓦齐的叛乱，在避暑山庄为厄鲁特四部贵族封爵，并仿效西藏桑鸢寺修建皇家寺庙。清政府希望边疆人民"安其居，乐其业，永永普宁"，故名"普宁寺"。1961年，普宁寺被国务院公布为全国重点文物保护单位；1985年，被国务院宗教局批准为宗教活动场所；2007年，被评为中国首批AAAAA级佛教圣地。

安远庙建于乾隆二十九年（1764），位于武烈河东岸的冈阜上，占地2.6万平方米。安远庙仿新疆伊犁河北部固尔扎庙而建，俗称伊犁庙。1988年，安远庙被国务院公布为全国重点文物保护单位。

殊像寺建成于清乾隆四十年(1775)，位于避暑山庄北面的普陀宗乘之庙之西，坐北朝南，占地2.3万平方米。1988年，殊像寺被国务院公布为全国重点文物保护单位。

普陀宗乘之庙建于乾隆三十二年（1767）至乾隆三十六年（1771），是乾隆帝为庆祝母后八十寿辰和自己六十寿辰，仿西藏布达拉宫而建，俗称"小布达拉宫"。其占地22万平方米，规模居外八庙之首。1961年，被国务院公布为全国重点文物保护单位。

普陀宗乘之庙形制为汉藏合璧式，坐北朝南，以琉璃牌坊为界，分前后两部分，共有大小建筑60余处。前半部沿中轴线依次为山门、碑亭、五塔门、琉璃牌坊，至此为汉式建筑风格；后半部主体建筑为大红台，依山就势，矗立山巅，仿布达拉宫红宫而建，有主殿万法归一。普陀宗乘之庙，意为观世音菩萨讲经说法之处。1771年，乾隆帝在这里接见过万里东归的土尔扈特部首领渥巴锡一行。乾隆帝在此曾举行讲经、说法、祝寿等活动。

1780年，乾隆帝七旬庆典，六世班禅到热河入觐朝贺。乾隆命人仿照日喀则扎什伦布寺建造"班禅行宫"，即须弥福寿之庙。1961年，须弥福寿之庙被国务院公布为全国重点文物保护单位。

广缘寺建于乾隆四十五年(1780)，位于普佑寺东侧，是外八庙中建成最晚、面积最小的寺庙，占地0.45公顷。乾隆御题"广缘寺"。今后殿已毁，其余建筑残存。

外八庙集汉、满、蒙古、藏等多民族建筑艺术、宗教艺术之大成，见证了"康乾盛世"的繁荣景象。外八庙呈半月形环绕避暑山庄，呈烘云托月之势，象征边疆各族人民与清朝中央政府的紧密关系，表现了中华各民族融合、统一的历史进程。

（作者：秦学武）

The Eight Outlying Temples refer to the eight royal temples surrounding Chengde Mountain Resort. Covering an area of 40 hectares, they are the largest royal temple complex that survives in the world. In 1982, the Eight Temples Surrounding Chengde Mountain Resort were designated by the State Council as a National Park of China.

The construction of the temples began in the 52nd year of Kangxi (1713), and was completed in the 45th year of Qianlong (1780). Chengde Mountain Resort is surrounded by a total of twelve temples, of which Puren Temple

普陀宗乘之庙、须弥福寿之庙、普宁寺、安远庙、殊像寺（摄影：王怀强）
Putuo Zongcheng Temple, Xumi Fushou Temple, Puning Temple, Anyuan Temple, Shuxiang Temple (Photographed by Wang Huaiqiang)

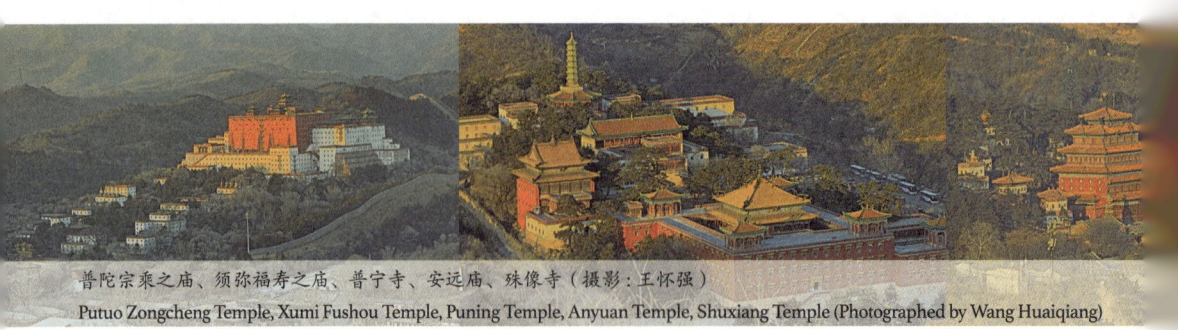

and Pushan Temple were built during the reign of Kangxi, and the other ten were built during the reign of Qianlong. Puning Temple, Puren Temple, Pushan Temple, Shuxiang Temple, Guangyuan Temple, Anyuan Temple, Putuo Zongcheng Temple and Xumi Fushou Temple were managed by the Qing government, hence their name Eight Outlying Temples. Pushan Temple is no longer extant.

Built in the 52nd year of Kangxi (1713), Puren Temple and Pushan Temple are the oldest of the Eight Outlying Temples. When Mongolian princes and nobles came for the 60th birthday of Kangxi, they sought permission for building temples to mark the occasion. Kangxi allowed two temples to be built on the east bank of the Wulie River for the Mongolian tribes when they gathered in Jehol. Puren Temple in front and Pushan Temple in back are largely the same in design and layout, with only a wall separating the two. In 2001, Puren Temple was designated by the State Council as a major historical and cultural site protected at the national level.

Built in the 24th year of Qianlong (1759), Puning Temple is located on the bank of the Wulie River to the north of the Mountain Resort. Covering an area of 33,000 square meters, it is the best preserved one of the Eight Outlying Temples. A gold-lacquered wood Buddha statue is housed in the temple, so it is also known as Buddha Temple. In 1755, the Qing government put down the rebellion of Tayiji Dawachi of the Mongolian

Dzungars. In Chengde Mountain Resort, the nobles of the four Eleuth tribes were awarded the title of dukes. A royal temple modelling after Bsamyas of Tibet was built. The Qing government wished the frontier people to pursue their livelihood peacefully, so the temple was named Puning (literally Universal Peace). In 1961, Puning Temple was designated as a Major Historical and Cultural Site Protected at the National Level by the State Council. In 1985, it was approved by the State Council as a religious place. In 2007, it became one of the first AAAAA Buddhist Holy Places in China.

Built in the 29th year of Qianlong (1764), Anyuan Temple sits on a hilly terrain on the east bank of the Wulie River, covering an area of 26,000 square meters. Colloquially called Yili Temple, it was modelled after the Kuldja Temple on the north side of the Yili River, Xinjiang. In 1988, Anyuan Temple was designated by the State Council as a Major Historical and Cultural Site Protected at the National Level.

Built in the 40th year of Qianlong (1775), Shuxiang Temple lies to the west of Putuo Zongcheng Temple, which is to the north of Chengde Mountain Resort. The temple faces south, covering an area of 23,000 square meters. In 1998, Shuxiang Temple was designated by the State Council as a Major Historical and Cultural Site Protected at the National Level.

Putuo Zongcheng Temple was built between the 32nd and the 36th year of Qianlong (1767–1771) in honor of the 60th birthday and the 80th birthday of the emperor and his mother. Colloquially known as "Small Potala Palace", the temple was modelled after the Potala Palace of Tibet. It covers an area of 220,000 square meters, coming top out of the Eight Outlying Temples. In 1961, Putuo Zongcheng Temple was designated by the State Council as a Major Historical and Cultural Site Protected at the National Level.

Putuo Zongcheng Temple, which faces south, combines the Han and the Tibetan architectural styles. It is divided by the glazed archway into front and rear parts, with over 60 buildings of varying sizes. The buildings in the front part are of the Han style, such as the gate, the tablet pavilion, the five-pagoda gate, and the glazed archway, which are aligned on the central axis. As the main architecture of the rear part, the Red Terrace stands on the hilltop. It was modelled after the Red Palace of Potala Palace to imply that all dharmas are one. Putuo Zongcheng Temple means the place where Avalokitesvara used to preach sutras. In 1771, Qianlong received the conquering heroes of the Torghuts led by Ubashi in the temple. The emperor had hold sutra lectures and celebrated his birthdays here.

When Emperor Qianlong celebrated his 70th birthday in 1780, the 6th Panchen Lama came to Jehol to offer his congratulations. A proclamation was sent out for the construction of Panchen's Temporary Palace—Xumi Fushou Temple, which was modelled after the Tashi Lhunpo Monastery in Shigatse. In 1961, Xumi Fushou Temple was designated by the State Council as a Major Historical and Cultural Site Protected at the National Level.

Built in the 45th year of Qianlong (1780), Guangyuan Temple is to the east of Puyou Temple. It is the latest and smallest one of the Eight Outlying Temples, merely covering an area of 0.45 hectares. "广缘寺", characters for the inscribed board, was written personally by Qianlong. The rear hall was destroyed, while the rest of the architectures still survive.

The Eight Outlying Temples feature the very essence of architectural art and religious art of Han, Manchu, Mongolian and Tibetan people. They attest to the glory of the High Qing Period. The temples encircle Chengde Mountain Resort in a crescent shape, signifying the close bonds between the frontier and the central government, and illustrating the sentiment of ethnic harmony and national unity.

(By: Qin Xuewu)

3. 遵化清东陵 Eastern Qing Tombs in Zunhua[1]

清东陵位于河北省遵化市，是中国现存规模最大、体系最完整、布局最规整的古代皇家陵园，1961年被国务院公布为国家重点文物保护单位。2000年，清东陵作为中国明清皇家陵寝[2]的一部分被联合国教科文组织列入世界文化遗产名录。2015年，被国家文化和旅游部评为AAAAA级旅游景区。

清东陵始建于顺治十八年（1661），完工于光绪三十四年（1908），历时247年。陵区在清代占地约2500平方千米，现在管理面积为78平方千米。共建有15座陵园，其中皇陵5座，后陵4座，妃园5座，公主陵1座；埋葬了5位皇帝、15位皇后、136位妃嫔、3位皇子、2位公主，共161人。

清东陵的陵寝布局以顺治帝的孝陵为中心，在昌瑞山南麓东西排列。辈分低的陵寝距孝陵较远，同一朝代的后陵和妃园均建在本朝帝陵的旁侧。清东陵的陵寝布局既体现了中国传统的居中而尊的理念，

1　秦雅梅：《新时代清东陵景区建设的思考》，《旅游纵览》2020年10期。
　Qin Yamei: "Thoughts on the Construction of Eastern Qing Tombs Scenic Area in the New Era", *Tourism Overview*, 2020, Issue 10.

2　清代皇室陵寝是清朝皇帝悉心规划营建的墓葬建筑，共有三处，即辽宁沈阳的北陵、河北遵化的东陵、河北易县的西陵。
　The royal tombs of the Qing Dynasty is the tomb architectures scrupulously planned and built by the Qing emperors. There're three sites: Northern Tombs in Shenyang, Liaoning, Eastern Tombs in Zunhua, Hebei, and Western Tombs in Yi County, Hebei.

清东陵（摄影：于文江）
Eastern Qing Tombs (Photographed by Yu Wenjiang)

又体现了尊祖归宗、一脉相承的兆葬之制。

清东陵的设计运用中国独创的风水理论，严格遵照"陵制与山水相称"的原则，既"遵照典礼之规制"又"配合山川之胜势"，将山川形胜的自然之美与陵寝建筑的人文之美有机结合，至于臻境，被联合国世界文化遗产专家誉为"人类具有创造性的天才杰作"。

清东陵已开放10座陵寝。顺治帝的孝陵规模堪称清代之最，既有长达6千米的神道，也有数量达18对的石像生；乾隆帝的裕陵，被誉为"石雕艺术宝库"和"庄严肃穆的地下佛堂"；慈禧太后的定东陵，以装修豪华、工艺精美著称，其"凤在上龙在下"的巨型石雕，凸显慈禧权倾一时的政坛地位。

清东陵是中国封建皇家陵园的集大成，是中华民族智慧的结晶，综合体现了中国传统的风水学、建筑学、美学、哲学、景观学，以及宗教、祭祀、丧俗等文化，具有重要的历史价值、艺术价值和科学价值，是中华民族和全人类的文化遗产。

（作者：秦学武）

Located in Zunhua of Hebei Province, the Eastern Qing Tombs are the largest, most sophisticated and most orderly imperial mausolea that survive in China. In 1961, They were designated by the State Council as a Major

Historical and Cultural Site Protected at the National Level. In 2000, the Eastern Qing Tombs, as a part of the Imperial Tombs of the Ming and Qing Dynasties, became a UNESCO World Heritage Site. In 2015, they were named a National AAAAA Level Tourist Attraction by the Ministry of Culture and Tourism of the People's Republic of China.

The construction of the Eastern Qing Tombs lasted 247 years from the 18th year of Shunzhi (1661) to the 34th year of Guangxu (1908). The tomb area covered 2,500 square kilometers in the Qing Dynasty, 78 square kilometers of which are under management today. There are 15 cemeteries in total, including 5 emperor cemeteries, 4 empress cemeteries, 5 concubine cemeteries and 1 princess cemetery, while 5 emperors, 15 empresses, 136 concubines, 3 princes and 2 princesses, which totalled 161 people, were buried here.

The cemeteries in the Eastern Qing Tombs, of which Xiaoling of Emperor Shunzi is the center, are aligned from east to west along the south foot of the Changrui Mountain. The cemeteries of younger generations are farther away from Xiaoling. The cemeteries of the empresses and concubines are next to the cemeteries of the contemporary emperors. The layout embodies the traditional idea of "center's superiority" in China, and reflects the honor people give to their ancestors.

The Eastern Qing Tombs blended geomancy (*feng shui*) in its design. They complied with the rule of "integrating into the landscape", and the "norms of etiquette" were embedded in the "mountainous terrain". The glories of nature and the beauty of humanities formed a consummate work of art. According to UN experts on world cultural heritages, the tombs "are masterpieces of human creative genius".

10 tombs are opened to the public. Xiaoling of Emperor Shunzhi, with a tomb passage of 6,000 meters long and 18 pairs of stone statues, is the

largest of all. Yuling of Emperor Qianlong enjoys the reputation for being a "treasure house of stone carving arts" and "solemn underground Buddha hall". Dingdongling of Empress Dowager Cixi is lavishly decorated with exquisite craftsmanship, and its giant stone carving featuring "the phoenix above the dragon" alludes to the woman in absolute power.

The Eastern Qing Tombs are an epitome of royal tomb complexes in China's feudal dynasties. As a crystallization of the wisdom of the Chinese nation, they embody *feng shui*, architecture, aesthetics, philosophy, landscape, religion, sacrificial rites and funeral customs altogether. With important historical, artistic and scientific values, they are the cultural heritage of China and the world.

(By: Qin Xuewu)

Panorama of Eastern Qing Tombs (Provided by the General Office of the Tangshan Municipal People's Government)

4. 卢龙永平古城 Yongping Ancient City in Lulong[1]

永平古城位于河北省卢龙县城，为明清永平府治所在地，是永平府的政治、经济、军事、文化中心。建于金代的大佛顶尊胜陀罗尼经幢，2006年被国务院公布为全国重点文物保护单位。永平府城墙，2013年被国务院公布为全国重点文物保护单位。

明洪武四年（1371），平滦府改为永平府，指挥费愚主持重修、扩建永平城。城池四周筑墙，由土城改建为砖城，东西长1165米，南北长1200米，城高3丈6尺，顶宽2丈，底宽3丈。设有四座城门和水门（水西门），东曰高明，南曰得胜，西曰镇平，北曰拱辰。门上设有城楼，规制相同。门边墙旁设有登城马道。明嘉靖、万历和清康熙、乾隆年间，永平城多次修葺，四门数易其名。

大佛顶尊胜陀罗尼经幢（摄影：王进勤）
Usnisa Vijaya Dharani Dhvaja (Photographed by Wang Jinqin)

永平城格局独特，四门并不对称，西门紧靠南门。古城依地势而建，城内有平山、阻山、永丰山三座山丘，掩映在楼阁、树丛中，城外无法看见山头，故有"三山不显，四门不对"之说。如今，永平城残存南门内门楼，西门瓮城和内城以及西城墙基本完好，北城墙尚有一段墙体完好，东门、北门及东、南城墙荡然无存。

---

1 参阅：宋坤主编：《京东第一府》，中国文史出版社2014年版。
See: Song Kun(ed.): *The First Prefecture to the East of the Capital*, China Culture and History Press, 2014.

明清之际，永平府号称"京东第一府"，是当地教育中心。明嘉靖年间，建有孤竹书院；隆庆年间，建有北平书院。清乾隆年间，建有敬胜书院，光绪年间改为新式学校——永平府立中学堂。还设有各种官学和私学。明清时期，永平城是县试、府试的考场所在地。现在城内三街有胡同，曰"考棚胡同"。

永平府是山海关与京师间的交通要冲。明清设永平卫，拱卫京师。永平府是清帝盛京（今辽宁沈阳）谒陵祭祖的必经之路。康熙1671年、1682年、1698年三次谒陵，路经永平城。乾隆1743年、1754年两次祭祖回銮，驻跸永平城外的夷齐庙。1778年，乾隆修建夷齐庙行宫。南门外的高大屏风，刻有"百代清风"；屏风两侧的石碑，右书"忠臣孝子"，左书"到今称圣"；南门楼石额，上书"贤人旧里"。

（作者：秦学武）

Located in Lulong County, Hebei Province, Yongping Ancient City was the seat of Yongping Prefecture in the Ming and Qing dynasties. It was also the political, economic, military and cultural center of the prefecture. In 2006, the Usnisa Vijaya Dharani Dhvaja, built in the Jin Dynasty, was designated by the State Council as a Major Historical and Cultural Site Protected at the National Level. In 2013, the city walls of Yongping Prefecture were designated by the State Council as a Major Historical and Cultural Site Protected at the National Level.

In the 4th year of Hongwu of Ming (1371), Pingluan Prefecture changed its name to Yongping Prefecture. Reconstruction and expansion of the city was headed by Fei Yu. The city was walled and built with bricks instead of earth. The new walls measured 1,165 meters long from east to west, 1,200 meters wide from north to south, and 3 *zhang* and 6 *chi* high. The top was 2 *zhang* wide and the bottom was 3 *zhang* wide. The city had four main gates—Gaoming in the east, Desheng in the south, Zhenping in the west, and Gongchen in the north—and a water gate in the west. Standing on the

West wharf (Photographed by Wang Jinqin)

top of the four gates were towers of the same design. Beside the walls near the four gates, there were bridle paths leading to the top. Yongping city was renovated during the reigns of Jiajing and Wanli of Ming, and Kangxi and Qianlong of Qing. The names of the four gates were changed several times.

The layout of Yongping city was unique. The four gates were asymmetric, with the west gate very close to the south gate. The ancient city was built according to the topography, and Pingshan Hill, Zushan Hill and Yongfeng Hill were half-hidden in the pavilions and trees, with the hilltops invisible outside the city. Thus, there is a saying that goes, "the three hills are invisible and the four gates are asymmetric." Today, the remaining arch over the south gateway, the barbican entrance and inner city connected to the west gate and the west wall of Yongping are undamaged; one section of the north wall is intact; the east gate, the north gate and the east and south walls are no longer extant.

From Ming to Qing, Yongping Prefecture was known as the "First Prefecture to the East of the Capital". It was the educational center of the locality. During the reigns of Jiajing and Longqing of Ming, Guzhu Academy and Beiping Academy were built. During the reign of Qianlong

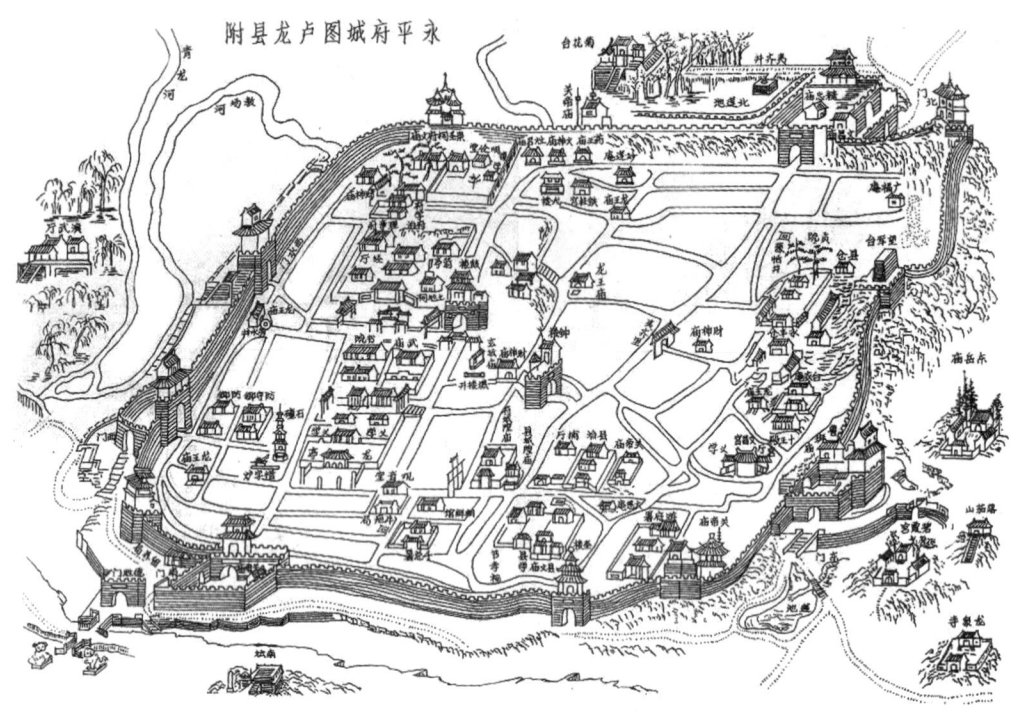

光绪年间永平府城平面图（摄影：王进勤）
Yongping city during the reign of Guangxu (Photographed by Wang Jinqin)

of Qing, Jingsheng Academy was built, which was changed into a new-type school—Yongping Prefecture Middle School—during the reign of Guangxu. Besides, there were various official and private schools. In the Ming and Qing dynasties, Yongping city was where the imperial examinations at county and prefecture levels were held. Today, we can see an Examination Room Alley in the Sanjie area of the city.

Yongping Prefecture was a thoroughfare between the Shanhai Pass and the Capital. Yongping Garrison was established in the Ming and Qing dynasties to defend the Capital. Yongping Prefecture was an essential route for journeys to and from Shengjing (today's Shenyang) when the Qing emperors honored their ancestors. In 1671, 1682 and 1698, Kangxi went to pay homage to his ancestors by way of Yongping. On the way back from the Royal Tombs in 1743 and 1754, Qianlong had a stopover in the Yi-Qi Temple outside the city. In 1778, Qianlong built a temporary palace near the Yi-Qi Temple. The tall screen outside the south gate was engraved with Chinese characters meaning "Incorruptible Governance". On either side of the screen stands a stone tablet. The one on the right reads "Loyal Officials and Dutiful Sons", and the one on the left reads "Would Be the Sages". The stone scribed board on the south arch reads "Birthplace of the Sages".

(By: Qin Xuewu)

5. 北戴河近代建筑群 Beidaihe Modern Architectural Complex[1]

北戴河近代建筑群位于河北省秦皇岛市北戴河区，以其独特的历史价值和艺术价值闻名于世，俗称"北戴河海滨别墅"。2006年，被国务院公布为全国重点文物保护单位。

北戴河近代建筑群，记录了北戴河乃至中国近代史的风云变幻。清光绪十九年（1893）英国传教士史德华在此首建别墅。光绪二十四年（1898），北戴河被清政府辟为首个"允中外人士杂居"的避暑地。津榆铁路修通后，北戴河的旖旎风光为世人发现，外国传教士、中外官僚政客、商人巨贾纷纷来此租地建屋。至1948年，北戴河海滨建有各类别墅719幢，其中外国人别墅482幢、中国人别墅236幢，无国籍别墅1幢，现存130余幢。

北戴河海滨别墅，是中国四大别墅区[2]中唯一的海滨别墅区。"蓝天绿树、红顶素墙、大阳台"是中国建筑学界对北戴河海滨别墅风格的定义。

---

1 王进勤:《秦皇岛古近代建筑》，海天出版社 2009 年版；刘强:《北戴河近代建筑简论》，《大众文艺》2016 年第 10 期。
Wang Jinqin: *Ancient and Modern Architectures in Qinhuangdao*, Haitian Publishing House, 2009; Liu Qiang: "On the Modern Architectures in Beidaihe", *Art and Literature for the Masses*, 2016, Issue 10.

2 一说为江西庐山、河北北戴河、福建厦门、山东青岛；一说为江西庐山、河北北戴河、河南鸡公山、浙江莫干山。

北戴河海滨别墅依联峰山而建，倚山瞰海，形成"层楼近水倚群峰"的建筑布局。别墅间以绿地花木相隔，成为意趣盎然的庭院。别墅建筑以西式为主，绝大多数为带有地下室的高台建筑。别墅内有回廊相连，内部结构、建筑纹饰多采取欧美风格，门窗多为弧形，装百叶窗，铺木质地板，有壁炉、阁楼等。别墅的墙体多以粗毛石砌就，取材于联峰山花岗岩。房顶多姿多态，红顶掩映于翠林间，形成浓郁的海滨田园情调。

北戴河近代建筑群，名人别墅众多。乔和别墅，为瑞士驻天津领事乔和为其女儿购置的生日礼物，俗称"瑞士小姐楼"；汉纳根别墅，为李鸿章的副官、德国贵族汉纳根的私人居所；海关楼，建于1903年，记录了英、美、法等国窃取中国海关治权的屈辱一页；傅作义别墅，建于1900年，原貌保存完好、充满维多利亚式风格；东金草燕别墅建于1942年，是日本风格与中式建筑的完美结合，因解放后何香凝曾在此居住，又称何香凝别墅；章家楼，又称张学良楼，为1925年天津巨商章瑞庭所建，以接待名人而声名远播，毛泽东、张学良等曾下榻此地；实业资本家吴鼎昌建于1914年的吴家楼，被誉为民国时期北戴河海滨"第一楼"；民族企业家周学熙之侄、启新洋灰公司总经理周叔韬为五个女儿分别建造的"五凤楼"，建筑风格统一，五座楼一字排开，颇有气势。

（作者：秦学武）

Located in Beidaihe District, Qinhuangdao City, Hebei Province, Beidaihe Modern Architectural Complex, known colloquially as "Beidaihe Seaside Villas", is famous for its unique historical and artistic values. In 2006, it was designated by the State Council as a Major Historical and Cultural Site Protected at the National Level.

Beidaihe Modern Architectural Complex is a witness to the tumultuous period in Beidaihe or even China in recent history. In the 19th year of Guangxu (1893), Stewart, a British missionary, built the first villa here. In

Beidaihe Modern Architectural Complex (Photographed by Yu Wenjiang)

the 24th year of Guangxu (1898), the Qing government designated Beidaihe as the first summer place where foreigners were allowed to live alongside the Chinese people. With the opening of the Tianjin–Yuguan Railway, the outstanding natural beauty of Beidaihe was discovered by people. A lot of foreign missionaries, Chinese and foreign bureaucrats and politicians, and well-heeled tradesmen came to the place and put up houses on the rented land. By 1948, 719 villas had been built in the seaside area, of which 482 were owned by foreigners, 236 by Chinese people, and 1 stateless. Today, there are more than 130 villas that survive.

Beidaihe Seaside Villas are the only seaside villa area among the Four Villa Areas in China[1]. In Chinese architectural circles, the villas are described with glowing terms, such as "a tree-lined area under the blue sky", "houses with plain walls and red roofs", and "large balconies".

---

1 Some think they are in Lushan of Jiangxi, Beidaihe of Hebei, Xiamen of Fujian and Qingdao of Shandong, while others think they are in Lushan of Jiangxi, Beidaihe of Hebei, Jigongshan of Henan and Moganshan of Zhejiang.

东金草燕别墅、东金草燕别墅外廊、五凤楼1号楼、张学良楼（摄影：王进勤）
Tokya Serna Villa and its veranda, Five Phoenix Villas No.1, Zhang Xueliang Mansion (Photographed by Wang Jinqin)

Beidaihe Seaside Villas lean against the Lianfeng Mountain and overlook the sea. The architectural layout features "buildings close to water and hills". The villas are spaced out with plants to become lively gardens. Mainly built in the Western style, they are mostly high-platform buildings with basements. The inside of a villa is connected by winding corridors, and the internal structures and decorations are also in the Western style. The houses are generally equipped with curved doors, blinds, floorboards, fireplaces and lofts. The walls of the villas are mostly built with coarse granites from the Lianfeng Mountain. The intriguing red roofs are half-hidden in green trees, creating a strong idyllic atmosphere near the coast.

In Beidaihe Modern Architectural Complex, there are many villas once inhabited by well-known figures. Joehee Villa, known colloquially as "Miss Switzerland Building", was a present from Joehee, the Swiss consul in Tianjin, for his daughter's birthday. Hanneken Villa was the private residence of von Hanneken, a German nobility serving as the adjutant of Li Hongzhang. Built in 1903, the Customs House bears witness to the humiliating period when China's customs was controlled by Britain, the

United States, France, etc. Built in 1900, Fu Zuoyi's Villa in Victorian style is preserved in good condition. Built in 1942, Tokya Serna Villa is a perfect combination of Japanese and Chinese architectural styles. It is also called He Xiangning Villa, because the madame had lived there after China's Liberation. Zhang's Mansion, aka Zhang Xueliang Mansion, was built in 1925 by Zhang Ruiting, a well-heeled Tianjin merchant. Great men such as Mao Zedong and Zhang Xueliang had stayed in this far-famed mansion. Built in 1914 by Wu Dingchang, an industrial capitalist, Wu's Mansion is known as the "First Mansion" in Beidaihe area in the Republic of China era. Zhou Shutao, nephew of the national entrepreneur Zhou Xuexi and General Manager of Chee Hsin Cement Company, built "Five Phoenix Villas" for his five daughters, which are aligned in a row with a unified style, looking quite impressive.

(By: Qin Xuewu)

二、自然风景 II. Natural Scenery

6. 北戴河鸽子窝公园 Beidaihe Dovecote Park[1]

鸽子窝公园位于秦皇岛市北戴河海滨东北角，又称鹰角石公园。公园建于1958年，占地20余公顷。公园是海鸥的栖息地，常有成群的海鸥朝暮相聚，或卧于海边岩石的缝隙之中。当地俗称海鸥为野鸽子，故名鸽子窝。公园内因地层断裂形成的临海悬崖上有一巨石，形似雄鹰屹立，故名鹰角石。公园由此得名。

1937年，"公益会"在海边石崖顶端修建一座凉亭，取名鹰角亭。1954年夏，毛泽东主席在北戴河写就名篇《浪淘沙·北戴河》，园内敬立高3.2米的毛主席雕像和《浪淘沙·北戴河》词碑。1985年，当地借鉴颐和园和避暑山庄的长廊，在园内东侧临海处修建一条长50米的望海长廊。

鸽子窝是中国九大观日出地之一，名曰"鹰亭迎日"。著名作家峻青曾撰文描绘鸽子窝观日出的壮景。

北戴河是享有国际盛誉的世界四大观鸟地之一，海边观鸟已成为当地生态旅游的重要内容。1936年，中国著名鸟类学家秦振黄等就曾到北戴河调查鸟类。1985年，英国剑桥大学学者、著名鸟类学家马丁·威廉姆斯来到北戴河并为这里丰富的鸟类资源所震撼。鸽子窝大潮坪[2]是东亚—澳大利亚候鸟迁徙路线上的重要驿站，被誉为"观鸟的圣地"。每到春秋季节，成千上万只候鸟南北迁徙途经此地。这里至今已发现20个目61个科400余种鸟类，包括东方白鹳、白鹳、灰鹤、丹顶鹤、白头鹤、灰头麦鸡、遗鸥等珍稀鸟类，还曾出现过14,700多只的鸟群，是国内外鸟类专家和观鸟爱好者的网红打卡地。

（作者：秦学武）

---

[1] 冯志远：《北戴河年鉴》，方志出版社2018年版。
Feng Zhiyuan: *Annals of Beidaihe*, Local Records Publishing House, 2018.

[2] 鸽子窝大潮坪，处于新开河入海口、鸽子窝公园北侧的海边滩涂，也称北戴河大潮坪或新开大潮坪。

The Dovecote Park, aka Eagle Park, is located in the northeast corner of Beidaihe seashore, Qinhuangdao. The park was built in 1958, covering an area of more than 20 hectares. It is home to flocks of seagulls. They either gather day and night, or perch in crevices of rocks by the sea. Seagulls are known locally as wild doves, hence the park got its name Dovecote Park. There is an eagle-shaped stone standing on the cliff which was created by the strata movement. That's how the park got its name Eagle Park.

In 1937, the Eagle Pavilion was built at the top of the seaside cliff by the "Public Welfare Association". In the summer of 1954, Chairman Mao composed the literary classic "Sand-Washing Waves · Beidaihe" in Beidaihe. A 3.2-meter-high statue of Chairman Mao and a stone tablet bearing the inscriptions of the poem are standing in the park. In 1985, after the fashion of the corridors in Beijing's Summer Palace and Chengde Mountain Resort, a 50-meter-long corridor was built in the east side of the park which is adjacent to the sea.

The Dovecote Park, specifically the Eagle Pavilion, is among the Nine Sunrise-viewing Spots of China. The splendid view of sunrise in Dovecote is the subject of an article of Jun Qing, a famous writer.

Beidaihe is one of the four greatest birdwatching sites in the world. Seaside birdwatching has become a major part of local ecotourism. In 1936, Qin Zhenhuang, a famous Chinese ornithologist, went to Beidaihe to investigate the birds. In 1985, Martin Williams, a scholar and famous ornithologist of Cambridge University, came to Beidaihe. He was impressed by the sheer amount of birds here. Hailed as the "Holy Land for Birdwatching", the Dovecote Tidal Flat[1] is an important rest station on the migration route of birds between East Asia and Australia. In spring and

---

1 The Dovecote Tidal Flat is located in the north of Dovecote Park and at the estuary of Xinkai River. It is also known as Beidaihe Tidal Flat or Xinkaihe Tidal Flat.

鸽子窝公园（摄影：于文江）
Dovecote Park (Photographed by Yu Wenjiang)

鹰角亭（摄影：王进勤）
Eagle Pavilion (Photographed by Wang Jinqin)

autumn, thousands of birds migrate across the place. More than 400 bird species falling under 61 families of 20 orders have been discovered here, including rare birds such as oriental white stork, white stork, grey crane, red crowned crane, hooded crane, grey-headed lapwing, and relict gull. Over 14,700 birds had once flocked together, creating an amazing sight to behold. As a result, it is now an internet-famous site for bird experts and bird watchers in China and abroad.

(By: Qin Xuewu)

7. 昌黎黄金海岸 Changli Gold Coast[1]

黄金海岸位于河北省昌黎县东部，海岸线长 52.1 千米，沙质松软，色如黄金。20 世纪 80 年代初，中国科学院地理研究所专家称这里可与澳大利亚昆士兰州的黄金海岸相媲美，故名"黄金海岸"。1990 年 9 月，昌黎黄金海岸自然保护区被国务院批准为国家级海洋海岸类型自然保护区之一，以海滩及近海生态系统为主要保护对象。

黄金海岸自然保护区占地 3 万公顷。这里的沙丘、沙堤、潟湖、林带和海洋生物等构成的沙质海岸自然景观及所在海区生态环境和自然资源，是研究海洋动力过程和海陆变化的典型岸段，具有重要的生态学、科学研究和旅游观赏价值。这里是文昌鱼分布密度最高的地区之一，有国家重点保护的鸟类 68 种。

黄金海岸分布有 40 余列天然海边沙丘，最高达 44 米，为中国海岸沙丘最高峰。沙丘每年在海潮、季风的作用下自然抬升。1986 年，这里建立了中国首家海边天然滑沙场——国际滑沙活动中心，被誉为"天下第一滑"。陡缓交错的沙丘、细软沙滩、碧蓝海水、小型湖泊和沙漠植物，构成了国内独有的海洋沙漠风光。

---

1 金照光，包宏伟:《昌黎黄金海岸国家级自然保护区内不同利益团体分析及其处措施》,《海洋开发与管理》, 2013 年 12 期。

Jin Zhaoguang and Bao Hongwei: "Analysis and Measures for the Coexistence of Different Interests in Changli Gold Coast National Nature Reserve", *Ocean Development and Management*, 2013, Issue 12.

单板五人滑沙（摄影：陈建国）
Five-person sand sliding (Photographed by Chen Jianguo)

翡翠岛位于黄金海岸南区，是黄色细沙与绿色植被相间的一座半岛，面积7平方千米，东、北、西三面由渤海和七里海环绕，被誉为"沙漠与大海的吻痕"。登高远眺，沙山横卧、碧海环绕、绿树葱茏，犹如镶嵌在金饰上的翡翠。翡翠岛集海洋大漠风光、戈壁绿洲景象、远古遗存物种、濒危珍稀鸟类等多种奇观于一体。

翡翠岛海浴场沙细、滩缓、水清、潮平，是天然优质海滨浴场，水质符合国家一级海水标准。这里是生态观光和滨海旅游休闲的优选之地，也是拓展训练和青少年夏令营的绝佳场所。

七里海是华北第一大潟湖，是秦皇岛沿海面积最大的天然鸟类栖息地。湖水富含鱼类、鸟类所需的矿物质和微生物，是鱼群生长、鸟类栖息的天堂，每年有400余种鸟类在此繁衍生息。七里海潟湖，是东亚—澳大利亚候鸟迁徙途中的重要驿站。

（作者：秦学武）

The Gold Coast is located in the east of Changli County, Hebei Province, featuring a 52.1-kilometer-long coast line and gold-like soft sand. In early 1980s, experts in Institute of Geographic Research, CAS said that the place could match the Gold Coast in Queensland of Australia, hene the name. In September 1990, Changli Gold Coast Nature Reserve was approved by the

State Council as a National Marine and Coastal Nature Reserve aiming to protect the beach and offshore ecosystems.

Changli Gold Coast Nature Reserve covers an area of 30,000 hectares. The sand dunes, sand banks, lagoons, forest belts and marine lives, of which its landscapes and natural resources are composed, are of great value to study ocean dynamics and geographic changes. With high ecological, scientific, and tourism significance, they are pleasing to behold. The place has the densest distribution of lancelets, and there are 68 bird species on the list of endangered and protected species of China.

The Gold Coast consists of over 40 natural coastal dunes, the tallest one of which measures 44 meters high—the peak of coastal dunes in China. The dunes are lifted by tides and monsoons each year. In 1986, Changli International Sand Sliding Center—the first seaside natural sand sliding ground in China, was

海边沙漠（摄影：张兴瑞）
Desert by the sea (Photographed by Zhang Xingrui)

established here. It was hailed as the "Finest Sand Sliding Ground in the World". With rolling sand dunes, fine sand beaches, blue sea, small lakes and desert plants, a unique desert scenery by the sea is formed.

Located in the south zone of the Gold Coast, the Jade Island is a peninsula featuring fine yellow sand and green vegetation. Covering an area of 7 square kilometers, it is hemmed in by Bohai Sea and Qilihai Lagoon in the east, north and west, and reputed to be the "love bite of desert and sea". Climbing to a high spot and looking around, one can see sand hills, blue sea and brilliant green trees lying around, shaped like a gold ornament studded with jade. The desert, oasis, ancient species and rare birds are all concentrated in this one place.

The Jade Island Seaside Resort, which offers fine sand, turquoise water and slow tides, is a natural high-quality bathing beach. With the water meeting the Sea Water Quality Standard (Grade I) of China, it is an ecotourism destination, a place for coastal recreation, and an ideal spot for outreach activities and summer camps.

Qilihai, as the biggest lagoon of North China, is the largest natural habitat of birds along the coast of Qinhuangdao. The rich minerals and microorganisms in the water serve as the main source of food for fish and birds. The place now attracts over 400 species of breeding birds every year. The Qilihai Lagoon is an important rest station on the migration route of birds between East Asia and Australia.

(By: Qin Xuewu)

8. 青龙祖山 Qinglong Zushan Mountain[1]

祖山位于河北省青龙满族自治县东南，距秦皇岛市区 25 千米，

---

1 张瑞华:《祖山风光》,《河北画报》, 2007 年 10 期。
Zhang Ruihua: "Zushan Scenery", *Hebei Pictorial*, 2007, Issue 10.

面积118平方千米。因燕山东段、渤海以北诸峰皆为此山余脉,故名"群山之祖",俗称老岭。1992年,被批准为市级森林生态自然保护区。2002年,祖山所在地被批准建立河北秦皇岛柳江国家地质公园。2010年,祖山景区被评为国家AAAA级景区。

祖山是典型的山岳型自然风景区,兼有泰山之雄、黄山之奇、华岳之险、峨眉之秀,以山、水、石、洞、花五奇著称。著名作家峻青题诗"劝君休夸五岳游,不登此山是虚生"。著名诗人臧克家赞其"画境诗天"。这里被誉为"塞北小黄山"。

祖山分天女峰、望海寺、画廊谷、飞瀑谷及乌龙谷五大景区。望海寺是祖山的中心景区,下山可观瀑布,上山可登主峰,西去可游花果山,东行可观画廊谷。

祖山山势陡峻,群峰竞秀,以山奇居首,1000米以上山峰达20余座。主峰天女峰,海拔1428米;响山,海拔1360米,悬崖峭壁处石缝纵横,山风掠过,如闻管弦之音;香瓜顶,海拔1200余米,南坡是百亩草甸,东坡为天然次生林带;背牛顶,沿悬梯攀爬直壁,令人惊心动魄;八仙顶,悬崖怪石环绕,云海下如游蓬莱。

祖山峰巅沟壑,怪石嶙峋,已命名的奇石美景60余处,如仙女云床、秀才观榜、山字峰、醉卧刘伶、龟兔赛跑、窟窿山、童戏驼峰、神龟探海、莲花出水等。仙女云床,是二三百万年前由巨型冰川冲蚀成的两个连体冰臼,犹如美女睡卧,堪称世界奇观。

祖山植被茂密,覆盖率达96%以上,植物达260余种。春季,繁花似锦,百鸟争鸣。5月前后,杜鹃、锦带花、紫丁香、八仙花、东陵绣球等山花次第开放。6月中旬,高山稀有花卉"天女木兰"[1]竞相吐蕊,素洁高雅,香气清淡,乃祖山盛景。夏季,风清气爽,云蒸霞蔚。云海、云流、云瀑,为夏季祖山特有景观。秋季,层林尽染,野果飘香,犹如巨幅油画。冬季,银装素裹,玉树琼花,一派北国风光。

---

[1] 天女木兰是太古第四纪冰川期幸存的珍稀植物,生长在海拔千米阴坡处。有植物活化石之称、被国家列入濒危物种保护名录。全国有野生植株3000多棵,祖山占一多半,且是唯一成片生长的地方。

祖山奇石（摄影：于文江）
Jagged rocks on Zushan (Photographed by Yu Wenjiang)

祖山受海洋气候影响，年降水量1000毫米左右，夏季平均气温低于20℃。溪流环绕，瀑布成群，成规模的瀑布达9处。花果山景区的瀑布落差80米，状如白蛇吐布。北龙潭瀑布落差60米，绝壁青苔密布，龙口喷玉吐珠。

祖山风景区东侧的铁瓦乌龙殿遗址，始建于隋唐或隋唐以前。1123年，奚族首领回离保在此建立奚国政权，8个月后为金所灭。祖山脚下的花厂峪村，曾是抗战时期凌（凌源）青（青龙）绥（绥中）联合县政府所在地，素有"铜墙铁壁花厂峪"之称。

（作者：秦学武）

Located in the southeast of Qinglong Manchu Autonomous County, Hebei Province, the Zushan Mountain is 25 kilometers away from downtown Qinhuangdao with an area of 118 square kilometers. As the "Origin of Mountains", Zushan, colloquially known as Laoling (literally Old Hill), stretches to the eastern part of Yan Mountains and the peaks to the north of Bohai Sea. In 1992, it was approved as a Municipal Forest Nature Reserve. In 2002, the establishment of Qinhuangdao Liujiang National Geopark with Zushan as part of it was approved. In 2010, the Zushan Scenic Area was named a National AAAA Level Tourist Attraction.

As a typical mountainous scenic area, Zushan combines the grandeur of

Flower of *Magnolia sieboldii* (Photographed by Wang Jinqin)

Mount Tai, the wonder of Mount Huang, the steepness of Mount Hua, and the beauty of Mount Emei. It is best known for the Five Wonders: peaks, streams, rocks, caves and flowers. Jun Qing, a famous writer, composed a poem which ran thus: "Don't you lavish praise on the Five Mountains; / You haven't lived without visiting Zushan." Zang Kejia, a famous poet, praised Zushan for its "picturesque scene and idyllic landscape". The place is hailed as the "North Equivalent of Mount Huang".

The Zushan Scenic Area is divided into five parts: Tiannü Peak, Wanghai Temple, Gallery Valley, Waterfall Valley, and Wulong Valley. As the center of the scenic area, the Wanghai Temple is surrounded by the waterfall below, the main peak above, Mount Huaguo in the west and Gallery Valley in the east.

The Zushan Mountain is precipitous with peaks in competing brilliance and rocks in curious shapes. There are more than 20 peaks above 1,000 meters in height. Tiannü, the main peak, is 1,428 meters above sea level. Xiangshan, 1,360 meters above sea level, is a steep peak riddled with stone crevices. Winds whistle through the crevices, creating music-like sounds. Xianggua Summit, with a hundred *mu* of meadow on the south slope and a natural secondary forest belt on the east slope, is more than 1,200 meters

Tiannü Peak (Photographed by Wang Huaiqiang)

above sea level. Beiniu Summit, with hanging ladders on the steep cliff, has a thrill of its own. Eight Immortals Summit, with jagged rocks and misty cloud, looks quite like a fairyland.

The Zushan Mountain has a lot of jagged rocks. There are over 60 stone sceneries that are nicknamed, such as Fairy Cloud Bed, Scholar Viewing the List, Mountain-shaped Summit, Drunken Liu Ling, Hare and Tortoise, Cave Mountain, Children Frolicking on the Hump, Supernatural Turtle Exploring the Sea, and Lotus Flower Rising from Underwater. The Fairy Cloud Bed, two conjoined pits created by glacial erosion two or three million years ago, looks like a sleeping beauty and is a great wonder in the world.

The Zushan Mountain is covered by a profusion of plants, with a vegetation coverage of over 96% and a variety of plants exceeding 260 species. In spring, flowers bloom brilliantly and birds chirp. Around

May, mountain flowers come out, such as azaleas, weigelas, lilacs and hydrangeas. In mid-June, the rare "*Magnolia sieboldii*"[1] trees open their buds, filling the mountain with subtle fragrance and contributing to an impressive sight. In summer, Zushan offers a splendid cloudscape with characteristic features such as cloud sea, cloud stream, and cloud waterfall. In autumn, the woods are tinged with red, and the aroma of wild fruits rises up through the air, creating a picturesque atmosphere. In winter, the mountain is snow-clad, and tree branches are covered by ice, forming a typical northern scenery.

The Zushan Mountain is affected by the oceanic climate, with 1,000 mm of rainfall per year and an average temperature lower than 20℃ in summer. Streams run zigzag through the mountain, and waterfalls cascade down the cliffs. There are 9 large-scale waterfalls. The one in Mount Huaguo, with a plunge of 80 meters, is like a white snake flicking a cloth. The one above Beilong Pond, spilling down the mossy cliff with a plunge of 60 meters, is like jades and pearls spewing from a dragon's mouth.

In the east of the Zushan Scenic Area, there lies the site of Tiewa Wulong Hall, which was built in or before the Sui and Tang dynasties. In 1123, Huilibao, leader of Xi people, established the State of Xi here. The state was annihilated by Jin eight months later. Located at the foot of the Zushan Mountain, Huachangyu Village had been the seat of the governing coalition of Lingyuan, Qinglong and Suizhong counties. It enjoys a reputation for being "an impregnable fortress".

(By: Qin Xuewu)

---

1 *Magnolia sieboldii*, a rare plant species first appeared during the Quaternary Glaciation, grows on shaded slopes at 1,000 meters above sea level. Known as a living plant fossil, it is on the list of endangered and protected species of China. Of the about 3,000 wild plants in China, more than half are found growing in clusters in the Zushan Mountain.

9. 兴隆雾灵山 Xinglong Wuling Mountain[1]

雾灵山位于河北省兴隆县境内，燕山山脉中段，主峰歪桃峰海拔2118米，被誉为"京东第一峰"。历史上曾称灵山、伏凌山、五龙山，明代始称雾灵山。1988年，雾灵山被批准为国家级自然保护区。1993年，河北省林业厅批准设立雾灵山省级森林公园。

雾灵山属暖温带湿润大陆季风区，东西长24千米，南北宽17千米，总面积14,246.9公顷，森林覆盖率84.68%，年均降水量863毫米。雾灵山地处潮白河、滦河上游，是密云水库、潘家口水库的重要水源涵养地，对北京、天津、承德、唐山的用水具有重要影响。

雾灵山地处华北、东北和内蒙古三大植被区系交汇区，属暖温带落叶阔叶林向温带针阔混交林的过渡地带。天然植被有针叶林、阔叶林、针阔混交林、灌丛、灌草丛、草丛、草甸、岩生植被、湿生植被和水生植被等10种类型。森林植被垂直分布明显，景观丰富多样。雾灵山是中国自然生态名山和京津地区的重要生态屏障。

雾灵山野生物种资源丰富，享有"华北物种基因库"美誉。这里有高等植物165科645属1870种，其中有红松、红景天、黄檗、紫椴、软枣猕猴桃、人参等国家二级保护植物14种，有雾灵丁香、雾灵景天等模式种[2]37个，有青檀、独根草等中国特有的单种属植物12种；有陆生脊椎动物247种，其中有金雕、金钱豹、秃鹫、猎隼和黄胸鹀等国家一级保护动物5种，勺鸡、红隼等国家二级保护动物35种；有大型真菌238种，昆虫3007种。

雾灵山是著名"雾山"，顾炎武《昌平山水记》云："其山高峻，有云雾蒙其上，四时不绝。"奇峰、林海、秀水、秋色、云海、日出、

---

1 马小欣：《京东绿色明珠——雾灵山省级森林公园》，《河北林业》，2021年10期；张希军：《雾灵山，京津绿色生态屏障》，《河北林业》，2020年04期。
Ma Xiaoxin: *A Green Pearl to the East of the Capital—Wuling Mountain Provincial Forest Park*, *Hebei Forestry*, 2021, Issue 10; Zhang Xijun: *Wuling Mountain, an Ecological Protective Screen for Beijing and Tianjin*, *Hebei Forestry*, 2020, Issue 04.

2 一个属中，首次被发现且被描述并发表的物种，定为模式种。

石海、佛光、冰雪、晚霞等奇观构成了美丽的山水画卷。雾灵山有龙潭、仙人塔、五龙头、清凉界四大景区，有歪桃峰、龙潭大峡谷、仙人塔、清凉界碑、龙潭瀑布、七盘井、古香杨树等著名景点。

雾灵山是文化名山。北魏郦道元《水经注》云："（伏凌）山高峻，严嶂寒深，阴崖积雪，凝冰夏结，事同《离骚》峨峨之咏，故世人因以名山也。"辽金时期庙宇众多，香火旺盛。强子岭关、白岭关、五虎（水）门、黑谷关等长城关隘为明将戚继光所建。明洪武年间，刘伯温巡边时题刻"雾灵山清凉界"碑。清康熙帝巡游此地，题诗《晓发古北口望雾灵山》。顺治二年（1645），雾灵山所在的兴隆县被划为清东陵"后龙风水禁地"，1915年解禁，封禁达270年。

2009年，雾灵山、兴隆溶洞、六里坪等景区和若干地质遗迹聚集地段，获批兴隆国家地质公园。

（作者：秦学武）

Located in Xinglong County, Hebei Province, the Wuling Mountain is in the middle section of the Yan Mountains. Reputed as the "First Peak to the East of the Capital", its main peak Crooked Peach is 2,118 meters above sea level. The Wuling Mountain was historically known as Ling Mountain, Fuling Mountain and Wulong Mountain. It began to be called Wuling Mountain in the Ming Dynasty. In 1988, the Wuling Mountain was approved as a National Nature Reserve. In 1993, Forestry and Grassland Bureau of Hebei Province approved the establishment of Wuling Mountain Provincial Forest Park.

The Wuling Mountain is lying in the humid warm temperate continental monsoon climate zone. 24 kilometers long from east to west and 17 kilometers wide from south to north, it covers an area of 14,246.9 hectares, with a forest coverage of 84.68% and an annual rainfall of 863 mm. At the head of Chaobai River and Luan River, the Wuling Mountain is an important water source conservation area for the Miyun Reservoir and the

Panjiakou Reservoir. It deeply affects the water supply of Beijing, Tianjin, Chengde and Tangshan.

The Wuling Mountain is situated at the confluence of North China, Northeast China and Inner Mongolian vegetation regions. It is a transitional zone from warm temperate broadleaved deciduous forests to temperate mixed forests, featuring 10 types of vegetation: coniferous forest, broadleaved forest, theropencedrymion, shrub, shrub-tussock, tussock, meadow, rock vegetation, hygrophilous vegetation and aquatic vegetation. The vertically distributed forest vegetation contributes to the abundance of plant species. The Wuling Mountain is a famous natural mountain in China and an important ecological screen for Beijing and Tianjin.

The Wuling Mountain, hailed as the Species Gene Bank of North China, is rich in wild species resources. It is home to 1,870 higher plant species falling under 645 families of 165 orders. Among them are 14 national second-class protected plants, such as *Pinus koraiensis*, *Rhodiola rosea*, *Phellodendron*, *Tilia amurensis*, *Actinidia arguta* and *Panax ginseng*; 37 type species[1], such as *Syringa wulingensis* and *Sedum wulingense*; 12 monotypic plant genera native to China, such as *Pteroceltis tatarinowii* and *Oresitrophe rupifraga*; 247 terrestrial vertebrates, among which 5 species— golden eagle, leopard, vulture, saker falcon and yellow-breasted bunting— are national first-class protected animals; 35 national second-class protected animals, including koklass pheasant and common kestrel; 238 species of macrofungi; and 3,007 species of insects.

The Wuling Mountain is a famous "Fog Mountain". According to the *Landscape Essay of Changping* by Gu Yanwu, "The lofty mountain is crowned with mist all the year round." A Chinese landscape painting of

---

1 A type species means the species under a genus first discovered, described and published.

Beautiful Wuling Mountain (Photographed by Wang Huaiqiang)

grotesque peaks, forests, waterscape, autumn scenery, cloud sea, sunrise, stone sea, Buddha light, ice and snow, and sunset is unfolded here. There are four scenic areas: Dragon Spring, Immortal Pagoda, Five Dragon Heads, and Refreshing World. Crooked Peach Peak, Dragon Spring Valley, Immortal Pagoda, Refreshing World Monument, Dragon Spring Fall, Seven-coil Well and Antique Poplar are among the prominent attractions.

The Wuling Mountain is a reputed cultural mountain. Here's what *Commentary on the Waterways Classic* by Li Daoyuan says: "The lofty (Fuling) Mountain is snow-clad. The cliffs are perennially covered with snow even in summer. Like mountains described in *Li Sao*, it towers majestically over the landscape as a magnificent mountain, hence its name." In the Liao and Jin dynasties, the temples in the mountain were well worshipped. Passes of the Great Wall, such as Qiangziling, Bailing, Wuhu (Wuhu Water) and Heigu, were built by General Qi Jiguang of Ming. During the reign of Hongwu of the Ming Dynasty, Liu Bowen, when he inspected the border areas, wrote the words "Refreshing World in Wuling Mountain" and had them inscribed on a tablet. In the Qing Dynasty, Emperor Kangxi travelled to the place and inscribed the poem "Depart in the Morning from Gubeikou for Wuling Mountain". For 270 years from the 2nd year of Shunzhi (1645) to 1915, Xinglong County where the Wuling Mountain was located was designated as an "off-limit area" of the Eastern Qing Tombs.

In 2009, The area including Wuling Mountain, Xinglong Karst Cave, Liuliping and a few other spots where geological heritages abound was approved as the Xinglong National Geopark.

(By: Qin Xuewu)

10. 木兰围场 Mulan Enclosure

木兰围场是集政治活动、军事训练、皇家娱乐等功能于一体的清代"皇家猎苑"，包括今河北围场满族蒙古族自治县全境，以及河北隆化县、内蒙古赤峰市、内蒙古多伦县三地的一部分。东西长约150千米，南北宽约100千米。

"木兰围场"是满汉混合语。"木兰"，即满语"哨鹿"之意，是皇家狩猎捕鹿时使用的一种状如牛角号的喇叭，以桦皮和树木制成，长五六寸，用嘴吹、吸，发出"呦呦"鹿鸣之声，以引诱鹿来；"围场"为汉语，即打猎场所。

木兰围场建于1681年，康熙为推行怀柔政策和训练军队在此设置皇家猎苑，乾隆时期达到鼎盛。清前半叶，皇帝秋季通常都要率王公大臣、八旗精兵来此射猎，最多时军队人数达1.2万人，史称"木兰秋狝"。康熙至嘉庆的140年间，这里举行"木兰秋狝"达105次。北京故宫博物院藏有多幅宫廷画家的《木兰秋狝图》，承德博物馆藏有满绣《乾隆木兰秋狝图》，生动地描绘了清代皇家狩猎的壮景。

现在的塞罕坝国家森林公园、御道口草原森林风景区和红松洼自

《弘历木兰图》（清人绘）
Emperor Hongli's Mulan Autumn Hunting (Painted in Qing Dynasty)

然保护区，是历史上木兰围场的一部分。

塞罕坝国家森林公园，面积9.4万公顷，森林覆盖率75.2%。这里动植物种类繁多，有高等植物81科312属659种，有以狍子为主的兽类11科25种，有以黑琴鸡为主的鸟类27科88种。浩瀚林海、广袤草原、清澈高原湖泊和清代历史遗迹，造就了独特的自然景观和人文景观。2007年，塞罕坝被批准为国家级森林生态类型自然保护区。

御道口草原森林风景区，面积10万公顷。景区有原始草原4.7万公顷，湿地1.3万公顷，天然次生林3.3万公顷，是滦河发源地之一。有植物659种，野生动物100多种。1982年，被批准为国家级风景名胜区；2005年，被评为国家AAAA级旅游景区。

红松洼风景区，面积 7.3 万公顷，森林覆盖率 78%。这里动植物种类繁多，山地高原交错，河湖星罗棋布，尤其是浩瀚林海与大面积天然草原浑然一体，优美壮观。1998 年，红松洼被批准为国家级草原草甸类型自然保护区。

（作者：秦学武）

The Mulan Enclosure was a royal hunting ground of the Qing Dynasty for political activities, military training and entertainment. It includes the entire Weichang Manchu and Mongolian Autonomous County of Hebei, and parts of Longhua County of Hebei, Chifeng City of Inner Mongolia, and Duolun County of Inner Mongolia. The enclosure measures 150 kilometers long from east to west and 100 kilometers wide from south to north.

"Mulan Enclosure" is a mixed phrase of Manchu and Chinese words. "Mulan", which means "Deer Whistle" in Manchu, is an ox-horn-shaped

牧秋（摄影：王怀强）
Herds in autumn (Photographed by Wang Huaiqiang)

trumpet used by the royal family when hunting deer. Made of birch bark and wood, it is 5–6 inches long. When blowing or sucking it, one could entice the deer by mimicking their calling sound. "Enclosure" is a Chinese word that means hunting ground.

Established in 1681 by Emperor Kangxi, the Mulan Enclosure was a royal hunting ground to press ahead with the policy of conciliation and train the army. During the reign of Qianlong, it reached the zenith of glory. In the first half of the Qing Dynasty, the emperors would hunt here in summer with dukes, ministers and elite troops of the Eight Banners. At its peak, there were 12,000 soldiers participating in the event, which was known historically as "Mulan Autumn Hunting". During the 140 years between the reigns of Kangxi and Jiaqing, the "Mulan Autumn Hunting" was held 105 times. Many versions of *Painting* of *Mulan Autumn Hunting*

Autumn scenery (Photographed by Wang Huaiqiang)

are collected in the Palace Museum. *Qianlong's Mulan Autumn Hunting*, a Manchu embroidery work, is kept in the Chengde Museum. They present a vivid picture of the grandeur of the autumn hunting.

Today's Saihanba National Forest Park, Yudaokou Grassland and Forest Scenic Area and Hongsongwa Nature Reserve had historically been parts of the Mulan Enclosure.

Saihanba National Forest Park covers an area of 94,000 hectares and has a forest coverage of 75.2%. It is home to a wide variety of animal and plant species, including 659 higher plant species falling under 312 families of 81 orders; 25 beast species falling under 11 orders, represented by roe deer; and 88 bird species falling under 27 orders, represented by black grouse. The vast forests and grasslands, clear plateau lakes and historical relics of the Qing Dynasty together make up the unique natural and humanistic landscapes. In 2007, Saihanba was approved as a National Forest Nature Reserve.

Yudaokou Grassland and Forest Scenic Area covers an area of 100,000 hectares, including 47,000 hectares of primary grassland, 13,000 hectares of wetland, and 33,000 hectares of natural secondary forest. As a source region of the Luan River, it is home to 659 plant species and more than 100 wildlife species. In 1982, it was approved as a National Park of China. In 2005, it was named a National AAAA Level Tourist Attraction.

Hongsongwa Scenic Area covers an area of 73,000 hectares and has a forest coverage of 78%. Featuring mountains and high lands and embedded with rivers and lakes, it is home to a variety of animals and plants and marks the dramatic coexistence of vast forests and sprawling natural grasslands. In 1998, Hongsongwa was approved as a National Grassland and Meadow Nature Reserve.

(By: Qin Xuewu)

第四章

民俗文化

Chapter IV Folk Culture

一、传统音乐 I. Traditional Music

1. 冀东民歌 Jidong Folk Song

民歌,是劳动人民口头创作、口头流传,并在流传过程中不断进行集体加工的传统音乐形式,具有鲜明的地域性、现实性和时代性。

冀东民歌,是指产生和流行在唐山、秦皇岛两市的民歌。冀东民歌的产生可追溯到辽金至明代,深受山西、山东、河南、安徽、江苏等地移民带来的外地民歌影响。

冀东民歌以"老呔话"[1]为基础,用"土嗓子"演唱,有浓郁的乡土气息。老呔话"先上挑、再下滑"[2]的语调特点,深刻影响了冀东民歌"高抛低落"的旋律线,形成了富有地方特色的长长拖腔。

冀东民歌不仅曲调丰富优美、婉转细腻,而且具有独特的润腔[3]技巧和发声方式,如卷舌音[4]、嘟噜音、喉控音、鼻控音、倚音[5]和滑音等,在河北民歌中独树一帜。

冀东民歌的唱腔,对乐亭大鼓、唐山皮影、评剧、冀东秧歌有直接影响。

冀东民歌体系齐全,有劳动号子、叫卖调、秧歌调、山歌、小调五大类。分秧歌调、单口唱、对口篇、表演唱等演唱形式。

1956年至1978年,经过4次大规模采风,挖掘、整理出冀东民歌近2000首。有影响全国的《茉莉花》《捡棉花》《绣灯笼》《梁山伯》《蒲连车》[6]《放风筝》《光荣榜》《渤海渔民号子》《刨花生》《闹花灯》,

---

1 学界称"昌黎方言",详见"滦州皮影"相关注释。

2 老呔话把普通话的阳平读为上声,上声又读为近似阴平、阳平。

3 所谓润腔,就是运用滑音、颤音、波音、顿音等装饰音对腔调或某些音进行润饰、装点。

4 老呔话常把儿化音拖长,使得"先上挑、再下滑"的语调特点更突出,更富有歌唱性。

5 倚音的演唱,通常要轻而短,冀东民歌为表达情感,要求"倚音扎实重唱"。

6 《蒲连车》,是流行于河北玉田的爱情民歌。蒲连车,是旧社会迎娶新娘的马拉婚车。婚车门帘用玉田南部盛产的香蒲草编成,故名。

昌黎民歌《小看戏》（摄影：乔景鹏）
"Going to Watch Opera", a Changli folk song (Photographed by Qiao Jingpeng)

以及稀有的唐山工人民歌《住锅伙》《窑工苦》《下煤窑苦难言》等。创作于1993年的《槐花海》[1]，是冀东新民歌的代表。《捡棉花》2002年入选全国义务教育七年级《音乐》教材。

民歌演唱家曹玉俭、刘荣德名满全国，还有王世杰、齐凤英、韩宫贤、解玉萍、魏淑君、徐盛茂、李丽茹、张小东等著名民歌手。唐山红玫瑰女子合唱团享誉国内外。

昌黎民歌是冀东民歌的代表，现有民歌189首。演唱形式有秧歌调、单口唱和对口篇。渔民号子《昌黎拉网调》，1957年获全国第二届文艺汇演优秀表演奖，曾在中南海演出。2006年，《昌黎拉网调》获第九届开渔节全国渔歌（号子）邀请赛二等奖。

2000年，昌黎县被文化部命名为"中国民间艺术之乡（民歌）"。2008年，昌黎民歌入选国家级非物质文化遗产代表性项目名录。

（作者：秦学武）

---

1 《槐花海》，刘麟作词，王志信、刘荣德作曲。

The folk song is a traditional musical form created by the working people. Delivered orally, it is constantly being refined over time. Regional characteristics, realistic tones and contemporary spirits are the most salient features of folk songs.

Jidong folk songs are created and popular in Tangshan and Qinhuangdao. Dating back to the Liao, Jin and Ming dynasties, the art form had been deeply influenced by the folk songs from Shanxi, Shandong, Henan, Anhui and Jiangsu.

Based on the "Laotai dialect"[1], Jidong folk songs are sung with a "folk-styled voice" suffused with a strong local flavor. The Laotai dialect accentuates the intonational characteristic of "rising and falling"[2] and gives Jidong folk songs a "rising and falling" rhythmic quality. The accent pronounced in a drawl is rich in local color.

The melody of Jidong folk songs is mellow and lingering. The art form has its own distinctive *run qiang*[3] and phonation skills, such as retroflex tone[4], vibrating tone, throat tone, nasal tone, appoggiatura[5] and portamento, which make it highly unique in Hebei folk songs.

The vocals of Jidong folk songs have a direct influence on Laoting bass drum, Tangshan shadow play, Pingju opera and Jidong Yangko.

Jidong folk songs cover a complete category, including work song,

---

1 Called "Changli dialect" in academic circles. More information can be found in the notes of "Luanzhou shadow play".

2 In the Laotai dialect, the rising tone in standard Mandarin is pronounced as the falling-rising tone, and the falling-rising tone is like the high and level tone or the rising tone.

3 The so-called *run qiang* is to lubricate the tone or certain sounds with grace notes such as portamento, trill, mordent and staccato.

4 In the Laotai dialect, the rhotic accent is used to be pronounced in a drawl to accentuate the intonation characteristic of "rising and falling", and give the words a musical quality.

5 Appoggiatura is usually light and brisk in pronunciation. In Jidong folk songs, appoggiatura has to be resonating and loud in order to manifest sentiments.

peddling song, Yangko tune, mountain song and popular tune. These songs can be performed in Yangko, solo, alternately, or with actions.

From 1956 to 1978, 4 major campaigns were mobilized to collect, search and organize nearly 2,000 Jidong folk songs. There are works widely known in China, such as "Jasmine", "Picking Cotton", "Embroidered Lantern", "Liang Shanbo", "Cattail Carriage"[1], "Flying the Kite", "The Honor Roll", "Bohai Fishermen's Work Song", "Harvesting Peanuts" and "Lantern Festival". Workers' songs of Tangshan, such as "Rough Houses", "Sufferings of Mine Workers" and "The Misery of Coal Mine Workers", are quite unusual works. Created in 1993, "Sophora Flower Sea"[2] is the representative of new Jidong folk songs. In 2002, "Picking Cotton" was selected into the music textbook for compulsory education (Grade 7) of China.

Cao Yujian and Liu Rongde are celebrated folk singers in China. Wang Shijie, Qi Fengying, Han Gongxian, Xie Yuping, Wei Shujun, Xu Shengmao, Li Liru and Zhang Xiaodong are also well-known. Tangshan Red Rose Women's Choir is known the world over.

The Changli folk song, with 189 songs currently, is the representative of Jidong folk songs. It can be performed in Yangko, solo, or alternately. In 1957, the fishermen's song "Changli Net-dragging Tune" received the Excellent Performance Award in the Second National Literature and Art Festival. The tune had been staged in Zhongnanhai. In 2006, "Changli Net-dragging Tune" won the second prize in the National Fishing Song (Chant) Invitational Competition held as a part of the 9th Fishing Festival.

In 2000, Changli County was named the "Hometown of Chinese Folk Art

---

1　"Cattail Carriage" is a folk love song popular in Yutian, Hebei. The cattail carriage was the wedding cart drawn by horses to pick up the bride in the old days. It got its name because the curtain was made of cattail abundant in the south of Yutian.

2　Lyrics by Liu Lin, music by Wang Zhixin and Liu Rongde.

(Folk Song)" by the Ministry of Culture of the People's Republic of China. In 2008, the Changli folk song was included in the List of Representative Items of National Intangible Cultural Heritage.

(By: Qin Xuewu)

2. 冀东吹歌 Jidong Trumpeting Song[1]

冀东吹歌，即冀东鼓吹乐，以唢呐为主奏乐器，鼓、钹为配奏乐器，吹奏牌子曲、汉吹曲、秧歌曲、杂曲等曲目的传统音乐形式。

唢呐是波斯语的音译，由哨片、气盘、芯子、杆子、碗子五部分组成，公元 3 世纪传入中国。唢呐艺人，俗称"吹鼓手"或"喇叭匠"。冀东鼓吹乐传于元末宫廷，《百鸟鸣》《万年欢》《满堂红》《句句双》《大姑娘美》等为宫廷乐曲牌。

冀东唢呐是河北吹歌的两大分支之一，分三个流派：抚宁派（昌黎、卢龙、抚宁），乐亭派（滦南、乐亭、唐海、丰南南部），迁安派（迁安、迁西、丰润、遵化、玉田、古冶大部）。二十世纪上半叶，冀东艺人的鼓乐班社遍及冀东、东北三省及内蒙古南部。

冀东唢呐，分海笛子、三机子、二唢呐、大唢呐四种。冀东唢呐有两个显著特点：一是大杆喇叭[2]的碗子比一般唢呐的碗子要长，碗子弧度较小，造成筒音和第一孔音不是大二度的关系，而是特有的小三度关系；二是托气盘比其他唢呐大且把嘴包住，演奏者循环换气，每曲一吹到底，形成独特的演奏风格。

冀东吹歌的演奏形式分五种：平吹、花吹、套吹[3]、大型平吹[4]、咔

---

1 参阅：王晓丹：《河北吹歌文化研究》，《通俗歌曲》2015 年 07 期；张强：《冀东地区唢呐流派研究》，天津音乐学院 2013 年硕士学位论文。
See: Wang Xiaodan: "Research on Hebei Trumpeting Song Culture", *Popular Song*, 2015, Issue 07; Zhang Qiang: "Research on Suona Schools in Jidong", 2013 Master's Thesis of Tianjin Conservatory of Music.

2 冀东鼓吹乐，常用二唢呐，很少用大唢呐，故习惯称二唢呐为"大杆喇叭"。因其杆子用铁梨木制成，又称"铁杆喇叭"。

3 由高音、次高音、中音、低音四种唢呐加鼓、钹一起演奏。

4 几十支大杆喇叭加大鼓、大钹一起吹奏，如大型庆典，气势恢宏。

奏[1]。主奏唢呐一般成双出现，这在全国独树一帜。乐队一般为4—6人，在河北鼓吹乐中最为精炼。乐队通常由两支同调大杆喇叭为主奏乐器，一人为掌曲之人（俗称"吹上手"），另一人为同度或低八度进行配奏（俗称"吹下手"）。鼓手掌控节奏和板式。

唢呐（供图：抚宁区文化馆）
Suona (Provided by Funing District Cultural Center)

鼓在头，音在后，故名鼓吹乐。广泛用于婚丧嫁娶、商业庆典、年节庙会、民间舞蹈的伴奏。

　　冀东吹歌的演奏技巧具有创新性。口吐鼻吸的循环换气法，是吹鼓手的必备演奏技巧。清末民初，杨元亨创立咔戏。民国初年，金财、姚卓雨在冀东开始演奏咔戏。金财创立的花吹《拔三节》，成为冀东花吹的代表节目。

　　冀东鼓吹乐名人辈出。清朝末年，有周柏祥、王大辫子、赵永利、赵永发、陈德、刘春玉等；民国时期，金财被誉为"天下第一吹"，还有赵会、顾炳珠、倪仕宽、张秉云、郭文田、吴殿奎、沈德、任福顺、刘逢春等。1938年，赵会的《满堂红》《绣红灯》录制成唱片；新中国成立后，任启瑞和孙俊元的"对喇叭"艺冠冀东，还有倪仕然、赵柏清、李春生、任启文、代文志、许同清、陆云起、陆云峰、吴庆生、吴庆余、沈金栋、张荣清、刘振声、王兴、贾占元、贾占恒、姚少林等。1958年，任启瑞、陆云起的唢呐曲在中央人民广播电台播出。

---

[1] 以咔碗为主奏乐器，配以口琴，模拟戏曲、曲艺中的人声。

1990年，崔占春、戴文治荣获"河北省吹歌艺术家"称号；新时期，有徐阁、刘桂存、任连义、赵立国、董连吉等。

抚宁鼓吹乐有400余年历史，在河北民间器乐中最具代表性。抚宁鼓吹乐曲目众多，有五大类共300余首，素有"牌子十四套，小曲赛牛毛，九辈吹喇叭，有曲没练着"之说。2006年，入选国家级非物质文化遗产代表性项目名录。

丰宁满族吵子会有300余年历史，分"吹打曲"和"杂曲"两种，曲牌大多为满族的。乐队包括2名吹鼓手和10名打击乐手。2008年，入选国家级非物质文化遗产代表性项目名录。

唐山花吹，由两支大杆喇叭、一个堂鼓和一副小钹组成。喇叭技巧有摘碗、转碗、甩碗、推拉碗等系列动作，以及在音孔上手的抹、点、剜、捻等俏皮动作17种；堂鼓技巧包括单点、双点、嘟噜点等20种；小钹技巧包括正反打、绕打、点打、边打等11种。2008年，入选国家级非物质文化遗产代表性项目名录。

（作者：秦学武）

The Jidong trumpeting song, aka Jidong percussion and wind music, is a traditional music form with suona as the main instrument and drums and cymbals in accompaniment. It features Qupai tunes, Han Yuefu tunes, Yangko tunes and miscellaneous tunes.

The suona, its name derived from the Persian language, consists of beating reed, air plate, slug, pole and bowl. The musical instrument entered China in the 3rd century. Suona performers were colloquially known as "trumpeter" or "bugler". Jidong trumpeting songs were popular in the court at the end of the Yuan Dynasty. "The Birds' Calls", "Eternal Happiness", "Triumph on All Fronts", "Repeated Sentences" and "Pretty Girls" were all palace *qupai* (literally named tune) at the time.

Jidong suona music, one of the two branches of the Hebei trumpeting song, is split into three sects: Funing Sect (Changli, Lulong and Funing),

Laoting Sect (Luannan, Laoting, Tanghai and southern Fengnan) and Qian'an Sect (Qian'an, Qianxi, Fengrun, Zunhua, Yutian and most parts of Guye). In the first half of the 20th century, drum clubs ran by Jidong artists were found throughout Jidong, northeastern China and southern Inner Mongolia.

There are four types of Jidong suona: *haidi* (sopranino) suona, *sanji* (alto) suona, tenor suona and bass suona. The Jidong suona has two salient features. First, the bowl of a big-pole trumpet[1] is larger than that of an ordinary suona, and the arc of the bowl is smaller. Therefore, there is not a major second relationship, but a peculiar minor third relationship, between the tube sound and the first hole sound. Second, the air plate of a Jidong suona, which is bigger than that of other suona, covers the mouth completely. By circular breathing, the performer would usually play a tune to the end, developing a unique performance style.

Jidong trumpeting songs are performed in five ways: common trumpeting, acrobatic trumpeting, ensemble trumpeting[2], large-scale trumpeting[3] and *kazou*[4]. The presiding suona generally appear in pairs, the first of its kind in China. The band is the smallest among the percussion and wind music bands in Hebei Province, with 4–6 members in the normal case. The main instruments are two big-pole trumpets of the same tone performed by two people: the tune leader (colloquially known as the "*chui shang shou*"), and

---

1 In Jidong percussion and wind music, the tenor suona is usually used, while the bass suona is scarcely used. People used to call the tenor suona "big-pole trumpet". As the pole is made of ironwood, it is also called "iron-pole trumpet".

2 The tune is played on sopranino, alto, tenor and bass suona, with a drum and cymbals as accompaniment.

3 The tune is played on dozens of big-pole trumpets, with drums and cymbals as accompaniment, creating a magnificent atmosphere.

4 The tune is played with kawan suona as the main instrument and harmonicas as accompaniment, simulating the human voice in opera and folk songs.

the accompanier in the same tune or an octave lower (colloquially known as the "*chui xia shou*"). The rhythm and metre are under the control of the drummer. As the drumming comes before the blowing, the art is called percussion and wind music. It is being used as the accompaniment of weddings, funerals, business celebrations, temple fairs and folk dances.

The Jidong trumpeting song is innovative in performance. A trumpeter must gain the circular breathing skill of exhaling through the mouth and inhaling through the nose. In the late Qing Dynasty and early Republic of China, Yang Yuanheng created Ka (Imitation) music. In the early Republic of China, Jin Cai and Yao Zhuoyu began to perform Ka music in Jidong. Created by Jin Cai, "Three-section Blowing" became a representation of Jidong acrobatic trumpeting.

There was a galaxy of talents in Jidong percussion and wind music, including Zhou Boxiang, Big Braid Wang, Zhao Yongli, Zhao Yongfa, Chen De and Liu Chunyu in the late Qing Dynasty. Jin Cai in the Republic of China was hailed as the "Greatest Trumpeting Song Performer under Heaven", and there were also Zhao Hui, Gu Bingzhu, Ni Shikuan, Zhang Bingyun, Guo Wentian, Wu Diankui, Shen De, Ren Fushun and Liu Fengchun in contemporary China. In 1938, "Triumph on All Fronts" and "Embroidered Lantern" by Zhao Hui were recorded. After the People's Republic of China was founded, Ren Qirui partnered with Sun Junyuan to form the "Trumpeting Twosome", which became a household name in Jidong. Celebrated performers include Ni Shiran, Zhao Baiqing, Li Chunsheng, Ren Qiwen, Dai Wenzhi, Xu Tongqing, Lu Yunqi, Lu Yunfeng, Wu Qingsheng, Wu Qingyu, Shen Jindong, Zhang Rongqing, Liu Zhensheng, Wang Xing, Jia Zhanyuan, Jia Zhanheng and Yao Shaolin. In 1958, the suona tune performed by Ren Qirui and Lu Yunqi was played on China National Radio. In 1990, Cui Zhanchun and Dai Wenzhi were named the "Trumpeting Song Artists of Hebei Province". In recent years, there are celebrated artists such as Xu Ge, Liu Guicun, Ren Lianyi, Zhao Liguo and Dong Lianji.

The 400-year-old Funing percussion and wind music is the most representative one among the Hebei folk instrumental music. The more than 300 songs fall under 5 categories. As a saying goes: "There are 14 sets of *qupai*, and the tunes are numerous as cow hair. Even people play suona for nine generations, there are still songs going unpracticed." In 2006, Funing percussion and wind music was included in the List of Representative Items of National Intangible Cultural Heritage.

The 300-year-old Fengning Manchu Chaozi music comes in "wind and percussion" and "miscellaneous" categories, and the *qupai* are mostly

Funing percussion and wind music (Provided by Funing District Cultural Center)

written in Manchu language. A band consists of 2 trumpeters and 10 percussionists. In 2008, Fengning Manchu Chaozi music was included in the List of Representative Items of National Intangible Cultural Heritage.

Tangshan acrobatic trumpeting is performed on two big-pole trumpets, one *tanggu* drum and a pair of small cymbals. The trumpeting techniques include bowl plucking, bowl turning, bowl flinging and bowl pulling, which are accompanied by 17 deft movements on the sound holes such as sweeping, touching, scooping and rolling. There are 20 techniques of playing the *tanggu* drum, including one-hand beat, double-hand beat and quickened beat. The small cymbals are displayed with 11 techniques, including reversible beat, surrounding beat, touching beat and side beat. In 2008, Tangshan acrobatic trumpeting was included in the List of Representative Items of National Intangible Cultural Heritage.

(By: Qin Xuewu)

二、传统舞蹈 II. Traditional Dances

3. 冀东秧歌 Jidong Yangko[1]

秧歌，是中国北方传统的民间舞蹈，集舞蹈、歌唱、戏剧、杂技、武术于一体。扭秧歌，也称闹秧歌、跑秧歌，是冀东的传统年俗，在农村广受欢迎。

秧歌，宋代称"村田乐"，是插秧时合着鼓点的群歌，后发展成一种带妆的场地舞蹈。今天，扭秧歌已由年俗变身广场舞，成为百姓健身、娱乐的新形式。

---

[1] 参阅：滕运涛、田国安：《昌黎地秧歌》，中国戏剧出版社 2012 年版；杨立新、郭秀芬：《滦州地秧歌》，香港新锐出版社 2013 年版。

See: Teng Yuntao and Tian Guoan: *Changli Field Yangko*, China Theatre Press, 2012; Yang Lixin and Guo Xiufen: *Luanzhou Field Yangko*, Hong Kong Xinrui Press, 2013.

满族寸子秧歌（摄影：王进勤）
Manchu *Cunzi* Yangko (Photographed by Wang Jinqin)

  冀东秧歌分地秧歌、高跷两种。地秧歌，流行于唐山、秦皇岛一带。昌黎、乐亭、滦州的地秧歌，先后入选国家级非物质文化遗产代表性项目名录。高跷，流行于承德、青龙一带，有三尺和一尺之别。一尺的高跷，称寸子[1]。青龙满族寸子秧歌，入选河北省级非物质文化遗产名录。

  冀东秧歌的行当，分妞（年轻女性）、丑（滑稽角色，表演的核心）、㧅（年长女性）、公子（书生）四类。妞和丑以扇子、手绢为道具，文㧅以团扇和烟袋为道具，武㧅以棒槌为道具。着装和表演有鲜明的地域差异。

  冀东秧歌的演出分过街和打场两种。过街，就是秧歌队在街巷中边走边舞地行进表演，动作简洁统一，强调扇花和队形的变化；打场，根据表演人数分大、中、小场。冀东地秧歌以规范严谨、只舞不歌的小场见长，昌黎地秧歌尤其讲究场面的调度、构图和造型。

  秧歌的伴奏一般由两支唢呐吹奏，伴以堂鼓、小镲。小镲掌握秧歌的节奏，堂鼓即兴加花击奏。乐停舞止，立即换大鼓、大镲敲打，

---

  [1] 古代满族妇女穿高底旗鞋，称"寸子鞋"。秧歌演员脚绑一尺的高跷代替旗鞋进行表演，故名"寸子"秧歌。

滦州地秧歌（摄影：钱兆福）
Luanzhou field Yangko (Photographed by Qian Zhaofu)

以烘托两个节目间的气氛。

"出子"[1]表演，是冀东地秧歌的重头戏，艺人通过亮绝活把演出推向高潮。昌黎地秧歌，以故事情节的完整和表演的幽默风趣取胜。清道光年间昌黎艺人王作云首创"秧歌演戏"，揭开秧歌戏剧化的序幕。1953年，周国宝、周国珍、张谦演出的《跑驴》被评为首届全国民间音乐、舞蹈汇演优秀节目并拍成电影，昌黎地秧歌一举成名。此外还有《捶布舞》《大秧歌》《卖花扇》《扑蝴蝶》《小放牛》《锔缸》《孟姜女》等著名"出子"。著名的"出子"艺人还有聂国和、宋荫村、田大迷糊、秦焕等。

冀东地秧歌流派众多，精彩纷呈，以滦州地秧歌和昌黎地秧歌为最。

滦州地秧歌，南派以唱舞结合闻名，妞和公子的演技高超；北派重在扭，以丑、扙的绝活见长。1956年，秧歌艺术家伦宝善和弟子高

---

[1] 指用哑剧形式表演的小折子戏或民间故事，舞者三至五人。

凤兰参加全国文艺汇演并获一等奖,受到毛主席、周总理接见。20世纪80年代,刘建平多次参加国家级民俗文化演出并获奖,演出的音像作品在全国发行。

昌黎地秧歌,以丑取胜,注重行当技巧展示,以细腻、风趣的戏剧化表演见长。1993年,获沈阳国际秧歌节金玫瑰奖。1996年,获全国广场舞蹈比赛铜奖。1996年,昌黎县被文化部命名为"中国民间艺术之乡(地秧歌)"。

(作者:秦学武)

As a traditional folk dance in northern China, Yangko combines dance, singing, opera, acrobatics and martial arts. The Yangko dance, aka Yangko spree or Yangko run, is a Spring Festival custom wildly popular in the rural areas of Jidong.

Yangko, known as "Farmland Music" in the Song Dynasty, was a group dance performed to the drumbeat when transplanting rice seedlings. It later evolved into a form of ground dance with makeup. Today, the Yangko dance has transformed from a folk custom to a form of square dance for the fitness and entertainment of people.

Jidong Yangko can be divided into field Yangko and stilt Yangko. The field Yangko was popular in Tangshan and Qinhuangdao. Changli, Laoting and Luanzhou's field Yangko was included in the List of Representative Items of National Intangible Cultural Heritage successively. The stilt Yangko, which falls into 3-*chi* and 1-*chi* categories, is popular in Chengde and Qinglong. The 1-*chi*-long stilt is called *Cunzi*[1]. Qinglong Manchu *Cunzi* Yangko was designated as an intangible cultural heritage of Hebei Province.

Jidong Yangko has four main roles: Niu (young woman), Chou (comic role, who is at the heart of performance), Kuai (old woman) and Gongzi

---

1 *Cunzi* shoes refer to the high bottom "banner shoes" of ancient Manchu women. Yangko dancers perform with stilts tied to their feet instead of wearing *Cunzi* shoes. The performance is named *Cunzi* Yangko.

昌黎地秧歌（摄影：左恭田）
Changli field Yangko (Photographed by Zuo Gongtian)

(scholar). Niu and Chou use fans and handkerchiefs as props, civil Kuai use round fans and tobacco pipes as props, and martial Kuai use mallets as props. The regional distinctions in dressing and performance are considerable.

There are two types of Jidong Yangko performance: street dance and circle dance. The street dance features the Yangko team walking and dancing in the streets with simple and orderly movements. The emphasis is on the changes in fans and formations. The circle dance is divided into large, medium and small ones based on the number of performers. Jidong field Yangko features dancers in small circles and neat formations without singing. Changli field Yangko is performed with an attention to scene scheduling, composition and posing.

Two suona are generally played to the rhythm of a Yangko dance, with *tanggu* drums and small cymbals as accompaniment. The small cymbals hold the rhythm of the dance, while the drums improvise drumbeats. When the music stops, the dance pauses as well, and then bass drums and large cymbals are played at once to fill the gap between the two programs.

Chuzi[1] performance is the highlight of Jidong field Yangko. The performance is boosted by the unique skills of the artists. Changli field Yangko is known for the complete scenarios and the witty and humorous performance. During the reign of Daoguang in the Qing Dynasty, Wang Zuoyun, a Changli artist, pioneered the "Yangko drama", which marked the beginning of the dramatization of Yangko. In 1953, *Running Donkey*, starring Zhou Guobao, Zhou Guozhen and Zhang Qian, was named Excellent Program of the First National Folk Music and Dance Show and made into a film. Changli field Yangko has become famous since then. There are also famous *Chuzi* plays such as *Hammering Cloth Dance*, *Large Yangko*, *Selling Flower Fans*, *Capturing Butterflies*, *The Boy Grazing the Cattle*, *Fixing the Water Vat* and *Meng Jiangnü*. Famous *Chuzi* artists include Nie Guohe, Song Yincun, Tian Damihu and Qin Huan.

There are numerous Jidong field Yangko sects, of which the Luanzhou sect and the Changli sect are most dazzling.

---

1 *Chuzi* refers to the opera highlights or folk stories in pantomime form with 3–5 performers.

昌黎地秧歌（摄影：赵秋洪）
Changli field Yangko (Photographed by Zhao Qiuhong)

昌黎地秧歌（摄影：左恭田）
Changli field Yangko (Photographed by Zuo Gongtian)

青龙地秧歌（摄影：王进勤）
Qinglong field Yangko (Photographed by Wang Jinqin)

高跷秧歌（供图：青龙县文化馆）
Stilt Yangko (Provided by Qinglong County Cultural Center)

Luanzhou field Yangko falls into two major groups—the southern group and the northern group. The southern group enjoys the reputation of combining singing with dancing, known for the brilliant performance of Niu and Gongzi. The northern group, emphasizing on swaying, features the acrobatic feats of Chou and Kuai. In 1956, Yangko artist Lun Baoshan and his disciple Gao Fenglan won the first prize in the National Art Show, and they were received by Chairman Mao Zedong and Premier Zhou Enlai. In the 1980s, Liu Jianping won a number of awards in many national folk culture performances. The audiovisual works of the performance were distributed nationwide.

Changli field Yangko, characterized by the performance of Chou, highlights the consummate skills of different characters and imparts a sense of subtlety and fun. In 1993, it won the Golden Rose Award of Shenyang International Yangko Festival. In 1996, it won the bronze medal of National Square Dance Competition. The same year, Changli County was named "Hometown of Chinese Folk Art (Field Yangko)" by the Ministry of Culture of the People's Republic of China

(By: Qin Xuewu)

4. 满族二贵摔跤 Manchu Ergui Wrestling[1]

满族二贵摔跤[2]是流传于河北省隆化县的一种传统民间道具舞蹈。它由传统体育项目"乔相扑"演化而来，形成于清道光末年（1850）前后，兴盛于清末至民国，至今170余年。2008年，入选国家级非物质文化遗产代表性项目名录。

---

1 参阅：https://www.ihchina.cn/project_details/13846/
See: https://www.ihchina.cn/project_details/13846/
2 摔跤是中国传统技艺，百戏中称"角抵"，南北朝谓"蚩尤戏"，唐宋时叫"相扑"，清代改称"摔跤"。

满族二贵摔跤（供图：隆化县文化馆）
Manchu Ergui wrestling (Provided by Longhua County Cultural Center)

  满族二贵摔跤为单人表演。表演者身背一个装扮成两人的木架，做摔跤架势。表演时需着不同颜色的服装，在道具围子的遮掩下，双腿全蹲，双臂拄地，形成两个矮人摔跤的夸张姿态，做出抢、转、滚、翻、摔、扫、踢、挡、下绊、托举等摔跤动作，在锣鼓点的伴奏下，生动展示两个满族武士摔跤的场面。全套动作一气呵成，是民间花会的"压街"节目。

  近年来，满族二贵摔跤已发展成 6—8 人的集体表演，并逐渐发展成地域文化品牌。

  20 世纪 80 年代以来，隆化县满族二贵摔跤五次代表河北省参加全国少数民族传统体育运动会表演项目并获金牌，先后在第一届国际民间艺术节、第三届全国少数民族艺术节、第三届全国农运会等国家级比赛中获奖。《二贵摔跤》纪录片曾在央视国际频道播出。

（作者：王海军，秦学武）

  Manchu Ergui wrestling[1] is a traditional folk prop dance popular in

---

  1 Wrestling is a traditional Chinese acrobatic feat. It was called "*jiaodi*" in ancient acrobatics, "Chiyou game" in the Northern and Southern dynasties, "sumo" in the Tang Dynasty, and "wrestling" in the Qing Dynasty.

Longhua County, Hebei Province. It evolved from "solo *xiangpu* (sumo)", a traditional sports activity. The 170-year-old tradition arose around the last year of Emperor Daoguang of the Qing Dynasty (1850) and prevailed in the late Qing Dynasty and early Republic of China. In 2008, Manchu Ergui wrestling was included in the List of Representative Items of National Intangible Cultural Heritage.

Manchu Ergui wrestling had been performed by one person. The performer bore a wooden frame on his back to impersonate two people wrestling. When performing on stage, the acrobat needed costumes of different colors. Under the cloak of prop curtain, he crouched down and kept his upper body straight with both arms to imitate the exaggerated postures of two wrestling dwarves. He danced to the accompaniment of gongs and drums, with wrestling movements such as swinging, turning, rolling, turning over, falling, sweeping, kicking, blocking, tripping and lifting. The scene of two Manchu warriors wrestling was thus vividly presented. During folk flower fairs, Manchu Ergui wrestling was usually a major event with its fluid movements.

In recent years, Manchu Ergui wrestling has developed from a one-person show into a collective show of 6–8 persons. Moreover, it has evolved into a representative of local culture.

Since the 1980s, the Manchu Ergui Wrestling Team of Longhua County had represented Hebei Province five times at the National Traditional Games of Ethnic Minorities and taken home gold medals. They had also won awards in other national competitions, such as the First International Folk Art Festival, the Third National Art Festival of Ethnic Minorities and the Third National Peasants' Games. The documentary *Ergui Wrestling* was shown on CCTV-4.

(By: Wang Haijun and Qin Xuewu)

5. 青龙猴打棒 Qinglong Monkey Dance[1]

猴打棒是一种满族民间舞蹈，俗称"猴打梆子"。流传于青龙满族自治县青龙镇、肖营子镇、七道河乡、三拨子乡、凉水河乡、八道河镇、娄杖子镇等地，有350余年历史。2006年，入选河北省级非物质文化遗产名录。

猴打棒源于满族传统舞蹈玛虎戏[2]。清康熙九年(1670)，满族正蓝旗马氏和陈氏的先祖来三拨子一带定居。先祖为保平安，夜晚在宅院击打两根短木棒以震虎狼；节庆日子，到各家房屋内外敲打以驱妖避邪。后来，马氏族人马长春将其融入花会表演。20世纪90年代初，青龙县文化馆进一步加工整理，将其定名"猴打棒"。

猴打棒有舞台演出、秧歌走街打场和广场演出等表演形式，一般由四人、八人或十二人组成，大型群体演出时达上百人。表演者头戴猴脸面具，身着黄衣黄裤，手持两根长约45厘米的短木棒，以各种舞姿和造型塑造出群猴嬉戏的艺术形象。

猴打棒以唢呐和打击乐器伴奏，表演者双手握棒，随着音乐节奏相互击打，铿锵有力，节奏明快。棒的基本打法有一击头、二击头、三击头、四击头等，花样打法有转花棒、挑花棒、云手花棒、轮棒、削棒、连环棒等。舞蹈步法主要有蹲步、虚步、蹲跳步、转跳步、跑跳步、弹跳步、跨转步等。唢呐多用《吵鸭子》《句句双》《满堂红》《柳青娘》等欢快曲调，配合木棒击打声及演员呼喊声[3]，热情奔放，韵味十足。

（作者：秦学武，王海军）

The monkey dance, colloquially known as "monkey clapper", is a

---

1 感谢青龙满族自治县文化馆提供相关资料。
We are thankful to Qinglong Manchu Autonomous County Cultural Center for providing the information.

2 满族人称"鬼脸""面具"为"玛虎"，称戴面具的舞蹈为"玛虎戏"。玛虎戏在清代宫廷和民间广为流传。

3 呼喊声多为满语"呼突依巴嘎干"（即鬼离开）、"那伊那叩"（表欢呼之意）等。

驱邪（供图：青龙县文化馆）
Dispel evil spirits (Provided by Qinglong County Cultural Center)

Manchu folk dance. The 350-year-old art form is popular in Qinglong Town, Xiaoyingzi Town, Qidaohe Township, Sanpozi Township, Liangshuihe Township, Badaohe Town, Louzhangzi Town, etc. of Qinglong Manchu Autonomous County. In 2006, it was designated as an intangible cultural heritage of Hebei Province.

The monkey dance originated from Mahu play, a traditional Manchu dance[1]. In the 9th year during the reign of Kangxi of the Qing Dynasty (1670), the ancestors of Ma Clan and Chen Clan of Manchu Plain Blue Banner settled in Sanpozi Township. To frighten the tigers and wolves away at night, they would make two short sticks clatter. On festivals, people would strike the sticks inside and outside houses to drive away ghosts and evil things. Afterwards, Ma Changchun, a member of Ma Clan, blended Mahu play into the flower fair. In early 1990s, Qinglong County Cultural Center reorganized and refined the art and named it "monkey dance".

---

1 The Manchus called the mask "Mahu", and the masked dance "Mahu play". This art form was popular both in the imperial court and among ordinary people of the Qing Dynasty.

百猴闹春（供图：青龙县文化馆）
100 monkeys welcoming the spring (Provided by Qinglong County Cultural Center)

The monkey dance can be performed on stage, with Yangko or in a square. A show usually musters 4, 8 or 12 people. For large group performance, there could be 100 people. The performers in monkey masks and yellow costumes hold two short wooden sticks about 45 centimeters long. With various dance movements and looks, they mimic the monkeys in play.

A monkey dance performance is accompanied by suona and percussion instruments. Performers hold the sticks in both hands and hit them to the rhythm of the music with vigor and in fast pace. The basic ways to manipulate the sticks include single punch, double punches, triple punches and quadruple punches, and the fancy ways include twisting, lifting up, waving hands like clouds, rotating, cutting and interlinking. The dance movements include crouching, empty step, squatting jump, turning jump, running jump, bouncing and straddling turn. Suona performance features cheerful songs, such as "Noisy Ducks", "Repeated Sentences", "Triumph on All Fronts" and "Lady Liu Qing". The beating of wooden sticks and the shouting of actors[1] are forceful with unrestrained passion and charm.

(By: Qin Xuewu and Wang Haijun)

---

[1] The performers utter the shouts mostly in Manchu language, such as "hutu ibagagan" (dispel evil spirits) and "nayi nakou" (cheer).

三、传统戏曲 III. Traditional Opera

6. 滦州皮影戏 Luanzhou Shadow Play[1]

皮影戏，是用灯光把影人[2]照射到影窗上来表演故事的传统戏剧形式。表演时，影匠[3]在白色幕布后面，一边操纵影人，一边用当地优美的唱腔演唱，并配以打击乐器和弦乐。影人多用驴皮制成，故称"驴皮影"。

皮影戏，肇始于汉代[4]，兴于唐宋，金代"南戏北渐"，普及于元明，清末民初达到鼎盛。13世纪起，中国皮影相继传入东南亚、西亚和土耳其。1767年，法国传教士把皮影带回国并在巴黎、马赛演出，被称为"中国灯影"，后改造为"法兰西灯影"。2011年，中国皮影戏入选联合国教科文组织人类非物质文化遗产代表作名录。

滦州皮影是中国三大影系之一，有400余年历史，又称乐亭皮影、唐山皮影、冀东皮影。流行于唐山、秦皇岛，辐射北京、天津、辽宁、吉林、内蒙古南部。

滦州皮影，以老呔腔[5]为特色，在明代定形并产生广泛影响力，滦州艺人黄素志有奠基之功。清代咸丰年间，郭老天开创了滦州皮影独有的"掐嗓"唱法。同属滦州影系的唐山、昌黎、乐亭、凌源的皮影戏，先后入选国家级非物质文化遗产代表性项目名录。

皮影戏，是集剧本、绘画、雕刻、音乐、歌唱、演奏、表演和布

---

1 参阅：张贵义、钱兆福：《滦州皮影》，大众文艺出版社2010年版；滕运涛、燕小锟主编：《昌黎皮影戏》，中国戏剧出版社2014年版；刘向权主编：《滦河文化研究文集》（第四卷），团结出版社2017年版。
See: Zhang Guiyi and Qian Zhaofu: *Luanzhou Shadow Play*, Mass Fine Art Publishing House, 2010; Teng Yuntao and Yan Xiaokun (ed.): *Changli Shadow Play*, China Theatre Press, 2014; Liu Xiangquan (ed.): *Collected Works on Luan River Culture* (Vol. 4), Unity Press, 2017.

2 皮影雕刻艺人用驴、牛等兽皮制成的人物剪影，俗称"影人"。

3 唱戏和操纵影人的艺人，俗称"影匠"。

4 有学者认为，皮影起源于春秋。本文取汉代说。

5 学界称昌黎方言，覆盖唐山市滦州、乐亭、滦南、曹妃甸区、路南区、路北区、开平区、古冶区、丰润区东部，以及秦皇岛市昌黎、卢龙南部。

皮影头茬（摄影：杨金波）
Shadow figure heads (Photographed by Yang Jinbo)

景于一体的综合艺术。

皮影剧本,俗称影卷,分单出和正卷。单出是情节简单的折子戏;正卷是连台剧本,情节复杂。一个皮影剧团,一般有十几部到几十部影卷。

冀东皮影的造型,包括行当脸谱、冠戴发髻、影人戳子和切末(道具、布景)造型四种。皮影的刻制,大体经过选料、雕刻、上色、涂漆、缝缀、装杆等工序。有杨德生、张老壁、聂春潮、王遇鸿、刘佳文、肖福成、居尚、田世民等雕刻名家。

滦州皮影戏班[1]一般为七至八人组成,演出有拿、打、拉、唱等分工,其中操纵二人,司鼓一人,还有琴师和唱戏的影匠,故有"七忙八闲"之说。男唱"小旦"须"掐嗓"。这些行规沿用至今。

皮影演出分堂会影戏、中台影戏、野台影戏。在影视不发达年代,皮影戏广受欢迎。谜语"远看灯火照,近看像个庙,里头人马喊,外边哈哈笑",生动再现了皮影演出的场景。

操纵分"上线"和"下线"。"上线"为主,是皮影演出总指挥;"下线"为辅,配合上线操纵,兼唱,同时为演唱者翻影卷。冀东皮影的操纵名家众多,张老壁、赵善元、赵紫阳、李云亭等被誉为"箭杆王"[2]。1980年代,"当代箭杆王"齐永衡到法、美、荷、日、德等国表演,《欧洲时报》称赞其操纵是"魔术般、闪电式的艺术"。张向东被称为"小箭杆王"。

滦州影的伴奏,文场以四胡为主,配以扬琴、二胡、笛子、大阮等;武场以鼓为主,还有板、镲、锣等。板式分大板、二板、三性板。伴奏为两人,一位司鼓,打鼓、板、锣、镲,兼演唱;一位琴师,拉四胡兼打堂鼓。其他乐器由伴声演员兼奏。

滦州影的唱腔属板腔体。调式分宫调式、商调式两类,俗称小嗓唱腔、大嗓唱腔。常用声腔有平调、花调、凄凉调、悲调、阴调、还

---

[1] 旧时俗称皮影戏班,抗日战争时期新建很多皮影社,新中国成立后改称皮影剧团。

[2] 影人操纵杆是用细高粱杆(俗称"箭杆")做成。民间对皮影操纵高手尊称"箭杆王"。

阳调。分生、小、髯、大、丑五个演出行当。唱腔是皮影的灵魂，是塑造人物的手段，也是区分皮影流派和衡量影匠唱功的标志。

近百年来，冀东皮影经历了清末民初、新中国初期两个繁荣期。既有誉满京东的杨寡妇班、聚德堂班、翠荫堂班、庆和堂班、乾利堂班、马家班等传统影班，也有声名远播的新长城影社、唐山皮影剧团等新式剧团。涌现了王华、冯凌生、张绳武、李紫兰、孙兆祥、张茂兰、韩增、苗幼芝、李秀、齐怀、周文友、汤子波、高荣杰、陈奎章、郑六、丁振耀、韩琢、曹辅全、孙品卿、刘景春等著名皮影艺术家。

中国皮影，是电影艺术的先导，对评剧的形成与发展有一定影响。1960年，唐山艺人在唐山皮影基础上创造出新剧种"唐剧"。

百灵剧团在2007年6月、2009年9月先后协助拍摄了电影《见龙卸甲》（刘德华主演）、《功夫梦》（成龙、贾登·史密斯主演）中的皮影片段。

（作者：秦学武）

Shadow play is a traditional dramatic art form of enacting stories by projecting the images of shadow figures[1] upon the screen. When performing, the shadow man[2] manipulates the figure from the back of a white curtain. He sings in fine local accent with the rhythmic accompaniment of percussion and string instruments. Shadow figures are usually made of donkey hide, so the art form is also called "donkey shadow play".

Shadow play started in the Han Dynasty[3] and flourished in the Tang and Song dynasties. In the Jin Dynasty, the art form spread from the south to the

---

1　Figure silhouettes made of donkey and cow hides by shadow play carvers, colloquially known as "shadow figure".

2　The singer and manipulator of shadow figures is known colloquially as "shadow man".

3　Some scholars believe that shadow play dates back to the Spring and Autumn Period. The Han Dynasty theory is adopted in this article.

昌黎皮影（摄影：左恭田、刘文军、乔景鹏）
Changli shadow play (Photographed by Zuo Gongtian, Liu Wenjun, Qiao Jingpeng)

Luanzhou shadow play (Photographed by Qian Zhaofu)

north. It became fashionable in the Yuan and Ming dynasties and reached the zenith in the late Qing Dynasty and early Republic of China. Since the 13th century, Chinese shadow play began to enter Southeast Asia, West Asia and Turkey. In 1767, French missionaries brought shadow play home and gave performances in Paris and Marseille. The art, originally called ombres chinoises (French for "Chinese shadows"), was later reinvented into ombres françaises (French shadows). In 2011, Chinese shadow play was included by UNESCO in the Representative List of the Intangible Cultural Heritage of Humanity.

The 400-year-old Luanzhou shadow play is among the three biggest shadow play schools of China. It is also called Laoting shadow play, Tangshan shadow play or Jidong shadow play. The art form prevails in Tangshan and Qinhuangdao, with influences over Beijing, Tianjin, Liaoning, Jilin and southern Inner Mongolia.

Luanzhou shadow play, featuring the Laotai accent[1], took form in the Ming Dynasty with wide influence. Huang Suzhi, a Luanzhou artist, was a founding figure of the art form. During the reign of Xianfeng in the

---

1 Called "Changli dialect" in academic circles, it is spoken in Tangshan (including Luanzhou County, Laoting County, Luannan County, Caofeidian District, Lunan District, Lubei District, Kaiping District, Guye District and the east of Fengrun District) and Qinhuangdao (including Changli County and the south of Lulong County).

Qing Dynasty, Guo Laotian created "*qia sang*", a unique throat-pinching singing method. The Tangshan, Changli, Laoting and Lingyuan schools, all falling under Luanzhou shadow play, have been included in the List of Representative Items of National Intangible Cultural Heritage.

Shadow play is a comprehensive art form combining scripts, painting, carving, music, singing, instrument playing, performance and set decoration.

The shadow play script, colloquially known as shadow scroll, is divided into two types: single scroll and multiple scrolls. The former features a simple opera highlight, and the latter features a complete and complex plot. A shadow play troupe usually has a dozen or dozens of scrolls.

A complete stage of Jidong shadow play includes four parts: facial makeups, headwear and hair, shadow figure bodies, and props and scenery. The making of a shadow figure has six procedures: material selection, carving, coloring, painting, stitching and rod installing. Yang Desheng, Zhang Laobi, Nie Chunchao, Wang Yuhong, Liu Jiawen, Xiao Fucheng, Ju Shang and Tian Shimin are among the famous carving masters.

A Luanzhou shadow play group[1] usually consists of 7–8 people, including two manipulators, one drummer, string players and singing shadow men. As they say, "The work is busy when there're only seven people, but relatively easy for eight." When a man imitates a woman to play *xiaodan*, he should pinch his throat when singing. The customs are still followed today.

A shadow play show can be performed in the courtyard, the theater or teahouse and the rural square. At the time when films had not yet reached out to common people, shadow play shows were very popular. There is a riddle that goes: "From a distance, a light illuminates the screen. Up close,

---

1 In the old days it was called a shadow play group. During the War of Resistance against Japanese Aggression, many shadow play groups were established. After the founding of the People's Republic of China, they were renamed as shadow play troupes.

皮影制作（摄影：王进勤）
Making of shadow figures (Photographed by Wang Jinqin)

it is like a temple. Inside, the horse whinnies. Outside, everyone laughs." A shadow play show may flash before our eyes with remarkable clarity when we read the riddle.

The figures are manipulated by the "upper thread" and the "lower thread". The former, as the chief conductor of a shadow play show, is assisted by the latter, who doubles as the coordinator, accompanier and scroll turner. Jidong has a galaxy of shadow play manipulators, such as Zhang Laobi, Zhao Shanyuan, Zhao Ziyang and Li Yunting who are honored as the "Kings of Arrow Rod"[1]. In the 1980s, Qi Yongheng, the "Contemporary King of Arrow Rod", performed on stage in France, the United States, the Netherlands, Japan and Germany. *Nouvelles D'Europe* had praised him, calling his performance "magical and lightning art". Zhang Xiangdong, another performer, is dubbed "Little King of Arrow Rod".

The accompaniment of Luanzhou shadow play is divided into civil and military types. The former, with *sihu* as the principal instrument, is accompanied by dulcimer, *erhu*, flute and large *ruan*. The latter, with drum as the principal instrument, is accompanied by clapper, cymbals and gong. There are three metre types for music: first metre, second metre and third

---

[1] Shadow figure manipulating rods are made of thin sorghum stalks (colloquially called "arrow rods"). The shadow play masters are honored as the "Kings of Arrow Rod" by the folks.

metre. The accompanists include a drummer, who douples as the singer while responsible for playing the drum, clapper, gong and cymbals, and a string player, who is responsible for playing the *sihu* and *tanggu* drum. Other instruments are played by the backing vocalist.

A Luanzhou shadow play singer sings in the *banqiang* style. The musical modes fall into *gong* and *shang*, colloquially called low musical mode and high musical mode. The widely used voice modes are male voice, female voice, mournful voice, sad voice, dreary voice and grave voice. The roles include *sheng* (youth males), *xiao* (females), *ran* (elderly males), *da* (the big-eyed or big-bearded) and *chou* (clowns). The singing part is the life and soul of a shadow play show, the means by which characters are portrayed, the distinction between different shadow play schools, and the yardstick to measure the singing skill of a shadow man.

Over the past century, Jidong shadow play had boomed in the late Qing Dynasty and early Republic of China, and the early days of the People's Republic of China. Troupes such as Widow Yang, Judetang, Cuiyintang, Qinghetang, Qianlitang and Majiaban were known throughout the Capital and areas to its east. Besides, there are far-famed modern troupes, such as New Great Wall Shadow Play Society and Tangshan Shadow Play Troupe. Numerous famous shadow play artists sprang up, such as Wang Hua, Feng

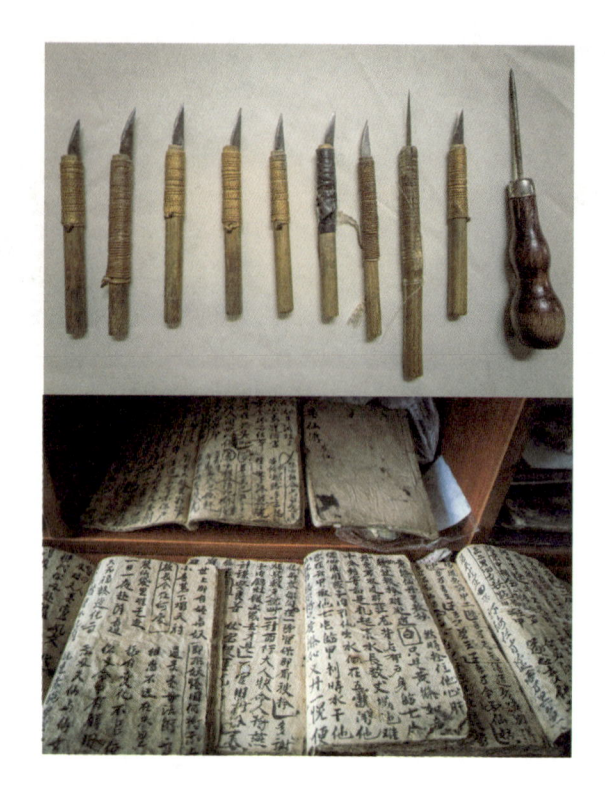

刻刀和影卷（摄影：王进勤）
Carving knives and shadow scrolls (Photographed by Wang Jinqin)

Lingsheng, Zhang Shengwu, Li Zilan, Sun Zhaoxiang, Zhang Maolan, Han Zeng, Miao Youzhi, Li Xiu, Qi Huai, Zhou Wenyou, Tang Zibo, Gao Rongjie, Chen Kuizhang, Zheng Liu, Ding Zhenyao, Han Zhuo, Cao Fuquan, Sun Pinqing and Liu Jingchun.

Chinese shadow play is the prelude to cinematography and has to some extent affected the evolution of Pingju opera. In 1960, Tangshan artists developed "Tang opera" on the basis of Tangshan shadow play.

In June 2007 and September 2009, Bailing Troupe provided assistance to the filming of shadow play scenes in *Three Kingdoms: Resurrection of the Dragon* (starring Andy Lau) and *The Karate Kid* (starring Jackie Chan and Jaden Smith).

(By: Qin Xuewu)

7. 评剧 Pingju Opera

评剧俗称"评戏",是我国北方地区群众喜闻乐见的地方戏,流行于华北、东北等地,是仅次于京剧的中国第二大剧种。2006年,入选国家级非物质文化遗产代表性项目名录。

莲花落,是清末滦县一带乞讨艺人创造的说唱艺术,俗称"落子"。评剧以莲花落为基础,汲取京剧、河北梆子、滦州皮影、乐亭大鼓的艺术成就逐步发展而成,经历了对口落子、拆出落子、平腔梆子戏、奉天落子、评剧等阶段。成兆才[1]是评剧事业最重要的奠基人。

1907年,成兆才等十余位艺人对莲花落进行改革。1908年,定名为"平腔梆子戏"。因其用真声,高弦低唱,故名"平戏"。评剧作为一个剧种基本形成。

1908年至1909年,成兆才率庆春班在冀东成功巡演,被称为"唐山落子"。

1913年底,在河北梆子、京剧艺人的帮助下,成兆才等四位艺人在剧本、人物行当、舞台表演、音乐伴奏、板式等方面对平腔梆子戏进行全面、系统的改革。

1919年,成兆才率戏社到营口、长春、哈尔滨等地热演,被称为"奉天落子"。1920年,张作霖特邀京剧名家梅兰芳、程砚秋和落子名家月明珠在奉天(今沈阳)同台演出。

1936年,"评剧皇后"白玉霜在沪拍摄影片《海棠红》,《大公报》新闻首用"评剧"[2]之名,评剧从此闻名全国。"时代艺人"喜彩莲在沪演出,受到著名戏剧家阿英、洪深、欧阳予倩的称赞。1930年代,评

---

[1] 成兆才(1874—1929),艺名东来顺,滦县绳各庄人(今属滦南县)。他是近百年来我国北方地方戏曲发展史上,贡献卓著的一位民间表演艺术家与剧作家,创作、改编、整理的剧本有102种,被誉为"东方的莎士比亚"。

[2] 评剧得名说法不一:一说,由著名女演员李金顺所起;一说,为调停平戏与京剧(平剧)的冲突,由李大钊所起;一说,1923年名宿吕海寰建议平腔梆子戏改称"评剧",获警世剧社采用。评剧,有"评古论今"之意。

《凤还巢》（罗慧琴饰演程雪娥）（供图：罗慧琴）
Phoenix Returning to Nest (starring Luo Huiqin as Cheng Xuee) (Provided by Luo Huiqin)

剧由地方小戏成为影响全国的大剧种。

经过1907年、1913年的两次改革，评剧逐渐形成生、旦、净、丑四个行当，每个行当又有更细的分支。

评剧表演，讲究"唱、做、念、打"四功和"手、眼、身、法、步"五法，以唱功见长。

评剧唱腔为板腔体，抒情性强，流畅自然，乡土味浓。有慢板、反调慢板、二六板、垛板、流水板、散板、尖板等常用板式。伴奏以板胡为主，打击乐器与京剧大体相同。

评剧唱腔流派众多，名家辈出。

月明珠等人开创了评剧女腔。以李金顺和刘翠霞为代表，使用真假声[1]两合水唱法；以白玉霜和爱莲君为代表，使用本声唱法；以新凤霞为代表，开创了评剧的"喜调"。小白玉霜，是20世纪50、60年代评剧界的旗帜。诞生了新凤霞、白玉霜、鲜灵霞、韩少云、花淑兰、筱俊亭等六大名旦，以及金开芳（男旦）、王金香、张凤楼（男旦）、碧莲花、刘翠霞、爱莲君、喜彩莲、陈桂秋、花连舫、花月仙、李忆兰、花玉兰、筱桂花等旦角流派。

倪俊生等人开创了男腔，还有魏荣元的花脸、老生唱腔，以及张

---

[1] 老艺人成国祯曾说"十句评剧九皮影"。评剧的真假声唱法和滦州皮影有着血缘关系。

德福、马泰、桂宝芬（女）、洪影（女）等小生流派。

评剧表演讲究师承。如旦角演出，中国评剧院、唐山评剧团和石家庄评剧团，以新派和白派为主；沈阳评剧院，以韩派、花派、筱派为主；天津评剧院，则以花派、鲜派为主。

评剧善于表观现实生活。成兆才的《杨三姐告状》，奠定了评剧以演现代戏为主的特长。小白玉霜、韩少云先后主演的《小女婿》，新凤霞主演的《刘巧儿》《小二黑结婚》《祥林嫂》，广受欢迎。电影《花为媒》风靡中国内地、中国香港和东南亚，新凤霞被评为亚洲最杰出艺人。新时期，又涌现出《山里人家》《贫嘴张大民的幸福生活》等优秀现代戏。

《成兆才》（张俊玲饰演成兆才）（供图：张俊玲）
Cheng Zhaocai (starring Zhang Junling as Cheng Zhaocai) (Provided by Zhang Junling)

中国戏剧奖·梅花表演奖是中国戏剧表演艺术最高奖。冯玉萍等22位评剧表演艺术家获此殊荣。2007年，唐山评剧团的新派传人罗慧琴、洪派小生张俊玲凭借《香妃与乾隆》一剧同获梅花奖。刘秀荣、洪影、张俊玲、罗慧琴为国家级非物质文化遗产代表性项目代表性传承人。

2000年，国家文化部艺术司、河北省文化厅和唐山市政府联合主办"中国评剧艺术节"，主办地设在评剧的发源地唐山市。

（作者：秦学武）

Pingju opera, colloquially called "Pingxi", is a local opera form well received by the audience of North China and Northeast China. In terms of popularity, it is second only to Peking opera in China. In 2006, Pingju opera was included in the List of Representative Items of National Intangible Cultural Heritage.

Lianhualao, colloquially called *"laozi"*, was an art form combining spoken dialogues with songs created by the begging artists in Luanxian County in the late Qing Dynasty. Evolved from *lianhualao*, Pingju opera also integrated the characteristics of Peking opera, Hebei clapper, Luanzhou shadow play and Laoting bass drum. Its evolution can be split into five periods: cross *laozi*, *chaichu laozi*, flat tone clapper, Fengtian *laozi* and Pingju opera. Cheng Zhaocai[1] is the chief founding figure of Pingju opera.

In 1907, Cheng Zhaocai and a dozen or so other artists pushed through a reform of *lianhualao*. In 1908, the art form was named "flat tone clapper". With natural voice, strained chords and soft tones, it was also called "flat opera". Pingju opera, as a drama type, basically took shape.

From 1908 to 1909, Cheng Zhaocai led the Qingchun Troupe on a successful tour in Jidong. Their performance was called "Tangshan *laozi*".

In the end of 1913, with the aid of Hebei clapper and Peking opera artists, Cheng Zhaocai and other three artists implemented comprehensive, systemic changes on flat tone clapper in terms of script, character, stage performance, musical accompaniment and metre type.

In 1919, Cheng Zhaocai led the troupe on a tour in Yingkou, Changchun and Harbin. Their performance was called "Fengtian *laozi*". In 1920, Zhang

---

1 Cheng Zhaocai (1874–1929), his stage name Dong Laishun, is a native of Shengge Village, Luanxian County (administered by Luannan County today). He was a folk performing artist and playwright who had made outstanding contributions to the development of local operas in northern China in the last hundred years. Hailed as the "Oriental Shakespeare", he created, adapted and sorted out 102 scripts.

Zuolin invited Mei Lanfang and Cheng Yanqiu, Peking opera masters, to join Yue Mingzhu, a *laozi* master, on stage in Fengtian (today's Shenyang).

In 1936, Bai Yushuang, later known as the "Queen of Pingju Opera", made the film *Begonia Red* in Shanghai, and *Dagong Daily* was the first to use the name "Pingju opera"[1] in its report. Since then, Pingju opera became famous throughout China. When Xi Cailian, an artist reflective of the times, went on stage in Shanghai, she was praised by famous dramatists A Ying, Hong Shen and Ouyang Yuqian. In the 1930s, Pingju opera, which started as a local drama, became a major type of drama with nation-wide influence.

After two reforms, one in 1907 and the other in 1913, *sheng*, *dan*, *jing* and *chou*, the four roles of Pingju opera, had gradually taken form, with each role subdivided into smaller branches.

With an attention to singing, performing, narrating and acrobatic feats by employing the techniques of hands, eyes, body and legs, Pingju opera performance boasts the art of singing.

Pingju opera is sung in the *banqiang* style , which is lyrically expressive and fluent with rich local characteristics. The common metre types include lento type, reversed lento type, 2/6 type, stacking type, water type, loose type and tip type. The performance is accompanied mainly by *banhu*, while the percussion instruments used are broadly the same as those of Peking opera.

There are many schools of Pingju opera and innumerable well-known artists.

---

1 Opinion is divided over how Pingju got its name. One theory is that the name was given by Li Jinshun, a famous actress. The other theory is that the name was given by Li Dazhao to stop the fight between Pingxi and Peking opera (Ping opera). Still, there's one theory that Lü Haihuan, a man of some distinction, proposed that flat tone clapper should change its name to "pingju" in 1923. His proposal was taken by Jingshi Opera Troupe. Pingju bears the meaning of "commenting on the past and the present".

《乾坤带》（罗慧琴饰演银屏公主）（供图：罗慧琴）
Qiankun Belt (starring Luo Huiqin as Princess Yinping) (Provided by Luo Huiqin)

Yue Mingzhu and others pioneered the female voice of Pingju opera. Li Jinshun and Liu Cuixia created the singing style combining natural voice and falsetto[1]; Bai Yushuang and Ai Lianjun created the true voice style of singing; Xin Fengxia created the "joyous tune" for Pingju opera. Junior Bai Yushuang was a pacesetter in Pingju opera circles in the 1950s and 1960s. During this period, a lot of famous *dan* performers had appeared, such as the Big Six (Xin Fengxia, Bai Yushuang, Xian Lingxia, Han Shaoyun, Hua Shulan and Xiao Junting), Jin Kaifang (male *dan*), Wang Jinxiang, Zhang Fenglou (male *dan*), Bi Lianhua, Liu Cuixia, Ai Lianjun, Xi Cailian, Chen Guiqiu, Hua Lianfang, Hua Yuexian, Li Yilan, Hua Yulan and Xiao Guihua.

Ni Junsheng and others pioneered the male voice of Pingju opera. Wei

---

1 Cheng Guozhen, a veteran artist, said that "Nine out of ten lines of Pingju come from shadow play". The natural voice and falsetto of Pingju opera and Luanzhou shadow play are closely related.

Rongyuan created the singing styles of *hua lian* (male character in Chinese opera with a painted face) and *lao sheng* (old gentleman in Chinese opera). Zhang Defu, Ma Tai, Gui Baofen (female) and Hong Ying (female) were representatives of *xiao sheng* (young man's role).

Pingju opera puts great emphasis on the succession of teachings. In terms of the *dan* performance, the Xin and Bai schools were in the dominant position in

Fragrant Concubine and Emperor Qianlong (starring Zhang Junling as Qianlong) (Provided by Zhang Junling)

China Pingju Opera Theatre, Tangshan Pingju Opera Troupe and Shijiazhuang Pingju Opera Troupe; the Han, Hua and Xiao schools were in the dominant position in Shenyang Pingju Opera Troupe; and the Hua and Xian schools were in the dominant position in Tianjin Pingju Opera Troupe.

Pingju opera is good at expressing the reality of life. Cheng Zhaocai's *Third Sister Yang Goes to Court* was a daring attempt in the modernization of Pingju opera. *Little Son-in-law*, starring Junior Bai Yushuang, and *Liu Qiaoer*, *Xiao Erhei Getting Married* and *Mistress Xiang Lin*, starring Xin Fengxia, were wildly popular. The film *Flower is a Go-between* became a hit in Chinese mainland, China's Hong Kong and Southeast Asia. For her performance in the film, Xin Fengxia was named the Most Outstanding Asian Artist. In recent years, excellent modern dramas sprang out, such as

Mountain Household* and *The Happy Life of Talkative Zhang Damin*.

The Plum Performance Award is the highest award for Chinese drama performance art. Feng Yuping and other 21 Pingju opera artists have won the honor. Luo Huiqin and Zhang Junling, inheritor of the Xin school and *xiao sheng* of the Hong school in Tangshan Pingju Opera Troupe, won the Plum Performance Award in 2007 for their excellent performances in *Fragrant Concubine and Emperor Qianlong*. Liu Xiurong, Hong Ying, Zhang Junling and Luo Huiqin are representative inheritors of Representative Items of National Intangible Cultural Heritage.

In 2000, the Arts Department of the Ministry of Culture of the People's Republic of China, the Department of Culture of Hebei Province and the Tangshan Municipal People's Government cohosted the China Pingju Opera Art Festival. The event took place in Tangshan, the birthplace of Pingju opera.

(By: Qin Xuewu)

8. 乐亭大鼓 Laoting Drum Ballad

大鼓是曲艺的一种。由一人自击鼓、板演唱，另一人用三弦等乐器伴奏。唱词多为民间流传的历史故事，用韵文编成。因地区、方言和曲调的不同而名称各异，如京韵大鼓、乐亭大鼓、东北大鼓、山东大鼓等，总称为大鼓书，简称大鼓。

乐亭大鼓是我国北方较有代表性的曲艺鼓书暨鼓曲形式。它发端于乐亭、滦州农村，流行于冀东、京津、东北三省等地。清初，乐亭人爱唱"清平歌"，艺人弦子李用三弦配奏，遂形成"乐亭腔"。道光、咸丰年间，定名为"乐亭大鼓"。[1] 温荣是主要创始人。

---

[1] 民间有两种说法：一是，1845年滦南（原属滦州）艺人冯福昌弃用木板、改用铁板击节伴唱后，乐亭大鼓在民间火了起来，遂名"乐亭大鼓"；另一是，1850年乐亭温荣进京献艺，恭亲王赐名"乐亭大鼓"。

乐亭大鼓是在当地民歌基础上，吸收皮影戏、叫卖调的某些唱腔，形成了独特的唱腔、板式。乐亭县、滦南县的"乐亭大鼓"，先后入选国家级非物质文化遗产代表性项目名录。王立岩、贾幼然、何建春、张近平，入选国家级非物质文化遗产代表性项目代表性传承人。

乐亭大鼓为板腔体结构，唱腔婉转、板式灵活。有四大口、四平调、流水、学舌、凄凉调、昆曲尾子、二黄腔等30余种调式。这些调式是乐亭大鼓与其他戏曲的区别所在。它的唱腔形式，对北京琴书、唐剧、东北大鼓等有较大影响。

书鼓和三弦（摄影：刘江涛）
Shugu and *sanxian* (Photographed by Liu Jiangtao)

乐亭大鼓，有大板（即4/4拍，多用在鼓书开始或中段）、二性板（即2/4拍，多用在锁板与叙事）、三性板（即1/4拍，用在鼓书高潮或情绪激烈的唱段）、散板等基本板式，还有"上字调"与"凡字调"两种不同调性的往复、转换。

乐亭大鼓，以说唱并重著称。伴奏乐器有书鼓、铁板、大三弦等。一般由两人合作演出。演唱传统曲目时，男演员着长衫，女演员穿旗袍；演唱近现当代曲目时，男演员多穿中山装，女演员穿旗袍或穿连衣裙、拖地裙。

乐亭大鼓，现有曲（书）目三百多个。传统曲目分长、中、短篇，多是警醒世人、锄强扶弱的故事；现代曲目以短篇为主，多为近现代革命事件。代表曲目有《东汉》《隋唐》《三侠五义》《呼延庆打擂》《金陵府》《小上坟》《蓝桥会》《古城会》《长生殿》等。乐亭大鼓的唱词，韵散相间、句式简练，有灵动儒雅之气。

乐亭大鼓名家辈出，有温荣、陈际昌、齐祯、冯福昌、王恩鸿、王德有、戚用武、戚文峰、韩香圃、靳文然、张云霞、贾幼然、姚顺悦等。以韩香圃为代表的韩派（即东路唱腔）、靳文然为代表的靳派（即西路唱腔）和王佩臣为代表的京津派最为著名。20世纪40年代末，西路唱腔完成了从曲牌体到板腔体的改革，被业内奉为正宗。

2008年，张近平获中国曲艺牡丹奖。刘书宇，2010年获巴黎中国曲艺节"卢浮"银奖，2012年获牡丹奖"提名奖"。

2002年，乐亭县被河北省命名为"民间艺术之乡——曲艺大鼓之乡"。2003年，乐亭县被文化部命名为"中国民间艺术之乡（乐亭大鼓）"。

（作者：秦学武）

The drum ballad is a form of *quyi* (literally melodious art), with one person singing while beating the drum and the clapper, and the other person playing the *sanxian* in rhythmic accompaniment. The ballad texts are mostly folk tales written in verse telling historical events. The name of the art form varies based on the regions, dialects and tunes, such as Beijing dialect drum ballad, Laoting drum ballad, Northeast drum ballad and Shandong drum ballad. They are known collectively as drum ballad storytelling and drum ballad for short.

The Laoting drum ballad, featuring drum storytelling and drum music, is a representative form of *quyi* in northern China. Originated from the rural areas of Laoting and Luanzhou, the art form is popular in Jidong, Beijing, Tianjin and the Northeast provinces. At the beginning of the Qing Dynasty, the natives of Laoting loved "Qingping tunes". They sang the songs to the *sanxian* accompaniment of an artist nicknamed String Li, and the

"Laoting tone" was formed. During the reigns of Daoguang and Xianfeng, the art form was named "Laoting drum ballad"[1]. Wen Rong was its chief originator.

Based on local folk songs and incorporating the singing styles of shadow play and peddling tune, the Laoting drum ballad has developed its unique voice and metre types. Laoting and Luannan schools of the art have been included in the List of Representative Items of National Intangible Cultural Heritage, and Wang Liyan, Jia Youran, He Jianchun and Zhang Jinping are named representative inheritors.

Laoting drum ballads, sung in the *banqiang* style, feature a flexibility of voice and metre types. There are more than 30 modes, such as four big mouths, four flat tones, flowing water, repeating, mournful tone, Kunqu ending and *erhuang* voice. They are the distinctive differences between the Laoting drum ballad and other types of drama. The singing style of the art form has a significant impact on Beijing *qinshu* storytelling, Tang opera and Northeast drum ballad.

Laoting drum ballads have several metre types: first metre (4/4 beat, usually used at the beginning or in the middle part), second metre (2/4 beat, usually used at the end or in narration), third metre (1/4 beat, used in the climax or in the emotional parts) and loose metre. The art form also features the alternation and conversion between "*shang*-character tone" and "*fan*-character tone".

The Laoting drum ballad is noted for its combination of speaking and singing with the accompaniment of *shugu* (small drum), iron clapper

---

1 There're two popular theories. First, in 1845, Feng Fuchang, an artist of Luannan (originally administered by Luanzhou), changed the wooden clapper for beating time into an iron one. Afterwards, the art form became a local trend and was named "Laoting drum ballad". Second, in 1850, Wen Rong, a native of Laoting, went to the Capital to perform his art. Prince Gong named the art "Laoting drum ballad".

乐亭大鼓表演（摄影：刘江涛）
Laoting drum ballad performance (Photographed by Liu Jiangtao)

and large *sanxian*. Usually, there are two performers. When singing traditional songs, the male performers wear long shirts, and the female ones wear cheongsams. When singing modern and contemporary songs, the male performers often wear Zhongshan suits, and the female ones wear cheongsams, one-piece dresses or floor-length gowns.

The Laoting drum ballad has more than 300 texts (scripts). The traditional texts are divided into long, medium and short sizes. They are mostly messages of warning or stories of helping the weak and fighting crime. The modern texts are mostly short revolutionary stories. Representative ballad texts include *The Eastern Han Dynasty*, *The Sui and Tang Dynasties*, *The Three Heroes and Five Gallants*, *Hu Yanqing's Challenge*, *Jinling Mansion*, *Grave Visitors*, *Blue Bridge Meeting*, *Ancient City Meeting* and *Changsheng Hall*. The rhyming and plain lines of Laoting drum ballads are delicate, elegant and brief.

There's a galaxy of famous Laoting drum ballad artists, such as Wen Rong, Chen Jichang, Qi Zhen, Feng Fuchang, Wang Enhong, Wang Deyou, Qi Yongwu, Qi Wenfeng, Han Xiangpu, Jin Wenran, Zhang Yunxia, Jia Youran and Yao Shunyue. The Han school (eastern style) embodied by Han Xiangpu, the Jin school (western style) embodied by Jin Wenran and the Jing-Jin school embodied by Wang Peichen are the most distinguished of all. By the end of the 1940s, the western style had made a full transition from *qupai* type to *banqiang* type, and it has been honored as the authentic type in this circle since then.

In 2008, Zhang Jinping won a China Quyi Peony Award. In 2010, Liu Shuyu won the "Louvre" Silver Prize at the Festival de Quyi de Paris; in 2012, he won a Nominee Award at the China Quyi Peony Awards.

In 2002, the Hebei Provincial Government named Laoting County "Hometown of Folk Art—Drum Ballad". In 2003, the Ministry of Culture of the People's Republic of China named Laoting County "Hometown of Chinese Folk Art (Laoting Drum Ballad)".

(By: Qin Xuewu)

四、传统体育 IV. Traditional Sports

9. 珍珠球 Pearl Ball[1]

"珍珠球"是满族传统体育项目，源于满族渔猎生活中的采珍珠，又称"踢核[2]""采核""扔核"。2008年，入选国家级非物质文化遗产代表性项目名录。

努尔哈赤时期，珍珠球运动就已在白山黑水之间的满族青年中开展。清军入关后，传入京畿和丰宁、承德一带。1980年起，丰宁县进行挖掘整理并予以推广。[3]1983年，民族传统体育专家借鉴篮球和手球的比赛规则，编制了"采珍珠"游戏规则，并将其定名"珍珠球"。北京、辽宁、河北、吉林、黑龙江等省市的少数民族传统体育运动会，均将其列入正式比赛项目。1991年，珍珠球被列为全国少数民族传统体育运动会竞赛项目。

珍珠球比赛的场地长28米，宽15米。比赛双方各为七名队员，其中一名队员站在一端准备持网捕捞，对方两名手持蚌形木拍的队员站在其前面拦截珍珠，其他四名队员与对方队员争夺珍珠，夺到珍珠后将其投向己方持网人，而对方持蚌人则设法用蚌形木拍截获珍珠。珍珠投入己方网里才得分，多者为胜。

围场满族蒙古族自治县珍珠球队，曾在河北省少数民族传统体育

---

[1] 参阅：https://www.ihchina.cn/project_details/13845/
See: https://www.ihchina.cn/project_details/13845/

[2] 在满语里"核"是"尼楚赫"的简音，即"珍珠"之意。

[3] 李景瑞、铁男：《承德满族民俗探源》，《满族研究》1998年04期。

A pearl ball game (Photographed by Jing Qiao)

运动会 5 次夺冠。1995 年，该队代表河北省参加第五届全国少数民族传统体育运动会并获亚军。

（作者：王海军）

Originated from pearl picking of the Manchu people, "pearl ball", aka nicuhe[1], is a traditional athletic activity of the ethnic group. In 2008, it was included in the List of Representative Items of National Intangible Cultural Heritage.

During the reign of Nurhachi, pearl ball had been popular among the Manchu youths in Northeast China. When the Qing army crossed the Shanhai Pass, the activity entered Fengning, Chengde and the surroundings of Beijing. Since 1980, the Fengning County Government had organized the exploration and promotion of the custom.[2] In 1983, traditional ethnic sports experts, by adopting the rules of basketball and handball, wrote the rules of "pearl picking" and gave it the name "pearl ball". In the Traditional Sports Games of Ethnic Minorities in Beijing, Liaoning, Hebei, Jilin,

---

1　In Manchu language, "nichuhe" is pronounced as "he" for simplicity. It means "pearl".

2　Li Jingrui and Tie Nan: "On the Origin of Manchu Folk Customs in Chengde", *Manchu Study*, 1998, Issue 04.

Heilongjiang, etc., pearl ball was listed as an official competitive sport. In 1991, pearl ball was designated as a competitive sport at the National Traditional Games of Ethnic Minorities.

The venue of pearl ball measures 28 meters long and 15 meters wide. Each team consists of 7 members. One stands at the end preparing to scoop up the pearl ball with the net, while two opponents holding the clamshell-shaped wooden rackets stand straight in front to stop him. The other four people compete with the opposing players for the ball. When grabbing the ball, one casts it to the net holder of his/her side. The opponents try to capture the ball with their rackets. A ball cast into the net of one's own side makes a point, and the side with more points win the game.

The Pearl Ball Team of Weichang Manchu and Mongolian Autonomous County has won five times at the Hebei Traditional Sports Games of Ethnic Minorities. In 1995, the team represented Hebei Province at the 5th National Traditional Games of Ethnic Minorities and finished second.

(By: Wang Haijun)

10. 陀螺 Top[1]

陀螺是少数民族传统体育项目，俗称"打陀螺""赶老牛""打冰猴儿"等，在满族、瑶族、佤族、壮族、哈尼族、拉祜族、基诺族等民族中流传已久，集对抗性、技巧性、趣味性为一体。1995年，陀螺成为全国少数民族传统体育运动会竞赛项目。

陀螺在北宋时期就已出现，宋代的《武林旧事》、清代的《通俗编》有相关记载。

民间打陀螺通常在冬春季进行，用鞭子连续抽打陀螺，使其在冰

1　感谢青龙县满族自治县文化馆提供相关资料。
We are thankful to Qinglong Manchu Autonomous County Cultural Center for providing the information.

打陀螺（供图：青龙县文化馆）
Top whipping (Provided by Qinglong County Cultural Center)

面或平滑地面不停旋转，或相互碰撞，以旋转的时间长短定胜负。

陀螺比赛须在平整无障碍的场地进行。比赛双方须按守、攻顺序进行互换。比赛从守方放陀螺开始，随后攻方将自己的陀螺抛掷入场，或触击守方陀螺、将其击出场区，或与守方陀螺在场区内比赛旋转时间的长短。比赛只计攻方轮次得分，累计得分多者获胜。

1995年，青龙满族自治县组建陀螺队，连续六届代表秦皇岛市参加河北省少数民族传统体育运动会，获18块金牌；五次代表河北省参加全国少数民族传统体育运动会，均进入全国八强。2004年6月，青龙被命名为河北省少数民族传统体育项目陀螺训练基地。

（作者：王海军、秦学武）

Top, a traditional sport of ethnic minorities, is colloquially called "whipping top", "driving the old ox" and "whipping the ice monkey". The sport has been around for a long time in Manchu, Yao, Va, Zhuang, Hani, Lahu and Jino ethnic groups. It features competition, skills and entertainment. In 1995, top was designated as a competitive sport at the National Traditional Games of Ethnic Minorities.

Top had appeared in the Northern Song Dynasty. Accounts of it could be found in *Former Events in Wulin* of Song and *Social Customs* of Qing.

Top whipping is a folk activity typically taking place in spring and

A top (Provided by Qinglong County Cultural Center)

winter. A player slashes the top with a whip to keep it spinning on the ice or the smooth ground. Sometimes, two tops crash into each other. The top spinning for the longest time wins.

The field for top competitions should be level and barrier-free. The two sides shift their positions to take the offensive alternatively. At the outset of a match, the defender releases the top. Then, the offender flings another top onto the ground. The top of the offender tries to force the top of the defender out of the ground, or the two tops vie with each other to see which could last longer. The points are added to the offender only, and the side with more points wins.

In 1995, Qinglong Manchu Autonomous County set up a top team. It represented Qinhuangdao for six times in a row at the Hebei Traditional Games of Ethnic Minorities and won 18 gold medals. It represented Hebei Province for five times at the National Traditional Sports Games of Ethnic Minorities and got into the last eight every time. In June 2004, Qinglong was designated as a top training base for ethnic minorities in Hebei Province.

(By: Wang Haijun and Qin Xuewu)

五、传统美术 V. Traditional Arts

11. 丰宁满族剪纸 Fengning Manchu Paper-cutting[1]

剪纸，又称刻纸，是一种以剪子或刻刀镂空出图案，用于装点生活或配合其他民俗活动的民间艺术。其载体可以是纸张、金银箔、布、皮、革等片状材料。2009年，中国剪纸入选联合国教科文组织人类非物质文化遗产代表作名录。

剪纸在中国有上千年的历史，汉唐时期的民间妇女就有使用金银箔和彩帛剪成装饰图案贴上鬓角的风尚。剪纸流传地域广，具有鲜明的地域特征、民族差异和时代特色。

从表现内容上看，剪纸可分传统剪纸和现代剪纸。传统剪纸的题材多反映现实生活、吉庆寓意、戏剧人物、传说故事和宗教祭祀等，以花鸟虫鱼、亭台楼阁、各种兽类、吉祥图案等最常见，多为民间艺人根据经验或图谱剪刻；现代剪纸，与时代生活结合较紧，具有鲜明的主题，或是艺人创作的剪纸画，或是小作坊根据需求进行批量刻制。

从创作形式看，剪纸又分单色剪纸和刀刻染色剪纸。前者多用红纸，根据图案进行折叠，然后剪刻而成；后者多用粉帘纸成沓刻制，通常是春夏秋季做刻制活，冬季或用前进行配色、点染。比较而言，单色剪纸更讲究造型与剪子工夫；刀刻染色剪纸，不仅讲究造型，还要讲究刀刻技巧和染色技巧。

剪纸的制作需要各式剪子、刻刀，刻法也有不同：阳刻，以线为主，留下造型的线条，线线相通，其余部分刻（剪）去；阴刻，以块为主，把图形的线条刻（剪）去，把造型剪空，线线相断；阴阳刻，阳刻与阴刻的结合，使作品更具观赏性。

冀东地区的剪纸丰富多彩，如承德市的丰宁、宽城、承德，唐山

---

[1] 门泽琪：《河北丰宁满族自治县剪纸艺术传承与保护》，2012年中央民族大学硕士学位论文。
Men Zeqi: "Inheritance and Protection of Paper-cutting Art in Fengning Manchu Autonomous County", *Hebei*, Master's Thesis of Minzu University of China, 2012.

丰宁满族剪纸（供图：丰宁县文化馆）
Fengning Manchu paper cuttings (Provided by Fengning County Cultural Center)

昌黎剪纸（摄影：乔景鹏）
Changli paper cuttings (Photographed by Qiao Jingpeng)

市的玉田、滦州、滦南、古冶、路北，以及秦皇岛市的抚宁、昌黎、卢龙、青龙等县（市、区）的剪纸，其中丰宁满族剪纸最具知名度，在中国民间剪纸中占有一席之地。

丰宁满族剪纸始于清康熙年间，乾隆年间形成鲜明的地域特征与民族风格，清末民初进入鼎盛时期。它以阳刻为主，阴刻为辅，批毛纤长，剪工精细。1993年，丰宁被命名为"中国民间剪纸艺术之乡"。2006年，丰宁满族剪纸入选国家级非物质文化遗产代表性项目名录。

丰宁满族剪纸主要用于窗花、祭神挂签、节令剪纸、婚庆剪纸、丧葬剪纸，以及室内装饰用顶棚花、风斗花、炕围花剪纸等。

张冬阁[1]的《满乡风情·正月初一出行》获全国首届剪纸大奖赛二等奖，《满乡情思》获中国旅游剪纸作品展金奖，《满乡育婴图》获全国民间艺术家书画展特别金奖。

此外，冀东皮影剪纸、昌黎剪纸画也是声名远播，承德县的乔杖

---

1 丰宁满族剪纸国家级非物质文化遗产代表性项目代表性传承人，国家工艺美术大师，国务院特殊津贴专家。

抚宁剪纸（供图：抚宁区文化馆）
Funing paper cuttings (Provided by Funing District Cultural Center)

子剪纸远销美、英、法、日、中国香港和中国台湾等 50 多个国家和地区。2003 年，乔杖子被命名为"中国民间艺术之乡（剪纸）"。

（作者：秦学武）

Paper-cutting, aka paper-carving, is a form of folk art by using scissors or knives to carve out patterns for gracing the houses or adding luster to folk activities. Sheet materials, such as paper, gold or silver foil, cloth, hide and leather, can be used for paper-cutting. In 2009, UNESCO included Chinese paper-cutting in the Representative List of the Intangible Cultural Heritage of Humanity.

Paper-cutting is a 1,000-year-old Chinese craft. In the Han and Tang dynasties, folk women began to cut gold and silver foils and colored silk into different shapes and plaster them on their temples. Paper-cutting is popular in many regions, imbued with distinctive local, ethnic and fashionable characteristics.

Paper-cutting comes in traditional and modern forms in content. Traditional paper-cutting is reflective of daily life, auspiciousness, dramatic characters, legends and religious sacrifices. They commonly feature flowers, birds, insects, fish, pavilions, beasts and auspicious patterns. The local craftsmen made paper cuttings by experience or according to design drawings. Modern paper-cutting keeps abreast of the times and has distinctive themes. The works are either handmade by craftspeople or mass-produced by small workshops based on demand.

As for the creative forms, paper cuttings could be classified into monochrome ones and carved-and-dyed ones. The former is typically made with red paper, which is folded and cut according to a pattern. The latter is typically made with *fenlian* paper (white and glossy on one side). Normally, carving is done in autumn, summer and fall, and color matching and details adding are done in winter. The emphasis of monochrome paper-cutting is on pattern designing and scissor work. The emphasis of carved-and-dyed paper cutting, besides pattern designing, is also on carving and dyeing skills.

In making paper cuttings, various scissors and knives are required. Besides, there are different carving methods. In Yang carving, the outline of a pattern is made with lines connected with each other, and the superfluous parts are carved or cut off. By contrast, the focus of Yin carving is on the block, and the lines of a pattern are carved or cut off so that there is no connected line. Yin-Yang carving, a combination of the two, is quite a delight to watch.

There are a variety of paper-cutting in Jidong, such as Fengning, Kuancheng and Chengde paper-cutting of Chengde City; Yutian, Luanzhou, Luannan, Guye and Lubei paper-cutting of Tangshan City; and Funing,

Changli, Lulong and Qinglong paper-cutting of Qinhuangdao City. The most famous one is Fengning Manchu paper-cutting, which holds a major place in Chinese folk paper-cutting.

Fengning Manchu paper-cutting started during the reign of Kangxi of the Qing Dynasty. In the years of Qianlong, it formed distinctive regional characteristics and ethnic styles. It experienced its heyday in the late Qing Dynasty and early Republic of China. The art form, with Yang carving as its main approach and Yin carving as a complementary method, features fine lines and delicate cuts. In 1993, Fengning County was named "Hometown of Chinese Folk Paper-cutting". In 2006, Fengning Manchu paper-cutting was included in the List of Representative Items of National Intangible Cultural Heritage.

Fengning Manchu paper-cutting is used mainly for window decorations, religious sacrifices, seasonal celebrations, weddings and funerals, as well as interior décor such as ceiling patterns, vent patterns and *kang*-side patterns.

Village Style · Travel on the First Day of the First Lunar Month, the work of Zhang Dongge[1], won the second prize in the 1st National Paper-cutting Competition. His *Homesickness* won the Gold Award in the China Tourism Paper-cutting Exhibition. His *Baby Nursing in a Manchu Township* won the Special Gold Award in the National Folk Artists Painting and Calligraphy Exhibition.

Moreover, Jidong shadow play paper-cutting and Changli paper-cutting are also widely popular. The Qiaozhangzi paper cuttings of Chengde County are exported to more than 50 countries and regions, such as the United States, Britain, France, Japan and China's Hong Kong and Taiwan.

---

1 Representative inheritor of Fengning Manchu paper-cutting—a Representative Item of National Intangible Cultural Heritage, master of Chinese arts and crafts, and recipient of Special Government Allowances of the State Council.

In 2003, Qiaozhangzi village was named "Hometown of Chinese Folk Art (Paper-cutting)".

(By: Qin Xuewu)

12. 玉田泥塑 Yutian Clay Sculpture[1]

泥塑，俗称"彩塑""泥玩""耍货"，是中国的一项传统民间手工艺。

玉田泥塑，俗称"泥人"或"泥笛儿"[2]，是一种用黏土塑造形象再经彩绘而成的玩具。2008年，入选国家级非物质文化遗产代表性项目名录。

玉田泥塑形成于清光绪年间，至今有100余年的历史，已传承五代，以吴玉成[3]、刘广田为代表。20世纪60年代，玉田泥塑进入成熟、兴盛期，鸦鸿桥大集的泥人一条街长达里许，吸引了众多京、津、东北等地的商家。

玉田泥塑是一种半塑半画、以画为主的小型泥塑，一般为椭形体，具有概括凝练、朴拙可爱的审美特征。制作工艺分两大步骤：一是"塑"，包括选土和泥、捏制泥胎、制作模具、合模装笛、修整晾晒、打磨等步骤；二是"画"，包括铺白粉底、调胶、敷彩等工序。其中，敷彩是玉田泥塑的最重要工序，决定了整个作品的气韵风貌。

根据把玩方式，玉田泥塑可分两类：一是"口吹类"，是指内部安装有苇笛，可产生声响；一是"手动类"，是指通过外力作用使之跳动或作响。

根据创作题材，玉田泥塑分为神话传说、飞禽走兽、戏剧和历史人物、时事风俗等四类。代表作为《八仙过海》《麒麟送子》等。这

---

1 王秀娟：《河北唐山玉田泥塑传承研究》，山西师范大学硕士学位论文，2013年。
Wang Xiujuan: "Study on the Inheritance of Yutian Clay Sculpture in Tangshan, Hebei Province", Master's Thesis of Shanxi Normal University, 2013.

2 玉田泥人内常装有可口吹的笛子，故称"泥笛儿"。

3 吴玉成，人称"泥人吴"，2009年入选国家级非物质文化遗产代表性项目代表性传承人。

些作品形象生动，寓意吉祥，乡土气息浓郁。

玉田泥塑，在河北首屈一指，在中国民间泥塑中占有一席之地。1993年，玉田县被命名为"中国民间艺术之乡（民间泥塑）"。1994年，刘广田的《小狮子戏绣球》和吴玉成的《骑毛驴走娘家》入选文化部举办的"中国民间艺术一绝大展"。

（作者：秦学武）

The clay sculpture, colloquially called "colored sculpture", "game clay" and "fun goods", is a traditional folk handicraft of China.

The Yutian clay sculpture, colloquially called "clay figurine" or "clay flute"[1], is a toy modelled with clay before being painted. In 2008, it was included in the List of Representative Items of National Intangible Cultural Heritage.

Appearing in the years of Guangxu of the Qing Dynasty, the 100-year-old Yutian clay sculpture represented by Wu Yucheng[2] and Liu Guangtian has been passed down for five generations. In the 1960s, Yutian clay sculptures came into full bloom. The cluster of clay figurine stalls in the Yahongqiao Fair, stretching up to 1 *li*, attracted buyers from Beijing, Tianjin and Northeast China.

Yutian clay sculptures are small sculptures half-sculpted, half-painted and typically fashioned in an ellipsoidal shape. They are characterized by conciseness, innocence and cuteness. The crafting process is divided into two steps: sculpting and drawing. The first step includes clay selecting, clay body making, mold making, mold assembling, reed flute installing, drying and polishing. The second step includes powder daubing, glue making and color applying. As the key procedure in clay sculpture making, color applying determines the general effect of the work.

1　A Yutian clay sculpture often has a flute inside, hence its name "clay flute".

2　Wu Yucheng, known as "Clay Man Wu", was named a representative inheritor of Representative Items of National Intangible Cultural Heritage in 2009.

Yutian clay sculptures (Photographed by Yao Wenhai)

According to the way of playing, Yutian clay sculptures fit into two types: blowing type and manual type. The former produces sounds through the reed flute installed inside. The latter leaps or produces sounds under external forces.

According to the theme, Yutian clay sculptures are divided into four groups: myths and legends, birds and animals, drama characters and historical figures, and current affairs and customs. Representative works such as *Eight Immortals Crossing the Sea* and *Kylin Bringing a Child* are vivid and auspicious with rich rustic characteristics.

The Yutian clay sculpture is the number-one sculpture type in Hebei and holds a place in Chinese folk clay sculptures. In 1993, Yutian County was named "Hometown of Chinese Folk Art (Folk Clay Sculpture)". In 1994, Liu Guangtian's *Little Lion Playing with the Silk Ball* and Wu Yucheng's *Riding a Donkey to My Parents' Home* were selected into the China Folk Art Exhibition hosted by the Ministry of Culture of the People's Republic of China.

(By: Qin Xuewu)

13. 丰宁布糊画 Fengning Cloth Painting[1]

丰宁布糊画，又称滕氏布糊画，是工艺美术大师滕腾[2]在满族传统工艺"补花"基础上发明的新型工艺美术画种。2014 年，入选国家级非物质文化遗产代表性项目名录。

满族"补花"起源于女真时期，先民常以不同颜色的布料为面，以棉毛填充，再用针线把布料缝制成花卉、兽头等，最后加以彩墨勾画，补在衣服、鞋帽等物件上。

丰宁布糊画以"补花"工艺为母体，融绘画、雕塑、刺绣、裱糊、剪裁等工艺为一体。作品既有油画的写实效果，又不失国画的意境；既有工笔重彩的观感，又有浮雕的立体效果；形成立体感强、色彩艳丽、画面逼真、乡土气息浓郁、取材广泛、做工细腻的艺术特色。

《凤凰宝相瓶》（供图：丰宁县文化馆）
Phoenix Vase (Provided by Fengning County Cultural Center)

丰宁布糊画有堆积法、凹凸法、抻扯法、褶皱法、拼凑法、悬空法、镶嵌法等制作工艺。1995 年，"布糊画制作方法"获国家发明专利（CN1087055A），主要有绘样、图纸分解、制板、整形、配料、布糊、组装、装饰、成画九道制作工序。布糊画用料繁多，以真丝面料和金

---

1 闫小荣:《略论滕氏布糊画的艺术价值和未来发展》，河北师范大学硕士学位论文，2013 年；吴雪雪:《布糊画艺术对民间工艺的传承与发展》，武汉纺织大学硕士学位论文，2013 年。

Yan Xiaorong: "On the Artistic Value and Future Development of Teng's Cloth Painting", Master's Thesis of Hebei Normal University, 2013; Wu Xuexue: "The Cloth Painting's Inheritance and Development of Folk Crafts", Master's Thesis of Wuhan Textile University, 2013.

2 2003 年，被联合国教科文组织授予"中国民间工艺美术大师"称号；2006 年，被国家授予"中国工艺美术大师"称号。

《和平昌盛图》（供图：丰宁县文化馆）
Picture of Peace and Prosperity (Provided by Fengning County Cultural Center)

丝银线为主料，以珠花、首饰、丝绒、海绵、木料、纸板等为辅料。产品远销美国、加拿大、澳大利亚、日本、新加坡、马来西亚等国家和地区。

滕氏布糊画的代表作有《九龙壁》《虞美人》《傲雪迎春》《花卉四扇屏》《孔雀春花园》《丰收硕果》《天下第一布糊寺》《大威德怖畏金刚》《正法明如来》等。2002 年，《和平昌盛图》《凤凰宝相瓶》被人民大会堂收藏。2005 年，《老鼠娶亲图》《十二生肖图》被国家博物馆收藏。

滕氏布糊画获得四次中国民间文艺山花奖，以及众多大赛、展会的金奖。2004 年 10 月，承德市龙腾艺术馆被批准为"中国滕氏布糊画传承发展基地"。

（作者：秦学武）

The Fengning cloth painting, aka Teng's cloth painting, is a new type of arts and crafts invented by Teng Teng[1], a master of arts and crafts, on the

---

[1] Recognized by UNESCO as a "Master of Chinese Folk Arts and Crafts" in 2003; recognized by the state as a "Master of Chinese Arts and Crafts" in 2006.

丰宁布糊画（供图：丰宁县文化馆）

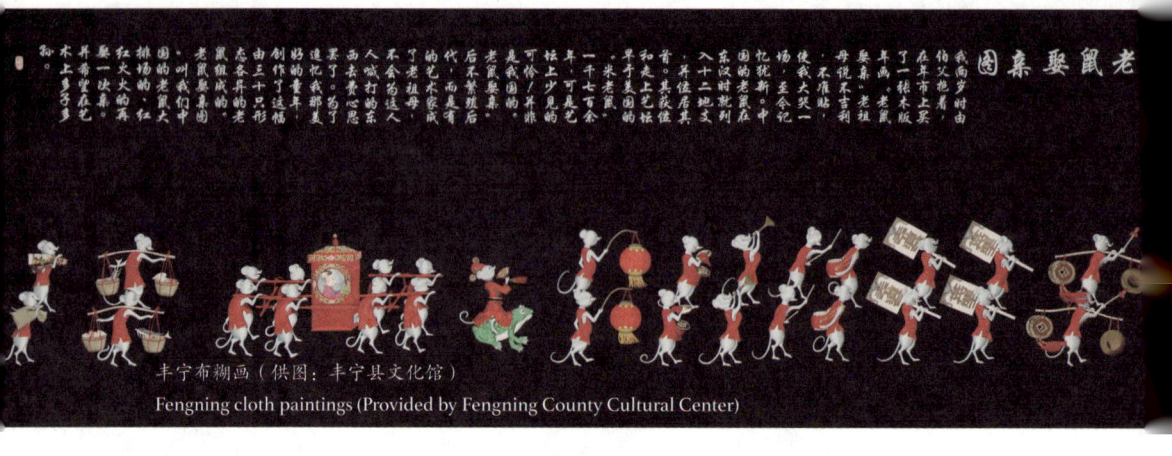

Fengning cloth paintings (Provided by Fengning County Cultural Center)

basis of the traditional Manchu craft "appliqué". In 2014, it was included in the List of Representative Items of National Intangible Cultural Heritage.

Manchu appliqué appeared in the Jurchen period. The ancient people used to stuff cloths of different colors with cotton wool, and stitch the cloths into flower and animal head patterns. The patterns would then be covered with colorful ink and sewn on clothes, shoes and hats.

The Fengning cloth painting, developed based on the craft of appliqué, integrates painting, sculpture, embroidery, pasting and cutting. The works are rendered with both the realistic style of oil paintings and the artistic conception of traditional Chinese paintings. They feature both the fine brushwork of traditional Chinese paintings and the stereoscopic effect of reliefs. The works are three-dimensional, colorful and exquisite, with extreme vividness, rich rustic characteristics and a broad range of topics.

The techniques of Fengning cloth painting making include stacking, concaving, stretching, folding, patching, hanging and embedding. In 1995, the "Making Method of Cloth Painting", which includes nine procedures—sketching, drawing dividing, plate making, shaping, material selecting, cloth pasting, assembling, decorating and painting, was granted a National Invention Pattern (CN1087055A). A variety of materials are used in cloth paintings, of which silk cloths and gold or silver threads function as the main materials, and bead flowers, jewelry, velvet, sponges, wood and cardboard are the auxiliary materials. The products are exported to many countries and regions, such as the United States, Canada, Australia, Japan, Singapore and Malaysia.

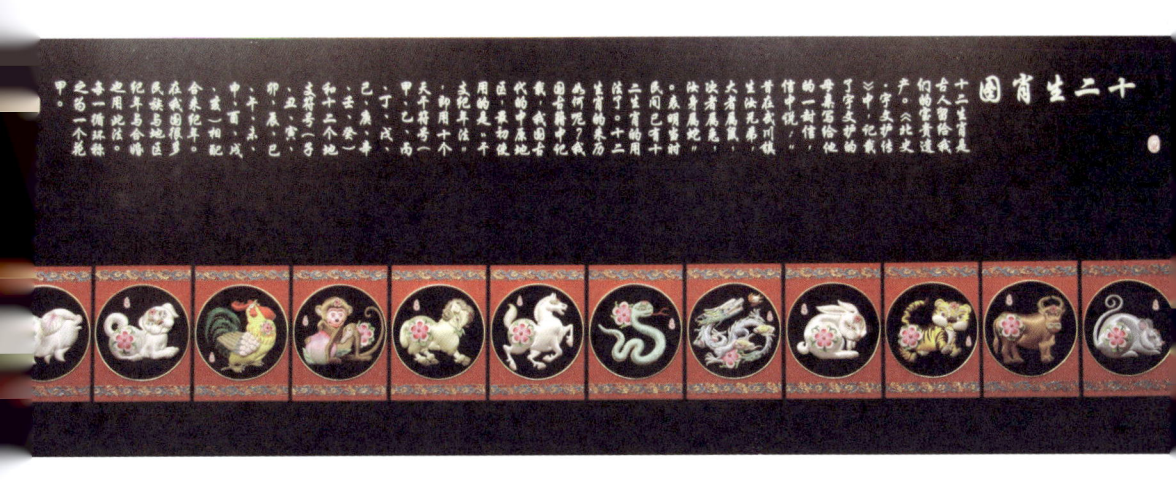

Teng's cloth painting masterpieces include *Nine-dragon Wall*, *Beauty Yu*, *Defying Snow and Looking Forward to Spring*, *Floral Quadruple Screen*, *Peacock in Spring Garden*, *A Bumper Harvest*, *Cloth Temple— The Greatest in the World*, *Yamāntaka* and *Zhengfaming Buddha*. In 2002, *Peace and Prosperity* and *Phoenix Vase* were collected by the Great Hall of the People. In 2005, the paintings *Mice Getting Married* and *Twelve Zodiac Animals* were collected by the National Museum of China.

Teng's cloth paintings have won the Chinese Folk Art Mountain Flower Awards four times and received the top awards of many competitions and exhibitions. In October 2004, Chengde Longteng Art Museum was approved as the "Inheritance and Development Base of Teng's Cloth Painting of China".

(By: Qin Xuewu)

六、节庆民俗 VI. Festivals and Folk Customs

14. 春节 Spring Festival[1]

春节是中国民间传统节日，也是一年中最盛大、最隆重的节日，俗称"过年"。2006 年，入选国家级非物质文化遗产代表性项目名录。

春节起源于商代岁末年初的祭神活动。汉武帝改用农历纪年后，中国历代都以立春日为春节，正月初一为新年。辛亥革命后，国民政府将正月初一定为"春节"。1949 年 9 月 27 日，中国人民政治协商会议第一届全体会议将元旦、春节等规定为法定假日。

在冀东的传统习俗中，腊月初八[2]即揭开过年的序幕。过了"小年"，生活开始步入春节的节奏，人们规划行程、置备年货，为过年做各种准备。大年三十，是春节的高潮。过完元宵节，春节遂告结束。民谚云："小孩小孩你别馋，过了腊八就是年。腊八粥，过几天，漓漓拉拉二十三。二十三，糖瓜粘；二十四，扫房子；二十五，做豆腐；二十六，割年肉；二十七，洗福禄；二十八，把面发；二十九，蒸馒头；三十晚上熬一宿，大年初一扭一扭。"这是传统年俗的生动写照。

（1）备年货，祭灶

腊月二十三，俗称"小年"。民间有"过小年"的传统，一家人小聚，谋划过年事宜。民间还有祭灶传统，祈望灶王爷上天言好事。

过完小年，各地年味儿渐浓，家家开始忙碌起来。赶大集，置办年货。贫困年代，冀东农村有杀年猪的习俗。如今人们生活富足，年前"赶大集"早已不是单纯采买，而是成为一方年俗。杀年猪、蒸年糕、备年货，更多是一种乡愁、一种春节仪式。

（2）扫房，祭祖

腊月二十四，冀东农村有"扫房子"的风俗。

1　参阅：https://www.ihchina.cn/project_details/14904/
　　See: https://www.ihchina.cn/project_details/14904/

2　腊月初八，俗称"腊八"，民间有吃"腊八粥"的习俗。

赶集（摄影：左恭田）
Spring Festival customs (Photographed by Zuo Gongtian)

20世纪90年代前，家庭居室大多没条件装修。这天，人们要对房屋院落大扫除，然后糊窗裱墙，张贴年画窗花，除旧布新。

中国人讲求慎终追远，有春节祭祖的传统。从腊月二十四到大年三十，冀东人家会择日到祖坟或墓地祭祀逝去的先人，表达缅怀之意。

（3）蒸馒头，贴春联

腊月二十八、二十九，冀东有蒸馒头、蒸年糕、蒸黏饽饽的习俗，以准备春节期间的主食，门窗还要贴上火红的春联、吉祥的福字、精美的窗花，以营造过年的气氛。

挂花灯是春节期间的传统习俗。红灯笼，代表喜庆、吉祥和对未来的美好追求。花灯起于汉代，盛于唐代，宋代以后在民间普及。沿街挂满火红的灯笼，过年的气氛更加浓厚。

（4）吃年饭，守岁

大年三十（闰年为二十九），吃年饭是最重要的年俗。在冀东，这顿团圆饭通常在中午进行，农村一般在下午两三点进行。俗话说"有钱没钱，回家过年"。忙碌一年的人们，从各地回到老家，全家人

春联（摄影：王洪涛）
Spring couplets (Photographed by Wang Hongtao)

欢聚一堂，互敬互爱，品味家乡味道，乐享团圆。

夜幕降临，家家宅院和屋舍灯火通明。全家人团聚在一起，边看"春晚"[1]，边守岁。子夜时分，伴随零点的钟声敲响和左邻右舍的爆竹声，吃过"年夜饭"的水饺，大人小孩才开始休息。意犹未尽的人们则要玩个通宵。

（5）拜年，压岁

拜年，是春节最重要的礼俗。这是人与人亲情、友情的体现，更是中华礼仪之邦的体现。

家中拜年，通常在大年三十就已开始。在吃年饭时，家中晚辈向长辈拜年，长辈要把提前准备好的压岁钱[2]分发给年幼的晚辈，这是千百年的习俗。

吃过年饭后，在外与熟人初次见面，彼此要道一声"过年好"，

---

1 中央广播电视总台春节联欢晚会始于1983年。看春晚，已成中国人的年俗。
2 压岁钱，又名压祟钱。祟，指不吉利的东西。压祟，有驱邪避灾、保佑平安之意。

以示祝福。

冀东地区还有正月里走亲戚、晚辈到长辈家拜年的习俗，一般从初二、初三开始。亲朋好友、同事邻里间也会相互祝福，互道"过年好""恭喜发财""恭贺新春"等吉祥话。

在资讯落后的年代，人们常在年前通过写信、寄贺卡等向远方的朋友亲人表达祝福。现在，人们多采用短信、微信、微博等方式即时拜年。亲朋好友间的互相拜年，常常是从大年三十就已开始，子夜时分达到高潮。

在冀东，还有两种特殊的拜年习俗：一是，刚结婚的小两口，正月里回娘家给父母和长辈拜年；二是秧歌队拜年。人们称正月扭秧歌为"办会"。秧歌队在会首的带领下，走街串巷给各家拜年，主人要给红包，俗称"赏钱"。大人小孩，常常追着秧歌跑，或地秧歌，或高跷秧歌，秧歌到哪里扭，哪里就是一片"人海"，俗称"跑秧歌"。

（6）逛花灯，吃元宵

正月十五日，元宵节。逛花灯、猜灯谜、吃元宵、放烟花，是冀东普遍的习俗。

中国幅员辽阔，各地的春节习俗因地域文化、城乡环境、时代变迁而有所不同。广大农村仍按传统方式过年，而城市过年更显简单，不如农村有年味儿。

（作者：秦学武）

Colloquially called "*guo nian*", the Spring Festival is the most ceremonious and solemn traditional festival of China. In 2006, it was included in the List of Representative Items of National Intangible Cultural Heritage.

The Spring Festival originated from the worship activities at the end of the year in the Shang Dynasty. When Emperor Wu of the Han Dynasty changed over to the lunar calendar, the day *lichun* (beginning of spring) was established as the Spring Festival, while the 1st day of the 1st lunar

Family dinner (Photographed by Liu Wenjun)

month was established as the New Year's Day. After the Revolution of 1911, the Kuomintang government made the 1st day of the 1st lunar month the "Spring Festival". On September 27, 1949, the New Year's Day and the Spring Festival were designated as national holidays in the First Plenary Session of the Chinese People's Political Consultative Conference.

By Jidong tradition, the 8th day of the 12th month[1] is the prologue to the Spring Festival. Right after the Little Spring Festival, people begin to make arrangements for the Spring Festival. They make travel plans and do shopping. The Spring Festival Eve is the culmination of the Spring Festival, and the Lantern Festival marks the end of it. As a Chinese proverb says: "Little children, little children, don't be greedy. Soon after Laba is the Spring Festival party. How many days do we eat Laba congee? Eat it until Day Twenty-three. Twenty-three, eat sticky candy. Twenty-four, sweep the house. Twenty-five, make bean curd. Twenty-six, buy some pork. Twenty-seven, have a bath. Twenty-eight, leaven the dough. Twenty-nine, steam the buns. Stay up late on the Spring Festival Eve, and visit relatives on

---

[1] The 8th day of the 12th lunar month is colloquially known as "Laba". On that day, it is customary for people to eat "Laba congee".

the Spring Festival day." This is a vivid characterization of the traditional Spring Festival customs.

(1) Shopping for the Spring Festival and Offering Sacrifices to the Kitchen God

The 23rd day of the 12th month is colloquially called the "Little Spring Festival". The folks have a custom of "celebrating the Little Spring Festival". On that day, the whole family get together to plan for the Spring Festival. It is customary for people to offer sacrifices to the Kitchen God. They beseech the god to put in a good word to the Jade Emperor.

When the Little Spring Festival is over, the Spring Festival atmosphere gets stronger day by day. Every household is busy shopping for the Spring Festival in the market. In the impoverished days, families in Jidong villages would butcher Spring Festival pigs. With the improvement of rural living conditions, people are no longer shopping for the Spring Festival out of necessity. The custom has become a folkway. Butchering Spring Festival pigs, steaming Spring Festival cakes and shopping for the Spring Festival are more of a vehicle for nostalgia and a Spring Festival rite.

(2) Sweeping the House and Honoring the Ancestors

Families in Jidong villages have a custom of sweeping the house on the 24th day of the 12th month.

Till the 1990s, most households didn't have the luxury of decorating the house. On that day, the house would be given a proper cleaning to welcome in the Spring Festival. The paper covering windows and walls would be replaced, and Spring Festival paintings and paper cuttings would be pasted for decoration.

Since ancient times, Chinese people have followed the custom of honoring the ancestors on the Spring Festival. The worship runs from the 24th day of the 12th month to the Spring Festival Eve. Villagers would

Guessing lantern riddles (Photographed by Liu Wenjun)

choose a day to visit their ancestral graves or cemeteries and honor their ancestors.

(3) Steaming Buns and Pasting Spring Couplets

On the 28th and 29th days of the 12th month, Jidong people have a custom of steaming buns, Spring Festival cakes and sticky cakes for the Spring Festival. Fiery red spring couplets, character *fu* (福) signifying good luck and exquisite paper cuttings for window decoration are pasted on the doors and windows to build up the mood for the Spring Festival.

Hanging the lanterns is a traditional custom of the Spring Festival. Red lanterns represent festivity, auspiciousness and the yearning for a better life. The festive lantern originated in the Han Dynasty, prospered in the Tang Dynasty, and became popular in the Song Dynasty. The red lanterns lining the streets add to the general gaiety of the Spring Festival.

（4）The Spring Festival Eve Dinner and the Spring Festival Stay

The Spring Festival Eve dinner is the most important Spring Festival custom on the Spring Festival Eve (the 30th day of the 12th month in normal years, and the 29th in leap years). In the urban areas of Jidong, the family dinner is usually held at noon. In rural areas, it is usually held at two or three o'clock in the afternoon. As a Chinese proverb says: "Go home for the Spring Festival, no matter if you're rich or not." After working all year long, people from all over the country come home. They taste the flavor of hometown in the family reunion gatherings.

As night falls, the houses and courtyards are sumptuously illuminated. The family members join in for the Spring Festival Stay while watching the CCTV Spring Festival Gala.[1] When the midnight bell rings, the Spring Festival comes around at the sound of fireworks in the neighborhood. After eating the Spring Festival dumplings, adults and children go to bed. Those feeling unfulfilled will play the whole night.

(5) Spring Festival Visits and Spring Festival Money

Spring Festival visits, the most important custom of the Spring Festival, strengthen the bond between family members and friends. It represents the characteristics of China as the "land of ceremony and propriety".

Family members usually start to visit each other on the Spring Festival Eve. At the Spring Festival Eve dinner, the junior members greet the senior members. The latter prepare the red envelopes containing Spring Festival money[2] ahead of time and hand them to the former. The custom has been followed for ages.

After the Spring Festival Eve dinner, acquaintances would say "Happy Spring Festival" when they come across each other outside.

Jidong people have the custom of visiting relatives from the second or third day of the Spring Festival to the end of the 1st lunar month. The

---

1 CCTV Spring Festival Gala began in 1983. It has become a Spring Festival custom for Chinese people to watch the program.

2 Spring Festival money is also called *yasui* money. *Sui* means inauspicious things, and *yasui* means exorcising those things to keep people peaceful.

年俗（摄影：左恭田）
Spring Festival customs (Photographed by Zuo Gongtian)

juniors would go to visit their seniors. Friends, kinfolks, colleagues and neighbors would say good-luck words to each other, such as "Happy Spring Festival", "Happy and Prosperous" and "Best Wishes for the Year".

In the era when telecommunication was underdeveloped, people used to write or send congratulation cards to friends and relatives living far away, which represented their sincerest blessing. People today would send Spring Festival greetings through SMS, WeChat and Weibo. Friends and kinfolks often greet each other starting from the Spring Festival Eve, and the Spring Festival celebration culminates with the ringing of the midnight bell.

In Jidong, there are two special Spring Festival customs. First, the wife would come back to her parents' home with her newly-married husband during the Spring Festival. Second, Yangko teams would go for the Spring Festival tour—"*banhui*" as they call it. Following the team leader, dancers go from village to village sending Spring Festival greetings to the households. The tips they receive are colloquially called "money reward". Men, women and children are often seen running after the Yangko teams, who usually perform field Yangko or stilt Yangko. Wherever a Yangko team goes, the street is at once thronged with people. This is colloquially called "Yangko Run".

(6) Viewing Festive Lanterns and Eating *Yuanxiao*

The 15th day of the Spring Festival is the Lantern Festival. Jidong people have the custom of viewing festive lanterns, guessing lantern riddles, eating *yuanxiao* and setting off fireworks.

China is a vast country with varied Spring Festival customs across the land as a result of diverse regional cultures, different urban and rural environments and changes of the times. In the rural areas, people are still

抢花表演（供图：滦平县政府办公室）
Lunhua performance (Provided by the Office of the People's Government of Luanping County)

keeping the Spring Festival traditions. In urban areas, the mood for the Spring Festival nowadays is less intense.

(By: Qin Xuewu)

15．滦平抢花 Luanping Lunhua (Spark Swinging)

抢花是流传于河北省滦平县火斗山镇及周边地区的传统民俗，每年元宵节或重要节庆活动时进行表演。2014年，滦平抢花入选国家级非物质文化遗产代表性项目名录。

清朝康熙年间，梁氏先祖迁至滦平，开始用抢花表演祭祀火神，祈求来年丰收、免于火灾，至今已三百余年。梁志福为国家级非物质文化遗产代表性项目代表性传承人。

抢花表演在夜晚进行，观赏效果最佳。观众以花架为中心围成大圆圈，须距离花架30米以上，以免被飞溅的铁水灼伤。

抢花的制作材料简单，但制作工艺较难。主要材料有锅铁、木炭、花筒，以及表演所用花架。首先，将花架固定在空旷的场地中央。花架高3米，两柱间距2—2.5米。花筒高约0.4米，直径约0.2米。其次，准备好桦木或柏木焖制的木炭，将锅铁轧成均匀的小碎片。最后，把木炭和锅铁按比例、分层装进花筒，投料不匀或比例失配会直接影响表演效果。花筒装好后，将上面木炭点燃，然后将花筒挂在花架的铁钩上，就可进行抢花表演。[1]

抢花表演时，整个场地中央金花四射、流光溢彩。开始时"流星"闪闪，继而"小鱼儿"飞蹿，高潮时则形成一片美丽光线交织的光环，远看像巨大金钵倒扣在地上发出万丈金光。

（作者：秦学武）

Lunhua (spark swinging) is a traditional folk custom popular in and around Huodoushan Town, Luanping County, Hebei Province. It is performed on the Lantern Festival and other special festivals. In 2014, Luanping Lunhua was included in the List of Representative Items of National Intangible Cultural Heritage.

During the reign of Kangxi of the Qing Dynasty, the ancestors of Liang clan moved to Luanping. They worshipped the God of Fire with Lunhua performance and prayed for plentiful harvest and deliverance from fire hazard. Lunhua is a 300-year-old custom, and Liang Zhifu is its representative inheritor.

Performed at night, Lunhua is a delight to watch. The spectators form a large circle around the Lunhua rack. There must be a space of no less than 30 meters between the rack and the spectators so that people wouldn't get hurt by the molten metal that spills out.

The materials for Lunhua are simple, but the preparing process is complex. The main materials are iron pot fragments, charcoal, Lunhua canisters and a Lunhua rack for the performance. First, fix the rack in the center of the open ground. The rack is 3 meters high and the two columns are spaced 2–2.5 meters apart. The canisters are about 0.4 meters high and

---

[1] 毛砚：《到滦平去看"抢花"》，《乡音》2015 年 08 期。

about 0.2 meters in diameter. Second, get the birch or cypress charcoal ready, and roll the iron pot fragments into even pieces. Last, put the charcoal and iron pieces into the canisters in certain proportions and in layers. Uneven placement or mismatched proportions will be detrimental to the effect of performance. When the Lunhua canisters are installed, ignite the charcoal on top, and put the canisters on the hooks of the rack. Then, the Lunhua performance begins.[1]

During the Lunhua performance, glittering sparks are sent flying around the center of the venue. At first, the sparks twinkle like "shooting stars". Then, the flame runs up like "little fish". The performance culminates with the sparks forming a beautiful halo. From a distance, it looks like a giant golden bowl put upside down glimmering through the darkness.

(By: Qin Xuewu)

16. 宽城背杆 Kuancheng Pole Carrying[2]

宽城背杆俗称"背歌"，是庙会和花会中的一种民俗巡游表演，流传于河北省宽城满族自治县宽城镇北村及周边地区。2008年，入选国家级非物质文化遗产代表性项目名录。

宽城背杆始于清代，兴盛于民国时期，至今二百余年。20世纪初，经一位山东小炉匠的改进、传承，奠定了宽城背杆的演出特色。据说，清同治帝到迁西县景忠山参加庙会，曾钦点宽城背杆表演《麒麟送子》。1990年，宽城满族自治县成立庆典，背杆成功复演。2014年春节，"背杆会"复出并到北京、承德等地演出。

宽城背杆，集武术、杂技、戏剧、魔术于一体。

1　Mao Yan: "Watching "Lunhua" in Luanping", *Local Accent*, 2015, Issue 08.

2　参阅：https://www.ihchina.cn/project_details/15184/
See: https://www.ihchina.cn/project_details/15184/

背杆表演者分上角和下角。上角指扭动的孩童[1]，俗称上架；下角为身强体壮的男子，俗称下架，负责托起扭童。背杆因此被称为"头顶上的秧歌"。

宽城背杆取材于古典戏剧，上下角均着传统戏装。乐器以唢呐为主，配有皮鼓和低鼓、苏锣、哑钹子等，常用《将军令》《小开门》等曲牌。

宽城背杆道具制作精细，上下角绑缚要求极高。主要道具为架杆[2]，重约27公斤，好背手能扛顶三四名扭童，负重一百多公斤。

宽城背杆表演场面宏大，演职人员约150人。开场时，旗队伴随音乐《将军令》首先入场并围成一个圆形表演场地。随后，背杆上下角色入场表演。背杆架高3—4米，每架由青壮男人顶架，架上有一至三名扭童舞动，上下角合演一出戏，共有"麻姑献寿""回荆州""韩湘子""算粮登殿""刘二姐逛庙"等十三架。表演时打叉、挑凳者若干人紧随其后，各尽其职，责任分明。

（作者：秦学武）

宽城背杆（摄影：赵生忠）
Kuancheng pole carrying (Photographed by Zhao Shengzhong)

---

1 扭童为5—8岁经过严格训练的孩童。旧时皆为男童，故称"背哥"或"背童子"。因其装束为格格，故有人称背杆是"背格格"的简语。

2 架杆必须避免摩擦挤压，上下角以活动自如、安全可靠为前提。新型架杆材质为轻质钛合金。

Colloquially called "carrying song", Kuancheng pole carrying is a folk parade performance staged in temple fairs and flower shows. It is popular in and around Zhenbei Village, Kuancheng Town, Kuancheng Manchu Autonomous County, Hebei Province. In 2008, it was included in the List of Representative Items of National Intangible Cultural Heritage.

The 200-year-old Kuancheng pole carrying started in the Qing Dynasty and prospered in the Republic of China era. In early 1900s, a tinker of Shandong improved and inherited the art form, establishing the characteristics of its performance. Emperor Tongzhi of Qing was said to have asked for *Kylin Bringing a Child* to be performed when attending the temple fair in the Jingzhong Mountain, Qianxi County. In the founding ceremony of Kuancheng Manchu Autonomous County in 1990, pole carrying returned. In the Spring Festival of 2014, the Pole Carrying Society staged a comeback and gave performances in Beijing and Chengde.

Kuancheng pole carrying combines martial arts, acrobatics, opera and magic.

Pole carrying performers are divided into upper and lower roles. The upper role, colloquially called *shangjia*, refers to the swaying children[1]; the lower role, colloquially called *xiajia*, refers to the strong men holding up the children. As a result, pole carrying is also called "Yangko on the head".

The subjects of Kuancheng pole carrying performance derive from classical operas, with the upper and lower roles all wearing traditional stage costumes. *Suona* is the main instrument, accompanied by leather drums, lower drums, bass gongs and low-pitch cymbals. "General's Order" and

---

[1] The swaying children are children aged between 5–8 years old after going through rigorous training. In the old days, they were all boys, thus known as "carried lads" or "carried boys". Since they are dressed like princesses, some people see pole carrying as the abbreviation of "princesses carrying".

背杆表演（摄影：赵生忠）
Pole carrying performance (Photographed by Zhao Shengzhong)

"Small Door" are among the commonly used *qupai*.

The props of Kuancheng pole carrying are finely made, and the binding of upper and lower roles should be highly secure. As the major prop, the pole[1] weighs about 27 kilograms. A good carrier can take 3–4 swaying children on his back weighing more than 100 kilograms.

The grand and spectacular Kuancheng pole carrying performance

---

1　Friction and extrusion must be avoided for the pole, and the conditions for upper and lower roles must be flexible, safe and reliable. The new type of pole frame is made of light titanium alloy.

features a cast of about 150 people. It opens with the flag team entering the ground and forming a circle to the music of "General's Order". Then the upper and lower roles come into the circle to perform. A pole of 3–4 meters high stands on the shoulder of a strong young man, and there are 1–3 swaying children on a pole. The upper and lower roles present a joint performance. There are 13 types of poles, such as "Magu Celebrating the Birthday", "Returning to Jingzhou", "Han Xiangzi", "Asking for Supplies and Ascending the Hall" and "Liu Erjie Going to the Temple Fair". The performers are followed by people taking forks and carrying stools, and everyone has his part to play.

(By: Qin Xuewu)

第五章

饮食文化

Chapter V Food Culture

一、塞外风味 I. Savory Foods Beyond the Great Wall

1. 平泉"五奎园"改刀肉 Pingquan "Wukuiyuan" Gaidao Meat

"五奎园"改刀肉是河北省平泉市的一道传统风味美食，重在刀工，制作精细，风味独特。2007年，入选河北省级非物质文化遗产名录。

改刀肉由御膳房刘德才主厨主创，是献给清道光皇帝的御菜，道光年间传入古镇八沟（今平泉），至今已近200年。据传，宫廷御厨刘德才年老体衰被赶出宫，后流落八沟。他在镇上开了一家小餐馆，经营改刀肉。当时平泉这座塞外山城是东北通向内地的重镇，颇为繁华。因其技艺精湛，许多外地客商常把改刀肉带给亲友品尝。

"五奎园"改刀肉（摄影：高少康）
"Wukuiyuan" Gaidao meat (Photographed by Gao Shaokang)

随着生意日渐兴隆，刘师傅连收了五个徒弟，把御膳改刀肉的做法传给他们，饭店因此取名"五奎园"。师兄弟五人又各收门徒，代代相传，历尽沧桑，终于使改刀肉流传了下来。改刀肉已成为承德最受国内外游客欢迎的佳肴之一。

改刀肉以猪肉和干笋片为主料，成品改刀肉呈浅黄色，外形犹如一座金字塔，菜形美观，入口绵软，咀嚼筋道，味道鲜美，干香适口，储存时间长。

（作者：赵桂华）

"Wukuiyuan" Gaidao meat is a traditional dish of Pingquan, Hebei Province. It is particular about knife skills, beautifully made and keenly aromatic. In 2007, the dish was added to the intangible cultural heritage List of Hebei Province.

Created by Liu Decai, head chef of the imperial kitchen, Gaidao meat was an imperial dish dedicated to Emperor Daoguang of the Qing Dynasty. The 200-year-old food entered Bagou Town (today's Pingquan) during the reign of Emperor Daoguang. It was rumored that Liu was driven away from the palace when he became old and feeble, and ended up in Bagou Town. He opened a little restaurant in the town selling Gaidao meat. Pingquan, a flourishing mountain town beyond the Great Wall, linked the Northeast and the inland. Made with extraordinary technique, Gaidao meat found favor with businessmen from out of town. They bought the meat as gifts for relatives and friends.

As his business grew, Liu Decai took on five (pronounced as wǔ in Chinese) apprentices and unreservedly passed on to them the recipe of Gaidao meat. Liu's restaurant was thus named "Wukuiyuan". The five people continued to take on apprentices to pass Gaidao meat from one generation to the next. The dish has become a favorite food for visitors at home and abroad.

Pork and dried bamboo shoots are the main ingredients of Gaidao meat. When it is served, the yellowish meat in pyramid shape looks beautiful. With nice chewiness and mellow flavor, the meat can be preserved for a long time.

(By: Zhao Guihua)

2. 平泉御膳糖饼 Pingquan Imperial Sugar Cake

平泉御膳糖饼原为清朝宫廷的一道御膳。1985 年载入《国家食品大全》，1992 年获河北省优秀食品"金鼎奖"，2009 年入选河北省级非物质文化遗产名录。

清道光年间，御厨中一位面点师傅为道光帝创制一道甜点，定名"御膳糖饼"。后来这位师傅跟大臣私访路过八沟（今平泉），遇到了早年在御膳房中共事的刘御厨的传人，并将御膳糖饼的制作技艺传给了他。御膳糖饼制作技艺，在平泉已流传近 200 年。

御膳糖饼（摄影：杨树海）
Imperial sugar cakes (Photographed by Yang Shuhai)

御膳糖饼以高筋面粉、白油（猪板油）、白糖等为主料，佐以香油、芝麻酱、赤小豆、葵花籽仁、核桃仁、花生仁、青丝、红丝、桂花等小料。

御膳糖饼采用纯手工制作，经和馅、和面、下剂、包饼、烤烙等多道工序。制作工艺为按 1 斤（500 克）面粉加 5 两（250 克）白油的比例和成油面，再按 1 斤面粉加 6 两（300 克）温水（30℃左右）的比例和成水面。用和好的水面包住油面，再和成油酥面。把和好的油酥面用手工揪成半两（25 克）大小的面剂子，擀成薄片状，包入半两馅，做成圆饼。上饼铛烙成虎皮色即可。

御膳糖饼呈圆形，色微黄，层数多，层薄如纸。糖饼香而不腻，酥甜可口。常温下可保存 3—4 个月。产品销往美国、加拿大、中国香港和中国台湾等国家和地区。

（作者：赵桂华）

The Pingquan imperial sugar cake was originally a dish consumed by the royal court. In 1985, it was listed in the *National Food Encyclopedia*; in 1992, it won the "Golden Tripod Award" of Celebrated Foods in Hebei

Province; in 2009, it was added to the Intangible Cultural Heritage List of Hebei Province.

During the reign of Emperor Daoguang, a pastry chef of the imperial kitchen created a dessert—imperial sugar cake, and dedicated it to the emperor. Afterwards, the chef accompanied the officials in a private visit. Going past Bagou Town (today's Pingquan), he met an apprentice of his fellow Liu Decai, and passed on to him the technique of imperial sugar cake making. The technique has continued for around 200 years since then.

High protein flour, white oil (lard), and white sugar are used as the main ingredients of the imperial sugar cake. They are seasoned with sesame oil, sesame paste, red beans, sunflower seeds, walnut kernels, peanuts, green and red dried fruit, and Osmanthus fragrans.

Imperial sugar cakes are handmade in several procedures: filling preparing, dough kneading, dough dividing, stuffing, and baking. First, mix 500 grams of flour and 250 grams of white oil together to make an oiled dough. Then, add 300 grams of warm water (about 30℃) to 500 grams of flour to make a watered dough. Wrap the oiled dough with the watered dough to make a pastry dough. Divide the pastry dough into small pieces weighing 25 grams each. Flatten a dough piece and stuff 25 grams of filling into it to make a round cake. Finally, bake the cakes in a hot pan until they start to singe.

An imperial sugar cake is round and golden with many layers, each as thin as a piece of paper. It is sweet but not greasy, tasting crisp and delicious. The cakes can be kept at room temperature for 3–4 months, and they are exported to the United States, Canada and China's Hong Kong and Taiwan.

(By: Zhao Guihua)

3. 隆化一百家子拨御面 Longhua One Hundred Households Royal Pushed Noodles

一百家子拨御面是河北省承德市隆化县张三营镇的一道美味面食。2007年，"一百家子拨御面"传统手工技艺入选河北省级非物质文化遗产名录。

拨御面（供图：隆化县文化馆）
Royal pushed noodles (Provided by Longhua County Cultural Center)

清代，张三营镇只有百十户村民，故称"一百家子"，以盛产白荞面闻名。承德吃荞麦的方法首推张三营镇。白荞面可制作成多种风味食品，以"拨面"最佳。

1762年，乾隆帝赴木兰围场狩猎驻跸张三营，在品尝姜家兄弟的拨面后，赞其"洁白如玉，赛雪欺霜"，并御封"一百家子拨御面"，从此拨御面进入宫廷食谱。

拨御面以白荞面为主要食材，和面手法独特，拨面方法考究。高级拨面师可将面拨到"细如针、白如雪"的程度，堪称中国民间手工技艺一绝。将拨面煮好后盛在碗内，浇上用老鸡汤、猪肉丝、榛蘑丁、木耳、盐做的卤，即可食用。

拨御面含有多种维生素和大量蛋白质，且含糖量极低。长期食用有助于化积，止汗，医治噎食、风眼、糖尿病、高血压、小肠疝气等多种疾病。

近300年来，拨御面的传承历经十几代，仍保持原始风味和独特技艺。1982年，一百家子拨御面传人辛占武应邀赴北京钓鱼台国宾馆为中央领导人和国外友人当场献技，和面、扬刀、拨面一气呵成，将传统的民间手艺展现得淋漓尽致。

（作者：赵桂华）

One Hundred Households royal pushed noodles are a delicious food in Zhangsanying Town, Longhua County, Chengde City, Hebei Province. In 2007, the traditional technique of One Hundred Households royal pushed noodles making was added to the Intangible Cultural Heritage List of Hebei Province.

In the Qing Dynasty, Zhangsanying Town had only about one hundred farmers' houses, hence its name One Hundred Households. It was well-known for its white buckwheat noodles. The most authentic and traditional method of buckwheat processing of Chengde is found in Zhangsanying. White buckwheat flour can be made into a variety of foods, of which the knife-pushed noodles taste best.

In 1762, Emperor Qianlong went to the Mulan Enclosure for hunting and had a stopover in Zhangsanying Town. He lavished his praise on the knife-pushed noodles made by the Jiang brothers after savoring the dish, saying that "as white as jade, the noodles surpass snow and frost". The dish was awarded the title "One Hundred Households royal pushed noodles" and added to the royal menu.

White buckwheat flour is used as the main ingredient of the royal pushed noodles, which feature unique dough kneading and noodle pushing techniques. A skilled chef could make the noodles "as thin as needles and as white as snow", contributing to a fabulous traditional skill. Once cooked, the pushed noodles are put into a bowl and poured with the sauce made of old chicken soup, pork shreds, diced honey mushrooms, jelly ears and salt.

There are various vitamins and proteins and little sugar in the royal

拨面条（供图：隆化县文化馆）
Pushing noodles (Provided by Longhua County Cultural Center)

pushed noodles. Regular consumption of the food would be helpful for improving digestion, reducing sweat, and treating a variety of diseases such as choking, wind-injured eyes, diabetes, hypertension, and intestinal hernias.

Over three centuries, the making of royal pushed noodles has been passed down for many generations, and the original flavor and technique are kept even today. In 1982, Xin Zhanwu, inheritor of One Hundred Households royal pushed noodles, was invited to perform noodle making in the presence of national leaders and foreign friends at Diaoyutai State Guesthouse. The dough kneading, knife wielding, and noodle pushing were all done with remarkable smoothness, fully displaying the essence of the traditional technique.

(By: Zhao Guihua)

4. 承德满族八大碗 Chengde Manchu Eight Bowls

满族八大碗是满族特有菜种，是山珍海味与地方风味的统一，集中了扒、焖、酱、烧、炖、炒、蒸、熘等烹饪手法，菜式多，食材珍贵，味道鲜美。

据《满族旗人祭礼考》记载，宴会用五鼎、八盏，俗称八大碗。相传，清乾隆时期，政局稳定，经济发展，饮食市场空前繁荣，"满汉全席"称雄饮食业。满汉全席又分为"上八珍""中八珍"和"下八珍"三种，满族八大碗则属于下八珍，满族地方风味也应运而生。

在清代，年节、庆典、迎送、嫁娶时，富家多以八大碗宴请。八大碗由雪菜炒小豆腐、卤虾豆腐蛋、扒猪手、灼田鸡、小鸡榛蘑粉、年猪烩菜、御府椿鱼、阿玛尊肉等八种菜组成。据说"阿玛尊肉"这道菜是努尔哈赤时期传下来的，又称努尔哈赤黄金肉。"阿玛尊肉"是清朝祭祀活动、庆典宴席上的必备菜，而且是第一道菜。

现在，八大碗是满族过年过节、婚丧喜庆不可或缺的餐品。宴客时，每桌八个人，桌上八道菜，上菜时都用清一色的大海碗，具有浓浓的乡土气息和满族特色。

（作者：赵桂华）

The Manchu eight bowls, a dish combination found exclusively in the Manchu ethnic group, combine dainty ingredients with local flavor. A variety of cooking methods are brought together, such as grilling, stewing, saucing, roasting, braising, stir-frying, steaming and quick-frying. With varied dishes and precious ingredients, the dish combination is delicious and refreshing.

According to *A Study on the Sacrificial Rites of Manchu Bannermen*, the five tripods and eight cups used in banquets were colloquially called "eight bowls". According to legend, China was stable and its economy was booming during the reign of Emperor Qianlong, and the catering market dominated by the Comprehensive Manchu-Han Banquet was prosperous like never before. The banquet was divided into upper, middle, and lower classes, of which the Manchu eight bowls belong to the last. The banquet fueled the boom of the Manchu local flavor.

In the Qing Dynasty, wealthy families would entertain the guests with the eight bowls during holidays and festivals, celebrations, welcoming parties and wedding ceremonies. The eight bowls are an eight-course meal featuring fried potherb mustard with bean curd dices, bean curd balls with shrimp sauce, braised pig trotters, roasted frogs, stewed chicken with honey mushrooms and cellophane noodles, stewed vegetables with Spring Festival pork, royal fried Toona sinensis leaves, and Ama meat. It is said that the Ama meat, aka Nurhachi golden meat, was passed down from the Nurhachi period. It was a necessary dish for sacrificial activities and celebrations in the Qing Dynasty and was often served as the first course.

Today, the eight bowls have become an indispensable dish combination for Manchu banquets in the Spring Festival, other festivals, weddings and funerals. In a banquet, there are eight people and eight courses at each table. The dishes are served in large bowls with rich local flavor and Manchu characteristics.

(By: Zhao Guihua)

5. 平泉羊汤 Pingquan Sheep Entrails Soup[1]

平泉羊汤是承德特色风味小吃，又称八沟羊汤，为康熙时期平泉清真寺阿訇张宏业所创。其味道鲜美清香，肥而不腻，无膻味。2017年，平泉羊汤制作工艺入选河北省级非物质文化遗产名录。

平泉羊汤的来历有多种传说，其中流传最广的是康熙皇帝在围场沟（今平泉党坝）设围打猎时偶然尝到羊杂汤，赞誉有加，并赋诗："喜峰口外远，塞北古道长。野鹿入柳林，八沟羊杂汤。"从此，八沟羊汤名声大振，关里关外无人不晓。

平泉羊汤制作工艺带有浓郁的地方特色和民族特色，有别于其他地区羊肉汤、羊骨汤的制作方法。羊汤以羊杂为主料，与羊骨、羊头

---

[1] 参阅：http://www.pingquan.gov.cn/art/2022/7/4/art_3126_368606.html
See: http://www.pingquan.gov.cn/art/2022/7/4/art_3126_368606.html

平泉羊汤（摄影：冯俊俞）
Pingquan sheep entrails soup (Photographed by Feng Junyu)

等共同熬制，在制作过程中有着选料精、辅料全、入锅细、汤要老等特点。

如今，平泉羊汤已遍及承德、北京、天津、石家庄、廊坊等大中城市。

（作者：赵桂华）

The Pingquan sheep entrails soup, aka Bagou sheep entrails soup, is a folk food of Chengde created by Zhang Hongye, an ahung of Pingquan Mosque, during the reign of Emperor Kangxi. The food is delicious but not greasy, with mellow flavor and no rank odor. In 2017, the technique of Pingquan sheep entrails soup making was added to the Intangible Cultural Heritage List of Hebei Province.

There are many stories about the origin of the Pingquan sheep entrails soup. According to the most widespread version, Emperor Kangxi once went hunting in Weichanggou (today's Dangba County, Pingquan City). He chanced to taste the sheep entrails soup and lavished his praise on the dish. The emperor composed a poem: "Xifengkou is so far away; / Beyond the border lies the ancient path. / In the wood wild deer disappear; / In Bagou the scent of sheep entrails travels far." Afterwards, the Bagou sheep entrails soup became famous within and beyond the Great Wall.

The technique of Pingquan sheep entrails soup making features strong local and ethnic characteristics, which is distinctively different from the techniques of mutton soup or sheep bone soup making in other areas. As the main ingredient, the sheep entrails are boiled together with bones and heads. With carefully chosen ingredients and a variety of seasonings, the making of the soup requires fine cutting and low-flame simmering.

Today, the Pingquan sheep entrails soup has become popular in large and medium-sized cities such as Chengde, Beijing, Tianjin, Shijiazhuang and Langfang.

(By: Zhao Guihua)

6. 青龙（宽城）水豆腐 Qinglong (Kuancheng) Soft Bean Curd

水豆腐，在青龙满族自治县、宽城满族自治县[1]一带，又称老豆腐。2020年，青龙东河水豆腐入选河北省第六批"燕赵老字号"。

满族人喜食豆制品，如水豆腐、黄豆腐、懒豆腐、豆腐脑等各种豆腐，以及豆片、豆浆、豆皮、豆芽、腐竹等。清康熙年间，水豆腐就随满族人一起来到青龙、宽城，至今已有300多年。在两县农村，许多家庭主妇都会做水豆腐。在困难时期，水豆腐是逢年过节、招待亲友时必不可少的一道菜肴。如今，水豆腐已成为一种家乡味道、一道乡野美食。

农家做水豆腐需要一套完整的工具，包括石碾、石磨、铁锅、吊杆、夹板、过滤包。原料为优质黄豆、山泉水及上好的卤水。制作工序包括精选黄豆、破碴子、磨豆腐、过豆汁、烧豆汁、卤水点豆腐等。俗话说"好水出好豆腐"，在青龙、宽城两县，祖山、都山一带的山泉水质最好，水豆腐也最有名。

做水豆腐，最讲究手艺，卤水点豆腐是最关键的环节。豆浆烧开

---

[1] 宽城县的大部分地区原属青龙县。1962年10月20日，国务院批准建立宽城县，以青龙、承德两县部分行政区域为宽城县行政区域。

青龙水豆腐（摄影：杨立壮）
Qinglong soft bean curd (Photographed by Yang Lizhuang)

后，要看准时间、火候，在适宜的温度，一边搅动豆汁一边用卤水点。卤水用多用少全凭经验。卤水用多了，豆腐就老了；少了，就凝不成豆腐了，味道也就不好吃了。在乡村传统中，做一手香嫩可口、汤汁四溢的水豆腐，是农家妇女的看家手艺。

青龙（宽城）的水豆腐颜色洁白、晶莹光亮，不仅入口爽滑细腻，还洋溢着原汁原味的豆香。吃法上，青龙、宽城两地也很有特点：水豆腐要用浅子[1]盛好，坐在汤盆上控浆，配着小米干饭或秫米干饭，搭配盐菁[2]或各式熟卤趁热吃。

剩余的水豆腐还有多种吃法，可以压制成豆腐块。豆腐块，既可做出炸丸子、麻婆豆腐、煎豆腐、肉末豆腐、白菜熬豆腐、小鱼炖豆腐、月子菜[3]等菜肴，也可揉进盐放到户外晾晒，制成豆腐干以便做出其他菜肴，还可冻成冻豆腐[4]，吃时浸泡，去掉冰碴，切成条、块，吃火锅或熬白菜时放进去一起熬煮。

---

1 用剥皮的细柳条编制的浅筐，俗称"浅子"。
2 盐菁为方言词，是咸菜的俗称，通常是红辣椒、香菜末、葱末、生咸菜相搭配。
3 青龙、宽城农村给产妇做的一道炒咸菜，食材为咸菜、小豆腐块、肉丝、粉丝，俗称"月子菜"。
4 夏天用冰箱或冰柜冷冻，冬季在室外阴处冷冻。

做豆腐时起的豆皮，营养丰富，是慰劳产妇的上好礼物。剩余的豆渣既可做酱，也可做豆渣炒饭。就连粘在锅上的锅巴，也是一道美食。

（作者：秦学武，赵桂华）

Soft bean curd, aka old bean curd, is popular in and around Qinglong Manchu Autonomous County and Kuancheng Manchu Autonomous County[1]. In 2020, Qinglong Donghe soft bean curd was added to the sixth batch of "Yanzhao Time-honored Brands" of Hebei Province.

The Manchu people love bean products, such as soft bean curd, yellow bean curd, lazy bean curd, jellied bean curd, bean curd slices, soybean milk, bean curd sheets, bean sprouts and bean curd sticks. During the reign of Emperor Kangxi, soft bean curd came to Qinglong and Kuancheng with the Manchu people. 300 years have passed since then. In the rural areas of the two counties, many housewives can make soft bean curd. In times of hardship, soft bean curd was an indispensable food for entertaining relatives and friends in the Spring Festival and other festivals. Today, soft bean curd is a special food with local flavor.

The making of soft bean curd requires a complete set of tools, including stone roller, stone mill, iron pot, hanger rod, clamp plate and filter bag. The ingredients are high-quality soybeans, spring water and fine brine. The food is made in several procedures: choosing soybeans, soaking, grinding, squeezing, boiling, and adding brine. A common saying goes, "Good water makes good bean curd." In and around Zushan and Dushan mountains in Qinglong and Kuancheng counties, the spring water is crystal clear, and the soft bean curd there is most popular.

1　Most parts of Kuancheng County were originally under the administration of Qinglong County. On October 20, 1962, the State Council gave its approval for the establishment of Kuancheng County. The county administers some original areas of Qinglong and Chengde counties.

The making of soft bean curd is very particular about adding brine. When the soybean milk is boiled, one should tend to the fire himself, and add brine while stirring it at the right temperature. The amount of brine needed all depends on one's own judgment. When it is overused, the bean curd would disappear. When it is underused, the bean curd would not curdle and the taste would be spoiled. Women in peasant households are very good at making soft bean curd. When the food is served, it is fresh and juicy.

The soft bean curd in Qinglong (Kuancheng) is snow-white. Just after taking a bite, you can feel an extremely fine texture and the aroma of soybeans. The natives of Qinglong and Kuancheng counties have a distinctive way of eating the food. They would put the bean curd in a *qianzi*[1], which is placed on a soup bowl, to filter out the soybean milk, and eat it with cooked millet or sorghum. The dish goes perfectly with salt vegetables[2] and cooked brine, and it tastes best while it is still warm.

There are a variety of recipes of processing the remaining soft bean curd, one of which is flattening. The flattened bean curd cubes can be made into deep-fried balls, stir-fried bean curd in hot sauce, fried bean curd, bean curd with minced pork, boiled bean curd with cabbage, stewed bean curd with small fish, and the lying-in dish[3]. Soft bean curd can also be salted and air-dried to make dried bean curd, or be frozen to make iced bean curd[4]. The iced bean curd should be soaked in water to thaw out the ice, and then it can be cut into strips or pieces and cooked in hotpot or with stewed cabbage.

---

1 Shallow basket made of peeled willow twigs, colloquially known as "*qianzi*".

2 Salt vegetables is a dialect phrase for pickles. It is usually a combination of red pepper, chopped coriander, chopped scallion and raw pickles.

3 A dish of fried pickles for lying-in women, colloquially called the "lying-in dish". The ingredients include pickled vegetables, small bean curd cubes, shredded pork and vermicelli.

4 Frozen in a refrigerator or freezer in summer; frozen in shady places outside in winter.

During the making of bean curd, a highly nutritious skin would form on it, which can help the lying-in women regain their strength. The residues from beans can be used to make sauce or fried rice. Even the bean crust on the pot is something appetizing.

(By: Qin Xuewu and Zhao Guihua)

7. 满族黏饽饽 Manchu Sticky Cake

黏饽饽，也称黏豆包，是一种满族特色面食，流传于青龙满族自治县、宽城满族自治县。2019 年，满族黏饽饽制作技艺入选河北省级非物质文化遗产名录。

满族人吃黏饽饽的习俗已有上千年历史。最初，黏饽饽是祭祀祖先的祭品。由于冬季易于储存、携带，黏饽饽成为满族人狩猎、耕种、行商、越冬以及战时的主要食品之一。满族入主中原，将其带入关内，逐渐形成居家日常也吃黏饽饽的习俗。

康熙年间，黏饽饽作为清朝军民特有的食物被带入青龙、宽城，距今已三百余年。农家制作黏饽饽，一般是在天寒地冻的腊月。否则，同样的食材也做不出那种味道。

农家做黏饽饽，先将黄米（或黏高粱米）用水浸泡淘好后磨成面粉，掺入少量玉米面或小米面，用水和好，发酵，包入豆馅，团成球形，下面垫以苏子叶、柞梸叶等，蒸熟食用。黄澄澄的黏饽饽味道香甜、软糯、劲道，是粗粮细作的典范。

蒸黏饽饽，一般用横柴（山上长的一种小叶植物）蒸。横柴好烧、火旺，如爆竹噼啪作响，寓意吉祥、发财。黏饽饽蒸熟后，上面点红点，寓意红运当头、四季平安。蒸好后要放室外晾，晾凉后装在缸里，放在户外冷冻。金黄透亮的黏饽饽，可随吃随取。

过去，很多农户一进腊月就开始蒸制黏饽饽，一蒸就要装两大缸，有的人家能吃到第二年开春。黏饽饽成了很多家庭的冬季主食。蒸黏饽饽那天，若是亲朋四邻赶上，一定会捡上刚出锅的黏饽饽吃个

做黏饽饽（摄影：张兴瑞）
Making sticky cakes (Photographed by Zhang Xingrui)

够，临走还要带些给家人尝尝鲜。

目前，黏饽饽生产已实现产业化、工厂化，产品销往国内各地及澳大利亚、新加坡、加拿大、美国、英国、韩国等多个国家。

（作者：秦学武，赵桂华）

The sticky cake, aka sticky bean paste-stuffed bun, is a special food of the Manchu people popular in Qinglong and Kuancheng Manchu autonomous counties. In 2019, the technique of Manchu sticky cake making was added to the Intangible Cultural Heritage List of Hebei Province.

Eating sticky cakes is a thousand-year-old tradition of the Manchu people. The food was initially a sacrifice offered to the ancestors. Sticky cakes were easy to store and carry in winter, so they were a staple food of the Manchu people in hunting, farming, trading, overwintering and wartime. When the Manchu people moved into the Central Plains, they took the food with them, and gradually they got into the habit of eating sticky cakes in daily life.

During the reign of Emperor Kangxi of the Qing Dynasty, the sticky cake came to Qinglong and Kuancheng as a special food for the military and the common people. 300 years have passed since then. In rural areas, sticky cakes are usually made in the twelfth lunar month when the weather is freezing cold, otherwise the flavor would not be the same.

Making sticky cakes includes several procedures. First, soak glutinous millet (or glutinous sorghum) in water and grind it into flour. Then, mix in a small amount of corn flour or millet flour. Then, add water and knead the dough. When the dough is fermented and cut into pieces, stuff them with bean paste and roll them into a ball shape. The cakes are steamed with Perilla or Quercus leaves under them. When they are served, the golden cakes taste sweet, soft and glutinous. The food is an example of making delicacies out of coarse grains.

Sticky cakes are traditionally steamed by burning *hengchai* (a kind of shrub growing in the mountains), which can make a good fire and is thought of as signifying auspiciousness and wealth with its crackling sound. When the sticky cakes are steamed, people would leave a red dot on it to obtain good omens for the year to come. The steamed cakes should be carried outside to cool, and then put in a vat outdoors to be frozen. The golden cakes are an appropriate food at any hour.

In the past, many farmers would make two vats of sticky cakes when the twelfth month came round, which could be kept till the next spring in some households. Sticky cakes have become a common staple food in winter. On the day when the cakes are steamed, some friends and relatives might happen to come over. While the sticky cakes are still fresh and hot, they would eat as much as they want. Before leaving, they would take a few cakes for their families.

Today, sticky cakes are produced on an industrial scale. They are sold across China and exported to Australia, Singapore, Canada, the United States, the United Kingdom, South Korea, etc.

(By: Qin Xuewu and Zhao Guihua)

8. 柞栎叶饼 Quercus Leaf Cake

柞栎叶饼是分布在长城沿线的地方名吃。东北的很多地方也有吃柞栎叶饼的习俗。2009 年，柞栎叶饼制作工艺入选秦皇岛市非物质文化遗产名录。先后荣获"河北省旅游美食名品""冀字号名吃""冀字号名点"等称号。

柞栎叶饼的由来，有两种说法。其一，柞栎叶饼是满族人在"虫王节"时制作的祭品。每年农历六月初六，家家户户都要制作柞栎叶饼来祭拜虫王爷，祈求风调雨顺、不闹虫灾。其二，相传明将戚继光率浙兵为主的"戚家军"镇守蓟镇长城，北方粗粮较多，为改善戍边南兵的生活，利用每年五月长城沿线柞栎叶鲜嫩时机，制成柞栎叶饼，粗粮细做。柞栎叶饼不但味道鲜美，还便于携带、贮存，后逐渐传到民间。

柞栎叶饼的主料为柞栎叶、面粉（玉米面或黍米面）和淀粉，馅料以韭菜、猪肉为主，也有豆馅。制作方法较为简单：先将鲜嫩的柞罗叶剪去叶柄，使其成圆形；将面粉和淀粉按一定比例混合，加水调制成面糊；再将面糊用铲刀均匀抹在洗净擦干的叶面上做皮儿；然后放上做好的馅，将叶片对折包好；最后放入笼屉中蒸熟。食用时须剥去叶子，能看到里面的馅，吃起来鲜美、有咬劲，还有一股柞栎叶的清香。

（作者：赵桂华）

The Quercus leaf cake is a famous local snack in places along the Great Wall. In many places of Northeast China, people keep the custom of eating the food. In 2009, the technique of Quercus leaf cake making was added to the Intangible Cultural Heritage List of Qinhuangdao. The cake was named Famous Tourist Food of Hebei Province, Famous Snack of Hebei Province and Famous Dessert of Hebei Province.

There are two theories on the origin of the Quercus leaf cake. First, the Quercus leaf cake was a sacrifice made by the Manchu people to celebrate the "Insect Lord Festival". On the sixth day of the sixth lunar month, families would offer Quercus leaf cakes as a sacrifice to the Insect Lord. They prayed to the Lord for favorable weather and no insect infestation. Second, legend has it that General Qi Jiguang of the Ming Dynasty led the Qi army—a fighting force composed mostly of Zhejiang soldiers—to stand guard in Jizhou. There were plenty of coarse grains in the north, and Quercus leaves along the Great Wall were tender in the fifth lunar month. To improve the diet of soldiers from the south, delicate coarse grain cakes wrapped with Quercus leaves were made. Quercus leaf cakes were delicious and easy to carry and store, so they gradually reached the common people.

Quercus leaves, flour (corn flour or millet flour) and starch are the main ingredients of Quercus leaf cakes, which are stuffed with shredded leeks and pork or bean paste. The cake is relatively simple to make. First, cut off the petioles and make the tender Quercus leaves into a round shape. Second, mix the flour and starch together in certain proportion before adding water and stirring to form a batter. Third, spread the batter evenly on the cleaned leaves with a spatula to make the wrappers. Fourth, stuff the wrappers with the filling and fold them together. Fifth and finally, Place the cakes into the steamer for steaming. When the leaves are striped off, the filling inside is visible, and the cakes are delicious and al dente with the natural fragrance of Quercus leaves.

(By: Zhao Guihua)

二、沿海美食 II. Coastal Foods

9. 抚宁白腐乳 Funing White Fermented Bean Curd[1]

抚宁白腐乳是产自秦皇岛市抚宁区的传统民间美食。2013 年，抚宁白腐乳制作技艺入选河北省级非物质文化遗产名录。

抚宁白腐乳，源自乐亭人左经达。新中国成立初期，他来到抚宁用祖传秘方制作腐乳，逐渐受到当地人欢迎。后来，抚宁陈家腐乳传承人陈福祥与左经达合作，吸取其制作优点，在保持香油白腐乳传统风味的基础上，改进制作方法，原料选用也更加考究。

抚宁白腐乳制作是传统工艺与现代技术的结合。它以优质黄豆为原料，经严格筛选除杂去残，再经浸泡、冲洗、磨煮、滤渣、点浆、压坯、划坯成型。将白坯放入竹笼后喷洒万分之二的毛霉菌种，在 20℃左右的气温下，进行 5 天左右的前期发酵。经显微镜检查无其他杂菌污染，毛坯即可腌渍，加盐量为毛坯的 30%，一层毛坯加盐一层，经 10 天腌渍即成腌坯。正常腌坯色泽黄亮、坚硬，四角方整，由毛霉形成一层表皮，即可装坛、灌汤、贮藏，进行后期发酵，使腐乳成熟，形成独特的色、香、味。

每年春节后，一解冻就开始生产，使发酵的时间赶上三伏天的高温期。

抚宁白腐乳是河北唯一的白方腐乳。它颜色白中微黄，质地细嫩，松软可口，风味独特，不但是下饭佳肴，也是烧汤做菜的好佐料。产品远销京津、山东和东北地区。

（作者：秦学武，赵桂华）

Funing white fermented bean curd is a local food popular in Funing District, Qinhuangdao. In 2013, the traditional technique of Funing white

---

[1] 感谢抚宁区文化馆提供相关资料。
We are thankful to Funing District Cultural Center for providing relevant information.

白腐乳（供图：抚宁区文化馆）
White fermented bean curd (Provided by Funing District Cultural Center)

fermented bean curd making was added to the Intangible Cultural Heritage List of Hebei Province.

Funing white fermented bean curd was created by Zuo Jingda, a native of Laoting. In the early days after the founding of the People's Republic of China, Zhao came to Funing and made fermented bean curd following the secret recipe handed down from his ancestors. The food gradually found favor with the locals. Afterwards, Chen Fuxiang, inheritor of Funing Chen's fermented bean curd, formed a partnership with Zuo Jingda and drew on the advantage of Zuo's bean curd. While retaining the traditional flavor of sesame oiled white fermented bean curd, Chen improved the making methods and was more particular about the choosing of ingredients.

The making of Funing white fermented bean curd is a combination of traditional techniques and modern technology. High-quality soybeans are used as the main ingredient. The beans are sifted through sieves to remove impurities, and then they are soaked, rinsed, grinded and boiled. After the dregs are filtered, the soybean milk is curdled, pressed and cut into cubes. The raw bean curd cubes are placed in a bamboo basket and sprayed with mucor at a concentration of 2:10,000. The pre-fermentation lasts about 5 days at 20 ℃. Then, the raw bean curd cubes are examined microscopically to avoid living contaminants before being pickled for 10 days, and the amount of salt added should be 30% of the weight of the bean curd, with bean curd and salt alternately layered. Under normal conditions, the pickled bean curd should be bright yellow, hard and square, and covered with a layer formed by mucor. After that, it is placed in jars, poured with brine and stored, entering the second stage of fermentation. When the bean curd is fully fermented, it features a unique color, smell and taste.

The production of white fermented bean curd begins every year after the spring thaw. In this way, the fermentation will happen right in the hottest days in summer.

Funing white fermented bean curd is the only kind of white fermented bean curd in Hebei. With a yellowish white color, it is tender, soft and delicious, serving both as a great appetizer and as a good seasoning for soups and dishes. Besides Hebei, it is also sold in Beijing, Tianjin, Shandong and Northeast China.

(By: Qin Xuewu and Zhao Guihua)

10. 刘美烧鸡 Liumei Roast Chicken

刘美烧鸡产于河北省乐亭县，是享誉百年的"唐山名食"，也是中国北方的一道名吃。2007 年，刘美烧鸡手工制作技艺入选河北省级非物质文化遗产名录。2019 年，刘美烧鸡入选河北省第三批"燕赵老字号"。

刘美烧鸡手工制作技艺的创始人刘俊，在继承祖传 200 多年的卤煮肉的基础上，经过潜心钻研，彻底改变传统烧鸡外形不雅的难题，开创了中国烧鸡整形之先河，并因此成名。2002 年 2 月，刘美烧鸡获国家知识产权局外观设计专利（CN3225202）。

据《乐亭县志》记载，1897 年，由乐亭县渔村李各庄迁至县城南关的刘俊与其祖父刘崇开始经营"刘记烧鸡铺"。1905年，光绪帝身边的二品带刀侍卫刘坦返乡省亲，品尝到刘记烧鸡后，甚感色、香、味好，只是外形看着不雅。经过潜心钻研，刘俊把白条鸡的一只翅膀从鸡脖刀口处穿入，从鸡嘴穿出，使鸡头与鸡脖随鸡翅紧贴于鸡背侧面，另一鸡翅自然折伏，再将鸡爪蜷曲折入腹腔，成形后再放入祖传老汤的锅内，加入28味名贵中草药。煮熏出来的烧鸡，摆在那里，竟如裸鸡卧睡。1906年秋，已任慈禧太后随身侍卫的刘坦再次返乡，带上几十只烧鸡回到北京。慈禧品尝后赞曰："天下烧鸡，刘美第一。"

刘美烧鸡选料为家常鸡，肉质优良。其做工精细，配料考究，鸡形美观，味香而不腻，肉烂而不脱骨，达到了色、香、味、形的统一。产品远销北京、天津、河北、福建、山东、甘肃、山西、河南、内蒙古、辽宁、吉林、黑龙江等18个省、市、自治区。

（作者：秦学武，赵桂华）

Originating in Laoting County, Hebei Province, the Liumei roast chicken is a famous food in Tangshan and North China with a century-long reputation. In 2007, the traditional technique of Liumei roast chicken making was added to the Intangible Cultural Heritage List of Hebei Province. In 2019, it was added to the third batch of "Yanzhao Time-honored Brands" of Hebei Province.

Liu Jun was the creator of the technique of Liumei roast chicken making. Inheriting the 200-year-old recipe of stewed meat making, he applied his mind to improving the appearance of roast chickens. He was the first to adjust the shape of chickens and became famous because of that. In February 2002, the Liumei roast chicken received an appearance design patent (CN3225202) granted by the China National Intellectual Property Administration.

According to *Local Records of Laoting County*, in 1897, Liu Jun and his grandfather Liu Chong moved from Ligezhuang, a fishing village in Laoting County, to the south of the county seat. There, they started the

Liu's Roast Chicken Shop. On his way home to see his parents in 1905, Liu Tan, a second-grade armed bodyguard of Emperor Guangxu, chanced to savor the roast chicken. He found that the chicken was excellent

刘美烧鸡（摄影：刘江涛）
Liumei roast chicken (Photographed by Liu Jiangtao)

in color, aroma and taste, but not elegant in shape. In an effort to make the chicken look beautiful, Liu Jun ran a wing of the chicken through the opened throat to the beak. In this way, the head and neck were laid on the side of the chicken. Meanwhile, the other wing was folded naturally, and the chicken claws were curled and stuffed into the abdominal cavity. When it took shape, the chicken was put into a pot of rich soup added with 28 rare medicinal herbs following a secret recipe. When it was served, the chicken was lying on the plate as if sleeping. In the autumn of 1906, Liu Tan, then the bodyguard of Empress Dowager Cixi, went home again and brought dozens of roast chickens back to Beijing. Cixi lavished her praise on the food: "The Liumei roast chicken is No.1 throughout the land."

Domestic chickens with fine quality are used to make the dish, which requires exquisite skills and specific ingredients. With a beautiful shape, the chicken is delicious but not greasy, and its meat is soft but not off the bone. The dish is attractive to the eye and appetizing to the taste. It is sold in 18 provinces, municipalities and autonomous regions, such as Beijing, Tianjin, Hebei, Fujian, Shandong, Gansu, Shanxi, Henan, Inner Mongolia, Liaoning, Jilin and Heilongjiang.

(By: Qin Xuewu and Zhao Guihua)

11. 吊桥缸炉烧饼 Diaoqiao Vat-baked Flatbread

吊桥缸炉烧饼是冀东四大名吃之一，系烤制的饼类面食。2012 年，吊桥缸炉烧饼被列入"中华老字号"会员单位。2013 年，吊桥缸炉烧饼传统制作技艺入选河北省级非物质文化遗产名录。2020 年，吊桥缸炉烧饼入选河北省第六批"燕赵老字号"。

吊桥缸炉烧饼（摄影：刘江涛）
Diaoqiao vat-baked flatbreads (Photographed by Liu Jiangtao)

缸炉烧饼始创于 1865 年。当时，乐亭县城北街有一位叫石老化的面食师傅，经营包子、饺子等。为更好利用做包子剩下的肥肉和白菜帮，他制馅做烧饼，放在吊炉烤制。因其味美价廉，十分畅销。之后，他不断增添肉馅，改进调料，特别是用缸炉取代吊炉，烤制出来的烧饼火头匀、颜色焦黄、外酥里嫩。20 世纪 30、40 年代，缸炉烧饼以乐亭东街左家烧饼铺最佳，因那里称吊桥，故称"吊桥缸炉烧饼"。

缸炉烧饼的灶具为一口大缸，平卧在砖砌的灶台上。面为上等小麦粉和精纯豆油。面粉和植物油调成糊状，俗称"制酥"。馅为肥猪肉、白菜切丁，加葱、姜、酱油、精盐、香油、五香面等佐料，搅拌均匀即成。包制后沾满略炒的芝麻仁，入缸烤制。

乐亭缸炉烧饼制作，要掌握包功和烤功。包功，即把醒好的面擀片，擦酥，卷成卷，揪成剂子；将剂子擀成片，包入肉馅。烤功，是指烤制烧饼时对火候的掌控技术。火大了，烧饼会烤煳；火小了，烧饼贴不住，还会夹生。掌握温度，全凭经验看炉色。以缸横卧、内壁贴饼、外温内烘是其独特的制作方法。

烤熟的烧饼呈圆形，皮焦黄酥脆，馅香而不腻。由于用果木炭烤

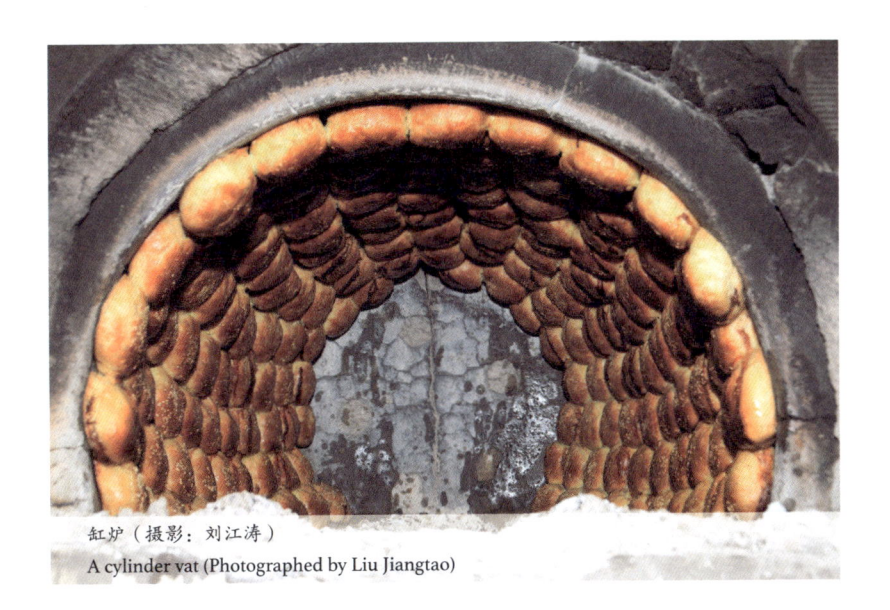

缸炉（摄影：刘江涛）
A cylinder vat (Photographed by Liu Jiangtao)

制，烧饼有独特的果香味。缸炉烧饼是烧烤、涮锅的佐餐佳品，享誉冀东、京津、东北一带。

（作者：秦学武，赵桂华）

The Diaoqiao vat-baked flatbread, one of the four famous foods in Jidong, is a kind of baked wheaten food. In 2012, it became a "China Time-honored Brand". In 2013, the technique of Diaoqiao vat-baked flatbread making was added to the Intangible Cultural Heritage List of Hebei Province. In 2020, it was added to the sixth batch of "Yanzhao Time-honored Brands" of Hebei Province.

The vat-baked flatbread was created in 1865. On the North Street of Laoting County, there was a cook named Shi Laohua who sold steamed stuffed buns and dumplings. He stuffed the leftover fat pork and cabbage after making buns into flatbreads and put them in the hanging oven for baking. The delicious flatbreads at an affordable price were sold very quickly. Afterwards, the filling and seasonings were constantly improved, and the hanging oven was replaced by a cylinder oven. Fresh from the oven, the light brown flatbreads were crisp and tasty. In the 1930s and 1940s, Zuo's Flatbread Shop located at Diaoqiao on the East Street of Laoting County made the best vat-baked flatbreads, thus the food got its name.

The cookware for making vat-baked flatbreads is a large cylinder vat lying on the brick-paved platform. The dough is made of high-quality wheat flour and pure soybean oil, which are rubbed together in the "paste making" process. The filling consists of diced fat pork and cabbage seasoned with chopped scallion and ginger, soy sauce, refined salt, sesame oil, and multi-spice powder, all of which are mixed evenly. When the flatbreads are prepared ready, they are covered with lightly fried sesame seeds before being baked in the vat.

The making of Laoting vat-baked flatbreads requires wrapping and baking skills. The dough should be rolled evenly, brushed with oil, wrapped up and divided into small balls, which are then flattened and stuffed with the filling. The baking of flatbreads requires precise control of heat. If the fire is too strong, the flatbreads would be overburnt. If the fire is too weak, the flatbreads would be undercooked. The control of heat depends on the judgment of the cook. The horizontally placed vat, the flatbreads being put on the inner surface, and the two-sided baking process are key to the making of flatbreads.

When it is served, a round flatbread is golden and crispy, and its filling is delicious but not greasy. The flatbreads have a unique fruit aroma as they are baked with fruitwood charcoal. The food goes perfectly with barbecues and hot pot. It is popular in Jidong, Beijing, Tianjin and Northeast China.

(By: Qin Xuewu and Zhao Guihua)

12. 唐山蜂蜜麻糖 Tangshan Honey Sesame Candy

蜂蜜麻糖是传统风味食品，是闻名中外的唐山特产。1999年，"蜂王牌"蜂蜜麻糖被授予"中华老字号"。2009年，唐山丰润区和新新麻糖厂的"蜂蜜麻糖制作技艺"入选河北省级非物质文化遗产名录。2019年，唐山蜂蜜麻糖入选河北省"燕赵老字号"。

蜂蜜麻糖（供图：付小芳）
Honey sesame candy (Provided by Fu Xiaofang)

（1）历史渊源

唐山蜂蜜麻糖始创于明万历四年(1576)。一户张姓人家从河北深县逃荒到丰润县，在七树庄定居。他依靠祖传手艺，制作糕点，研制出蜂蜜麻糖。民国时期，张家传人之一张凤舞创立"广盛号"。现在，第十七代传人张国荣继承祖业，创立公司。

1931年，唐山新新麻糖公司成立。1935年，"广盛号"蜂蜜麻糖技艺传入唐山。20世纪60年代，袁广义将"广盛号"麻糖技艺传给女弟子董淑媛。1986年，唐山市重建新新麻糖厂。

唐山蜂蜜麻糖现有很多分支品牌，以"广盛号"历史最悠久。

（2）工艺传承

唐山蜂蜜麻糖是由冀东一带的节日食品"排叉"演变而来。油炸"排叉"硬而脆，蜜汁"排叉"软而皮。"广盛号"融合这两种排叉的做法，借鉴京城糕点"蜜供"的浇浆法，研制出风味名吃——蜂蜜麻糖。被誉为"麻糖第一家"。

新新麻糖厂引进"广盛号"制作技艺，形成一整套独特的工艺流程，被誉为"麻糖大王"。

（3）食品特色

蜂蜜麻糖由精面粉、优质白砂糖、纯净蜂蜜、香油、花生油、糖桂花等原料，经一套复杂的传统工艺制作而成。产品形似团花，色泽淡黄、薄如蝉翼、松软酥脆、香甜适口。

唐山蜂蜜麻糖广销河北、北京、天津及东北地区，远销日本和东南亚国家。多次获得省部国家级奖项，受到党和国家领导人及中外宾朋的交口称赞。

（作者：秦学武，赵桂华）

Honey sesame candy is a special food of Tangshan well-known both in China and abroad. In 1999, Queen Bee Honey Sesame Candy was recognized as a "China Time-honored Brand". In 2009, the technique of honey sesame candy making of Tangshan's Fengrun District and Xinxin Sesame Candy Plant was added to the Intangible Cultural Heritage List of Hebei Province. In 2019, Tangshan honey sesame candy was added to the "Yanzhao Time-honored Brands" of Hebei Province.

(1) Historical origin

Tangshan honey sesame candy was created in the 4th year of Wanli of the Ming Dynasty (1576). A Mr. Zhang fled from Shenxian County to Fengrun County in Hebei Province and sought refuge in Qishuzhuang Village. Following the recipes passed down from his ancestors, he earned a living by making sweets and cakes, and developed the honey sesame candy. In the Republic of China era, Zhang Fengwu, a descendant of the Zhang clan, founded Guangshenghao. Today, Zhang Guorong, the seventeenth-generation inheritor, founded a company.

In 1931, Tangshan Xinxin Sesame Candy Company was founded. In 1935, the technique of Guangshenghao's honey sesame candy making was introduced to Tangshan. In the 1960s, Yuang Guangyi passed the technique to his female apprentice Dong Shuyuan. In 1968, Xinxin Sesame Candy Plant was reestablished in Tangshan.

Among the many branches of Tangshan honey sesame candy,

Honey sesame candy (Provided by Fu Xiaofang)

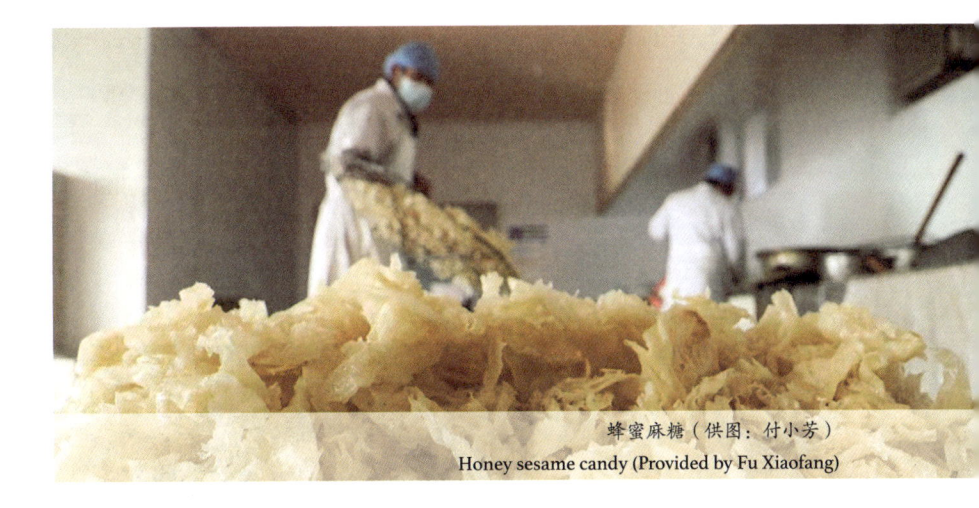

Guangshenghao is the oldest one.

(2) Inheritance of the technique

Tangshan honey sesame candy evolved from *paicha*, a festival food in Jidong. The fried *paicha* is crisp, and the honey *paicha* is soft. By blending the two kinds of *paicha* and drawing on the syrup-pouring method of *migong*, a pastry from Beijing, Guangshenghao developed the unique honey sesame candy. It is known as the "No.1 Sesame Candy Maker".

Xinxin Sesame Candy Plant introduced the traditional technique of Guangshenghao and developed a unique production process. It is renowned as the "King of Sesame Candy".

(3) Characteristics

The ingredients of honey sesame candy are refined flour, high-quality white sugar, pure honey, sesame oil, peanut oil, and sugar osmanthus, which are handled following a complex set of traditional techniques. The food looks like a thin, yellowish ballflower, and tastes crisp and delicious.

Tangshan honey sesame candy is sold in Hebei, Beijing, Tianjin and Northeast China, and even exported to Japan and Southeast Asian countries.

It has won provincial and national awards for many times and received complimentary remarks from the Party and state leaders and other people in China and abroad.

(By: Qin Xuewu and Zhao Guihua)

13. 饹馇 Gezha Pancake[1]

饹馇是冀东一带的特色副食品，也叫粉格子。饹馇的传统做法是先把绿豆破碎，浸泡去皮，加姜黄后用石磨磨成豆浆，然后用尖锅（俗称"煎饼闹子"）摊熟，俗称"摊饹馇"。

焦熘饹馇（摄影：杨立壮）
Fried Gezha (Photographed by Yang Lizhuang)

关于饹馇的名字，据说清王朝在遵化建东陵后，守陵人为讨得皇家欢心，就把这一特产送进皇宫请慈禧品尝。御膳房做了醋熘饹馇，慈禧太后吃了两口，还没吃够，见太监想往下撤，说了句"搁着"。太监以为是太后赐的菜名，马上传令下去："老佛爷赐此菜名为饹馇。"饹馇与"搁着"谐音，从此，饹馇的叫法在民间广为流传。

按制作工具，饹馇分大锅饹馇、尖锅（或平锅）饹馇。前者用普通的铁锅摊制，锅面擦食用油，文火加热，先将绿豆汁用铲刀搅拌至五六成熟，再摊成薄片，加热至熟，又称"熟汁子饹馇"；后者用尖锅摊制，锅面擦食用油，文火加热，将绿豆汁舀到锅上，马上用"拉子"[2]拉平摊薄，加热至熟，又称"生汁子饹馇"。

---

1 参阅：刘向权主编：《滦河文化研究文集》（第一卷），团结出版社 2017 年版。
See: Liu Xiangquan (ed.): *Collected Works on Luan River Culture* (Vol. 1), Unity Press, 2017.

2 竹筷的一端按上光滑的木片，也称"拉耙"。

按浆汁用料，饹馇分三种：过罗饹馇，是指将磨制好的绿豆汁用细密的纱布过滤掉豆渣，做出来的煎饼更加口感细致、劲道、耐熬；混浆饹馇，是指原浆的绿豆汁做出的饹馇；混合饹馇，是指以绿豆为底料，掺入黄豆等其他豆类，磨成浆，再加入姜黄上色。一般是 5 份豆浆、2 份淀粉、3 份面粉进行调和。

饹馇是冀东百姓逢年过节、红白喜事时的必备食物，也是招待宾客的地方美食。民间甚至有"没吃饹馇宴,不算到冀东"的说法。

饹馇宴，是以饹馇作原料进行二次烹饪，煎、炒、熘、炸、烩均可，能做出几十道菜，比如饹馇熬白菜、饹馇千子、烩饹馇、菠菜炒饹馇、醋熘饹馇、焦熘饹馇、糖醋饹馇、饹馇汤等。过去，吃饹馇是解馋；现在，吃饹馇是怀旧，是家乡的味道。

（作者：秦学武，赵桂华）

烩饹馇（供图：迁安市政府办公室）
Stewed Gezha (Provided by the Office of the People's Government of Qian'an City)

The Gezha pancake, aka Fengezi, is a characteristic non-staple food in and around Jidong. In the traditional process, first, the mung beans are smashed, soaked and peeled; then, turmeric is added and bean milk is made with a stone mill; finally, after being fried with a pan (colloquially called "pancake maker"), the food is done.

The Gezha pancake got its name for a reason. Legend has it that when the Eastern Qing Tombs were built, a tomb keeper, to gain the favor of the royal family, carried the food to the palace for Empress Dowager Cixi. The imperial kitchen processed it by adding a dash of vinegar and quick-

饹馇、炸千子（供图：迁安市政府办公室）
Gezha, fried Gezha puff pastry (Provided by the Office of the People's Government of Qian'an City)

frying. When the dish was placed in front of Cixi, she took a few bites but didn't feel full. Seeing that the eunuch was about to clear away the dish, she uttered a word "gezhe", which meant "leave it here". Thinking it was the name given to the dish, the eunuch sent word to the chefs, "Her Majesty called the dish Gezha." Gezha shared a similar pronunciation with Gezhe, and the name became popular among common people.

According to the cooking utensils, Gezha pancakes can be divided into pot-made Gezha and pan-made Gezha. The former is made in an ordinary iron pot. First, brush the pot with edible oil and heat it with a low fire before adding the mung bean milk. Then, stir the bean milk with a spatula until it is parboiled. Finally, flatten and heat it until it is fully cooked. This type is also called Boiled Gezha. The latter is made in a pan. First, brush the pan with edible oil and heat it with a low fire. Then, spoon the mung bean milk on to the pan and immediately flatten it with a "*lazi*"[1]. Finally, heat the food until it is fully cooked. This type is also called Unboiled Gezha.

According to the bean milk used, Gezha pancakes fall under three categories: Filtered Gezha, Unfiltered Gezha, and Mixed Gezha. In making Filtered Gezha, the mung bean milk is filtered with fine gauze to remove the bean dregs, and the fried pancakes have a tender and pliable texture. Unfiltered Gezha, just as its name implies, refers to Gezha made with unfiltered mung bean milk. For Mixed Gezha, the basic mung beans are mixed with soybeans and other beans, grounded into bean milk, and colored with turmeric. Normally, the proportion of bean milk, starch and flour is 5:2:3.

The Gezha pancake is an indispensable food in Jidong in the Spring Festival, other festivals, weddings and funerals. It is also a food with local flavor for entertaining guests. There is a popular saying that goes, "If you haven't tasted the Gezha Banquet, you haven't seen the true Jidong."

Gezha pancakes are used as the main ingredient of the Gezha Banquet, which has dozens of courses made by frying, stir-frying, quick-frying, deep-frying and stewing. There are, for example, cabbage stewed with Gezha, Gezha puff pastry, stewed Gezha, stir-fried Gezha with spinach, quick-fried Gezha with vinegar, crisp Gezha, sweet and sour Gezha, and Gezha soup. In the past, people ate Gezha pancakes to fill their bellies. Today, the food has become a flavor of hometown.

(By: Qin Xuewu and Zhao Guihua)

1　A smooth wood chip attached to the end of a bamboo chopstick, also called "scraper".

14. 赵家馆饺子 Zhaojiaguan Dumpling

赵家馆饺子是盛誉冀东、京津、东北一带的百年老店，也是当地的传统名吃。1999年，赵家馆荣获河北省著名商标企业。2007年，昌黎赵家馆饺子制作技艺入选河北省级非物质文化遗产名录。2011年，赵家馆入选"中华老字号"。

赵家馆饺子（摄影：李静）
Dumplings in Zhaojiaguan (Photographed by Li Jing)

"赵家馆"始创于1921年。创始人赵福元（俗称赵老二），是一代著名的饺子大师。他自幼承担起养家的重担，从事饮食行业，冬卖煮饺、夏卖冷食。是年，清末老秀才高云山为其饺子店题写匾额，定名"赵家馆"。

赵家馆饺子以圆笼蒸饺为主，选料讲究，皮薄馅散，味道鲜美，香而不腻，水灵可口。有海鲜、素馅、肉馅、什锦四大系列，十三类品种，并常年随节令的变化，分别掺拌对虾、蟹肉、虾籽、鱼骨、海参、干贝、鲍鱼、八爪鱼、皮皮虾等各种海味，使饺子具有独特的风味。制作方法为开水烫面，肉馅喂鸡汤，全部手工制作。

20世纪50年代，赵家馆饺子就已蜚声关内外，赵福元多次参加全国性、行业性及省、市、地区的表演和比赛并屡获大奖。在天津参加表演赛时，时任国家主席刘少奇题写牌匾，赞为"京东第一家"。茅盾、廖沫沙、荀慧生、尚小云等知名人士曾品尝过赵家馆饺子并给予高度评价。《人民日报（海外版）》《河北日报》《经济日报》《秦皇岛日报》等都有报道。

赵家馆饺子以其"清香能引洞中仙，美味偏招云外客"的独特魅力，吸引着天南地北的美食家来此品尝。

（作者：赵桂华，秦学武）

Zhaojiaguan Dumpling is a century-old restaurant well-known in Jidong, Beijing, Tianjin and Northeast China, and the namesake food is a famous traditional local food. In 1999, Zhaojiaguan got the Hebei Famous Trademark Certificate. In 2007, the technique of Zhaojiaguan dumpling making was added to the Intangible Cultural Heritage List of Hebei Province. In 2011, Zhaojiaguan was recognized as a "China Time-honored Brand".

Zhaojiaguan was founded in 1921 by Zhao Fuyuan (nicknamed Zhao the Second), a dumpling master of his generation. Taking on the burden of supporting his family from an early age, he opened a small eatery selling dumplings in winter and cold dishes in summer. In 1921, he invited Gao Yunshan, an old scholar in the late Qing Dynasty, to write the words "Zhao Jia Guan" for the board of his eatery.

Dumplings in Zhaojiaguan are steamed in a round steamer. The

在赵家馆包饺子（摄影：赵秋洪）
Making dumplings in Zhaojiaguan (Photographed by Zhao Qiuhong)

ingredients are of very high quality, and while the fillings are properly steamed, the wrappers would not collapse. When they are served, the white and shiny dumplings are delicious but not greasy. There are four types of fillings—seafood, vegetable, meat and assorted, with 13 varieties changing according to the seasons. Marine products, such as prawn, crab, shrimp roe, fish bone, sea cucumber, scallop, abalone, octopus and mantis shrimp, are added to the fillings, intensifying the flavor of the dumplings. The dumplings are all handmade, featuring dough kneaded with boiled water and fillings infused with chicken soup.

In the 1950s, Zhaojiaguan Dumpling was already widely renowned. Zhao Fuyuan had triumphed in many industrial performances and competitions at national, provincial, municipal and regional levels. During an exhibition match in Tianjin, Liu Shaoqi, then President of China, personally wrote the words "Jing Dong Di Yi Jia" (literally No. 1 Restaurant to the East of the Capital) for an inscribed board. High-profile individuals such as Mao Dun, Liao Mosha, Xun Huisheng and Shang Xiaoyun had savored the dumplings and spoke highly of the food. *People's Daily (Overseas Edition)*, *Hebei Daily*, *Economic Daily* and *Qinhuangdao Daily* had all published articles about it.

As a Chinese proverb says: "The immortals in the cave can't resist its temptation with that aroma in the air." The unique flavor of dumplings in Zhaojiaguan is appealing to the most discerning gourmets from across the country.

(By: Zhao Guihua and Qin Xuewu)

15. 应季海鲜 Seasonal Seafoods

唐山、秦皇岛位于渤海湾西岸，附近海域及沿岸滩涂盛产鱼、虾、蟹、贝等百余种海鲜。随着四季时令更替，到海边吃应季海鲜，是当地居民和外地游客的美食首选。

二月底三月初，雪虾上市。它通体雪白，大小犹如虾皮儿，只有约20天的捕捞期。本地人用雪虾与鸡蛋或韭菜一起烹炒，味道鲜美。

三月，冷水板（高眼鲽鱼）、小黄鱼（小黄花鱼）上市。冷水板体侧扁，呈长圆形，鳞细小。此时的冷水板，鱼子金黄板结，越嚼越香。或清蒸，或红烧，出锅就是飘香的美味。小黄鱼冬季在深海越冬，春季向沿岸洄游。其肉质细腻，呈蒜瓣状，味道鲜美，可干炸、红烧或家常炖等。

三月底四月初，面条鱼上市。它是一种白色的小鱼，比小拇指略细，捕捞期为半个月左右。多与豆腐、鸡蛋搭配烹炒或做汤，鲜美无比。

四月初，皮皮虾上市。皮皮虾俗称"虾爬子"，是本地主要海鲜食材。其特点是形体长壮，呈浅青色。此时的皮皮虾味道鲜美，清蒸、辣炒、椒盐、蒜香、涮锅均宜，尤以满籽儿的母皮皮虾最好吃。还可包皮皮虾肉饺子、做皮皮虾鲜肉馄饨等。

四月下旬，螃蟹上市。本地蟹有花盖蟹和红夹子蟹两种。花盖蟹，体小但肉质发甜，膏肥黄满；红夹子蟹个大，大红夹子是其招牌。螃蟹以清蒸为佳，蘸着醋汁，更加鲜美。

五月和六月，鲅鱼、鳎目鱼、海蛎子、毛蚶子、生蚝、蛏子、海虹、花蛤、黄蛤、海肚脐（猫眼螺）、海螺、八爪鱼（章鱼）等纷纷上市。或清蒸，或水煮，或家常炖，或辣炒，或涮锅，吃法多多。可做出鲅鱼饺子、毛蚶子大馅饺子、辣炒花蛤、碳烤生蚝、八爪鱼炖肉等美食。

七八月为禁渔期。养殖的基围虾开始上市。基围虾以壳薄、体肥、肉嫩、味美而著称，白灼基围虾、干锅基围虾、香辣基围虾、椒盐基围虾、油爆基围虾等都是上乘美味。

秋天是近海捕捞大虾的时节。清水煮大虾是最通行的吃法，还可加工成水饺以及油焖大虾、烤大虾、糖酥大虾、盐焗虾、腰果虾仁、水晶虾球、土豆虾球、茄汁开背大虾、青笋炒虾仁、虾仁蒸蛋、南瓜

红夹子蟹、花盖蟹、皮皮虾、生蚝、蛏子（摄影：张兵）
Red-pincer crab, flower-covered crab, mantis shrimp, oyster, razor clam (Photographed by Zhang Bing)

虾仁炒饭等多种菜肴。

中秋节前后，是吃海蟹的最佳时节。海蟹肉肥膏满，或清蒸，或辣炒，美味难得。

九月至十一月，鲅鱼最常见。因为鱼身刺少，本地人常做成鱼丸或饺子馅，还可家常炖。

当地民谚云："一鲆二镜三鳎目。"是指排在前三位的鱼。此时，鲆鱼、镜鱼、鳎目鱼、偏口鱼、多宝鱼等鱼类，都值得品尝。

十一月和十二月，扇贝上市。它味道鲜美，营养丰富，与海参、鲍鱼齐名。蒜蓉扇贝、清蒸扇贝，是最地道的当地吃法。

（作者：赵桂华）

Tangshan and Qinhuangdao are located to the west of the Bohai Bay. The sea areas and coastal beaches offer more than 100 kinds of seafoods, such as fish, shrimps, crabs and shellfish, through the varying seasons of the year. Seasonal seafoods are the must-haves of local residents and tourists.

In late February and early March, snow shrimps come into the market. With snowy white bodies, they are as big as the dried small shrimps. The fishing period lasts only about 20 days. The locals fry the snow shrimps with eggs or leeks, and the dish is deliciously refreshing.

In March, cold-water flatfish (*Cleisthenes herzensteini*) and little yellow croakers (*Larimichthys polyactis*) come into the market. A cold-water flatfish is flat, oblong and fine-scaled, and its golden roes are delicious. Fresh from the pot, the aroma of steamed or braised fish rises up in the air. Little yellow croakers spend winter in the deep sea and swim back to the coastal areas in spring. The fish in the shape of a garlic clove are fresh and delicate, and they can be fried, braised or stewed.

In late March and early April, noodle fish (*Ammodytes personatus*) come into the market. It is a small white fish slightly thinner than the little finger. The fishing period lasts about half a month. As an exceptional delicacy, they are usually cooked with bean curd or eggs or made into soup.

In early April, mantis shrimps, a major local seafood of finest quality at this time of the year, come into the market. The light blue shrimps are long and strong, and they can be steamed, stir-fried, baked with pepper, salt or garlic, or put directly into the hot pot. The roe-carrying female mantis shrimp tastes best. Besides, mantis shrimps can also be used as the filling of dumplings and wontons.

In late April, crabs come to the market. There are two types of local crabs: flower-covered crab and red-pincer crab. The former is small but tasty, often carrying plenty of roes, while the latter is large with two big pincers. A crab is best served by steaming, and a dash of vinegar can add a mellow flavor to it.

In May and June, the market is full of seafoods, such as seerfish (Spanish mackerel), tonguefish, clam, oyster, razor clam, mussel, flower clam, yellow clam, sea navel (tapestry turban), conch and octopus. These seafoods can be steamed, boiled, stewed, stir-fired or put into the hot pot. The cooks are also inspired to make mackerel dumplings, clam dumplings, spicy stir-fried clams, grilled oysters, and stewed meat and octopus.

In the closed fishing period in July and August, farm-raised shrimps, with thin shell, fat body, tender flesh and delicious taste, come into the market. Boiled shrimps, griddled shrimps, spicy shrimps, pepper and salt shrimps, and quick-fried shrimps are all very delicious.

In autumn, the fishermen go to catch prawns. The prawns are tasty enough after simply being boiled. Besides, there are prawn dumplings, braised prawns, baked prawns, sweet crisp prawns, salt-baked prawns, fried prawns with cashew nuts, prawn balls, prawn and potato balls, open-back prawns in tomato sauce, fried prawns with green bamboo shoots, steamed egg custard with prawns, and stir-fried rice with pumpkin and prawns.

The period around the Mid-autumn Festival is the best time to taste sea crabs. The fat sea crabs can be either steamed or stir-fried.

From September to November, Spanish mackerels are commonly seen in the market. The fish with very few small bones are usually made into fish balls or dumpling filling. Stewed mackerel is also a popular home-made dish.

As a local proverb says, "flounder first, slivery pomfret second, and tonguefish third." Beyond them, olive flounder and turbot are also tasty.

In November and December, scallops come to the market. As famous as the sea cucumber and the abalone, the food tastes delicious and is highly nutritious. Scallops with minced garlic and steamed scallops are traditional recipes adored by the natives.

(By: Zhao Guihua)

第六章

冀东文学

Chapter VI Jidong Literature

一、明清文苑 I. Literary World of the Ming and Qing Dynasties

1. 谷应泰 Gu Yingtai

谷应泰 (1620—1690)，字赓虞，号霖苍，直隶丰润 (今河北丰润) 人。清代历史学家，被称为"清代文苑第一人"。做过户部主事、员外郎、学政佥事等官职。

青少年时期，谷应泰在丰润县学读书，便已显示过人才华。明崇祯十三年（1640），中举人。清顺治四年（1647），中进士。1656 年，在杭州延揽张岱、陆圻、徐倬等学者编撰《明史纪事本末》，1658 年末撰成并刊行。

《明史纪事本末》以时间为序，记载了自 1352 年朱元璋起兵到 1644 年李自成攻克北京近三百年间的历史。不同于传统的编年、纪传体史书，《明史纪事本末》采用纪事本末体。全书仿照南宋袁枢《通鉴纪事本末》的体例，分 80 个专题，每题为 1 卷，共 80 卷。谷应泰广集明代资料，博采众长，记述了自认为重要的历史事件的始末。民国时期，《明史纪事本末》便被列为"国学基本丛书"，至今仍是明史研究的重要文献。

谷应泰编撰《明史纪事本末》的目的是"使读者审理乱之大趋，迹政治之得失"。故该书对明末农民大起义叙述得十分详尽，记录了大量统治者残酷剥削与被压迫者奋起抗争的珍贵史料。每卷末尾附"谷应泰曰"，是他对该卷所记史事的评论，反映了谷应泰以官吏身份为清朝统治提供经验教训的立场。《四库全书总目提要》评曰："其排比篡次，详略得中，首尾秩然，于一代事实，极为淹贯，每篇后各附论断，皆仿《晋书》之体，以骈偶行文，而遣词抑扬，隶事亲切，尤为曲折详尽。"

谷应泰还著有《筑益堂诗集》，后散佚，仅有少量诗作存世。

（作者：李文钢）

Gu Yingtai (1620–1690), his courtesy name Geng Yu and his literary name Lin Cang, was a native of Fengrun, Zhili (today's Fengrun, Hebei). As a historian of the Qing Dynasty, he was called the "First Man in the Literary Circles of Qing". He had been Director of Ministry of Revenue, Ministry Councilor, and Supervisor of Academic Affairs.

Gu showed exceptional talent as a youth when he studied in the county school. In the 13th year of Chongzhen of the Ming Dynasty (1640), he passed the imperial examination. In the 4th year of Shunzhi of the Qing Dynasty (1647), he became a successful candidate at the metropolitan examination. In 1656, he commissioned scholars Zhang Dai, Lu Qi and Xu Zhuo in Hangzhou to compile the *Chronicle of the Ins and Outs of the Ming History*. The book was published at the end of 1658.

Chronicle of the Ins and Outs of the Ming History, in a chronological format, tells the history of nearly 300 years from Zhu Yuanzhang's declaring war in 1352 to Li Zicheng's taking Beijing in 1644. Unlike the traditional chronological or biographical historical books, it presents the history in separate accounts of important events. Adopting the style of *Chronicle of Events in History as a Mirror* by Yuan Shu of the Southern Song Dynasty, the book breaks down into 80 volumes, each focusing on a specific topic. Gu Yingtai collected many materials of the Ming Dynasty and fused them into the narration of historical events he considered important. In the Republic of China era, *Chronicle of the Ins and Outs of the Ming History* was counted among the "Rudimentary Books of Chinese Study". Today, it is still an important material for studying the history of the Ming Dynasty.

The purpose of *Chronicle of the Ins and Outs of the Ming History* is "for readers to take an in-depth look at history and politics". The Peasant Uprisings at the end of the Ming dynasty are elaborated in the book. As a valuable window on history, it has described the cruelness of the rulers and the resistance of the oppressed people. At the end of each volume is appended "Gu Yingtai says"—Gu's comments on the historical events. They reflect the stance of the author as an official to provide lessons for the rulers of the Qing Dynasty. Here's what *Summary of the General Catalogue of the Complete Library of the Four Branches of Literature* says: "The materials are put together in good order, with relatively important events described in more detail. They give a holistic insight into the history. At the end of each volume is appended the comments written in rhythmic prose after the style of *The History of the Jin Dynasty*. With an emphasis on wording and phrasing and an attention to quotations and allusions, the facts have been so plainly stated."

Gu Yingtai also wrote the *Poetry Collection of Zhuyi Hall*, which was lost later with only a few poems surviving today.

(By: Li Wengang)

2. 曹雪芹 Cao Xueqin

曹雪芹（约 1715—约 1763），名霑，字梦阮，号雪芹，祖籍河北丰润[1]，中国古典名著《红楼梦》的作者。

曹雪芹出生于江宁（今江苏南京），是江宁织造曹寅之孙。康熙、雍正时期，曹家三代主政江宁织造 58 年，为当地豪门。曹雪芹早年生活富贵，博览群书，尤爱诗赋、戏文、小说之类的文学书籍。雍正五年（1727）十二月，其父曹頫因罪入狱，次年正月元宵节前被抄家。此后，全家迁居北京，家道日衰。为复兴家族，曹雪芹一度勤奋读书，多方干谒权贵，但因是罪臣之后，困难重重。他便知难而退，专心著书，结合家世兴衰与个人感悟写成《红楼梦》。乾隆二十八年

---

[1] 关于曹雪芹的祖籍，学界有河北丰润说、辽宁辽阳说、辽宁铁岭说，本书采用河北丰润说。

（1763），幼子夭亡，曹雪芹悲伤过度，是年除夕病逝。

曹雪芹写就《红楼梦》的前八十回，八十回以后的手稿佚失。今天通行的一百二十回本，为程伟元、高鹗根据残稿和他人续稿整理而成。清代得舆《京都竹枝词》云："闲谈不说《红楼梦》，读尽诗书是枉然。"道出了《红楼梦》在读者心目中的受欢迎程度。

《红楼梦》以贾宝玉和林黛玉的爱情悲剧为主线，讲述了以贾府为代表的四大家族由盛而衰的故事，塑造了众多性格鲜明、声情毕现的艺术形象——似傻如痴的贾宝玉、心细多疑的林黛玉、圆通平和的薛宝钗、宽容大度的贾母、斩钉截铁的王熙凤、爽直浪漫的史湘云、精明干练的探春、谙于世故的刘姥姥、严正古板的贾政、粗俗霸道的薛蟠、贫嘴滑舌的贾蓉……小说融入了作者悲切凄凉的人生体验，规模宏大，情节生动。

《红楼梦》采用鲜活的北方口语，又融汇传统文言，达成极高的语言成就；它以写实叙事为主，又融入诗化的情韵；它突破了中国传统小说叙事全知全能的模式，在外视角的叙事中嵌入人物的内视角，从而更灵活地展现人物的内心世界，人物形象更加立体。鲁迅《小说史大略》赞曰："至清有《红楼梦》，乃异军突起，驾一切人情小说而远上之，较之前朝，固与《水浒》《西游》为三绝，以一代言，则三百年中创作之冠冕也。"

《红楼梦》是中国古典小说的巅峰之作，在世界文学史上占有重要地位。专门研究《红楼梦》的学问——红学，成为当代学术的显学。

（作者：李文钢）

Cao Zhan (ca. 1715–1763), his courtesy name Mengruan and his literary name Xueqin, was a writer whose ancestral home was in Fengrun[1], Hebei. He wrote *Dream of the Red Chamber*, a classical Chinese novel.

1　Opinions are divided over the ancestral home of Cao Xueqin, which is believed by scholars to be in Fengrun of Hebei, Liaoyang of Liaoning or Tieling of Liaoning. This book accepts the theory that his ancestral home was in Fengrun, Hebei.

曹雪芹雕像（摄影：付小芳）
Statue of Cao Xueqin (Photographed by Fu Xiaofang)

Born in Jiangning (today's Nanjing, Jiangsu), Cao Xueqin was the grandson of Cao Yin, head of the Jiangning Weaving Bureau. During the reigns of Kangxi and Yongzheng, as a noble family in the local community, the Cao family had supervised the Jiangning Weaving Bureau for three generations over 58 years. In his early life, Cao Xueqin led an affluent life. He was well-read and particularly fond of literary books such as poems, dramas and novels. In the 12th month of the 5th year of Yongzheng (1727), his father Cao Fu was thrown into prison, and the family's property was confiscated before the Lantern Festival in the first month of the following year. Then, the whole family moved to Beijing and began to decline. To bring honor and glory back to his family, Cao Xueqin studied hard and tried to establish connections with powerful people, but there were difficulties because he was the son of a guilty official. Cao shrank back before the difficulties and applied his mind to writing. Based on the ups and downs of his life and his sensibility, *Dream of the Red Chamber* was written. In the 28th year of Qianlong (1763), Cao Xueqin's young son died. Prostrate with grief, he died after an illness on the last day of the same year.

The first 80 chapters of *Dream of the Red Chamber* were composed by Cao Xueqin, while the manuscript after the 80th chapter had been lost. The 120-chapter book we read today was compiled by Cheng Weiyuan and Gao E based on the incomplete manuscript and sequels by others. Here's what *Folk Romantic Songs in the Capital* by De Yu of the Qing Dynasty says: "Trying to be a wordsmith without reading *Dream of the Red Chamber* will prove to be futile." The popularity of *Dream of the Red Chamber* among readers was captured by the sentence.

The love tragedy of Jia Baoyu and Lin Daiyu is a consistent thread running through *Dream of the Red Chamber*. The book focuses on the rise and decline of the four big families represented by the Jia family. It has shaped many characters with strong personalities and rich emotions—Jia Baoyu for his seeming idiocy, Lin Daiyu for her skeptical disposition, Xue Baochai for her gentle demeanor, Grandmother Jia for her generousness, Wang Xifeng for her resolute attitude, Shi Xiangyun for her straightforwardness, Tanchun for her wits and abilities, Grannie Liu for her sophistication, Jia Zheng for his sternness, Xue Pan for his vulgarity and cruelness, Jia Rong for his artful speeches…The hefty novel mirrors the miserable life of its author in a dramatic and vivid account.

Dream of the Red Chamber, combining the vibrant colloquial language of the north with the traditional classical Chinese, is a great achievement in terms of linguistic art. Principally a realistic novel, it also integrates the element of poetry. As a breakthrough from the traditional mode of narrative fiction featuring omniscience and omnipotence, it embeds the internal perspective of characters into the narrative from an external perspective, allowing the book to more flexibly capture the innermost thoughts of the characters and make them incredibly lifelike. Lu Xun gave complimentary remarks on the book in *A Brief History of Fiction*: "In the Qing Dynasty,

Dream of the Red Chamber sprang up above all romance novels. Compared with the works of the previous Ming Dynasty, it could be juxtaposed with *Outlaws of the Marsh* and *Journey to the West* as the Three Great Classical Novels. In the three hundred years of the Qing Dynasty alone, it was the most beautiful pearl in the literary crown."

As the acme of classical Chinese novels, *Dream of the Red Chamber* occupies an important position in the history of world literature. Redology, which is devoted to studying *Dream of the Red Chamber*, has drawn much attention of the modern academic circle.

(By: Li Wengang)

3. 史梦兰 Shi Menglan

史梦兰（1813—1899），字香崖，号砚农，晚清著名学者，编撰有《永平府志》等著作，慈禧称其为"京东第一人"，亦有"直隶一人"的美誉。

明万历年间，史氏祖辈由江阴迁居直隶乐亭。嘉庆十八年（1813），史梦兰在乐亭西南乡大港村出生。半岁时丧父，在母亲和祖父的教育下成长。道光二十年（1840），中举人。后多次参加会试，均落第。道光三十年（1850），他以举人身份被派任山东朝城知县，以母亲年迈为由未就，遂绝意仕途，潜心学术。咸丰十年（1860），英法联军犯京。史梦兰招募乡勇团练保卫家乡，后获奖五品官衔。他在碣石山购田百亩，修建"止园"别墅，藏书4万余卷，以著述自娱，并与曾国藩、李鸿章、吴汝纶等往来密切。光绪十七年（1891），因其才学、人品卓异，获加四品卿衔。光绪二十三年（1897），又获加国子监祭酒衔。

史梦兰一生著作甚多，大多关乎世道人心，希冀产生现实功用。除为光绪《永平府志》《乐亭县志》《抚宁县志》总纂编外，还著有《全史宫词》《永平诗存》《止园诗话》《止园笔谈》《叠雅》《异号类编》《图书便览》《舆地韵编》《史肪》《氏族考异》《古今风谣拾遗》等40

多种。其中，《叠雅》《抚宁县志》《尔尔书屋诗草》《尔尔书屋文钞》《止园笔谈》收录于《续修四库全书》，《全史宫词》收录于《四库未收书辑刊》。

  史梦兰的诗作《尔尔书屋诗草》八卷，突显了关怀现实的人文精神，以及重义轻利的人生态度，恰如《旐言》所言："名如画饼充饥，利似望梅止渴。早谙过眼空花，何待当头棒喝？"诗集中的《登澄海楼》，盛赞了云霞之下山海关澄海楼的壮观、宏伟。

（作者：李文钢）

Shi Menglan (1813–1899), his courtesy name Xiangyan and his literary name Yannong, was a distinguished scholar in the late Qing Dynasty. As the author of *Local Records of Yongping Prefecture*, Shi was praised by Empress Dowager Cixi as the "First Man to the east of the Capital". He also enjoyed a reputation for being the "First Man of Hebei".

During the reign of Wanli of the Ming Dynasty, the ancestors of Shi clan came from Jiangyin to Laoting in Hebei Province. In the 18th year of Jiaqing (1813), Shi Menglan was born into a family in Dagang Village, Xi'nan Township, Laoting. Shi's father died when he was barely six months old, and he was brought up by his mother and grandfather. In the 20th year of Daoguang (1840), he became a candidate at the metropolitan examination (*juren*) but did not make the list after several attempts. In the 30th year of Daoguang (1850), he was appointed county magistrate of Chaocheng, Shandong while still being a *juren*. To look after his old mother, he declined the offer and devoted himself to academic study. In the 10th year of Xianfeng (1860), the Anglo-French Allied Forces invaded Beijing. Shi Menglan recruited a militia to defend the hometown. Later, he was granted the title of a fifth-grade official. In the Jieshi Mountain, he bought a hundred acres of land and built the "Stay Garden". The villa, where Shi entertained himself with writing, housed more than 40,000 volumes of books. He was personally acquainted with Zeng Guofan, Li Hongzhang and Wu Rulun. In the 17th year of Guangxu (1891), Shi Menglan was promoted to a fourth-grade official for his profound learning and uprightness. In the 23rd year of Guangxu (1897), he was awarded the title of Chief of the Imperial Academy.

In his life, Shi Menglan had many works to his credit, most of which were associated with the way of the world with realistic significance. In addition to compiling *Local Records of Yongping Prefecture*, *Local Records of Laoting County*, and *Local Records of Funing County* during the reign of Guangxu, he also composed more than 40 books, such as *Palace Poems on the Whole History*, *Poems of Yongping*, *Remarks on Poetry in Stay Garden*, *Essays in Stay Garden*, *Elegant Reduplication*, *List of Names*, *Brief Guide of Books*, *Rhymed Compilation of the Land*, *History on the Paper*, *A Study of Clans*, and *Folk Rhymes from Ancient to Modern Times*. Among them, *Elegant Reduplication*, *Local Records of Funing County*, *Collection of Poems in Erer Study*, *Literary Trifles in Erer Study*, and *Essays in Stay Garden* were included in the *Continuation of the Four Branches of Literature*, while *Palace Poems on the Whole History* was included in the *Collection of Uncollected Books under the Four Branches of Literature*.

The eight volumes of *Collection of Poems in Erer Study* epitomize the realistic humanity spirit and underline the righteous attitude to life of Shi Menglan. As "Superfluous Words" says, "Fame is like drawing cakes to appease hunger, and profit is like quenching thirst by looking at plums. If you had seen through the illusion, life couldn't have taken you head-on." The collection also features the poem "Ascending the Chenghai Tower", which marvels at the Chenghai Tower for being a fine, imposing place under the slanting sunbeams.

(By: Li Wengang)

4. 张佩纶 Zhang Peilun

张佩纶（1848—1903），字幼樵，又字绳庵，号篑斋，祖籍河北丰润齐家坨，晚清名臣李鸿章之婿，近代才女张爱玲之祖父。

张佩纶清同治九年（1870）中举人，次年中进士。同治十三年（1874）授职编修，光绪元年（1875）擢为侍讲，次年兼任日讲起居注官。他慷慨好论天下大事，主张"外御列强，内整政纲"，与黄体芳、张之洞、宝延合称"翰林四谏"。光绪五年至七年（1879—1881），张佩纶入李鸿章幕府，在天津参议海防事务。光绪八年(1882)，被委任左副都御史一职，次年补授翰林院侍讲学士。

中法战争爆发后，他多次上奏主战，并受命以三品卿衔办理福建海疆事宜，兼任船政大臣。1884 年 7 月 15 日，法军舰入侵马尾港，8 月 23 日福建水师覆灭，马尾船厂被毁。张佩纶因此获罪，被遣往察哈尔充军。1888 年获释后，他复入天津李鸿章幕府，并娶其女李菊耦为第三任妻子。中日甲午战争期间，因"干预公事"之罪被弹劾并逐回原籍。

张佩纶学问渊博，藏书丰富，编有藏书目录《管斋书目》《丰润张氏书目》。他致力于研究《管子》，著有《管子注》《庄子古义》《涧于集》。

张佩纶的诗歌以苏轼为宗，兼学杜甫、李商隐。他曾为居庸关写有《居庸》一诗："落日黄沙古堠台，清时词客几人来？八陉列成风云阔，重驿通商锁钥开。暮兽晓禽催旅梦，长枪大戟论边才。从今咫尺天都远，疲马当关首屡回。"表现了他内心的无限悲凉之感，体现了豪壮与凄婉兼具的美学特征。

（作者：李文钢）

Zhang Peilun (1848–1903), his courtesy name Youqiao (or Sheng'an) and his literary name Kuizhai, was a native of Qijiatuo Village, Fengrun, Hebei. He was the son-in-law of Li Hongzhang, a famous official of the late Qing

Dynasty, and the grandfather of Eileen Chang, an accomplished woman in modern times.

Zhang Peilun became a candidate at the metropolitan examination in the 9th year of Tongzhi of the Qing Dynasty (1870), and passed the metropolitan examination in the following year. In the 13th year of Tongzhi (1874), he was assigned the post of Document Compiler. In the 1st year of Guangxu (1875), he was promoted to the position of Imperial Tutor. The following year, he doubled as the Imperial Commentator on History. Known collectively as the "Four Admonitors of the Imperial Academy" with Huang Tifang, Zhang Zhidong and Bao Yan, Zhang liked to discuss affairs of state and argued in favor of "defending the nation against the big powers while tidying up the government from inside". From the 5th to the 7th year of Guangxu (1879–1881), Zhang Peilun entered the office of Li Hongzhang and participated in coastal defense affairs in Tianjin. In the 8th year of Guangxu (1882), he was appointed Deputy Imperial Censor. The following year, he was retroactively recognized as Tutor of the Imperial Academy.

When the Sino-French War broke out, Zhang Peilun appealed repeatedly to go to the front. As a result, he was granted the title of a third-grade official to deal with the affairs in the coastal areas of Fujian while doubling as Minister of Ship Affairs. On July 15, 1884, the naval vessels of France invaded the Mawei Port. On August 23, the Fujian Fleet was annihilated, and the Mawei Shipyard was destroyed. Zhang Peilun was convicted and banished to Chahar. When he was released in 1888, he entered the office of Li Hongzhang again and married Li Juou, Li Hongzhang's daughter, as his third wife. During the Sino-Japanese War of 1894–1895, Zhang Peilun was impeached on the charge of "meddling in official affairs". He was ousted and sent back to the hometown.

Zhang Peilun was an accomplished and profound scholar with a huge collection of books, which were classified in *Bibliography of Guan Study* and *Fengrun Zhang's Bibliography*. He devoted himself to the study of *Guanzi*, with *Notes on Guanzi*, *Ancient Meaning of Zhuangzi*, and *Collection of Works by Zhang Jianyu* to his credit.

Zhang Peilun mainly studied the poems of Su Shi, as well as those of Du Fu and Li Shangyin. He once wrote the poem "Juyong" for the Juyong Pass: "The setting sun glows on the dusty ancient beacon tower, which is little frequented by Qing poets. The eight passages, heavily guarded with clouds rolling, see merchants coming and going. Beasts and birds waken the travelers from their dreams, while soldiers armed with spears and swords are fighting in the border. The hometown is near yet immeasurably distant, and I, on the horseback, look back repeatedly on the tough road." There is a feeling of sadness in the poem, which embodies the aesthetic characteristics of being both heroic and melancholic at the same time.

(By: Li Wengang)

二、现当代作家 II. Contemporary Writers

5. 李尔重 Li Erchong

李尔重（1913—2009），原名李育三，河北丰润人。著有《李尔重文集》《新战争与和平》《赵四小姐》等作品。毛主席称赞他是"我们的作家和才子"。

他出身农家，幼年丧母，祖母养大。1925年，入读丰润车轴山中学。1930年，参加中共地下党组织的"唐山暴动"，失败后被迫逃往外地。曾先后在南京中央政治学校、北平大学农学院、北京大学哲学系、日本仙台帝国大学社会经济专科学习。因参加革命活动，曾三次入狱。1937年参加八路军，亲历抗日战争和解放战争。新中国成立后，先后担任中共武汉市委第二书记、湖北省委常委、中南局党委宣传部长、广东省委常委革委会副主任、海南区党委书记、陕西省委常务书记、河北省委书记兼省长等职。

李尔重在工作之余，勤于文学创作。1983年，他开始创作《新战争与和平》，1993年出版，共八卷500万字。这是一部反映中华民族抵抗日本侵略、争取民族解放的长篇小说。它以时间为经，书写了从"九·一八"东北沦陷到抗战全面胜利的恢宏历史画卷。全书遵循史实，刻画了上至毛泽东、蒋介石，下到普通士兵、农民的众多人物形象。小说长于白描手法，采用大众化语言，以事写人，具有鲜明民族特色，堪称"民族史诗"。

李尔重曾说："我之所以要写这部小说，就是要从本质上再现一下二次世界大战的内涵，使人们有机会重新思考：战争到底是怎么来的，怎样才能消灭战争的根源。"魏巍认为李尔重的写作"体现了中国人民坚韧不拔的品质和共产党员的革命精神"。李先念在《新战争与和平》（第二版）序言中，称其为"社会主义文艺园地里的一朵奇葩"。

2001年，《新战争与和平》获第五届国家图书奖二等奖（一等奖空缺）。

（作者：李文钢）

Li Erchong (1913–2009), originally named Li Yusan, was a native of Fengrun, Hebei. His works include *Collected Works of Li Erchong*, *New War and Peace*, and *The Fourth Daughter of Zhao Family*. Chairman Mao praised him as "a writer and talent of the people".

Li Erchong was born of a peasant family. His mother died when he was a child, and it was his grandmother who had brought him up. In 1925, Li attended Fengrun Chezhoushan Middle School. In 1930, he was involved in the "Tangshan Riot" organized by the Underground Communist Party of China. Upon the loss of the riot, he was forced to flee away. He had studied in

Central School of Governance in Nanjing, School of Agriculture of Peiping University, Department of Philosophy of Peking University, and Department of Socioeconomics of Sendai Imperial University. Li Erchong went to prison for three times for involving in revolutionary activities. In 1937, he was enlisted into the Eighth Route Army and served in the War of Resistance against Japanese Aggression and the War of Liberation. After the founding of the People's Republic of China, Li had served as Second Secretary of Wuhan Municipal Committee of the Communist Party of China, Member of the Standing Committee of Hubei Provincial Committee, Propaganda Director of the Central South Bureau Party Committee, Deputy Director of the Revolutionary Committee of the Standing Committee of Guangdong Provincial Committee, Secretary of the Party Committee of Hainan Region, Standing Secretary of Shaanxi Provincial Committee, and Secretary of Hebei Provincial Party Committee and Governor of Hebei Province.

Li Erchong was keen on writing in his spare time. In 1983, he began to compose *New War and Peace*. The book with 8 volumes and 5 million words was published in 1993. It is a novel about the Chinese nation's resistance against Japanese aggression and its struggle for national liberation. In the order of time, it tells the history from the fall of Manchuria in the September 18 Incident to the final victory of the War of Resistance. Honoring the historical facts, the book has successfully portrayed the images of Mao Zedong, Chiang Kai-shek, common soldiers, peasants, etc. It features a simple, straightforward style of writing in plain language. The characteristics of people are shown through events. With a distinctive ethnic flavor, the book is acclaimed as a "national epic".

Li Erchong once said, "The purpose of the novel is to reflect the World War II in essence. We should reflect on one thing: why is war happening, and how can we ensure that there is no war in future?" Wei Wei considered that Li Erchong's work "embodies the fortitude of the Chinese people and the revolutionary spirit of the communists". In the preface to the *New War and Peace* (Second Edition), Li Xiannian called it "a wonderful flower in the garden of socialist literature and art".

In 2001, *New War and Peace* won the second prize of the 5th Book Award of China (first prize: none).

(By: Li Wengang)

6. 宋之的 Song Zhidi

宋之的（1914—1956），原名宋汝昭，河北丰润人，剧作家。

宋之的出生于农民家庭。11岁时，父亲将其寄养到绥远（今内蒙古呼和浩特）的二伯家。1929年，宋之的被送回家乡，在车轴山中学继续读书。1930年夏，他在朋友帮助下考入北平大学法学院俄文经济系，结识了于伶、陈沂等人，并在他们影响下参加左翼剧团呵莽剧社的反帝公演。1932年6月，宋之的与于伶等人成立苞莉芭剧社，并加入左翼戏剧家联盟北平分盟，主编机关刊物《戏剧新闻》。

1933年，白色恐怖加剧，宋之的中断学业离京赴沪，参加上海左翼剧联，组织并领导新地剧社、大地剧社，同时参加夏衍领导的左翼影评小组，开始职业文学活动。1948年，参加解放军。新中国成立后，他曾担任解放军总政治部文化部文艺处处长、《解放军文艺》主编，并当选中国戏剧家协会常务理事。

宋之的一生创作戏剧40部，其中以多幕话剧《雾重庆》《祖国在召唤》《保卫和平》、独幕讽刺喜剧《群猴》影响最大。他的剧作大多紧密配合现实斗争，具有鲜明的民族化特征。《雾重庆》通过表现林卷妤、沙大千、苔莉、万世修等流亡重庆的大学生在腐败、黑暗的"政治迷雾"下渐渐走向沉沦的悲剧，有力控诉了国民党政府的反动统治。《雾重庆》排演时，得到了在重庆工作的周恩来的热情支持，公演后在社会上引起热烈反响。

宋之的还创作了大量报告文学、小说和散文作品。《一九三六年春在太原》表现了国民党统治下太原城的恐怖气氛，揭露了"春天被关在了太原城外"的现实，是其报告文学代表作。

（作者：李文钢）

Song Zhidi (1914–1956), originally named Song Ruzhao, was a native of Fengrun, Hebei. He was a playwright.

Song Zhidi was born of a peasant family. When he was 11 years old, his father sent him to his second uncle's family in Suiyuan (today's Hohhot, Inner Mongolia). In 1929, Song was taken home, and he continued his study in Fengrun Chezhoushan Middle School. In the summer of 1930, with the aid of a friend, he was admitted to Department of Russian Economics, School of Law, Peiping University. There, he met Yu Ling and Chen Yi, among others. Under their influence, he joined the Hemang Theatre Society, a leftist theatre group, and participated in the anti-imperialism public performances. In June 1932, Song Zhidi and Yu Ling founded the Bor'bá Theatre Group. They joined the Leftist Dramatist League Peiping Branch and served as the editors of its flagship magazine *Drama News*.

In the universal white terror that darkened the time in 1933, Song Zhidi withdrew from university and went to Shanghai. There, he joined the Shanghai Leftist Drama Federation to become the organizer and leader of Xindi Drama Group and Dadi Drama Group. He also joined the leftist film review group led by Xia Yan and started his career as a professional writer. In 1948, Song was enlisted into the Chinese People's Liberation Army (PLA). After the founding of the People's Republic of China, he had served as Director of the Literature and Art Division of the Culture Department of the General Political Department of the PLA and Chief Editor of *People's Liberation Army Literature and Art*, and was elected Standing Director of the Chinese Dramatist Association.

Song Zhidi created 40 dramas throughout his life, of which multi-act dramas *Foggy Chongqing*, *Call of Motherland* and *Defend Peace*, and single-act satirical comedy *Monkeys* were most influential. Most of his works have parallels with events in real life and feature distinctive ethnic characteristics. *Foggy Chongqing*, as a tragedy describing the degeneration of college students such as Lin Juanyu, Sha Daqian, Tai Li and Wan Shixiu living in exile in Chongqing in the political scene haunted by corruption and darkness, is a powerful indictment of the reactionary rule of KMT. The rehearsal of *Foggy Chongqing* had engaged the support of Zhou Enlai who was working in Chongqing. It got an overwhelming response after public performance.

Song Zhidi also produced a large number of literary reportages, novels and proses. *Taiyuan in the Spring of 1936* illustrates the terror in the air of Taiyuan City under the rule of KMT, underscoring the fact that "the spring was blocked outside Taiyuan City". It was the magnum opus of his literary reportages.

(By: Li Wengang)

7. 张爱玲 Eileen Chang

张爱玲（1920—1995），本名张煐，祖籍河北丰润，现代著名作家。

张爱玲出生在上海租界，家世显赫。其祖父张佩纶是清末名臣，祖母李菊耦是晚清重臣李鸿章的长女，父亲张志沂是典型的遗少，母亲黄素琼是长江水师提督黄翼升的孙女。但童年的张爱玲因父母分居而变得性格内向，唯有在孤独中向文学寻求慰藉，小学时便在刊物上发表习作，展现了不凡的艺术才华。

中学时期的张爱玲已被视为天才，通过了伦敦大学的入学考试，后因战乱而选择香港大学，但毕业前夕又逢香港沦陷，只得返沪，靠写作渡过难关。1943年，她发表了成名作《沉香屑·第一炉香》和《沉香屑·第二炉香》，成为当时上海最负盛名的女作家。1952年赴中国香港，1966年后定居美国，晚年主要从事中国文学评价和《红楼梦》研究。

张爱玲的作品主要有散文集《流言》、散文小说合集《张看》、中短篇小说集《传奇》、长篇小说《倾城之恋》《半生缘》。其作品大多以上海和香港两大都市为背景，描写当时那些没落的封建世家和半新半旧的资产阶级家庭人物，尤其注意挖掘庸常生活里的寂寞、悲凉、自私乃至变态的精神世界。她的写作在总体上呈现出敏锐深切的"苍凉"感，恰如她的名言："生命是一袭华美的袍，爬满了虱子。"

其代表作《金锁记》，生动刻画了上海姜公馆病态的二少奶奶曹七巧的形象。曹七巧出身卑微，因家人贪图富贵，被嫁给了姜公馆久患骨痨病的二少爷。在这场金钱与门第的交易中，曹七巧因不能正常满足的生理欲望渐趋变态，得不到幸福的她也以残忍的方式处心积虑地破坏儿女的婚恋，表现出被虐—自虐—虐子的心理蜕变过程。曹七巧被害而又害人的一生，在张爱玲营造出来的凄怆情调中愈显苍凉。《金锁记》发表不久，便被傅雷誉为"我们文坛最美的收获之一"。

（作者：李文钢）

Eileen Chang (1920–1995), her real name Zhang Ying, was a famous modern writer whose ancestral home was in Fengrun, Hebei.

Eileen Chang was born of a distinguished family in the foreign concession in Shanghai. Her grandfather Zhang Peilun was a famous official of the late Qing Dynasty; her grandmother Li Juou was the eldest daughter of Li Hongzhang, a high official of the late Qing Dynasty; her father Zhang Zhiyi was a typical person loyal to the former dynasty; and her mother Huang Suqiong was the granddaughter of Huang Yisheng, the Yangtze River Navy Commander. Eileen Chang was very introverted in her childhood as her father and mother were separated, and she turned to literature for comfort in solitude. In elementary school, she began to publish articles in journals and show extraordinary artistic talent.

In high school, Eileen Chang was regarded as a genius. She passed the entrance examination of University of London, but chose to study in University of Hong Kong because of war. Just before her graduation, however, Hong Kong fell. Chang had to return to Shanghai and make a living by writing. In 1943, her signature works *Eaglewood Ashes: The First Incense* and *Eaglewood Ashes: The Second Incense* were published. Since then, Chang became the most prestigious female writer in Shanghai. Eileen Chang went to China's Hong Kong in 1952 and settled down in the United States in 1966. In her later years, she focused on the review of Chinese literature and the study of *Dream of the Red Chamber*.

Eileen Chang's works consist mainly of *Rumors*, a collection of proses; *Looking Around*, a collection of proses and fictions; *Legends*, a collection of novelettes and short stories; and *Love in a Fallen City* and *Half a Lifelong Romance*, full-length novels. Her works are mostly set against the background of declining feudal nobilities and half-modern bourgeois families in Shanghai and Hong Kong, focusing on revealing the loneliness, sadness, selfishness and even abnormality in the innermost thoughts of people through matters in ordinary life. There is always this feeling of profound "desolation" in her writing. As her famous saying goes, "Life is a gorgeous robe crawling with lice."

In *The Golden Cangue*, a magnum opus of Eileen Chang, the morbid psychology of Cao Qiqiao, wife of the Second Master of the Chiang family, is perceptively portrayed. As a low-born woman, she is forced by her materialistic parents into marrying the second son of the Chiang family who is a cripple. As a victim to wealth and social status, her mind is twisted for being deprived of a normal marriage life. With no happiness in life, she calculates to spoil the marriages of her children by brute means. Her psychology has undergone a transforming process from being tormented to self-imposed torment, then to tormenting her children. *The Golden Cangue* is a rueful, wry observation about the life of Cao Qiqiao, which ends up being a tragedy. Shortly after its publication, Fu Lei praised *The Golden Cangue* as "the most important harvest in our literary world".

(By: Li Wengang)

8. 管桦 Guan Hua

管桦（1922—2002），原名鲍化普，河北丰润人，当代著名诗人、作家。

管桦生于丰润县三女河乡女过庄村，童年在本村读书。1938年，因父亲参加冀东抗日大暴动，全家避居天津，入读天津志达中学。1940年，回冀东参加八路军，进入晋察冀华北联合大学文学系学习。1942年，任冀东军区救国报社记者，后调冀东军区尖兵剧社，期间创作了大量以战斗生活为题材的文艺作品。东北解放后，他转任东北鲁迅文艺学院文学研究所研究员，后调往中央音乐学院创作组。1952年，转任中央乐团创作员，曾在抗美援朝战争中到前线访问，并与他人合作了一些音乐作品。1957年，他响应号召，带全家回故乡女过庄村安家，为日后创作积累了丰富素材。1963年，调往北京市作协工作。1970年起，他用二十多年时间完成了反映冀东军民团结抗日的长篇历史小说《将军河》。

管桦著作丰富，代表作有长篇小说《将军河》《深渊》、中短篇小说《小英雄雨来》《葛梅》《暴风雨之夜》《辛俊地》等、歌曲作品《快乐的节日》《我们的田野》《听妈妈讲那过去的事情》等、诗歌《望长城》《天空》等。

《小英雄雨来》以"抗日反扫荡"为背景，描写12岁的少年雨来，在一次日寇扫荡中，英勇地掩护交通员老李并机智地逃脱敌人追击的故事。作品洋溢着深厚的爱国主义情感和浓郁的乡土气息，深得少年读者的喜爱。小英雄雨来，是抗战时期冀东少年儿童的缩影。管桦从小就与村里伙伴一起站岗放哨，给八路军送鸡毛信，为写作这篇小说积累了原始素材。

《辛俊地》刻画了个人主义严重的游击队员辛俊地的形象。他没有听从队长的命令，就私自打响了一场伏击战的第一枪，结果使游击队遭受很大损失。最后，他也因个人主义而丢掉性命。作品发表后曾引起广泛争议，但也得到了巴金等著名作家的赞誉。

"大风高歌壮士曲，浪花飞写英雄篇"（《将军河》），准确反映了管桦的写作风格。

（作者：李文钢）

Guan Hua (1922–2002), his real name Bao Huapu, was a native of Fengrun, Hebei. He was a famous modern poet and writer.

Guan Hua was born in Nüguozhuang Village, Sannühe Township, Fengrun County. As a child, he studied in the village school. In 1938, his father was involved in the Uprising against Japanese Aggression in Jidong, his family moved to Tianjin for safety, and Guan attended Tianjin Zhida Middle School. In 1940, Guan Hua was enlisted into the Eighth Route Army in Jidong, and he attended the Literature Department of Jin-Cha-Ji Huabei Associated University. In 1942, he worked as a reporter of *National Salvation News* in Jidong Military Region. Later, he was transferred to the Jianbing Theatre Group in Jidong Military Region. During this period, he had written a large number of literary works about the army life. After the liberation of Northeast China, he was transferred to Luxun Academy of Fine Arts and served as a researcher in its Institute of Literature. Then he was transferred to the creative group of Central Conservatory of Music. In 1952, Guan Hua served as a composer of the Central Orchestra. During the War to Resist US Aggression and Aid Korea, he visited the soldiers in the front line and composed some musical works with others. In answer to the summons of the state, Guan Hua moved his family back to his hometown

Nüguozhuang Village, where he collected abundant materials for his literary creation. In 1963, he was transferred to Beijing Writers Association. Since 1970, it took him more than 20 years to create *General River*, a historical novel showing the soldiers and civilians standing united in the War of Resistance against Japanese Aggression.

Guan Hua was a prolific writer. His magnum opuses include full-length novels *General River* and *Abyss*; novelettes and short stories *Yulai Little Hero*, *Ge Mei*, *Stormy Night* and *Xin Jundi*; songs *Happy Festivals*, *Our Fields* and *Listening to Mom Telling the Stories of the Past*; and poems *Looking at the Great Wall* and *Sky*.

Yulai Little Hero is set against the background of "Counter-campaign against the Japanese Mopping-up". Yulai, a lad of twelve, heroically guarded the underground messenger Old Li in a Japanese mopping-up campaign. In the end, he cleverly got away from the pursuit of the enemy. There is a profound sense of patriotism and a strong rustic feeling in the work well-liked by little readers. Little hero Yulai was a miniature of children in Jidong during the War of Resistance against Japanese Aggression. Guan Hua and his village playfellows had served as sentries and messengers for the Eighth Route Army, and the novel was inspired by his childhood experience.

Xin Jundi portrays the image of Xin Jundi, an individualistic guerrilla warrior. Disobeying the orders of the team leader, he fired the first shot in an ambush and inflicted heavy casualties on the guerrilla detachment. In the end, he lost his life because of his personal individualism. When the work was published, it became highly controversial, but famous writers such as Ba Jin were very complimentary about it.

"The wind sings the heroic song, and the waves write the heroic chapter." (*General River*) These words give an accurate picture of the writing style of Guan Hua.

(By: Li Wengang)

9. 葛翠琳 Ge Cuilin

葛翠琳（1930—2022），又名葛翠林，笔名婴林，河北乐亭人，当代儿童文学作家。《野葡萄》《翻跟头的小木偶》《会唱歌的画像》《核桃山》曾获中国作协全国优秀儿童文学奖。《野葡萄》在第二次（1954—1979）全国少年儿童文艺创作评奖中获一等奖。

葛翠琳出身书香门第，曾祖父、祖父、父亲都是教师，童年在乐亭县立小学上学，因成绩优异，进北京崇慈女子中学免费读书。中学毕业后，她考进燕京大学，积极参加革命宣传活动。她经常自编自演节目，这是其文艺创作的开端。解放后，她曾在北京市委文艺工作委员会、北京市文联工作，一度担任作家老舍的秘书。"文革"结束后，她重回北京市文联工作，并担任中国作协儿童文学委员会委员。1990年，她与韩素音等人创办冰心奖，着力培养儿童文学作者。

她创作广泛，包括诗歌、小说、散文、报告文学、剧本、童话、文艺评论等，尤以童话创作影响最大。代表作《野葡萄》发表于1956年，是中国当代童话的名篇之一，讲述了善良的"白鹅女"的故事：

"白鹅女"因帮家里放鹅，又喜欢白鹅而得名。不幸的是，在她十岁时，父母意外离世，婶娘霸占了她的家产并开始虐待她。婶娘生了一个女儿，眼睛却是瞎的，因而十分嫉妒白鹅女那双美丽的大眼睛。一天，婶娘突然抓起一把沙子，揉进了白鹅女的眼睛，把她的眼睛也弄瞎了。白鹅女坐在河边整夜伤心流泪，突然想起妈妈曾对她说过，深山里有一种野葡萄，盲人吃了就能重见光明。于是，她让白鹅带路，去深山里寻找野葡萄。历经艰险，她终于找到了野葡萄，并治好了自己的眼睛。她拒绝了山神让她在山上当仙女的好意，采摘了很多野葡萄，又历经艰险回到家乡，让她的妹妹和很多盲人重见光明。充满爱心的白鹅女，感动了许许多多的读者。

葛翠琳几十年来坚持写童话，在童话创作中追求真善美的境界。老作家冰心曾盛赞："她写的童话，人物很鲜明，故事很生动，语言很优美，具有她自己的细腻活泼的风格。"

（作者：李文钢）

Ge Cuilin (1930–2022), alias 葛翠林, her pen name Yinglin, was a native of Laoting, Hebei. She was a contemporary children's literature writer. Her *Wild Grapes*, *Little Puppets Turning Somersaults*, *A Portrait that Sings* and *Walnut Mountain* won the National Excellent Children's Literature Award of China Writers Association. Her *Wild Grapes* won the first prize of the 2nd National Award for Children's Literature (1954–1979).

Ge Cuilin came from a cultured family. Her great grandfather, grandfather and father were all teachers. In her childhood, she attended Laoting County Primary School. With good grades, she was admitted by Beijing Chongci Women's Middle School as a tuition-free student. After graduation, Ge tested into Yenching University and actively publicized revolutionary ideas there. She often wrote a play and starred herself, which was the beginning of her literary creation. After liberation, she had worked first in the Literature and Art Working Committee under Beijing Municipal Party Committee and then in the Beijing Federation of Literary and Art Circles, and was once a secretary of Chinese writer Lao She. After the Cultural Revolution, Ge Cuilin got a transfer back to the Beijing Federation of Literary and Art Circles, and became a member of the Children's Literature Committee of China Writers Association. In 1990, she established the Bingxin Award with Elisabeth Comber (Han Suyin) to cultivate writers of children's literature.

Ge Cuilin's works cover a wide range of genres, including poetry, novel, prose, literary reportage, script, fairy tale and literary review, with her fairy tales being the most influential of all. *Wild Grapes*, a magnum opus published in 1956, is a famous piece of contemporary Chinese fairy tales. It tells the story of the kind "white goose girl".

The "white goose girl" used to herd geese for her family, and she loved geese, hence her name. Unfortunately, her parents accidentally died when she was ten years old. The girl's aunt took over her property and mistreated her. The aunt had a blind girl and was jealous of the white goose girl who possessed a pair of big, tender eyes. One day, the aunt suddenly picked up a handful of sand and rubbed it in the eyes of the white goose girl, making her a blind girl too. The girl sat by a river and cried desolately all night. She suddenly recalled the words of her mother. Deep in the mountains, there was a species of wild grape which could make the blind people see again. Thus she went deep into the mountains following a white goose. Going through many dangers, she finally found the wild grapes with which she cured her blindness. She declined the favor of the Mountain God for her to be a mountain fairy. She gathered a lot of wild grapes and brought them home going through many dangers again, curing her sister and many other blind people. The white goose girl, who was full of love, has touched numerous readers.

Ge Cuilin had been engaged in the creation of fairy tales for decades. In the process, she was always in pursuit of the true, the good and the beautiful. The veteran writer Bingxin once praised Ge: "In her fairy tales, the characters have striking personalities, the stories are vivid, and the language is beautiful. She writes with a unique sentiment that is coupled with a spirited style."

(By: Li Wengang)

10. 浩然 Hao Ran

浩然（1932—2008），本名梁金广，笔名白雪、盘山，祖籍河北宝坻县（今天津宝坻区），被称为"生活在农民中间、为农民而写作的作家"。1990年，长篇小说《苍生》荣获首届中国大众文学奖特别奖。

浩然出生在唐山市赵各庄煤矿。他10岁丧父，12岁丧母，14岁参加革命，16岁入党。1951年到河北省团校学习，1954年起任《河北日报》《中苏友好报》记者，1961年任《红旗》杂志编辑，1964年调北京市文联从事专业创作。曾任中国作协理事、北京市文联副主席、北京市作协主席等职。1986年11月，他携妻子到河北省三河县长期生活并挂职。

浩然誓言"深入一辈子农村，写一辈子农民，给农民当一辈子忠实代言人"，创作了大量农村题材作品，包括短篇小说集《喜鹊登枝》《苹果要熟了》《新春曲》《杏花雨》、长篇小说《艳阳天》《金光大道》《山水情》《晚霞在燃烧》、中篇小说《西沙儿女》《浮云》《赵百万的人生片断》《男大当婚》等。尽管浩然的创作因时代政治观念的影响而有所局限，但他始终心怀农民，关心民生疾苦，作品充满泥土气息。

代表作《艳阳天》通过叙述1957年前后发生在北京郊区东山坞农业生产合作社的故事，表现新的时代语境下农村阶级斗争的新特点。主人公萧长春作为党的基层干部，与潜藏的资本主义势力代表马之悦等人展开了激烈斗争。萧长春在品德和人格方面堪称完美，马之悦、马小辫等人则老奸巨猾、笑里藏刀，因而双方的斗争也变得十分复杂。作品还生动刻画了一系列农民形象：韩百仲、马老四、喜老头、福奶奶等乐观积极的先进农民，马学怀、韩百安、马大炮、弯弯绕等不明是非的落后农民，真实表现了他们在时代巨变面前的困惑与抉择。

著名学者叶嘉莹曾评价《艳阳天》："……从我个人的观念来看，《艳阳天》这部小说所叙写的情事，与我一向所研读的古典诗歌中所叙写的一些情事，就外表看来其内容虽然有很大的不同，然而作为一部出色的作品，《艳阳天》的某些品质，与古典诗歌中的某些优秀作品，却是颇有相似之处的。那就是它们既都具含有作者内心中一份真正感动的情意，而且更写出了对社会大我的一种关怀和理想。"当然，由于作品中浓厚的政治色彩和阶级斗争观念,《艳阳天》在改革开放后曾一度引起广泛争议。

(作者:李文钢)

Hao Ran (1932–2008), his real name Liang Jinguang and his pen names Baixue and Panshan, was a native of Baodi County, Hebei (today's Baodi District, Tianjin). He was called "a writer of the peasants and for the peasants". In 1990, his full-length novel *Men on the Earth* won the Special Prize of the 1st China Popular Literature Award.

Hao Ran was born in the Zhaogezhuang Coal Mine, Tangshan. His father and mother died when he was 10 and 12 years old. He participated in the revolution at 14 and joined the Party at 16. In 1951, he attended Hebei Youth League School; in 1954, he became a reporter of *Hebei Daily* and *Sino-Soviet Friendship News*. He served as an editor of *Red Flag* magazine in 1961, and was transferred to the Beijing Federation of Literary and Art Circles in 1964 to engage in literary creation. Hao Ran had been Director of China Writers Association, Vice Chairman of Beijing Federation of Literary and Art Circles, and Chairman of Beijing Writers Association. In November 1986, he settled down in Sanhe County, Hebei Province with his wife and took a temporary post.

Hao Ran vowed to "devote his life to the countryside and make writing of farmers his life's work", and he wrote about the countryside prolifically. His works include short stories *Magpie Climbing the Branch*, *Apples Getting Ripe*, *New Spring Song* and *Apricot Blossom Rain*; full-length novels *Sunny Days*, *Golden Avenue*, *Mountains and Rivers* and *Sunset Glowing*; and novelettes *Children of Xisha*, *Clouds*, *Life of Zhao Baiwan* and *A Man Thinks of Marriage*. Hao Ran's writing was limited by the political ideas affecting the time, but he always had the peasants on his mind and was sensitive to the plight of people. His works have a rustic flavor.

Sunny Days, the magnum opus of Hao Ran, is a story set against the background of Dongshanwu Agricultural Production Co-operative in Beijing Suburb. It mirrors the class struggle of rural areas in the new era. Xiao Changchun, hero of the book who was a grassroots cadre of the CPC, engaged in a heated battle against the underlying capitalist force represented by Ma Zhiyue. Xiao Changchun was a perfectly virtuous man, while Ma Zhiyue and Ma Xiaobian were crafty, cunning fellows. There was a complicated struggle between the two sides. Hao Ran meticulously portrayed the images of many peasants in the work: Han Baizhong, Ma Laosi, Oldster Xi and Grandma Fu, who were advanced, optimistic peasants; and Ma Xuehuai, Han Bai'an, Ma Dapao and Wanwanrao, who were unenlightened, amoral peasants. The work accurately portrays the confusions and choices of people in the great transformation of times.

Florence Chia-ying Yeh, a famous scholar, once commented on *Sunny Days*: "…This is my opinion of *Sunny Days*. The stories in this novel are, externally, quite different from those in the classical poems I have always studied. As a great work, however, *Sunny Days* seems much like some excellent classical poems in certain aspects, which is that they all feature genuine emotions that touch our heartstrings and reflect a care and expectation for the society at large." After the Reform and Opening Up, *Sunny Days* once caused controversy for its intense political overtone and class struggle concept.

(By: Li Wengang)

11. 从维熙 Cong Weixi

从维熙（1933—2019），河北玉田人，当代著名作家。曾任作家出版社社长、总编辑。

从维熙出生于玉田县代官屯，4岁时丧父。民间传说和家中散落的文学经典引发了他对文学的兴趣。他靠母亲在北平当保姆的微薄收入在北平读完了初中，1950年考入北京师范学校并开始写作。1953年，他放弃保送北京大学的机会，到青龙桥小学任教。1954年调北京日报社任编辑、记者。1955—1956年，出版短篇小说集《七月雨》和《曙光升起的早晨》。他的早期作品大多取材于农村的新人新事，师法孙犁的诗情画意，有一股清新的乡土气息，被视为"荷花淀派"的代表作家之一。

从维熙1957年被错划为"右派"，1978年重返文坛。《大墙下的红玉兰》《远去的白帆》《风泪眼》先后获全国第一、二、四届优秀中篇小说奖，编剧电影《第十个弹孔》1980年获文化部优秀故事片奖，长篇小说《北国草》获北京市优秀文学奖。"文革"结束后，他率先描写了监狱和劳改生活，反映极"左"路线造成的危害，被称为"大墙文学"之父。

《大墙下的红玉兰》是其代表作，表现了1976年早春时节一个劳改农场内善恶之间的激烈斗争。葛翎原是省劳改局的老干部，因被打成"现行反革命分子"而被关进劳改营。关在同一劳改营的恰好有曾被葛翎镇压过、审问过的恶霸地主和流氓分子，他们借机对葛翎展开了疯狂报复。一天，劳改营传来首都人民在天安门广场自发纪念周总理的消息，葛翎想与狱友一起做花圈献给总理，却在打算采摘几朵从大墙外伸到墙内的玉兰花时被开枪打死。葛翎的好友唯有怀揣几朵被鲜血染红的玉兰花连夜坐火车进京告状。

当代评论家张炯认为："从维熙'大墙'内的小说，把矛盾始终放在正义与邪恶、崇高与卑下斗争的风口浪尖，突出精神的搏斗与一种峻峭高远之志。'大墙文学'始终保持着一种紧张感，而悲剧性的结尾，又使作品悲壮的涵义和崇高精神如火一般地喷出。"这段话很好概括了从维熙的创作特色。

（作者：李文钢）

Cong Weixi (1933–2019), a native of Yutian, Hebei, was a famous contemporary writer. He had been the Director and Editor-in-chief of Writers Publishing House.

Cong Weixi was born in Daiguantun Village, Yutian County, and his father died when he was 4 years old. The folk tales and literary classics found at home were an interest for him. His mother paid for him to finish junior high school in Peiping with her small income from being a nurse. In 1950, Cong tested into Beijing Normal University and started writing. In 1953, he declined the recommendation for admission to Peking University and became a teacher in Qinglongqiao Primary School. In 1954, he was transferred to *Beijing Daily* and worked as an editor and journalist. From 1955 to 1956, he published short story collections *July Rain* and *First Light of Day*. His earlier works were mostly based on rural people and events in the new era, featuring a poetic quality in the manner of Sun Li and a rustic flavor. He was considered as a representative of the "Lotus Lake School".

Cong Weixi was falsely taken as a "rightist" in 1957, and he came back to the literary scene in 1978. *Magnolias under the High Wall*, *Departing White Sail* and *Wind Tears* won the 1st, 2nd and 4th National Excellent Novelette Awards. In 1980, the feature film *The Tenth Bullet Scar* scripted by him won the Excellent Feature Film Award of Ministry of Culture of the People's Republic of China. The full-length novel *Grass in the Northern Lands* won the Beijing Excellent Literature Award. When the Cultural Revolution ended, Cong Weixi was the first to depict the life of imprisonment and reform-through-labor. Those works reflect the harm done by the ultra-leftists, and he was thus called the father of "High Wall Literature".

Magnolias under the High Wall, the magnum opus of Cong Weixi, is about the bitter conflict between good and evil in a reform-through-labor farm in the early spring of 1976. Ge Ling, who had been a veteran cadre of the Provincial Bureau of Reform-through-Labor, was branded as a "modern counter-revolutionary" and sent to a reform-through-labor camp. The despotic landlords and local riffraff whom Ge Ling had cracked down on and interrogated happened to be in the same camp. They took the chance to engage in a frenzied revenge. One day, the message of people in the capital organizing an impromptu memorial to Premier Zhou came to the reform-through-labor camp, and Ge Ling and his fellow prisoners wanted to make a wreath for the Primer. When Ge was about to pluck the magnolias stretching across the high wall, he was shot dead. Carrying the blood-stained magnolias, A friend of Ge's travelled by train overnight to Beijing to file a lawsuit.

Zhang Jiong, a modern literary critic, once said, "The struggle between justice and evilness, between sublimity and humbleness, has been at the forefront of the central conflict of Cong Weixi's 'High Wall' novels. They shed light on the lofty will and ambition of people. There's a sense of tension throughout the 'High Wall Literature' works, and the tragic endings invest those works with a fiery sense of solemnness and sublimity." The words best sum up the writing style of Cong Weixi.

(By: Li Wengang)

12. 何申 He Shen

何申（1951—2020），本名何兴身，当代著名小说家。他与关仁山、谈歌，并称河北文坛"三驾马车"。

何申出生于天津市，1969年到承德山区插队，1973年入河北大学中文系学习。1976年9月后，长期在承德地区的党校、文化局、宣传部、承德日报社等单位工作。曾任中国作协全委会委员、河北省作协副主席、第九届全国人大代表。

何申从 1981 年开始小说创作，著有长篇小说《梨花湾的女人》《多彩的乡村》等、中篇小说集《年前年后》《穷县》《乡村英雄》《七品县令和办公室主任》等、电视连续剧剧本《一村之长》《一乡之长》《青松岭后传》《男户长李三贵》《乡村女法官》《大人物李德林》等。中篇小说《秘书长》获《中篇小说选刊》优秀作品奖，并获 1993 年度庄重文文学奖。中篇小说《年前年后》获鲁迅文学奖（1995—1996）。他的小说将熟悉的乡镇生活栩栩如生地展现在读者面前，凸显时代面貌和世态风情，彰显现实主义文学的永恒魅力。

代表作《年前年后》生动刻画了基层乡镇干部乡长李德林的形象。他一心为公，在临近春节时，仍为乡里的小流域治理项目去找县领导。大年初一，他又把自己的饺子送给了那些吃不上饺子的农民工。但他也有着自己的小算盘：期盼着能早点干出一番业绩然后调往县城。为此，他还专门去县城送礼走后门。小说对人物的刻画真实可信，能让读者感同身受，被誉为"现实主义冲击波"的代表作。

（作者：李文钢）

He Shen (1951–2020), his real name He Xingshen, was a famous contemporary novelist. He Shen, Guan Renshan and Tan Ge were known collectively as the "Big Three" of the Hebei literary scene.

He Shen was born in Tianjin. He came to the mountain areas of Chengde as a production team member in 1969. In 1973, he attended the Chinese Department of Hebei University. Since September 1976, he had been working in Chengde for the Party School, Cultural Bureau, Publicity Department and *Chengde Daily*. He was a former Member of the Committee of the Whole of China Writers Association, Vice Chairman of Hebei Writers' Association, and Representative of the Ninth National People's Congress.

He Shen became a novel writer since 1981. He was the author of full-length novels *Women of Pear Blossom Bay* and *Colorful Countryside*;

novelette collections *Before and After the Spring Festival*, *Poor County*, *Village Heroes* and *Seventh-graded County Magistrate and Office Director*; and TV series screenplays *The Head of a Village*, *The Head of a Township*, *The Sequel of Pine Mountains*, *The Male Head of Household Li Sangui*, *The Female Judge in the Village* and *The Great Man Li Delin*. His novelette *Secretary General* won the Outstanding Works Award of *Selective Periodical of Novelettes* and the 1993 Zhuang Zhongwen Literature Prize. His novelette *Before and After the Spring Festival* won the Lu Xun Literature Award (1995–1996). He Shen's works vividly present the familiar township life in front of the readers, and they are reflective of the times and the permanent charm of realistic literature.

Before and After the Spring Festival, the magnum opus of He Shen, gives a graphic description of the character of Li Delin, a grassroots township head who served the public good with his whole heart. Before the Spring Festival, he still went looking for the county leaders for the minor drainage basin management project in the town. On the first day of the year, he brought his dumplings to the migrant workers who couldn't get home. But Li Delin also had a personal reason for doing so. He wished he could make a success in his post and get transferred to the county. For that, he went to the county specially to pull some strings. The characters portrayed in the work are alive and readers might find it easy to relate to their experiences. *Before and After the Spring Festival* is known as the representative work of the "shock waves of realism".

(By: Li Wengang)

13. 关仁山 Guan Renshan

关仁山（1963—），河北丰南人，当代著名小说家，河北文坛"三驾马车"之一。

关仁山出生在唐山丰南县东田庄乡谷庄子村。在昌黎师范学校读书时加入"碣石文学社"任编委，1981年毕业。先后当过小学语文教师、乡文化站站长、县政府秘书。1999年，调河北省作协任专业作家。现为河北省作协主席。

1984年，关仁山在《唐山劳动日报》发表处女作《亮晶晶的雨丝》。主要作品有长篇小说《天高地厚》《麦河》《日头》《白纸门》《风暴潮》《福镇》《权力交锋》《金谷银山》等、中短篇小说《大雪无乡》《九月还乡》《蓝脉》《红旱船》《落魂天》《平原上的舞蹈》《红月亮照常升起》《苦雪》等。2004年，获第九届庄重文文学奖。长篇小说《天高地厚》荣获第十四届中国图书奖、第八届全国少数民族文学创作骏马奖，小说《船祭》获香港《亚洲周刊》第二届世界华文小说比赛冠军奖，报告文学《感天动地——从唐山到汶川》获第五届鲁迅文学奖（2007—2009）、中宣部第十一届精神文明建设"五个一工程"奖。

关仁山的小说长期关注农民题材，长篇小说《天高地厚》《麦河》《日头》被称为农村三部曲。代表作《天高地厚》背景宏阔，以冀东平原上的蝙蝠村为背景，书写了荣家、梁家、鲍家三个家族三代人的生动故事，全景式反映了中国农村20世纪70年代以来近三十年的社会变迁——从实施家庭联产承包责任制到21世纪初中国加入世贸组织对农村的影响，既展现了时代风貌，又充满了浓郁的乡土气息。作品中人物众多，矛盾纠葛复杂，但各具神采，尤其是对老一代农民荣汉俊和农村新人鲍真、梁双牙的塑造，丰富了当代文学农民形象画廊，令人印象深刻。

诚如关仁山在《天高地厚》后记所言："农民可以不管文学，但是文学永远不能不关心农民的生存。"评论家雷达称其为"现实主义冲击波"的代表人物。

（作者：李文钢）

Guan Renshan (1963–), a native of Fengnan, Hebei, is a famous contemporary novelist. He is among the "Big Three" of Hebei literary scene.

Guan Renshan was born in Guzhuangzi Village, Dongtianzhuang Township, Fengnan County, Tangshan. While studying in Changli Normal School, he was a member of the editorial board of "Jieshi Literature Society". After graduating in 1981, he had been the Chinese teacher of a primary school, head of the township cultural station, and secretary of the county government. In 1999, he was transferred to Hebei Writers' Association as a professional writer. He is currently the chairman of Hebei Writers' Association.

In 1984, Guan Renshan published his first work *Shiny Rain* in *Tangshan Workers' Daily*. He is the author of full-length novels *High Heaven and Deep Earth*, *Barley River*, *Daytime*, *White Paper Gate*, *Storm Surge*, *Fuzhen County*, *Power Clash* and *Golden Millet and Silver Mountain*; and novelettes *Snowy Hometown*, *Returning Home in September*, *Blue Mountain*, *Red Land Boat*, *Lost Heaven*, *Dance on the Plain*, *The Red Moon Rises as Usual* and *Bitter Snow*. In 2004, Guan Renshan won the 9th Zhuang Zhongwen Literature Prize. The full-length novel *High Heaven and Deep Earth* won the 14th China Book Award and the 8th National Minority Literature Creation Gallant Horse Award. The short story *Boat Sacrifice* won the first prize of the 2nd World Chinese Fiction Competition of *Asia Weekly* of Hong Kong. The literary reportage *Astonishing Heaven with Faith—From Tangshan to Wenchuan* won the 5th Lu Xun Literature Award (2007–2009) and the 11th Spiritual Civilization Construction "Five-One Project" Award of the Publicity Department of the CPC Central Committee.

The life of peasants has been a constant topic of Guan Renshan's novels. His full-length novels *High Heaven and Deep Earth*, *Barley River* and *Daytime* are known as the "Rural Trilogy". His magnum opus *High Heaven and Deep Earth* is set against a vast background. It concerns the interesting stories of the Rong, Liang and Bao clans for three generations going on in

Bat Village on the Jidong Plain. The work is a panoramic reflection of the change in rural China over nearly three decades from the implementation of household contract responsibility system in the 1970s to China's accession to the World Trade Organization in the early 21st century. Besides, there is a strong rustic flavor in the work. It features an abundance of characters and complicated relationships, and the characters are all distinctive. Rong Hanjun, a farmer of the old generation, contrasts well with Bao Zhen and Liang Shuangya, farmers of the new generation, and they have opened the readers' minds to a whole new and very impressive way of viewing the modern farmers.

Just as Guan Renshan said in the postscript of *High Heaven and Deep Earth*, "Literature could be beyond the concern of farmers, but it never could be indifferent to the living of farmers." Lei Da, a literary critic, called Guan Renshan a representative of the "shock waves of realism".

(By: Li Wengang)

14. 张楚 Zhang Chu

张楚（1974—），原名张小伟，河北滦南人，当代著名小说家。

张楚出生于滦南县周夏庄村，并在家乡读完了小学和中学。1997年，辽宁税务高等专科学校毕业后到滦南县国税局工作。2011年春季到夏季，到鲁迅文学院学习。2014年，调往河北省作协任专业作家。2020年11月，当选为天津作协副主席。

张楚从1993年开始写作，著有中短篇小说集《樱桃记》《七根孔雀羽毛》《夜是怎样黑下来的》《野象小姐》《在云落》《风中事》《梵高的火柴》《中年妇女恋爱史》、散文集《秘密呼喊自己的名字》等。2003年，作品《曲别针》获第十届河北省文艺振兴奖，引发文坛关注。2004年，《长发》获《人民文学》短篇小说奖。2012年，获首届林斤澜短篇小说奖优秀短篇小说作家奖。2014年，短篇小说《良宵》获第六届鲁迅文学奖。2016 年,《野象小姐》获第四届郁达夫小说奖短篇小说奖。2017 年,获第二届茅盾文学新人奖;《风中事》获第十七届百花文学奖中篇小说奖。2018 年,《水仙》获第三届华语青年作家奖短篇小说类主奖。

张楚的小说诚挚深沉,擅长细节处理,刻画了一系列社会底层人物。《良宵》讲述了一个退隐的京剧名旦救助艾滋病患儿的凄美故事:

冀东平原的麻湾村,住进了一个奇怪的租户,她是曾"红极一时"的戏剧名旦,在大病之后选择来此避居。一天夜里,她家突然来了一个小偷,在厨房偷吃她剩下的食物。当她得知小偷的孤苦身世——小男孩的家人因艾滋病均已离世,自己也遗传艾滋病时,便在乡亲的不解中做出了陪伴孩子的决定。每天晚上,她会故意留出精心准备的饭菜,等待他的到来,让那些夜晚成为真正的"良宵"。作品细腻温暖,传递出令人感动的悲悯情怀。

第六届鲁迅文学奖颁奖词云:"张楚的叙事绵密、敏感、抒情而又内敛,在残酷与柔情中曲折推进,虽然并不承诺每一次都能抵达温暖,但每一次都能发现至善的力量。"这精准概括了张楚小说的创作特色。

(作者:李文钢)

Zhang Chu (1974–), his real name Zhang Xiaowei, is a native of Luannan, Hebei. He is a famous contemporary novelist.

Zhang Chu was born in Zhouxiazhuang Village, Luannan County, where he finished primary and secondary schools. After graduating from Liaoning Taxation College in 1997, he began to work in Luannan County State Tax Bureau. From spring to summer of 2001, he studied in Lu Xun Literature Institute. In 2014, Zhang was transferred to Hebei Writers' Association. In November 2020, he was elected Vice Chairman of Tianjin Writers' Association.

Zhang Chu began to write fictions in 1993. He is the author of novelette and short story collections *Records of Cherry*, *Seven Peacock Feathers*,

How the Night Is Growing Dark, *Miss Wild Elephant*, *Falling in the Clouds*, *Things in the Wind*, *Van Gogh's Match* and *Middle-aged Women's Love Affairs*; and prose collection *Calling My Name in Secret*. In 2003, *Paper Clip* won the 10th Hebei Provincial Literature and Art Promotion Award and attracted the notice of the literary world. In 2004, *Long Hair* won the Short Story Award of *People's Literature*. In 2012, Zhang Chu won the 1st Lin Jinlan Short Story Award for Outstanding Writers. In 2014, the short story *Fine Evening* won the 6th Lu Xun Literature Award. In 2016, *Miss Wild Elephant w*on the Short Story Award of the 4th Yu Dafu Prize for Fiction. In 2017, Zhang Chu won the 2nd Mao Dun Award for the New Generation; *Things in the Wind* won the 17th Baihua Literature Award for Novella. In 2018, *Narcissus* won the Main Prize for Short Stories of the 3rd Young Writer Award.

Zhang Chu's fictions, with deep-seated emotions, depict a variety of low-status people in detail. *Fine Evening* tells a melancholy story of a famous retired Peking opera actress who spared no effort to save a child with AIDS. It goes like this:

A strange tenant moved into Mawan Village on the Jidong Plain. She had been a famous artist in the opera scene, but fell gravely ill later. Upon recovery, she lived in solitude in the village. One night, a little boy stole into her home and ate what was left in the kitchen. When she learned the history of the boy — an AIDS patient whose parents had died of AIDS, she decided to accompany the boy in spite of the perplexity of the fellow villagers. Every evening she would carefully prepare a meal for the boy, making it a "fine evening" indeed. Readers are touched by the emotional warmth and empathy perceptively written in the work.

Here is what the congratulatory speech at the 6th Lu Xun Literature Award says, "Zhang Chu's narration bespeaks a certain meticulousness, sensitivity, lyricalness and restraint. His work carries a mixture of cruelty and tendernes. It might not lead to a happy result every time, but we can always feel the underlying supreme virtue." The words best sum up the characteristics of Zhang Chu's fictions.

(By: Li Wengang)

三、当代诗人 III. Contemporary Poets

15. 郭小川 Guo Xiaochuan

郭小川（1919—1976），河北丰宁人，当代著名诗人。

郭小川的父母都是教师。1933 年 3 月，全家逃难至北平。1937 年，他到山西太原参加了八路军，后在延安中央研究院进修。1945 年 8 月，郭小川回到丰宁县担任首任县长，与国民党反动派开展游击斗争。1948 年夏，转战新闻宣传工作。1949 年 5 月随军南下武汉，与陈笑雨、张铁夫合作，以笔名"马铁丁"撰写了大量"思想杂谈"。新中国成立后，他又创作了大量诗歌与报告文学作品，出版了《致青年公民》《月下集》《将军三部曲》《甘蔗林——青纱帐》等 10 部诗集，成为当代中国著名诗人。

郭小川是当代政治抒情诗的代表，诗风激越高亢，富有鼓动性和感染力，同时又擅长人物复杂心理的刻画。叙事长诗《白雪的赞歌》，描写了一位与被俘丈夫离散的妻子在内心深处所经历的道德与情感的冲突。在充满磨难的生活里，她与来给孩子看病的医生产生了微妙复杂的情感，但对丈夫的爱和对革命事业的忠诚，使她最终走出了生活的"陷阱"。她的丈夫在敌人的严刑拷打下也经受住了考验，夫妻终于团聚。这对革命夫妻，在各自经历的严峻考验面前，证明了"一个共产党员可以攀登得多么高"。

在诗体形式方面，郭小川做过多种尝试。他用过"楼梯体""半格律体",探索过古典词曲在现代诗中的融入,为当代诗歌形式的建构积累了宝贵经验。正如《甘蔗林——青纱帐》中的名句:"南方的甘蔗林哪,南方的甘蔗林!/你为什么这样香甜,又为什么那样严峻?/北方的青纱帐啊,北方的青纱帐!/你为什么那样遥远,又为什么这样亲近?"一节诗行,通过两两相对的对句,营造出了独特的韵律节奏,充满热情而又朗朗上口,形成了被人们称为"新赋体"的独特风格。

毛泽东曾这样评价郭小川:"我一向认为他是'中国的马雅可夫斯基'。"

(作者:李文钢)

Guo Xiaochuan (1919–1976), a native of Fengning, Hebei, was a famous contemporary poet.

Guo Xiaochuan's father and mother were both teachers. In March 1933, Guo's family sought refuge in Peiping. In 1937, he was enlisted into the Eighth Route Army in Taiyuan, Shanxi, and afterwards he studied in Yan'an Central Research Institute. In August 1945, Guo Xiaochuan served as the first county magistrate of Fengning, and he launched a guerrilla war against the KMT reactionaries. In the summer of 1948, he started to work to spread revolutionary messages. In May 1949, he went south with the army to Wuhan, where he worked with Chen Xiaoyu and Zhang Tiefu and wrote many "essays on thoughts" under the pseudonym "Ma Tieding". After the founding of the People's Republic of China, he wrote a large number of poems and reportages and published 10 poetry collections, such as *To the Young Citizens*, *Under the Moon*, *The General Trilogy* and *Sugarcane Forest—A Green Curtain*, thus becoming a famous poet in contemporary China.

Guo Xiaochuan was a representative figure of contemporary political lyric poetry. His works feature an emotive, appealing language, and he was adept at portraying the complicated mental mechanism of characters. The narrative poem "Praise of the Snow" depicts the interplay between ethics and emotions of a woman who was forced to be separated from her captured husband. In the face of the painful situations, she developed a subtle and complex feeling toward the doctor called in to see her son. The love for her husband and the loyalty to revolution helped her break the "trap" of life. Meanwhile, her husband, subjected to the brutality of the enemies, remained steadfast. At last, they were finally reunited. The revolutionary couple came through the test and demonstrated "how high a communist could get".

Many attempts had been made by Guo Xiaochuan in terms of poetic forms. He had employed the "stair style" and "semi-metrical style" and blended classical *ci* and *qu* into modern poetry, accumulating valuable experience for contemporary poetry writing. Here's what "Sugarcane Forest—A Green Curtain" says: "Sugarcane forest in the south, sugarcane forest in the south! / Why are you so sweet? Why are you so stern? / Green curtain in the north, green curtain in the north! / Why are you so far away? Why are you so intimate?" The lines manifested by unique, rhythmic antitheses are enthusiastic and memorable, and this very original style developed by Guo is called the "new *fu* poetry".

This is what Mao Zedong had said of Guo Xiaochuan: "I always think he is the 'Chinese equivalent of Mayakovsky'."

(By: Li Wengang)

16. 李瑛 Li Ying

李瑛（1926—2019），河北丰润人，当代著名诗人。诗集《我骄傲，我是一棵树》获1983年全国首届优秀诗集奖一等奖，《生命是一片叶子》获1999年首届鲁迅文学奖，长诗《我的中国》获"五个一工程"

奖暨全国优秀图书奖。

　　李瑛生于辽宁锦州的一个铁路工人家庭，7岁时被送回丰润农村老家读书，10岁时又随父亲到天津读书。中学时代他开始写诗并发表作品。1945年，考入北京大学中文系，在此任教的冯至、卞之琳等著名诗人对其创作产生了影响。1949年初，李瑛参加解放军，任新华通讯社第四野战军总社记者并随军南下。新中国成立后，曾任《解放军文艺》社社长、中国人民解放军总政治部文化部部长、中国文联第五届副主席、中国诗歌学会副会长等。

　　李瑛以军旅生活为主要书写对象，创作了大量政治抒情诗，风格大多清新单纯，具有强烈的爱国主义情怀与乐观主义精神。

　　20世纪50年代，李瑛的诗歌大多刚健激昂，如《戈壁日出》："太阳醒来了／它双手支撑大地，昂然站起，／窥视一眼凝固的大海，／便拉长了我们的影子。／我们匆匆地策马前行，／迎着壮丽的一轮旭日，／哈，仿佛只需再走几步，／就要撞进它的怀里。"晚年，李瑛的诗转向深沉细腻，如《蟋蟀》："产后的田野疲倦地睡了／喧闹如雨的秋声已经退去／夜，只剩一个最瘦的音符／执著地留下来／代替油盏，跳在／秋的深处，夜的深处，梦的深处。"

　　长诗《一月的哀思》是李瑛的名作。全诗500多行，情景相生，时空交错，善用排比，悲怆有力地表达了诗人在周恩来总理逝世后的哀思之情，引发全社会的广泛共鸣。

　　当代著名诗评家谢冕高度评价李瑛的诗歌创作："李瑛出现在中国社会方生未死的重要时刻，他的写作结束了战争时代未能回避的、可以说本有的粗粝本色，他在沿袭战时诗歌雄健风格的同时，坚持并引领了细致、华美的诗风，他的诗开辟了戍边卫国的士兵心目中的一片新鲜而美丽的天空。"

（作者：李文钢）

　　Li Ying (1926–2019), a native of Fengrun, Hebei, was a famous contemporary poet. His poetry collection *I'm Proud to Be a Tree* won the first prize of the 1st National Excellent Poetry Collection Award in 1983, *Life is A Leaf* won the 1st Lu Xun Literature Award in 1999, and long poem "My Home China" won the "Five-One Project" Award and National Excellent Book Award.

Li Ying came from a railway worker family in Jinzhou, Liaoning. At the age of 7, he was sent back to Fengrun and studied in his rural hometown. At the age of 10, he followed his father to Tianjin and studied there. In middle school, he began to write and publish poems. In 1945, he tested into the Department of Chinese Language and Literature of Peking University, where famous poets such as Feng Zhi and Bian Zhilin had profound influence on him. In early 1949, Li Ying joined the People's Liberation Army. He served as a reporter of the Xinhua News Agency in the Fourth Field Army and went down south. After the founding of the People's Republic of China, Li had been the President of the magazine *People's Liberation Army Literature and Art*, Head of the Culture Department of the PLA General Political Department, 5th Vice Chairman of the China Federation of Literary and Art Circles, and Vice President of the Poetry Institute of China.

Li Ying's creation was centered on the army life. His political lyric poems, composed in great abundance, were written in a refreshing and pure style and have an intense sense of patriotism and optimism.

Li Ying's poems created in the 1950s were marked by his fiery passions, such as "Sunrise in the Gobi" which goes like this, "The sun is waking up. / It stands up with its hands supporting the earth. / With a glance at the still sea, / It throws on the earth our elongated shadows. / We gallop off there, / Toward the glorious morning sun. / Seemingly, a few paces farther down the road, / We'd run into its arms." In his later years, Li Ying changed his poetry style to profundity and subtlety, such as "Cricket" which goes like this, "The field after harvest, weary, falls asleep. / The noisy autumn, like rain, has receded. / A last note barely grazes the silence of the night. / It keeps tinkling / In place of the oil lamp, / In the deepest recess of autumn, night, and dream."

The long poem "Sorrow in January" is a masterpiece of Li Ying. With more than 500 lines, it is lyrically expressive in space and time, and the parallel sentences powerfully express the sorrow of the poet over the death of Premier Zhou Enlai. The poem struck a chord in the whole society.

Li Ying's works were highly praised by Xie Mian, a famous contemporary poetry critic. He put it this way, "Li Ying came at an important moment when the new was just born and the old was not yet dead in China. Putting an end to the intrinsic, inescapable coarseness of war literature while carrying on the grandness of wartime poetry, he pioneered a meticulous and gorgeous poetic style. His poems forged a new path to portray a glistening sky in the eyes of frontier soldiers."

(By: Li Wengang)

17. 刘章 Liu Zhang

刘章（1939—2020），原名刘玺，河北兴隆人，当代著名诗人。著有诗集《燕山歌》《葵花集》《南国行》《北山恋》等30余部。1981年，组诗《北山恋》获中国作协全国中青年诗人（1979—1980）优秀新诗奖。

刘章生于兴隆县上庄村，未满周岁丧父，初中时开始写诗并发表作品。1958年，因母亲患病，他从承德高中肄业回农村劳动并坚持写诗，10月在《诗刊》发表《日出唱到太阳落——新民歌20首》，引起诗坛注意，不久调到半壁山公社文化馆工作。1975年到兴隆县文化馆任副馆长，1976被《诗刊》社借调当编辑，1977年到河北省歌舞团写歌词。1982年调到石家庄市文联，后任文联副主席。

20世纪50年代，刘章就以"农民诗人"闻名。农村生活的体验和家乡的风土人情，是其创作源泉。刘章的诗大多简约如话、风格清新，有着接近民歌的轻松活泼，如他的《牧场上》："花半山，/草半山，/白云半山羊半山，/挤得鸟儿飞上天。//羊儿肥，/草儿鲜，/羊吃青草如雨响，/轻轻移动一团烟。//榛条嫩，/枫叶甜，/春放沟谷夏放坡，/五黄六月山头转。//抓头羊，/带一串，/羊群只在指掌间，/隔山听呼唤。"他的新诗，大多践行了"用乡亲们喜欢的形式和语言写"的理念。

刘章创作了大量旧体诗词，出版有《刘章诗词》等。"让新诗有旧体诗的韵味，让诗词有新诗的生命元素"是其创作追求。他还写作了大量歌词、散文作品。2007年，他的歌词《知音歌》获中宣部第七届"五个一工程"奖。评论家谢冕曾把刘章的创作比喻为"燕山山下一葵花"："葵花，一种朴素、热情、朝气蓬勃的花，一种向阳花。"

（作者：李文钢）

Liu Zhang (1939–2020), his real name Liu Xi, was a native of Xinglong, Hebei. As a famous contemporary poet, he had published more than 30 poetry collections, including *Song of Yan*, *Sunflower Collection*, *Travel to the South*, and *Romance of Beishan Mountain*. In 1981, "Romance of Beishan Mountain", a suite poem, won the National Excellent New Poetry Award (1979–1980) for Young and Middle-aged Poets of the China Writers Association.

Liu Zhang was born in Shangzhuang Village, Xinglong County, and his father died before he reached the first birthday. In middle school, he began to write and publish poems. When his mother fell ill in 1958, he quitted Chengde High School and returned to the countryside to do manual labor while continuing to write poems. With the publication of *From Sunrise to Sunset—20 New Folk Songs* in *Poetry Periodical* in October, Liu Zhang attracted attention in the poetry scene. Before long, he was transferred to the Banbishan Commune Cultural Center. In 1975, he was transferred to the Xinglong County Cultural Center as Deputy Director. In 1976, he was temporarily assigned to *Poetry Periodical* as an editor. In 1977, he worked in Hebei Song and Dance Troupe as a songwriter. In 1982, he was transferred to the Shijiazhuang Federation of Literary and Art Circles and later became its Vice Chairman.

In the 1950s, Liu Zhang had become known as a "peasant poet". The life and customs in the countryside had inspired him to write many poems. Liu's poems are characterized by simplicity, freshness and ballad-like vivacity. This is what "On the Pastureland" says: "Flowers are blooming, / Grass is lush, / Clouds and sheep form a white blanket. / The birds are edged out into the sky. // Sheep are fat, / Grass is fresh, / Sheep graze on grass like rain. / They move gently like smoke cloud. // Hazelnut twigs are tender, / Maple leaves are sweet, / Herd sheep to valley in spring and to slope in summer, / Let them eat yellow grass in May and run on hill in June. // The alpha sheep, / leads the herd, / controlling all the sheep with ease. / They listen to the call even across the mountain." Most of Liu Zhang's new poems are written in exactly the "form and language loved by his fellow villagers".

Liu Zhang had written many ancient-style poems and published the *Ancient-style Poems of Liu Zhang*. The general focus of his works is to "give an ancient charm to new-style poems, and a new life to ancient-style ones". Liu had also written many lyrics and proses. In 2007, *To Our Bosom Friends* written by him won the 7th "Five-One Project" Award of the Publicity Department of the CPC Central Committee. Xie Mian, a poetry critic, likened the works of Liu Zhang to "a sunflower at the foot of the Yan Mountains"—"a simple, warm and vigorous flower always facing the sun".

(By: Li Wengang)

18. 张学梦 Zhang Xuemeng

张学梦（1940—），河北丰润人，当代著名诗人。代表作长诗《现代化和我们自己》，获 1979—1980 年全国中青年诗人优秀诗歌奖。曾任河北省作协副主席。

1957 年初中毕业后，为减轻家庭负担，他先到唐山市话剧团做杂工，后在唐山市冶金矿山机械厂、唐山市劳动局生产服务队、唐山机械制造厂等单位工作。1979 年开始发表诗作，1982 年加入中国作协，1983 年调入唐山市文联任专业作家。

长诗《现代化和我们自己》发表于《诗刊》1979 年 5 月号，结集出版后获 1983—1984 年全国优秀新诗集奖。全诗以饱满的激情、磅礴的气势、强劲有力的"楼梯体"诗行，集中表现了一代青年向愚昧开战、向现代化进军的昂然奋进心态："跟上队伍的 / 一同前进，/ 掉队的 / 终被丢弃。/ 怎能设想 / 叫奔驰的时代列车 / 停下来，/ 再等你 / 半个世纪？！ / 问题是尖锐的，/ 谁也不能回避！ / 那么，思考这个问题吧，/ 现代化和我们自己。"诗中，张学梦以敏锐的艺术直觉感受到中国社会现代化的步伐，提出了"现代化和我们"这一时代命题，这既是对"五四"时期沿承下来的人的自由与解放主题的积极回应，也具有重要的文学史意义。长诗奠定了张学梦的文学地位。

张学梦多年笔耕不辍，诗作《祖国振兴的时刻》《胚芽骚动的城市》分获 1982 年、1987 年河北省文艺振兴奖。2019 年 7 月，长诗《伟大的思想实验》在《诗刊》发表，延续了其诗作兼容思想性、时代性和艺术性的复合特征。张学梦希望自己的诗能产生现实作用："我从现实中采撷一切。我固执地坚信，离开了现实，诗就失去了生命力。我希望诗着眼于今天和未来。"其诗作也以贴近时代政治的现实感和论辩性见长，多为政治抒情诗。其诗作擅长于对抽象理论问题的思考，但有时也带有理念化的缺陷。

（作者：李文钢）

Zhang Xuemeng (1940–), a native of Fengrun, Hebei, is a famous contemporary poet. The long poem "Modernization and Ourselves", his magnum opus, won the National Excellent New Poetry Award for Young and Middle-aged Poets (1979–1980). Zhang had been the Vice Chairman of Hebei Writers' Association.

After he graduated from middle school in 1957, to help ease the family burden, Zhang Xuemeng first became an odd-job man in Tangshan Opera Troupe, then worked in Tangshan Mining & Metallurgical Machinery Plant, Tangshan Labor Bureau Production Service Team, and Tangshan Machinery Factory. Zhang started publishing poems in 1979 and joined the China Writers Association in 1982. In 1983, he was transferred to the Tangshan Federation of Literary and Art Circles as a professional writer.

The long poem "Modernization and Ourselves" was published in the May 1979 issue of *Poetry Periodical*. After being published as a book, it won the 1983–1984 National Excellent New Poetry Collection Award. The poem, mighty and awe-inspiring, took on a feverish intensity. The forceful lines in the "stair style" is a reflection of the enterprising mood of the youths fighting against ignorance and moving toward modernization. Here is what it says: "Keep pace, / And we can advance together. / Unable to keep up, / You'll be left behind. / How is it possible / To stop the running train of times / And wait for another half a century?! / This is a sharp question / That there's no getting around! / Now, let's work at this question / Of modernization and ourselves." With an acute artistic sense, Zhang Xuemeng felt China's march to modernization and put forth the proposition of "modernization and ourselves". It is as much a positive response to the freedom and liberation of humanity passed down from the May 4th Movement as a hallmark with a great significance in literary history. Long poems established Zhang Xuemeng as a master in the literary scene.

Zhang Xuemeng has been engaged in writing for many years. His poems "Moments of Revitalization of the Motherland" and "A Sprouting City" won the Hebei Provincial Prize for the Revitalization of Literature in 1982 and 1987 respectively. In July 2019, his long poem "The Great Thought Experiment" was published in *Poetry Periodical*. The work features a combination of ideological contents, characteristics of times and artistic quality, all of which are the trademarks of Zhang's poems. Zhang Xuemeng hopes his works could have realistic significance: "I draw nourishment from reality. I strongly believe that when poetry gets away from the real world, it will be taken out of life. I hope that poetry could focus on the present and the future." The works of Zhang, mostly political lyric poems, are close to real life with strong argumentation. His poems, while sometimes too idealized, are characterized by the reflections on abstract theories.

(By: Li Wengang)

19. 大解 Da Xie

大解（1957—），原名解文阁，河北青龙人，当代著名诗人。

大解出生于青龙县双山子镇的一户农家。1973年高中毕业后，他与同乡创办了文学民刊《幼苗》。1979年清华大学水利工程系毕业，他先后在青龙县水利局、文化馆工作，期间一直坚持文学创作。1988年8月借调到河北省文联《诗神》月刊任编辑，1991年1月调入秦皇岛市党史研究室，1991年11月正式调入河北省文联《诗神》编辑部。现为河北省作协副主席。

大解著有长诗《悲歌》、诗集《岁月》《诗歌笔记》《个人史》《河之北》《群峰无序》《山水赋》等、小说集《长歌》《他人史》、寓言集《傻子寓言》《别笑，我是认真的》等。叙事长诗《悲歌》被称为新诗的重要收获；具有独创性的寓言系列被誉为"超越荒诞"的开先河之作；小说集《他人史》以开创性的写作手法受到文学界的广泛关注和好评。

诗集《个人史》获首届中国屈原诗歌奖金奖和第六届鲁迅文学奖诗歌奖。鲁迅文学奖授奖词准确概括了大解诗歌的特色："大解与人生、历史、现实进行心灵对话，建构兼具个人体验和智慧哲思的精神世界，在传统精神和当下立场的相互支撑中生发诗意。朴素自然的语言，富于质感的意象，丰盈的细节，深厚的文化和哲学背景，使他的诗开阔苍茫，具有本质性力量。"诗作《衣服》颇具代表性：

"三个胖女人在河边洗衣服 / 其中两个把脚浸在水里 另一个站起来 / 抖开衣服晾在石头上 // 水是清水 河是小河 / 洗衣服的是些年轻人 // 几十年前在这里洗衣服的人 / 已经老了 那时的水 / 如今不知流到了何处 // 离河边不远 几个孩子向她们跑去 / 唉 这些孩子 / 几年前还呆在肚子里 / 把母亲穿在身上 又厚又温暖 / 像穿着一件会走路的衣服。"

（作者：李文钢）

Da Xie (1957–), his real name Xie Wenge, is a native of Qinglong, Hebei. He is a famous contemporary poet.

Da Xie was born into a peasant household in Shuangshanzi Town, Qinglong County. After he graduated from high school in 1973, he founded the literary magazine *Seedling* with his fellow villagers. After he graduated from the Department of Hydraulic Engineering of Tsinghua University in 1979, he worked in the Water Conservancy Bureau and the Cultural Center of Qinglong County. During this period, he persisted with literary creation. In August 1988, he was transferred to the Hebei Federation of Literary and Art Circles, where he served as the editor of the monthly magazine *God of Poetry*. In January 1991, he was transferred to Qinhuangdao Party History Research Office. In November 1991, he was formally transferred to the Editorial Department of *God of Poetry* under the Hebei Federation of Literary and Art Circles. He is now the Vice Chairman of Hebei Writers' Association.

Da Xie is the author of long poem "Sad Melody"; poetry collections

Years, *Poetry Notes*, *Personal History*, *North of the River*, *Disordered Peaks* and *Ode of the Landscape*; novelette collections *Long Songs* and *History of Others*; and fable collections *The Fables of Fools* and *Don't Laugh, I Mean It*. His narrative poem "Sad Melody" is praised as an important achievement of new poetry, his original fables are known as the pioneer "transcending absurdity", and his novelette collection *History of Others* has received wide attention and appreciation in the literary scene with its innovative style.

The poetry collection *Personal History* won the Gold Award of the 1st Chinese Qu Yuan Poetry Award and the Poetry Award of the 6th Lu Xun Literature Award. Here is what the congratulatory speech on the Lu Xun Literature Award says of Da Xie's poems: "Da Xie, by communicating spiritually with life, history and reality, has constructed a spiritual world combining personal experience with philosophical wisdom. His poetic quality is generated through the interaction between the traditional spirit and the modern standpoint. The plain language, striking imageries, rich details, and profound cultural and philosophical background make his poems broad, vast and inherently powerful." Here is what his representative work "Clothes" goes:

"Three fat ladies are washing their clothes by the river. / Two of them bathe their feet in the water, while the third lady stands up. / She shakes the clothes and puts them on the stone. // The water is clear, and the river is small. / There are young people washing clothes. // People who washed clothes here decades ago / Have grown old, and I don't know / Where the water at that time has flowed. // Not far from the river are several children running to them. / Oh, these children / Were developing embryos several years ago. / They had their mothers around them, thick and warm / Like wearing walking clothes."

(By: Li Wengang)

第七章

产业文化

Chapter VII Industrial Culture

一、工业文化 I. Industry

1. 秦皇岛港 Qinhuangdao Port

秦皇岛港，位于渤海湾西岸、河北省沿海的东北端，拥有12.2千米长的码头岸线，陆域面积11.3平方千米，水域面积226.9平方千米，是中国北方天然良港。

秦皇岛港开埠于清光绪二十四年（1898），为中国北方首个自开通商口岸，主要承担开平矿务局的煤炭运输业务。1912年，港口更名为开滦矿务局秦皇岛经理处。1949年至1978年，秦皇岛港由单一煤码头发展成综合性港口。1983年，自主建成中国第一座大型煤炭输出专业码头，确立了中国能源输出大港的地位。

秦皇岛港全景图（摄影：王进勤）
Panorama of Qinhuangdao Port (Photographed by Wang Jinqin)

秦皇岛港是世界最大的煤炭输出港和干散货港，是中国"北煤南运"的主枢纽港。现有泊位50个，最大可接卸15万吨级船舶。分东、西两大港区。东港区以能源运输为主，拥有原油、成品油和世界一流的现代化煤炭码头；西港区以杂货、集装箱运输为主，拥有装备先进的杂货和集装箱码头。

秦皇岛港是综合性国际贸易大港，具有完善的集疏运条件。京山、沈山、京秦、大秦等国铁干线与自营铁路连接，京沈高速、102国道、205国道、秦承公路与疏港路相通；与100多个国家和地区建立通航往来；已开通秦皇岛至龙口、秦皇岛至旅顺至烟台的海上客运航线；开辟了秦皇岛至日本、韩国等 4 条国际集装箱航线。

秦皇岛港是历史悠久的百年大港。2008 年秦皇岛港股份有限公司成立，分别于 2013 年和 2017 年在香港联交所、上海证券交易所上市。

开滦矿务局办公楼（摄影：王进勤）
Kaiping Mining Bureau's office building (Photographed by Wang Jinqin)

2009 年成为河北港口集团的控股子公司，现已形成秦皇岛港、唐山曹妃甸港、沧州黄骅港三个港区的发展格局。2018 年启动"蒙中韩大陆桥海铁过境"项目，为融入"一带一路"倡议开辟了新途径。

2013 年，秦皇岛港口近代建筑群被国务院公布为全国重点文物保护单位。2018 年，秦皇岛市确立建设国际一流旅游城市的发展战略，这为秦皇岛港的转型发展带来了新机遇。

（作者：秦学武）

Qinhuangdao Port is located on the west coast of Bohai Bay and the northeast end of Hebei coastal area. With a wharf shoreline of 12.2 kilometers, a land area of 11.3 square kilometers and a water area of 226.9 square kilometers, it is a superior natural seaport in northern China.

Qinhuangdao Port was opened in the 24th year of Guangxu of the Qing Dynasty (1898). As the first non-treaty port in northern China, it was responsible for transporting the coal of Kaiping Mining Bureau. In 1912, the port was renamed to Kaiping Mining Bureau Qinhuangdao Management Office. From 1949 to 1978, Qinhuangdao Port developed from a coal wharf to a comprehensive port. In 1983, the first self-built large-scale wharf for transporting coal was completed, which established the status of

20世纪初的秦皇岛港（供图：王进勤）
Qinghuangdao Port in the early 20th century (Provided by Wang Jinqin)

Qinhuangdao Port as a large energy transportation port in China.

As the world's largest coal transportation port and dry bulk port, Qinhuangdao Port is the major pivotal port for the "transportation of coal from the north to the south". Currently, there are 50 berths for vessels with a maximum deadweight of 150,000 tons. The port is divided into east and west port areas. The east port area, of which the major function is to transport energy resources, has crude oil, refined oil and world-class modern coal terminals. The west port area, of which the major function is general cargo and container transportation, has advanced general cargo and container terminals.

Qinhuangdao Port is a comprehensive international port with perfect conditions for inland transportation. Its self-operated railway line links national railway trunk lines such as Beijing–Shanhaiguan Railway, Shenyang–Shanhaiguan Railway, Beijing–Qinhuangdao Railway and Datong–Qinhuangdao Railway. Beijing–Shenyang Expressway, National Highways 102 and 205 and Qinhuangdao–Chengde Highway offer easy access to the port. Qinhuangdao Port has established direct links with more than 100 countries and regions. Maritime passenger routes linking

Qinhuangdao with Longkou, Lüshun and Yantai, and 4 international container routes linking Qinhuangdao with Japan, South Korea, etc., have been opened to navigation.

    Qinhuangdao Port is a time-honored port with a century-long history. In 2008, Qinhuangdao Port Co., Ltd. was founded. The company got listed on Hong Kong Stock Exchange and Shanghai Stock Exchange in 2013 and 2017. In 2009, the company became majority-owned by Hebei Port Group Co., Ltd, and now the coordinated development of Qinhuangdao Port, Tangshan Caofeidian Port and Cangzhou Huanghua Port has been established. In 2018, the Sea–Rail Transit Route Program for the Mongolia–China–South Korea Land Bridge was officially kicked off, exploring a new way for the port to integrate into the Belt and Road Initiative.

    In 2013, the modern architectural complex in and around Qinhuangdao Port was designated by the State Council as a Major Historical and Cultural Site Protected at the National Level. In 2018, Qinhuangdao proposed the strategy of building a world-class tourist city, which represents a new opportunity for the transformation and development of Qinhuangdao Port.

(By: Qin Xuewu)

2. 中铁山桥集团有限公司 China Railway Shanhaiguan Bridge Group Co., Ltd.

中铁山桥集团有限公司前身为山海关桥梁厂，肇始于1894年成立的山海关造桥厂，是中国第一家钢结构制造企业。中铁山桥，是中国历史最悠久的钢桥梁、钢结构制造企业和铁路道岔制造企业，被誉为"中国钢桥的摇篮，道岔的故乡"。

中铁山桥已通过ISO9000质量管理体系认证、ISO14000环境管理体系认证、ISO18000职业健康安全管理体系认证和UKAS国际标准认证，覆盖管理、制造与服务的全过程。2016年，通过美国钢结构协会（AISC）认证审核。

中铁山桥是世界著名的钢桥制造商，从建造中国第一座钢桥——滦河大桥至今，已累计建造钢桥3200余座，包括19座长江大桥、12座黄河大桥，以及香港昂船洲大桥、港珠澳大桥等，还承建了摩洛哥阿尤恩栈桥、挪威哈洛加兰悬索桥、柬埔寨北线铁路、孟加拉国帕德玛大桥等重大工程。创造众多中国之最：第一孔钢桥、第一座长江大桥、第一座焊接钢拱桥、第一座全断面焊接铁路钢混结合梁、第一座跨度接近1500米的悬索桥。创造多项世界之最：苏通长江大桥和朝天门长江大桥，建成时分别为世界主跨最大的斜拉桥和拱桥。

中铁山桥是享誉国内外的钢结构制造商，产品用于工业与民用建筑、电站等，如山东石横电站、唐山陡河电站、北京石景山电站、上海宝钢、人民大会堂、洛阳电站、吉林电站、大连星海会展中心等工程。钢桥梁、钢结构还出口到日本、越南、缅甸、坦桑尼亚、巴基斯坦、孟加拉国、菲律宾等国家和中国港澳台地区。

中铁山桥是中国最大的铁路道岔研发制造基地，中国的第一组铁路钢轨道岔、第一组高锰钢辙叉、第一组地铁道岔、第一组准高速道岔、第一组提速道岔、第一组城市高架铁路道岔、第一组高速铁路道岔、第一组高锰钢辙叉与钢轨焊接道岔等都由中铁山桥制造。产品出口到美国、俄罗斯、日本、加拿大、泰国、韩国、朝鲜、印度尼西亚、坦桑尼亚、赞比亚、博茨瓦纳等国家和中国港澳台地区。

中铁山桥是中国重要的大型工程机械专业修造商,产品覆盖起重机械、装卸机械,铺架机械和其他施工机械等,制造了中国第一台架桥机、第一台液压门座式起重机、第一套铸造真空造型设备、第一台100吨全液压铁路起重机、第一台大吨位自行式箱梁架桥机等设备。

中铁山桥荣获全国科学大会奖、国家技术发明奖、国家科技进步奖等多项国家级奖项,参建工程摘得国家优质工程金奖、鲁班奖、詹天佑奖、全国优秀焊接工程一等奖等国内奖项以及乔治·理查德森奖、古斯塔夫斯·林德撒尔奖、菲迪克工程奖等国际奖项。2022年,参建的港珠澳大桥赢得国际焊接最高奖——乌戈·圭雷拉奖。

中铁山桥是中国现代民族造桥、铁路机械工业的代表,是中国与世界知名行业企业角逐的"王牌",代表了中国品牌和中国质量。

(作者:王妹娟,秦学武)

China Railway Shanhaiguan Bridge Group Co., Ltd. had originally been Shanhaiguan Bridge Factory. Founded in 1894, the latter was the first steel structure manufacturer in China. China Railway Shanhaiguan Bridge Group is the oldest manufacturer of steel bridges, steel structures and railway switches. It is praised as the "Cradle of Steel Bridges and Hometown of Railway Switches in China".

China Railway Shanhaiguan Bridge Group is an ISO 9000 (Quality Management System, QMS), ISO 14000 (Environmental Management System, EMS), ISO 18000 (Occupational Health and Safety Management Systems, OHSMS) and UKAS (United Kingdom Accreditation Service) certified company. These certifications cover the whole process of management, manufacturing and service. In 2016, the company became an AISC (American Institute of Steel Construction) certified enterprise.

China Railway Shanhaiguan Bridge Group is a world-famous steel bridge manufacturer. Since the Luan River Bridge—China's first steel bridge, it has manufactured more than 3,200 steel bridges, including 19 Yangtze River bridges, 12 Yellow River bridges, Stonecutters Bridge in Hong Kong, and Hong Kong–Zhuhai–Macao Bridge. The company also undertook major overseas projects such as Laayoune Bridge in Morocco, Hålogaland Bridge in Norway, Northern Railway in Cambodia, and Padma Multipurpose Bridge in Bangladesh. China Railway Shanhaiguan Bridge Group has set many Chinese records: first steel bridge, first Yangtze River bridge, first welded steel arch bridge, first all-welded railway steel-concrete composite beam, and first suspension bridge with a span of nearly 1,500 meters. It has also set many world records: Sutong Yangtze River Bridge and Chaotianmen Yangtze River Bridge were a cable-stayed bridge and an arch bridge with the longest main spans in the world at the time of their completion.

China Railway Shanhaiguan Bridge Group is a steel structure manufacturer famous both in China and abroad. Its products are used in industrial and civil buildings and power stations, such as Shandong Shiheng Power Plant, Tangshan Douhe Power Plant, Beijing Shijingshan Power Plant, Shanghai Baosteel, Great Hall of the People, Luoyang Power Plant, Jilin Power Plant, and Dalian Xinghai Convention & Exhibition Center. Its steel bridges and steel structures are exported to Japan, Vietnam, Myanmar, Tanzania, Pakistan, Bangladesh, Philippines and China's Hong Kong, Macao and Taiwan, among others.

China Railway Shanhaiguan Bridge Group is China's largest railway switch research, development and manufacturing base. China's first steel railway switch, high manganese steel frog, subway switch, quasi-high-speed switch, speed-raising switch, urban elevated railway switch, high-speed railway switch, and railway switch welded with a high manganese steel frog are all manufactured by the company. The company's products are exported to the United States, Russia, Japan, Canada, Thailand, South Korea, the DPRK, Indonesia, Tanzania, Zambia, Botswana and China's Hong Kong, Macao and Taiwan, among others.

China Railway Shanhaiguan Bridge Group is an important manufacturer and repairer of large engineering machines. Its product line covers a series of construction machines such as crane, loader-unloader and laying machine. It has manufactured China's first bridge girder erection machine, hydraulic portal crane, vacuum casting and molding equipment, 100-ton full hydraulic railway crane, and large-tonnage self-propelled box girder bridge erection machine.

China Railway Shanhaiguan Bridge Group has won many national awards, such as National Science Conference Award, State Technological Invention Award and State Science and Technology Progress Award. The projects it worked on have won many domestic awards, such as National Quality Engineering Award (Gold), Luban Prize, Tien-yow Jeme Civil Engineering Prize and National Excellent Welding Engineering Award (First Prize); and many international awards, such as George S. Richardson Medal, Gustav Lindenthal Medal and FIDIC Project Award. In 2022, the Hong Kong–Zhuhai–Macao Bridge it worked on won the Ugo Guerrera Prize—the highest international welding award.

China Railway Shanhaiguan Bridge Group is the representative in the bridge building and railway machinery industries of modern China. It is a "trump card" in the competition between Chinese and top international companies on the world stage, building an image of "Chinese brand" and "Chinese quality".

(By: Wang Meijuan and Qin Xuewu)

3. 中国耀华玻璃集团有限公司 China Yaohua Glass Group Co., Ltd.

中国耀华玻璃集团有限公司俗称"耀华玻璃厂",被誉为"中国玻璃工业的摇篮"。原址位于秦皇岛市海港区道南片区,2001年底搬迁至北部工业区。2013年,耀华玻璃厂旧址[1]被公布为全国重点文物保护单位。

耀华玻璃厂始建于1922年,是由20世纪中国著名民族实业家、滦州矿务公司董事长周学熙与比利时乌得米财团共同出资创建,时称"耀华机器制造玻璃股份有限公司"。耀华玻璃厂,是中国第一家机器生产平板玻璃[2]企业,开创了亚洲玻璃工业的先河,打破了外国玻璃在中国的垄断,奠定了秦皇岛市"玻璃城"的称号。

耀华玻璃厂于1923年建成,1924年9月一号窑投产。1924年4月,耀华玻璃注册"阿弥陀佛"商标,1925年10月改为"双套金刚钻"并沿用至今。1999年1月,"耀华"牌浮法白玻璃被评为"改革开放二十年最具影响力著名品牌"。2002年2月,"耀华"牌浮法玻璃商标被评定为"中国驰名商标"。2004年1月,"耀华"牌浮法玻璃被评定为建筑玻璃类首批国家免检产品。

耀华玻璃厂是中国玻璃工业的旗舰,深受国家重视。毛泽东、周

---

1 耀华玻璃厂旧址,占地1.33公顷,由水塔、水泵房、电灯房三座独立建筑组成。其他建筑作为秦皇岛市玻璃博物馆园区保留了下来。

2 即"弗克法"生产技术,也称有槽垂直引上法。彼时,耀华玻璃厂以6万英镑购买比利时"弗克法"玻璃生产专利,为周学熙的创举。这一做法对耀华乃至中国玻璃工业的发展产生了决定性的影响。

恩来、刘少奇、朱德、杨尚昆、李鹏、朱镕基、尉健行、吴邦国、胡锦涛等国家领导人莅临耀华视察。1951年，毛主席指示有关部门邀请苏联专家来厂解决技术难题；1954年4月21日，毛主席到厂视察。1998年，江泽民主席乘坐耀华制造的冲锋舟亲临"98抗洪"一线。2005年10月29日，胡锦涛主席在金正日的陪同下视察耀华援建的朝鲜大安友谊玻璃厂。

1921年以来，耀华玻璃厂变革求存，数易其名，历经耀华机器制造玻璃股份有限公司（1921—1944）、耀华玻璃股份有限公司（1944—1955）、公私合营秦皇岛耀华玻璃厂（1955—1966）、秦皇岛玻璃厂（1966—1997）、秦皇岛耀华玻璃厂（1977—1988）、秦皇岛耀华玻璃总厂（1988—1994）、中国耀华玻璃集团公司（1994—2011）、中国耀华玻璃集团有限公司（2011至今）等不同阶段。2015年7月至2017年11月，耀华集团完成战略重组，归中国建材集团公司旗下凯盛科技集团管理。百年耀华，涅槃重生。

建厂百年来，耀华玻璃厂创新发展，创造中国玻璃工业众多第一：1924年9月15日，中国第一条机制平板玻璃连续生产线投产，产品出口美国、印尼、马来西亚、新加坡、菲律宾、印度等国；1955年至1956年，建造中国第一座自主设计、自主装备的大型玻璃熔窑；1958年，生产中国第一根机制玻璃管；1965年，建成中国第一条军用航空玻璃生产线；1966年，建成中国第一座无槽垂直引上工艺玻璃熔窑；1985年，生产中国第一片彩色平板玻璃；1989年，生产中国第一片建筑用镀膜平板玻璃；2004年，成为中国第一家成功生产在线低辐射玻璃的企业；2006年，生产中国第一块硼硅浮法玻璃；2018年，中国第一条5200毫米板宽"宽板等速"薄玻璃生产线投产；2021年，中国第一块"耀华灰"颜色玻璃商业化生产。获全国科技大会奖状、国家发明二等奖、国家金质奖章、国家新产品奖、国家科技进步二等奖、全国五一劳动奖状等多项国家级荣誉。

耀华玻璃厂现有5条浮法玻璃生产线和2条具有自主知识产权的

高硼硅特种浮法玻璃生产线，主要生产优质浮法玻璃、汽车玻璃、节能玻璃、本体着色玻璃及在线镀膜玻璃、硼硅玻璃等。在国外设计与总包的生产线有40余条，产品远销60多个国家和地区。

2012年，秦皇岛市玻璃博物馆在耀华玻璃厂老厂区建成，成为传承城市文脉、保留城市记忆的一道风景。

（作者：秦学武，王妹娟）

水塔泵房（摄影：王进勤）
Pump house (Photographed by Wang Jinqin)

China Yaohua Glass Group Co., Ltd., colloquially called Yaohua Glass Factory, is reputed to be the "Cradle of China's Glass Industry". Originally located in Daonan Area, Haigang District, Qinhuangdao, it was relocated to the Northern Industrial Zone at the end of 2001. In 2013, the site of Yaohua Glass Factory[1] was designated as a Major Historical and Cultural Site Protected at the National Level.

Yaohua was founded in 1922 with funds supplied by Zhou Xuexi, a famous national industrialist in the 20th century serving as the Chairman of Luanzhou Mining Company, and the Udmi Consortium of Belgium. It was called Yaohua Machinery Manufacturing Glass Co., Ltd. at the time. Yaohua was the first machine-made plate glass[2] manufacturer in China. It

---

1 The site of Yaohua Glass Factory, covering an area of 1.33 hectares, consists of three individual buildings: water tower, pump house, and electric light room. Other buildings are kept as a part of the Qinhuangdao Museum of Glass.

2 The glass was manufactured using the "Fourcault" process—a vertical draw process that requires a pit or drawing area. Back then, Yaohua bought the patent of the Fourcault process from Belgium with 60,000 pounds. The pioneering effort by Zhou Xuexi had a decisive influence on the development of the company and China's glass industry.

pioneered the glass industry in Asia, broke the monopoly of foreign glass manufacturers in China, and endowed Qinhuangdao with the title of "Glass City".

The Yaohua Glass Factory was built in 1923 and the Furnace 1 began production in September 1924. In April 1924, the company registered the "Amitabha" trademark. In October 1925, the trademark was changed to "Double Diamonds" which is still used today. In January 1999, "Yaohua" white float glass was named the "Most Influential Brand over the 20 Years since the Reform and Opening Up". In February 2002, "Yaohua" float glass was designated as a "Famous Trademark of China". In January 2004, it was listed among the first batch of national inspection-free architectural glass products.

As the flagship of China's glass industry, Yaohua is valued by the state. Many national leaders, such as Mao Zedong, Zhou Enlai, Liu Shaoqi, Zhu De, Yang Shangkun, Li Peng, Zhu Rongji, Wei Jianxing, Wu Bangguo and Hu Jintao, had visited and inspected the place. In 1951, Chairman Mao Zedong gave an instruction to the authorities for seeking the opinions of Soviet experts on the technical difficulties encountered in the factory. On April 21, 1954, Mao Zedong came to the factory for an inspection. In 1998, President Jiang Zemin took the assault boat made by Yaohua to the scene of the "1998 Floods". On October 29, 2005, President Hu Jintao, accompanied by Kim Jong-Il, inspected the Tae-an Friendship Glass Factory in the DPRK which was built with the aid of Yaohua.

Since 1921, Yaohua has been changing to stay alive. It went by the names Yaohua Machinery Manufacturing Glass Co., Ltd. (1921–1944), Yaohua Glass Co., Ltd. (1944–1955), Qinhuangdao Yaohua Glass Factory Under Public-Private Joint Management (1955–1966), Qinhuangdao Glass Factory (1966–1997), Qinhuangdao Yaohua Glass Factory (1977–1988),

Qinhuangdao Yaohua Glass General Factory (1988–1994), China Yaohua Glass Group Company (1994–2011), and China Yaohua Glass Group Co., Ltd. (2011–present). From July 2015 to November 2017, the strategic restructuring of Yaohua Group was completed, and the company was put under Triumph Science & Technology Co., Ltd. owned by China National Building Material Group Co., Ltd. The century-old enterprise is revitalized.

Over the past century, Yaohua has been sticking to innovation, creating many firsts in China's glass industry. On September 15, 1924, China's first continuous production line for machine-made plate glass came into operation. The products were exported to the United States, Indonesia, Malaysia, Singapore, Philippines and India. From 1955 to 1956, China's first independently designed and equipped large glass furnace was built. In 1958, China's first machine-made glass tube was manufactured. In 1965, China's first military aircraft glass production line was built. In 1966, China's first pit-less vertical draw glass furnace was built. In 1985, China's first colored plate glass was manufactured. In 1989, China's first coated plate glass for building purposes was manufactured. In 2004, Yaohua became China's first manufacturer of online LOW-E glass. In 2006, China's first borosilicate float glass was manufactured. In 2018, China's first 5,200 mm "wide plate & constant speed" thin glass production line came into operation. In 2021, China's first "Yaohua Grey" colored glass went into commercial production. Yaohua has won many national honors, such as National Science and Technology Conference Award, National Invention Award (Second Prize), National Gold Medal, National New Product Award, State Science and Technology Progress Award (Second Prize) and National May 1st Labor Certificate.

Yaohua has 5 float glass production lines as well as 2 special high borosilicate float glass production lines with proprietary intellectual property rights. Its main products include high-quality float glass, automotive glass, energy-saving glass, noumenon coloring glass, body-tinted glass and borosilicate glass. The company has more than 40 production lines designed and contracted abroad, and its products are exported to over 60 countries and regions.

In 2012, the Qinhuangdao Museum of Glass was inaugurated on the site of the old Yaohua Glass Factory. It has become a scene carrying on the heritage of the city.

(By: Qin Xuewu and Wang Meijuan)

4. 山海关船舶重工有限责任公司 Shanhaiguan Shipbuilding Industry Co., Ltd.

山海关船厂位于秦皇岛经济技术开发区东区，是中国三大造船基地之一。1972年开始兴建，1986年正式投产，2007年转股改制为山海关船舶重工有限责任公司，2016年并入大连船舶重工集团有限公司。

公司通过了ISO9001:2000质量体系认证，1995年获得对外贸易进出口经营权，2001年获得独立的港埠经营权和指泊权。现有6座大型干船坞和19个码头，并有600吨龙门吊、拖轮、1250吨油压机等各类大型设备。年承修大中型船舶200余艘，年造船能力140万载重吨。已形成船舶修理改装、船舶建造为主，海洋工程、军工产品和非船产业协调发展的经营格局。

40余年来，公司累计完成世界首艘海洋风车安装船、7万吨举力浮船坞、3.5万吨半潜式驳船、12万吨散货船、6.5万吨原油轮、3.7万吨化学品船、2万吨水泥自卸船、1100箱集装箱船等24个船型逾百艘船舶的建造工程，曾参与"中油海3号"平台、"胜利作业二号"平台的建造工程。现与韩国、希腊、新加坡、印度、丹麦、美国、中国

1922年耀华玻璃厂外景（供图：王进勤）
Yaohua Glass Plant in 1922 (Provided by Wang Jinqin)

香港和中国台湾等 30 多个国家和地区的航运公司保持着良好的业务关系。

山船重工是中国乃至全球修船市场中脱硫系统加装项目承接的先行者，其工期、价格等备受业界瞩目，曾服务希腊、韩国、伊朗等多个国家，在全球船舶市场占有一席之地。

（作者：王姝娟）

Located in the east area of Qinhuangdao Economic & Technological Development Zone, Shanhaiguan Shipyard is one of the top three shipbuilding bases of China. Its establishment got underway in 1972, and it was put into operation in 1986. After the restructuring in 2007, it became Shanhaiguan Shipbuilding Industry Co., Ltd. (SHGSIC). In 2016, the company was merged into Dalian Shipbuilding Industry Co., Ltd.

The company is an ISO 9001:2000 certified company. In 1995, it was granted the foreign trade import and export rights. In 2001, it was granted the independent port management right and berth assigning right. Currently, there are 6 large dry docks and 19 wharves, together with heavy equipment such as 600-ton gantry girders, tugboats and 1,250-ton oil hydraulic presses. The company maintains over 200 large- and medium-sized ships annually, and has an annual shipbuilding capacity of 1.4 million dead weight tonnage. A business pattern of ship building, repairing and refitting, coupled with marine engineering, military products and non-shipbuilding business, has formed.

Over the past 40-some years, SHGSIC has completed the construction of more than 100 ships of 24 types, including the world's first wind turbine installation vessel, 70,000-ton floating dock, 35,000-ton semi-submersible barge, 120,000-ton bulk freighter, 65,000-ton crude oil tanker, 37,000-ton chemical tanker, 20,000-ton cement self-discharging ship, and 1,100-TEU container ship. The company has worked on the construction of the "CPOE No.3" Platform and the "Shengli No.2" Platform. It has established business relationships with shipping companies in more than 30 countries and regions, including South Korea, Greece, Singapore, India, Denmark, the United States and China's Hong Kong and Taiwan.

SHGSIC is a pioneer in desulfurization system installation in the Chinese and even global ship repair market. Its schedule and price setting attract much attention in the industry. The company has provided service to Greece, South Korea, Iran, etc., securing a place in the global ship market.

(By: Wang Meijuan)

5. 唐山陶瓷 Tangshan Ceramics[1]

唐山是中国北方瓷都。明代永乐年间至今，唐山陶瓷有近 600 年历史。陶瓷业是唐山的四大支柱产业之一。2012 年 3 月，"唐山骨质瓷"被列入国家地理标志保护产品。

唐山是中国现代卫生陶瓷的诞生地。1915 年，唐山启新洋灰有限公司成立启新磁厂，生产卫生陶瓷和日用陶瓷。1923 年，启新磁厂

---

[1] 参阅：马永平：《唐山陶瓷业百年回眸》，《中国建材》，2021 年 11 期。
See: Ma Yongping: "Review of Tangshan Ceramic Industry over the Past Century", *China Building Materials*, 2021, Issue 11.

从德国引进陶瓷生产机械设备，结束唐山手工制造陶瓷的历史。1924年，生产出中国第一件现代卫生陶瓷，带来了中国的马桶革命。1927年，启新磁厂由德国人汉斯·昆德租赁经营[1]，生产出中国第一件彩色铺地砖。1930年，民族实业家秦幼林创办德盛窑业厂，最先用电动机取代柴油机，生产卫生瓷、建筑瓷和各种日用细瓷产品，发展成唐山陶瓷业的首户。

20世纪20年代至30年代初，唐山陶瓷业出现一段兴旺期。有陶瓷厂约60家，生产的卫生陶瓷销往我国的上海、广州、香港和新加坡、马来西亚等地，始有"北方景德镇"之誉。20世纪40年代，启新磁厂、德盛窑业厂入围"唐山八大厂矿"。

解放前夕，唐山陶瓷工业濒临崩溃，全市88家陶瓷企业有36家破产。1948年12月唐山解放，唐山陶瓷工业重获新生。1949年6月，启新磁厂被政府接管，成为唐山第一家国营瓷厂，1955年改名为唐山陶瓷厂。1953年，唐山成为中国最早、最大的理化瓷生产基地。1956年，唐山市陶瓷工业公司成立，产能进一步扩大。1963年，唐山开始研制骨质瓷，翌年开始生产釉面砖。至1966年，唐山形成门类较为齐全的综合性陶瓷工业生产体系，成为当时全国陶瓷行业的标杆。1973年，骨质瓷在唐山诞生，填补中国高档瓷生产的空白。

20世纪80年代，唐山陶瓷进入鼎盛期，日用瓷在中国同行中率先打入美国市场，卫生瓷和工业理化瓷独揽中国市场大半。1987年，"唐陶"牌卫生陶瓷摘得陶瓷行业唯一国家金质奖牌，奠定了唐山陶瓷在国内外的声誉和地位。90年代，唐山形成了完善的日用瓷、卫生瓷、建筑瓷、工业特种瓷、工艺美术瓷及相关配套产品等门类齐全的陶瓷产业体系。

唐山陶瓷技术水平始终走在全国前列。2005年，唐山率先研制出国家级技术创新产品——无铅骨质瓷，荣获国家科技进步二等奖，引

---

[1] 1935年后，启新磁厂由昆德父子独立经营。

领中国骨质瓷进入无铅时代;唐山"红玫瑰"骨质瓷以第一名成绩入选日用瓷行业首批、骨质瓷行业唯一的"中国名牌产品"。

唐山陶瓷的装饰技法主要有雕金、喷彩、釉中彩等,形成了唐山陶瓷的独特风格。骨质瓷瓷质润泽、光灿莹洁、胎质细致,白玉瓷瓷质细腻、釉面光润、白中泛青,是唐山陶瓷的代表。日用瓷有"红玫瑰""隆达"和"海格雷"等著名品牌。

唐山惠达陶瓷(集团)有限公司是中国卫生陶瓷的旗舰。"惠达"商标为中国驰名商标,"惠达"牌卫生陶瓷为中国名牌。惠达产品遍及全中国,远销美国、加拿大、英国、澳大利亚等100多个国家和地区。卫浴产品曾荣获德国红点奖、IF设计奖、A'设计大奖、日本优良设计奖等国际行业奖项。

(作者:王姝娟,秦学武)

Tangshan is the ceramic capital of northern China. Starting from the Yongle years of the Ming Dynasty, ceramic making is a 600-year tradition in the city. The ceramic industry is one of the four mainstays of Tangshan's economy. In March 2012, Tangshan bone china was listed as a Protected Geographical Indication Product of China.

Tangshan is the birthplace of modern sanitary ceramics in China. In 1915, Chee Hsin Ceramic, a subsidiary plant of Chee Hsin Cement Co., Ltd., was founded to manufacture sanitary ceramics and domestic ceramics. In 1923, the plant imported from Germany the mechanical equipment for ceramic production, marking the end of handmade ceramics in Tangshan's history. In 1924, the first modern sanitary ceramic in China was produced, spurring the Toilet Revolution in China. In 1927, Dr. Hans Gunther from Germany rented Chee Hsin Ceramic[1] and produced China's first colored floor tile. In 1930, Qin Youlin, a national industrialist, founded Desheng Ceramic

---

[1] After 1935, Chee Hsin Ceramic was independently run by Dr. Hans Gunther and his son.

唐山陶瓷（供图：唐山市政府办公厅）
Tangshan ceramics (Provided by the General Office of the Tangshan Municipal People's Government)

Factory. The factory was the first to replace diesel engines with electric motors. As a manufacturer of sanitary ceramics, architectural ceramics and various domestic fine ceramics, it became the top enterprise in Tangshan's ceramic industry.

Between the 1920s and the early 1930s, Tangshan witnessed a boom in the ceramic industry. Sanitary ceramics manufactured by about 60 ceramic factories were sold to Shanghai, Guangzhou and Hong Kong, and exported to Singapore and Malaysia, earning Tangshan the name "Northern Jingdezhen". In the 1940s, Chee Hsin Ceramic and Desheng Ceramic Factory were listed among the "Eight Top Factories and Mines in Tangshan".

Before liberation, the ceramic industry in Tangshan was on the verge of collapse, with 36 out of 88 ceramic enterprises going out of business. After the liberation of Tangshan in December 1948, Tangshan's ceramic industry took on a new lease of life. In June 1949, Chee Hsin Ceramic was taken over by the government and became the first state-owned ceramic factory in Tangshan. In 1955, its name was changed to Tangshan Ceramic Factory. In 1953, Tangshan became the earliest and largest production base of chemical ceramics in China. In 1956, Tangshan Ceramic Industry Company was established, further expanding the manufacturing capacity. In 1963, the development of bone china began in Tangshan. In the next year, the production of glazed tiles began. By 1966, Tangshan had established a comprehensive ceramic production system with various categories, setting a benchmark for the ceramic industry across the country. In 1973, the emergence of bone china in Tangshan filled up the blank of high-grade ceramic production in China.

The 1980s was the heyday of Tangshan's ceramic industry. Its domestic ceramics became the first to gain access to the US market among its contemporaries, and its sanitary ceramics and industrial chemical ceramics occupied the majority of China's ceramic market. In 1987, "TSTC" sanitaryware took the only gold medal for national high quality products in the ceramic industry, establishing the reputation of Tangshan ceramics in China and abroad. By the 1990s, Tangshan had established a comprehensive ceramic industry system with various categories, including domestic ceramics, sanitary ceramics, architectural ceramics, industrial special ceramics and art ceramics, as well as their supporting products.

Tangshan is at the cutting edge in China in the development of ceramic manufacturing technologies. In 2005, Tangshan successfully developed lead-free bone china, a technologically innovative product at the national level winning the Second Prize of the State Science and Technology Progress Award, promoting the Chinese bone china industry into a lead-free era; Tangshan "Red Rose" bone china was recognized as one of the first batch of China Top Brands in the domestic ceramic industry and the only China Top Brand in the bone china industry with top marks.

The unique decorative techniques of Tangshan ceramics mainly include gold carving, color spraying and in-glaze coloring. As the best representatives of Tangshan ceramics, bone china is sleek, glossy and exquisite, and jade porcelain has an extremely fine texture, a smooth glaze and a beautiful white color with a tinge of green. "Red Rose", "Longda" and "Haigelei" are famous brands of domestic ceramics.

Tangshan Huida Ceramics (Group) Co., Ltd. is the flagship of Chinese sanitary ceramics. Huida is a well-known trademark, and Huida Sanitary Ware is a famous brand in China. The products of Huida are sold across China and exported to more than 100 countries and regions, including the United States, Canada, Britain and Australia. Its sanitary products have won the Red Dot Design Award of Germany, IF Design Award, A' Design Award, Good Design Award of Japan, etc.

(By: Wang Meijuan and Qin Xuewu)

6. 开滦煤矿 Kailuan Coal Mine[1]

开滦煤矿是开滦（集团）有限责任公司的前身，位于河北省唐山市境内，被誉为"中国煤炭工业源头"和"中国近代工业摇篮"。

开滦煤矿始建于1878年，已有140多年历史。开滦煤矿以建设"中国第一佳矿"唐山矿为肇始，促进了周边地区的经济近代化，托举了唐山和秦皇岛两座城市的兴起。

井下作业场所（供图：唐山市政府办公厅）
Underground working site (Provided by the General Office of the Tangshan Municipal People's Government)

（1）诞生与劫掠

清光绪三年（1877），直隶总督李鸿章委派唐廷枢以官督商办的形式在永平府开平镇（今唐山开平）成立开平矿务局。1878年，在开平镇乔家屯创建大型现代化煤矿"唐山矿"。1881年，煤矿全面投产。1898年，产煤量达到73万吨。19世纪末，开平矿务局总资产已近600万两，与江南制造局一起成为洋务运动中的典型。

1901年，开平矿务局被英商骗占，改名为开平矿务有限公司。为遏制英商垄断，在直隶总督袁世凯的支持下，1907年，周学熙等人成立滦州矿务股份有限公司。次年，滦州煤矿的实力规模与开平煤矿已势均力敌。1912年1月，英商开平煤矿迫使滦州煤矿与其合并，成立开滦矿务总局。此后近半个世纪，开滦煤矿一直被英国人掌管。

1　刘晓慧：《开滦矿工为何"特别能战斗"》，《中国矿业报》2022年2月10日第001版。
　　Liu Xiaohui: "Why Are the Kailuan Miners 'Always Combat-ready'", *China Mining Industry News*, February 10, 2022, Page 001.

（2）70年的变迁

1948年12月12日，唐山解放。1949年，开滦煤矿收归国有。1952年5月，人民政府接管开滦煤矿，一方面对原有林西、赵各庄矿进行恢复和改造，另一方面新建吕家坨、范各庄、荆各庄等矿。范各庄矿是新中国第一座年产180万吨的大矿井。开滦矿区机械化采煤程度较高，水力采煤技术达到世界先进水平。

1999年12月，开滦（集团）有限责任公司成立，标志着中国最老的煤炭企业——开滦矿务局开始建立现代企业制度。2004年，组建"开滦股份"上市公司。2005年，获批建设开滦国家矿山公园。2018年，开滦煤矿入选第一批中国工业遗产保护名录。

开滦集团现为综合性大型能源集团，形成了以煤炭、煤化工、现代服务和新兴产业为支撑的产业发展格局。2021年，排名中国企业500强第248位，企业总资产913亿元。

（3）"特别能战斗"精神

开滦煤矿是一个"特别能战斗"的集体，孕育了"特别能战斗"精神。2019年，"特别能战斗"精神入选"新中国70年中国企业精神"。

创办人唐廷枢[1]克服重重困难，曾连续几日骑毛驴或步行由天津到开平，终于成功开办开平矿务局。他通过在华商中招股解决了巨大资金问题，这是中国最早发行的股票。

1920年，中国共产党早期工人运动领袖邓中夏，通过罗章龙结识唐山工运领袖邓培。1922年10月，罗章龙、王尽美、邓培组织开滦五矿[2]同盟大罢工，持续25天，最终迫使资本家同意提高工人工资待遇，减轻对工人的剥削，沉重打击了资本家与封建反动势力。这是开滦工人由自发斗争进入自觉斗争的一个伟大转折，在中国工人运动史上写下光辉的一页。毛泽东在《中国社会各阶级的分析》一文称赞开滦工人阶级"特别能战斗"。

1　2022年5月19日，纪念唐廷枢诞辰190周年暨香山商帮与洋务运动学术年会在澳门举行。

2　开滦五矿，是指唐山、林西、马家沟、赵各庄、唐家庄五个煤矿。

1938年春，开滦煤矿工人在中国共产党的领导下举行五矿同盟大罢工，给日本侵略者"以战养战"策略以极大打击。同年7月，开滦矿工参加冀东抗日大暴动，3000多工人加入抗日游击队，有力支援和配合了冀东地区的抗日斗争。毛主席称赞煤矿工人节振国是"民族英雄式的人物"。

开滦煤矿是中国煤炭行业的主力矿。在不同历史时期，开滦煤矿为中国经济社会发展做出了重要贡献。1975年，原煤产量达2563万吨，居全国煤炭系统之首。全国劳模赵国峰发明"台阶式推采法"等先进操作方法，极大提高了煤矿产量。周总理表扬开滦为国家"出了力，救了急，立了功"。邓小平高度评价"大庆的经验要学，开滦的经验也要学"。

开滦煤矿开创了众多中国或行业第一：是中国最早使用机器开采的大型煤矿；有亚洲第一、世界第二洗煤厂；有中国最早的标准轨距铁路——唐胥铁路，中国第一台蒸汽机车——"龙号"；创办的细棉土厂生产出中国第一桶机制水泥；建造了中国企业首个煤炭码头——秦皇岛港，驶出了中国企业最早的自营海运船队……改革开放以来，开滦共获得十余项国家发明奖、国家科技进步奖。

（作者：秦学武，王妹娟）

The Kailuan Coal Mine, predecessor to Kailuan (Group) Limited Liability Corporation, is located in Tangshan, Hebei. It is known as the "Source of China's Coal Industry" and the "Cradle of China's Modern Industry".

Founded in 1878, Kailuan has been around for more than 140 years. Start with building the Tangshan Mine into the "best mine of China", it boosted the economic modernization of surrounding areas and accelerated the rise of Tangshan and Qinhuangdao.

(1) Birth and Suffering

In the 3rd year of Guangxu of the Qing Dynasty (1877), Li Hongzhang, Viceroy of Zhili, sent Tang Tingshu to establish the Kaiping Mining Bureau in Kaiping Town, Yongping Prefecture (Today's Kaiping, Tangshan) in a government-supervised and merchant-managed form. In 1878, the Tangshan Mine, a large modern coal mine, was established in Qiaojiatun Village, Kaiping Town. In 1881, the mine came on stream. In 1898, its coal output reached 730,000 tons. In the end of the 19th century, the total assets of Kaiping Mining Bureau were nearly 6,000,000 silver taels. Together with Jiangnan Manufacturing Bureau, it became a model in the Self-Strengthening Movement.

In 1901, the Kaiping Mining Bureau was cheated out by British businessmen, and its name was changed to Kaiping Mining Co., Ltd. To disrupt the monopoly of British businessmen, Zhou Xuexi and others established the Luanzhou Mining Co., Ltd. with the support of Yuan Shikai, Viceroy of Zhili. The next year, the Luanzhou Coal Mine could match the Kaiping Coal Mine in scale. In January 1921, the British businessmen forced the Luanzhou Coal Mine to merge with the Kaiping Coal Mine, and they established the Kailuan Mining Administration. For nearly half a century, the Kailuan Coal Mine was under the control of the British people.

(2) Changes over 70 Years

Tangshan was liberated on December 12, 1948. In 1949, the Kailuan Coal Mine was nationalized. In May 1952, the mine was taken over by the people's government. Linxi and Zhaogezhuang mines were restored and reconstructed. In the meantime, Lüjiatuo, Fangezhuang and Jingezhuang mines were built. The Fangezhuang Mine was the first mine reaching an annual output of 1.8 million tons in new China. The Kailuan Mining Area was highly mechanized, and its hydraulic coal mining technology had reached the world-class level.

In December 1999, the Kailuan (Group) Limited Liability Corporation was established, which marked the establishment of a modern enterprise system for Kailuan Mining Bureau—the oldest coal enterprise of China. In 2004, Kailuan launched its IPO. In 2005, the construction project of Kailuan National Mine Park was approved. In 2018, the Kailuan Coal Mine was selected into the first batch of China's Industrial Heritage Protection List.

The Kailuan Group is a large, comprehensive energy enterprise. Its development pattern features coal mining, coal chemical industry, modern services and emerging industries. In 2021, it ranked 248th in China's top 500 companies with assets of 91.3 billion yuan.

(3) The "Combat-ready" Spirit

Kailuan is a "combat-ready" collective where the "combat-ready" spirit was nurtured. In 2019, the "combat-ready" spirit was named an "Enterprise Spirit of New China over the 70 Years".

Tang Tingshu[1], founder of the mine, overcame various difficulties. For several days in a row, he rode a donkey or went on foot from Tianjin to Kaiping, where he started the Kaiping Mining Bureau. He raised a large amount of capital by issuing shares among the Chinese merchants, which was the first stock in China.

In 1920, Deng Zhongxia, leader of the early Workers' Movement of the CPC, got acquainted with Deng Pei, leader of the Tangshan Workers' Movement, through Luo Zhanglong. In October 1922, workers of the Five Mines of Kailuan[2] staged a strike lasting 25 days following the lead of Luo Zhanglong, Wang Jingmei and Deng Pei, which eventually forced the capitalists to improve the wages and working conditions of workers. The strike dealt a heavy blow to the reactionary capitalists and feudalists. It was

---

1　On May 19, 2022, the Celebration of the 190th Anniversary of Tang Tingshu's Birth and the Academic Annual Conference on Xiangshan Merchants and Self-Strengthening Movement were held in Macao.

2　The Five Mines of Kailuan refer to the mines in Tangshan, Linxi, Majiagou, Zhaogezhuang and Tangjiazhuang.

Original Kailuan Coal Mine (Provided by the General Office of the Tangshan Municipal People's Government)

a turning point from spontaneous struggle to voluntary participation for the Kailuan workers, marking a glorious chapter in China's history of workers' movement. In his "An Analysis of the Various Classes in Chinese Society", Mao Zedong praised the Kailuan workers for being "combat-ready".

In the spring of 1938, the Kailuan workers staged the Five Mines Strike under the leadership of the CPC, dealing a heavy blow to the Japanese aggressors who "sustained the war by means of war". In July, the Kailuan workers were involved in the Uprising against Japanese Aggression in Jidong. More than 3,000 workers joined the guerrillas, giving strong support to the struggle against Japanese aggression in Jidong. Jie Zhenguo, a coal miner, was praised by Chairman Mao as a "national hero".

Kailuan, being at the frontier of the coal industry of China, had made important contributions to the economic and social development of the country in different historical periods. In 1975, the mines here produced 25.63 million tons of raw coal, coming top among the Chinese coal mines.

Zhao Guofeng, a national model worker, invented the "Stepped Pushing Mining Method", an advanced approach which greatly increased the coal output. Premier Zhou praised Kailuan for its "indelible contributions" to the country. Deng Xiaoping urged people to "study the advanced experiences of not only Daqing but also Kailuan".

Kailuan boasts many firsts in China and abroad: the first large-scale coal mine in China to achieve mechanization, Asia's largest and the world's second largest coal washery, the earliest standard-gauge railway in China—Tangshan–Xugezhuang Railway, China's first steam locomotive—"Dragon", China's first barrel of machine-made cement produced by its cement plant, Chinese enterprise's first coal wharf—Qinhuangdao Port, and China's first self-operated marine fleet…Since the Reform and Opening Up, Kailuan has won the State Award for Inventions and the State Science and Technology Progress Award for a dozen times.

(By: Qin Xuewu and Wang Meijuan)

7. 启新水泥 Chee Hsin Cement[1]

启新水泥公司是中国水泥工业的发祥地、最早的机制水泥厂和最大的水泥厂之一，生产了中国第一桶机制水泥及中国第一台水泥烘干机和水泥旋窑。2018年，启新水泥公司（现为中国水泥工业博物馆）入选第一批中国工业遗产保护名录。

启新公司肇始于唐山细棉土厂。1889年，唐廷枢创办该厂，后因原料成本高、产品质量次，于1893年关闭。1900年8月，周学熙[2]聘用德国人汉斯·昆德负责技术，组织复产。1906年8月，他从英商开平矿务局赎回唐山细棉土厂，改名为"唐山洋灰公司"。1907年8

---

1 方强：《启新洋灰公司生产经营述论（1906—1937）》，2007年河北大学硕士学位论文。
Fang Qiang: "On the Production and Operation of Chee Hsin Cement Company (1906–1937)", Master's Thesis of Hebei University, 2007.

2 周学熙（1866—1947），中国北方近代民族工业奠基人，与实业家张謇并称"南张北周"。

月，更名为"启新洋灰有限公司"，以"龙马负太极图"为商标，俗称"马"牌。

1906年至1924年，周学熙出任总理。他充分利用政商关系获取设厂、赋税、运输、销售和燃料等多方面的经营特权，还聘用中外技术人才，引进开发技术，引进更新设备，探索出成功的经营之道，迅速将启新建成当时中国最大的水泥厂，独霸水泥市场达20年之久。

在此期间，启新洋灰公司两次扩建，形成甲、乙、丙、丁四厂，在上海、天津、沈阳、汉口设立四个总批发所，水泥行销全国。1914年，公司兼并湖北水泥厂，开始垄断国内水泥市场。1919年，启新水泥占全国销量的92.02%，还出口东南亚和北美国家。1923年，产量达150万桶。1924年，公司资本达880万元，占全国水泥业资本总额的55.7%。

从1909年起，公司投资建立了马家沟机器制砖厂（今马家沟耐火材料厂）、启新磁厂（今唐山陶瓷厂）、启新机修厂（今唐山水泥机械厂），奠定了近代唐山建材工业的格局。

1949年至1955年，毛主席、朱总司令、周总理曾视察启新洋灰公司。

1954年公私合营，组建唐山启新水泥公司。1995年4月，公司与香港越秀企业（集团）有限公司合资，组建唐山启新水泥有限公司。公司现已成为拥有固定资产7.5亿元，具有现代化的自动控制生产线，年产水泥110万吨的大型水泥企业。

启新水泥质量优良，多次荣膺国际、国内大奖。1904年，获美国圣鲁意赛会（圣路易斯世界博览会）头等奖；1911年，获意大利都朗（都灵）博览会优等奖；1915年，获巴拿马赛会（巴拿马万国博览会）头奖和农商部国货展览会特等奖；1929年，获天津特别国货展览会特别奖；近年，连获省优、部优和国家银质奖。

启新水泥在中国建筑史上留下了浓重一笔。从20世纪初的北平图书馆、辅仁大学、燕京大学、南京中山陵、上海外滩，到新中国成立后的人民大会堂、历史博物馆、天安门广场等著名建筑，以及青岛、厦门等地码头，津浦铁路淮河铁路桥、黄河大桥、京汉铁路洛河铁桥，陇海铁路渭河铁桥等重大工程，无不留下它的身影。

（作者：秦学武，王妹娟）

The Chee Hsin Cement Company, as the birthplace of China's cement industry, the earliest machine-made cement plant, and one of the largest Chinese cement plants, had produced China's first barrel of machine-made cement, first cement dryer, and first rotary cement kiln. In 2018, the Chee Hsin Cement Company (today's China Cement Industry Museum) was selected into the first batch of China's Industrial Heritage Protection List.

Chee Hsin had been the Tangshan Cement Plant founded in 1889 by Tang Tingshu. It was closed down in 1893 due to the high raw material cost and inferior product quality. In August 1900, Zhou Xuexi[1] hired Dr. Hans Gunther as the technical director, and the plant resumed operation. In August 1906, Zhou bought back the Tangshan Cement Plant from the Kaiping Mining Bureau run by the British businessmen and changed its name to Tangshan Cement Company. In August 1907, the company's name was changed to The Chee Hsin Cement Company Limited. Its trademark featured "a dragon horse carrying the *taiji* diagram" and was colloquially known as the "Horse" brand.

From 1906 to 1924, Zhou Xuexi served as the president of the company. He drew upon his extensive network in government and business to gain privileges in terms of factory establishment, taxation, transportation, sales and fuel. Besides, he hired Chinese and foreign technical talents and introduced development technologies and new equipment. With its success in business, Chee Hsin Cement quickly became China's largest cement

---

1 Zhou Xuexi (1866–1947), founder of modern national industry in northern China. He and industrialist Zhang Jian were called "South Zhang and North Zhou".

plant, and its supremacy in the cement market had continued for 20 years.

After two expansions during this period, the Chee Hsin Cement Company established four plants in Tangshan and set up four general wholesale offices in Shanghai, Tianjin, Shenyang and Hankou respectively, with its cement sold across the country. In 1914, the company merged with Hubei Cement Plant and began to monopolize the domestic cement market. In 1919, the cement produced by Chee Hsin made up 92.02% of the domestic market, and the products were exported to Southeast Asia and North America. In 1923, the company produced 1.5 million barrels of cement. In 1924, the company's capital reached 8.8 million silver yuan, accounting for 55.7% of the total capital of the cement industry in China.

Since 1909, Chee Hsin had invested in Majiagou Machine-made Brick Factory (today's Majiagou Refractory Factory), Chee Hsin Ceramic (today's Tangshan Ceramic Factory) and Chee Hsin Machine Repair Plant (today's Tangshan Cement Machinery Factory). They laid the foundation of the modern building materials industry of Tangshan.

Between 1949 and 1955, Chairman Mao, Commander-in-chief Zhu and Premier Zhou had inspected the Chee Hsin Cement Company.

As the government pushed through the public-private joint management in 1954, Tangshan Chee Hsin Cement Company was established. In April 1995, the company established a joint venture—Tangshan Chee Hsin Cement Co., Ltd.—with Yuexiu Group of Hong Kong. The company has evolved into a large cement enterprise holding fixed assets of 750 million yuan, and, with its modern automatic production lines, it can produce 1.1 million tons of cement every year.

The high-quality cement produced by Chee Hsin had won many domestic and international awards and prizes. In 1904, it won a bronze medal at the Louisiana Purchase Exposition; in 1911, it won the Award of Excellence

Original Chee Hsin Cement Company (Provided by the General Office of the Tangshan Municipal People's Government)

at the Italian Turin International; in 1915, it won the First Prize at the Panama–Pacific International Exposition and the Grand Prize at the Chinese Products Exhibition hosted by the Ministry of Agriculture and Commerce; in 1929, it won the Special Prize at the Tianjin Special Chinese Goods Exhibition; in recent years, it won many silver awards at provincial, ministerial and national levels.

Chee Hsin had made quite a mark in the history of Chinese architecture. In early 1900s, its products were used in Peiping Library, Fu Jen Catholic University, Yenching University, Sun Yat-sen Mausoleum in Nanjing, and the Bund in Shanghai. After the founding of the People's Republic of China, the contribution of Chee Hsin could be seen in famous buildings such as Great Hall of the People, History Museum and Tiananmen Square, and massive projects such as wharfs in Qingdao, Xiamen and other places, Huaihe River Bridge and Yellow River Bridge of Tianjin–Pukou Railway, Luohe River Bridge of Beijing–Hankou Railway and Weihe River Bridge of Long–Hai Railway.

(By: Qin Xuewu and Wang Meijuan)

8. 唐胥铁路 Tangshan–Xugezhuang Railway[1]

唐胥铁路是指开平矿务局于 1881 年在唐山至胥各庄（今属唐山丰南）间修建并运行的一条长 9.67 千米的铁路。这是中国最早的标准轨距铁路，也是中国人自建的第一条铁路，距今已 140 余年，在洋务运动史和中国铁路史上具有重要意义。

唐胥铁路从筹划到修建，其决策是在唐廷枢和李鸿章之间进行的。光绪六年（1880）九月和七年（1881）二月，唐廷枢两次禀报李鸿章修建唐山至胥各庄之间的"快车路"，即骡马曳车在铁轨上行走的马车铁路，从而连接芦台至胥各庄之间的河路，以解开平矿务局运煤之需。七年四月，李鸿章奏请清廷。唐胥铁路建成之初，尚无蒸汽机车可用，朝野上下也普遍不支持修建火车铁路，在得到醇亲王奕譞的暗中支持后，开平矿务局才敢先以骡马拉车旋即改为机车牵引。至于民间所传慈禧以机车"震动东陵"为由只准马拉火车，或清廷以"喷出黑烟，有伤禾稼"为由勒令停驶，当为不确。

为更好满足开平煤矿的运煤需求，1887 年唐胥铁路延修至芦台，1888 年展筑至天津，全长 130 千米，命名为"津唐铁路"。1889 年，铁路向东北延伸，1892 年建至滦河段，遂有滦河铁桥[2]建设工程。1894 年，唐山至山海关段建成通车。1897 年，由天津通到北京城外马家堡。1901 年，这条铁路又延展至北京正阳门，改称京榆铁路，即今京山铁路。

唐山是中国铁路零起点城市，开创了中国铁路兴建的新时代。从唐胥铁路建成到 1949 年新中国成立的六十余年间，全国建成铁路共约 2.7 万千米。截至 2022 年，中国铁路营业里程已达到 15.5 万千米，

---

[1] 潘向明：《唐胥铁路史实考辨》，《江海学刊》2009 年 04 期。
Pan Xiangming: "Textual Research on the Historical Facts of Tangshan–Xugezhuang Railway", *Jianghai Academic Journal*, 2009, Issue 04.

[2] 1892 年，詹天佑首次采用气压沉箱法解决了滦河铁桥在河底打桩的难题。2018 年，滦河铁桥入选第一批中国工业遗产保护名录。

北洋大臣李鸿章等巡视铁路（供图：付小芳）
Li Hongzhang and others inspecting the railway (Provided by Fu Xiaofang)

其中高铁达 4.2 万千米，居世界第一。

（作者：王妹娟，秦学武）

The Tangshan–Xugezhuang Railway was a 9.67-kilometer-long section of railway from Tangshan to Xugezhuang (in today's Fengnan, Tangshan) built and operated by the Kaiping Mining Bureau in 1881. The 140-year-old railway was the earliest standard gauge railway in China as well as the first railway built by Chinese people. It has had profound significance in the Self-Strengthening Movement and the development of railway in China.

The planning and construction of the Tangshan-Xugezhuang Railway were decided by Tang Tingshu and Li Hongzhang. In the 9th month of the 6th year (1880) and the 2nd month of the 7th year (1881) of Guangxu, Tang Tingshu submitted two memorials to Li Hongzhang for building an "express road" between Tangshan and Xugezhuang—a railway with horses and mules pulling the carts along the track—to connect Lutai with Xugezhuang, allowing the Kaiping Mining Bureau to deliver its coal. In the 4th month of the 7th year of Guangxu, Li Hongzhang submitted a memorial on this

津榆铁路基址与滦河铁路桥（摄影：王进勤）
Site of Tianjin–Yuguan Railway roadbed and Luan River Railway Bridge (Photographed by Wang Jinqin)

issue to the court. When the Tangshan–Xudezhuang Railway was newly built, there was no steam locomotive available, and the program was almost universally opposed by the court and the commonalty. With the backing of Yixuan, Prince Chun, the Kaiping Mining Bureau was finally emboldened to go on. They first used mules and horses to pull the carts and then switched to locomotives. It was rumored that Cixi originally allowed only the horse-drawn trains to be used due to concerns of "disrupting the Eastern Tombs", and that the Qing court once ordered the railway to stop operation because "the black smoke could harm the crops", but these rumors proved groundless.

To better meet the delivery demand of the Kaiping Coal Mine, the Tangshan–Xugezhuang Railway was extended to Lutai in 1887 and Tianjin in 1888. The railway stretching for 130 kilometers was named "Tianjin–Tangshan Railway". Starting from 1889, the railway was extended northeast, and the Luan River section was built in 1892, which led to the construction of the Luan River Railway Bridge. In 1894, the Tangshan–Shanhaiguan section was opened to traffic. In 1897, the railway was extended from

Tianjin to Majiapu outside the city of Beijing. In 1901, the railway was extended to the Zhengyang Gate of Beijing, and its name was changed to Beijing–Yuguan Railway (today's Beijing–Shanhaiguan Railway).

Tangshan marked the beginning of China's railway era and inaugurated an age of railway construction. For over 60 years from the completion of the Tangshan–Xugezhuang Railway to the founding of the People's Republic of China, a total of 27,000 kilometers of railway had been built. Today, the operating mileage of China's railway has reached 155,000 kilometers, of which 42,000 kilometers are high-speed railways, ranking first in the world.

(By: Wang Meijuan and Qin Xuewu)

9. 唐钢集团 Tangsteel Company[1]

唐山钢铁集团有限责任公司地处河北省北部，总部位于唐山市。公司始建于 1943 年，前身为日本东洋纺织株式会社创办的唐山制钢所，1948 年唐山解放后收归国有。

唐钢集团被誉为"转炉的故乡"。1952 年 11 月，碱性侧吹转炉炼钢法试验成功，此后 20 年被中国冶金行业普遍采用。1976 年，唐山大地震后 28 天，公司炼出第一炉"志气钢"，有力支持了灾后重建工作。1979 年，公司粗钢产量突破 100 万吨，跻身全国十大钢行列。2005 年，公司钢产量达 1006 万吨，跻身千万吨级大钢行列。同年，唐钢与宣钢、承钢联合组建唐山钢铁集团有限责任公司，年钢产量达 1607 万吨，位居中国第二位。

2008 年 6 月 30 日，由唐钢集团和邯钢集团组建的河北钢铁集团有限公司揭牌成立，唐钢集团成为其子公司。由"唐钢股份""邯郸

---

[1] 张龙：《唐山钢铁集团资本运营战略研究》，2014 年山东大学硕士学位论文。
Zhang Long: "Research on the Capital Operation Strategy of Tangsteel", Master's Thesis of Shandong University, 2014.

钢铁""承德钒钛"三家上市公司合并组建的特大型钢铁企业——河钢股份有限公司，是目前中国最大钢铁上市公司之一。2021年，河钢集团位列《财富》世界500强排行榜第200名。

2008年以来，唐钢实施大规模厂容环境综合治理工程，成功打造了"世界最清洁钢厂"，赢得业内广泛赞誉。同时，唐钢投资31.8亿元实施节能和技术改造，使公司吨钢能源成本每年降低50元至100元，2010年至2013年累计降本增效40亿元。2017年，唐钢被国家工信部命名为全国第一批"绿色工厂"。

郑久强是唐钢产业工人的代表。他坚守炉台28年，练就目测钢水温度一度不差的绝活，成为"华夏第一炼钢工"。他总结出"三二四"炼钢操作法，结束炼钢厂50多年来完全靠经验炼钢的历史，成长为全国劳模、首席操作技能专家。

唐钢产品广泛用于汽车、家电、机械制造、基建工程、桥梁建设等重要领域，销往100多个国家和地区，主要装备进入国际先行列，工艺技术达到行业先进水平，成为中国具有重要影响力的汽车板、家电板生产商和综合服务商。

2020年9月，公司本部迁往乐亭县，开启了向海图强、转型升级的新征程。

（作者：王妹娟，秦学武）

The Tangshan-based Tangsteel Company is located in northern Hebei Province. First established in 1943, it was originally the Tangshan Steel Works founded by Toyobo of Japan. After the liberation of Tangshan in December 1948, the company was nationalized.

Tangsteel was known as the "Birthplace of Converter Steelmaking" in China. In November 1952, the side-blown alkaline converter steelmaking process was successfully experimented, which had been used on a huge scale in the metallurgical industry for two decades in China. 28 days after the 1976 Tangshan Earthquake, the company produced the first furnace of

"Aspiration Steel", offering strong support to the post-earthquake recovery. In 1979, the company produced more than 1 million tons of crude steel, joining the rank of top 10 steel producers in China. In 2005, the company produced 10.06 million tons of steel, joining the rank of 10-million-ton steel producers. In the same year, Tangsteel merged with Xuanhua Steel and Chengde Steel to form Tangshan Iron and Steel Group Co., Ltd., which was the second largest steel company in China with an annual steel output of 16.07 million tons at that time.

On June 30, 2008, Hebei Iron and Steel Group Co., Ltd. was established by the merger of Tangsteel and Hansteel, and HBIS Tangsteel Company became its subsidiary. Listed companies Tangshan Steel, Handan Steel, and Chengde Vanadium Titanium also consolidated to form HBIS Company Limited, a super large iron and steel enterprise, which has become one of the largest listed steel companies in China. In 2021, HBIS ranked 200th in the Fortune Global 500.

In 2008, HBIS Tangsteel started a large-scale project to comprehensively improve the factory environment, successfully building the company into "the cleanest steel plant in the world" and gaining wide acclaim in the industry. Meanwhile, the company invested 3.18 billion yuan on energy conservation and technological transformation, reducing the energy cost per ton of steel by 50–100 yuan annually with a total cost reduction of 4 billion yuan from 2010 to 2013. In 2017, Tangsteel Company was listed among the first batch of "Green Factories" by the Ministry of Industry and Information Technology of the People's Republic of China.

Zheng Jiuqiang is the representative of industrial workers in Tangsteel. Standing fast in his position for 28 years, he had mastered the skill of measuring the temperature of molten steel by eye. Enjoying the fame as China's No.1 Steelworker, Zheng made his own experience into the "3-2-

4" rule (3 calculations, 2 controls, and 4 observations), marking the end of the 50-year-long tradition of making steel by experience. Today's Zheng Jiuqiang has become a national model worker and chief expert on operating skills.

Tangsteel's products, which are widely used in automobiles, household appliances, machinery manufacturing, infrastructure construction and bridge construction, are exported to more than 100 countries and regions. Its major equipment has entered the world's leading ranks, and its processing technologies have reached the advanced level in the industry. Today, HBIS Tangsteel Company has developed into a manufacturer and comprehensive service provider in the automobile and household appliance sectors with significant influence in China.

In September 2020, the company relocated its headquarters to Laoting County, starting a new venture of going global and transforming itself.

(By: Wang Meijuan and Qin Xuewu)

10. 唐山机车车辆厂 Tangshan Locomotive and Rolling Stock Works

唐山机车车辆厂始建于 1881 年，俗称"南厂"。其前身是开平矿务局胥各庄修车厂，伴随唐胥铁路的修筑而诞生。它是中国轨道交通装备制造业的发祥地，生产了中国第一台蒸汽机车（"龙号"）和设计制造了中国第一辆客车（"銮舆"[1]）。

唐山机车车辆厂具有光荣的革命传统，度过 140 余年的风雨沧桑。1891 年 4 月，广东籍工人棒打洋技师伯恩，揭开工人斗争的序幕。1920 年，这里诞生唐山地区第一名共产党员（邓培）和第一个党组织。抗美援朝时期，工厂多次派员支援前线并修复大量机车。2006 年 7 月

---

[1] 1889 年为慈禧太后制造的一辆豪华专用客车，俗称"龙车"。

龙号和銮舆（供图：付小芳）
Dragon and Luanyu (Provided by Fu Xiaofang)

29 日，时任国家主席胡锦涛视察该厂。

从胥各庄修车厂成立至今，公司历经 20 余次更名、数次改隶。1907 年 8 月，更名为京奉铁路局唐山制造厂。1994 年 5 月，更名为唐山机车车辆厂。2007 年 7 月，更名为唐山轨道客车有限责任公司。2016 年 1 月，更名为唐山机车车辆有限公司。

唐山机车车辆有限公司是中车股份有限公司核心子企业，主要从事轨道交通装备的研发、制造、服务和检修以及工程总包、污水处理等多元化产业，总部位于唐山市。

公司先后通过了国家级企业技术中心、国家级工业设计中心、国家地方联合工程研究中心认定，拥有博士后科研工作站、院士工作站，曾获 2012 年度国家科技进步奖一等奖、2015 年度国家科技进步奖特等奖。自主研制的 CJ-2 型时速 250 千米城际动车组，获中国设

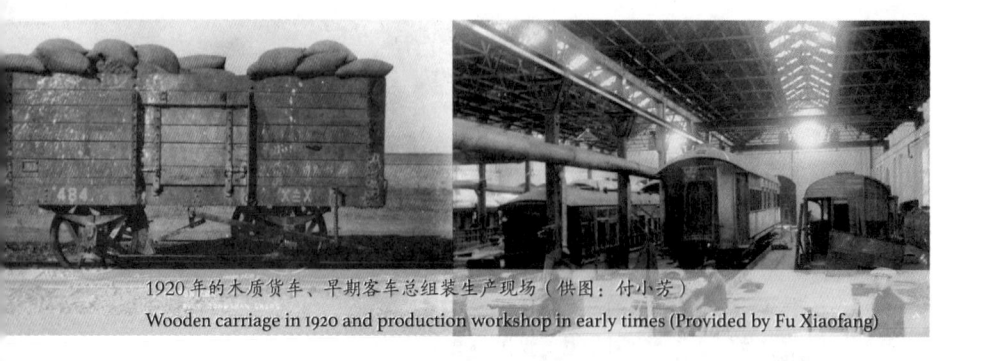

1920年的木质货车、早期客车总组装生产现场（供图：付小芳）
Wooden carriage in 1920 and production workshop in early times (Provided by Fu Xiaofang)

计奖最高奖——红星奖金奖；新研制的 CRH3X 型可变编组动车组，获中国优秀工业设计奖金奖，闪耀柏林展会；新型高速卧铺动车组，获红星奖金奖。

公司先后研制了国内首列双层内燃动车组（1998）、首列时速 160 千米摆式客车（2003）。2005 年，开始与德国西门子公司合作生产时速 300 千米高速动车组。2008 年 6 月，生产的 CRH3 型动车组创造时速 394.3 千米的当时中国铁路第一速；2011 年 1 月，自主研制的 CRH380BL 型高速动车组创造时速 487.3 千米的世界高速铁路运营试验最高速。

公司客车产品遍及国内 18 个铁路局集团公司及金温、黑河、威海等地方铁路公司，并先后为北京、天津、福州、石家庄、厦门等城市提供城轨系列产品。产品远销美国、加拿大、葡萄牙等 20 个国家和地区。

（作者：王姝娟）

Colloquially called the "South Factory", Tangshan Locomotive and Rolling Stock Works was founded in 1881. Formerly known as Xugezhuang Repair Depot of Kaiping Mining Bureau, it was born with the construction of Tangshan–Xugezhuang Railway. As the cradle of China's rail transportation equipment manufacturing industry, the company produced China's first steam locomotive (Dragon), and designed and manufactured Chin's first passenger railway car (Luanyu[1]).

Tangshan Locomotive and Rolling Stock Works, experiencing the vicissitudes of more than 140 years, has glorious revolutionary tradition. In April 1891, foreign technician Burne was beaten by Cantonese workers, kicking off the workers' struggles. In 1920, the first member of the Communist Party of China (Deng Pei) and the first Party Organization in Tangshan appeared here. During the War to Resist US Aggression and Aid Korea, the factory sent its workers to the front line for many times to fix the locomotives. On July 29, 2006, Hu Jintao, then president of China, inspected the factory.

So far, the factory has experienced more than 20 name changes and many structural reforms. In August 1907, its name was changed to Peking–Mukden Railway Bureau Tangshan Manufacturing Factory. In May 1994, its name was changed to Tangshan Locomotive and Rolling Stock Works. In July 2007, its name was changed to Tangshan Rail Passenger Train Co., Ltd. In January 2016, its name was changed to CRRC Tangshan Co., Ltd.

CRRC Tangshan Co., Ltd., a Tangshan-based core subsidiary of CRRC Corporation Limited, is mainly involved in R&D, manufacturing, service and overhaul of rail transportation equipment, as well as some other diversified businesses such as general contracting and sewage treatment.

The company is certified as a National Enterprise Technology Center, National Industrial Design Center and National-Local Joint Engineering Research Center, with a Post-doctoral Research Center and an Academician Workstation established here. It has won the First Prize of the 2012 State Science and Technology Progress Award and the Special Prize of the 2015 State Science and Technology Progress Award. Its independently developed

---

1 A luxury car made for Empress Dowager Cixi in 1889, commonly known as "Dragon Car".

Four types of high-speed trains (Photographed by Wu Kechao)

CJ-2 Intercity EMU, with a maximum speed of 250 km/h, won the Gold Prize of the Red Star Design Award—the most important award for industrial design in China, its new CRH3X Variable Marshalling EMU won the Gold Prize of China Excellent Industrial Design Award and attracted much attention at InnoTrans, and its new high-speed sleeper EMU won the Gold Prize of the Red Star Design Award.

The company developed China's first double-deck DMU (1998) and first 160 km/h tilting train (2003). In 2005, it started to work with Siemens to develop a 300 km/h high-speed train. In June 2008, the CRH3 high-speed train set a speed record of 394.3 km/h in China. In January 2011, its independently developed CRH380BL high-speed train reached a top speed of 487.3 km/h, which was the world's fastest railway test speed at the time.

Passenger trains produced by the company can be found in the 18 regional subsidiaries of China Railway, as well as local railway companies in Jinwen, Heihe, Weihai, etc. The company has been providing urban rail transit products for Beijing, Tianjin, Fuzhou, Shijiazhuang, Xiamen, etc. Its products are exported to 20 countries and regions, such as the United States, Canada and Portugal.

(By: Wang Meijuan)

11. 唐山港 Tangshan Port

唐山港位于河北省唐山市东南沿海，分京唐港区和曹妃甸港区，是中国对外开放口岸、沿海地区性重要港口，能源、原材料等大宗物资专业化运输系统的重要组成部分，华北及西北部分地区经济发展和对外开放的重要窗口。

京唐港区位于乐亭县王滩镇。1989年8月开工建设，1992年7月国内通航，1993年7月国际通航，2001年跻身千万吨级大港。1993年7月17日，北京市和唐山市签署联合建港协议，唐山港更名为京唐港。2003年，港口吞吐量2083万吨。2005年，河北省、唐山市决定恢复唐山港港名，京唐港改称京唐港区。2009年，完成吞吐量1.0541亿吨。2013年，吞吐量2.01亿吨。运输货种包括煤炭、矿石、钢铁、集装箱、水泥、粮食等10多大类、100多个品种。

曹妃甸港区位于曹妃甸区，是孙中山《建国方略》中"北方大港"的港址所在地，是渤海沿岸唯一不需开挖航道和港池即可建设40万吨级大型泊位的天然港址，2005年正式对外通航。曹妃甸港是国际能源、工业原材料集疏与贸易大港，承揽矿石、钢铁、集装箱、焦煤、液体化工、机械设备、滚装汽车及其他散杂、件杂等货物装卸及增值业务。

唐山港现已形成港口、铁路、公路、高速公路交叉纵横的综合交通运输体系，通达70多个国家（地区）、200多个港口。2021年，唐山港完成货物吞吐量7.22亿吨，位居全国沿海港口第2位；集装箱吞吐量329万标箱。

2010年7月，唐山港集团在上海主板上市，累计募集资金60.1亿元用于港口建设，根本改变了港口的发展速度和质量。唐山港集团先后获得全国五一劳动奖状、国家科技进步二等奖、全国文明单位等多项殊荣。

（作者：王姝娟）

Located on the southeast coast of Tangshan, Hebei, Tangshan Port is

京唐港区和曹妃甸港区（供图：唐山市政府办公厅）
Jingtang Port Area and Caofeidian Port Area (Provided by the General Office of the Tangshan Municipal People's Government)

composed of two separate port areas: Jingtang and Caofeidian. It is an important coastal port open to the outside world, an important part of the specialized transportation system for energy resources, raw materials and other bulk materials, and an important window for the economic development and opening up of North China and parts of Northwest China.

The Jingtang Port Area is located in Wangtan Town, Laoting County, and its construction began in August 1989. In July 1992 and July 1993, it was opened to domestic shipping and international shipping respectively. In 2001, the area became a ten-million-ton port. On July 17, 1993, Beijing and Tangshan signed an agreement for jointly building the port, and Tangshan Port changed its name to Jingtang Port. In 2003, the handling capacity of the port reached 20.83 million tons. In 2005, Hebei Province and Tangshan City decided to resume the former name of the port, and Jingtang Port changed its name to Jingtang Port Area. In 2009 and 2013, the handling capacity of the port reached 105.41 and 201 million tons respectively. Today, the port area deals with over 100 types of goods under a dozen categories, such as coal, ore, steel, containers, cement and grains.

The Caofeidian Port Area, located in Caofeidian District, is where the "Great Northern Port" in Sun Yat-sen's *Plans for National Reconstruction* is located. Officially opened to shipping in 2005, it is the only natural port area along the coast of Bohai Sea where berths for 400,000-ton ships can be built without excavating channels and harbor basins. As an international port for the collection, distribution and trade of energy resources and industrial raw materials, the Caofeidian Port Area undertakes the loading and unloading of ore, steel, containers, coking coal, liquid chemical products, machinery and equipment, ro-ro vehicles and other miscellaneous goods while providing value-added services for clients.

Tangshan Port has been developed into an integrated transport system featuring port areas, railways, highways and expressways, with access to more than 200 ports in over 70 countries and regions. In 2021, its cargo throughput reached 722 million tons, coming second among the coastal ports of China, and its container throughput reached 3.29 million TEU.

In July 2010, Tangshan Port Group got listed on the main board of Shanghai Stock Exchange and raised a total of 6.01 billion yuan for port construction, fundamentally changing the speed and quality of its development. Tangshan Port Group has won many national honors, such as National May 1st Labor Certificate, State Science and Technology Progress Award (Second Prize), and National Civilized Unit.

(By: Wang Meijuan)

二、农业文化 II. Agriculture

12. 京东板栗 Jingdong Chestnut[1]

板栗，果实称栗子，壳斗科栗属植物。李时珍《本草纲目》云：

---

[1] 郝福为，张法瑞：《中国板栗栽培史考述》，《古今农业》2014 年 03 期。
Hao Fuwei, Zhang Farui: "Research on the History of Chinese Chestnut Cultivation", *Ancient and Modern Agriculture*, 2014, Issue 03.

"栗之大者为板栗，中心扁子为栗楔（xiè）。稍小者为山栗。山栗之圆而末尖者为锥栗。"板栗在中国被称为"千果之王"，国外称之为健康食品。

（1）板栗的栽培

板栗原产于中国，至今有六千余年的栽培史。板栗适应性强，生长力强，极易推广，生长周期短，结果时间长，有"铁杆庄稼"之称。

京东板栗（摄影：王爱军）
Jingdong chestnuts (Photographed by Wang Aijun)

古代的板栗栽培技术主要有实生繁殖、移栽繁殖和嫁接繁殖。《齐民要术》《物理小识》《农政全书》《便民图纂》等有详载。

（2）板栗的利用价值

板栗有很高的食用价值，《吕氏春秋》《韩非子》《战国策》已有记载。《齐民要术》将其与桃、杏、李、枣并称"五果"。板栗的淀粉含量为56%—72%，蛋白质含量为5.7%—10.7%，脂肪含量为2%—7.4%，含有多种维生素。它与红枣、柿子并称三大"木本粮食"。

板栗有很高的药用价值。常食栗子可益气血、养胃、补肾、健肝脾，生食有舒筋活络、驱寒止泻的功效。陶弘景《名医别录》云："主益气，厚肠胃，补肾气，令人耐饥。"孙思邈《千金方》云："生食之，甚治腰脚不遂。"李时珍《本草纲目》所述甚详。栗楔、栗荴（fū）、栗壳、毛球、栗花、栗树皮、栗树根等均有药用功效。

板栗树高大、挺直，木材坚实、抗冲击、抗腐、耐湿，是制作建筑和家具的优质木材。《公羊传》《左传》有相关记载。

（3）京东板栗的栽培

京东板栗是指生产于河北省燕山山脉的迁西、遵化、迁安、抚宁、卢龙、青龙、兴隆、宽城、平泉、承德、滦平等11个县（市、区）的板栗。2006年，被国家质检总局审核批准为地理标志保护产品。

京东板栗在汉代已大规模栽培，至今有约2000年历史。《战国策·燕策》云："（燕）南有碣石、雁门之饶，北有枣栗之利，民虽不由田作，

青龙县肖营子镇的板栗古树群（摄影：张京政）
Old chestnut trees in Xiaoyingzi Town, Qinglong County (Photographed by Zhang Jingzheng)

枣栗之实，足食于民矣，此所谓天府也。"《史记》《全辽文》《辽史》也有记载。青龙县有树龄100年以上的板栗古树2000多株。宽城、青龙、昌黎等地均有树龄千年的"栗树王"。

燕山山脉土壤母质多为片麻岩，呈微酸性，通透性好，且含有多种微量元素。年均气温7.7—11.5℃，年降雨量351.1—804毫米，年日照时数2600—2745小时，无霜期135—198天。得天独厚的土壤及气候条件，生长出优质京东板栗：果型端正，色泽鲜艳，果实均匀，营养丰富，香、甜、糯可口，耐贮性强，[1]有"东方珍珠"之美誉。

目前，京东板栗有燕山早丰、燕山短枝、替码珍珠、遵玉、紫珀、燕山魁栗、东陵明珠、遵化短刺、塔丰栗、遵达栗、大板红等优良品种。

（4）京东板栗产业

京东板栗是中国著名果品品牌，在国内外久负盛名。曾获"全国林业博览会金奖""中国国际农业博览会名牌产品"。产品远销日本、东南亚等30多个国家和地区。

京东板栗是冀东地区的支柱产业，种植面积460余万亩，年产值逾60亿元，惠及300万栗农。青龙满族自治县板栗栽培面积近100

---

[1] 李小新等:《京东板栗生产中存在的问题与对策》,《中国园艺文摘》2018年01期。

万亩，居全国第一。遵化市年产板栗 5 万吨，板栗加工品产值达 100 亿元。

（作者：秦学武，王妹娟）

Castanea mollissima, its fruit called Chinese chestnut, is a member of the genus Castanea, family Fagaceae. According to *Compendium of Materia Medica* by Li Shizhen, "In terms of the nuts in a cupule, the large ones are called chestnuts, and the central flat one is called the nut wedge. Small chestnuts are called mountain chestnuts, and round, pointed mountain chestnuts are called cone chestnuts." Chestnuts are renowned as the "King of Fruits" in China and recognized as a health food abroad.

(1) The Cultivation of Chestnuts

Chinese chestnuts have been cultivated for more than 6,000 years. The plant has strong adaptability and vigorous vitality, and, with a fast growth rate and a long fruiting period, it can be widely planted as an "iron-like crop".

Back in the ancient times, chestnut trees were cultivated mainly through seed propagation, transplanting propagation and grafting propagation, which are well documented in *Essential Techniques for the Welfare of the People*, *Innate Laws of Things*, *Complete Treatise on Agriculture* and *An Illustrated Book for the Convenience of People*.

(2) The Values of Chestnuts

Chestnuts are highly nutritious, which has already been described by *Master Lü's Spring and Autumn Annals*, *Hanfeizi* and *Strategies of the Warring States*. In *Essential Techniques for the Welfare of the People*, chestnuts, peaches, apricots, plums and jujubes are known as the "Five Fruits". Chestnuts contain 56–72 grams of starch, 5.7–10.7 grams of protein and 2–7.4 grams of fat in a 100-gram reference, and provide a variety of vitamins. Chestnuts, jujubes and persimmons are called "Three Major Woody Grains".

Chestnuts have medicinal properties. Regular consumption of the food can replenish *qi* and blood, nourish the stomach, tonify the kidney, and strengthen the liver and spleen. When eaten raw, the fruit can stimulate the circulation of blood, relax the muscles and joints, expel cold and stop diarrhea. According to *Supplementary Records of Famous Physicians* by Tao Hongjing, "Chestnuts can tonify the *qi*, thicken the stomach and intestines, invigorate the kidney *qi* and help control hunger." Here is what *Thousand Golden Prescriptions* by Sun Simiao says: "Eaten raw, chestnut can strengthen the waist and legs." Li Shizhen gave a detailed record of the fruit in *Compendium of Materia Medica*. Chestnut wedges, peels, shells, cupules, flowers, bark and roots all have medicinal properties.

Chestnut trees are tall and straight, and chestnut wood is solid and resistant to impact, corrosion and moisture, making it a perfect building and furniture material. Relevant records can be found in *Gongyang's Commentary on The Spring and Autumn Annals* and *Zuo's Commentary on The Spring and Autumn Annals*.

(3) The Cultivation of Jingdong Chestnuts

Jingdong chestnuts refer to the chestnuts produced in Qianxi, Zunhua, Qian'an, Funing, Lulong, Qinglong, Xinglong, Kuancheng, Pingquan, Chengde and Luanping in the Yan Mountains of Hebei Province. In 2006, it was approved by the General Administration of Quality Supervision, Inspection and Quarantine of the People's Republic of China as a Protected Geographical Indication Product.

Jingdong chestnuts have been planted on a large scale for about 2,000 years since the Han Dynasty. According to *Strategies of the Warring States*, "To the south (of the State of Yan), there lies the fertile land of Jieshi and Yanmen; to its north, there lies the land for jujubes and chestnuts. The people there don't do farm work. They feed themselves on jujubes and chestnuts. This is

Deep processing of chestnuts (Photographed by Liu Xinming)

what we call the Land of Abundance." Similar records can also be found in *Records of the Historian*, *A Whole Collection of Liao Literature* and *History of Liao*. In Qinglong County, there are more than 2,000 ancient chestnut trees over 100 years old. The "Kings of Chestnut Trees" of over 1,000 years old can be found in Kuancheng, Qinglong and Changli.

The parent material in the Yan Mountains is mostly gneiss, and the soil there is slightly acidic with good aeration and multiple micronutrients. The average annual temperature is 7.7–11.5℃, the annual rainfall is 351.1–804 millimeters, the annual sunlight duration is 2,600–2,745 hours, and the frost-free period is 135–198 days. Blessed with the unique combination of soil and climate, the Jingdong area produces superior chestnuts that are regularly shaped, fresh-looking, well-proportioned and highly nutritious. Fragrant, sweet and soft, Jingdong chestnuts can be preserved for a long time[1] and are reputed to be the "Pearls of the East".

---

1 Li Xiaoxin, etc.: "Problems and Countermeasures in Jingdong Chestnut Production", *Chinese Horticultural Abstracts*, 2018, Issue 01.

There are a variety of Jingdong chestnuts, such as Yanshanzaofeng, Yanshanduanzhi, Timazhenzhu, Zunyu, Zipo, Yanshankuili, Donglingmingzhu, Zunhuaduanci, Tafengli, Zundali and Dabanhong.

(4) Jingdong's Chestnut Industry

Jingdong chestnuts are well-known both in China and abroad, winning a Gold Medal at the Forestry Expo China and being named a Famous Product at the China International Agricultural Exhibition. The chestnuts and processed products are exported to more than 30 countries and regions, such as Japan and Southeast Asia.

As a mainstay of Jidong's economy, Jingdong chestnuts are cultivated in an area of over 4.60 million *mu* and have an annual output value of over 6 billion yuan, benefiting about 3 million farmers. In Qinglong Manchu Autonomous County, the cultivated area of chestnuts is nearly 1 million *mu*, ranking first in China. In Zunhua, 50,000 tons of chestnuts are produced every year, and the output value of processed chestnut products has reached 10 billion yuan.

(By: Qin Xuewu and Wang Meijuan)

13. 山海关大樱桃 Shanhaiguan Cherry[1]

大樱桃为蔷薇科李属植物，别称迎庆果、樱珠、车厘子，是中国乃至全世界人们最喜爱的重要水果之一。欧洲、西亚、东亚、北美、南美和大洋洲均有栽培。

大樱桃原产于西亚和东南欧，主要生长在北纬 30—45° 地区。大樱桃的栽培特点为喜温暖、好湿润、忌寒冷、怕霜冻，最佳栽培区域年均温度在 10—12℃。秦皇岛市位于北纬 40° 附近，背山向海、气候

---

[1] 姜涛等:《秦皇岛大樱桃产业现状与发展对策》,《河北果树》2022 年 02 期。
Jiang Tao, etc.: "Current Situation and Development Countermeasures of Cherry Industry in Qinhuangdao", *Hebei Fruits*, 2022, Issue 02.

萨米拖、美早、雷尼（摄影：张立彬）
Summit, Tieton, Rainier (Photographed by Zhang Libin)

温和、热量充足、雨水充沛，年均降雨量约700毫米，处在我国大樱桃栽培的北线，地理环境适合大樱桃的发展。

19世纪70年代中国开始栽植大樱桃，主要分布在华中、华北及两广地区，以辽宁大连、山东烟台、河北秦皇岛为最。目前，秦皇岛市大樱桃栽培面积3850公顷，其中山海关区面积2000公顷，是中国著名的大樱桃产区。

大樱桃是山海关区的支柱产业，1985年开始栽培。露地樱桃及设施樱桃现有红灯、萨米拖、早大果、沙王、俄罗斯8号、美早等20多个品种，年产量超3万吨，产值5亿元以上。

山海关区依托现有旅游资源，建立了集观光采摘、休闲度假、餐饮娱乐、产品加工为一体的新型农业综合体，年吸引游客40万人次，旅游收入近6千万元。借助互联网优势，山海关大樱桃已走出河北，远销上海、广州等城市。

近年来，山海关大樱桃产业已由传统的生产型向特色型、规模化、综合性的现代农业转变。2001年，山海关区被国家林业局授予"中国樱桃之乡"。2020年，"山海关大樱桃"通过国家知识产权局的地理标志证明商标注册。

（作者：王姝娟，秦学武）

A cherry, aka yingqing fruit, cherry pearl or chelizi in China, is the fruit of many plants of the genus Prunus, family Rosaceae. It is one of the most popular fruits in China and around the world. The fruit is cultivated in

Europe, West Asia, East Asia, North America, South America and Oceania.

Cherry trees, originating in West Asia and Southeast Europe, grow mainly between 30° N and 45° N. They are thermophilic, suited to a humid climate and vulnerable to cold and frost, and the ideal annual average temperature for them is 10–12℃. Qinhuangdao, located around 40° N and surrounded by mountains and sea, has a mild and warm climate and an average annual rainfall of about 700 millimeters, thus becoming an area suitable for the cultivation of cherries in North China.

China began to plant cherry trees in the 1970s in Central China, North China and Guangdong and Guangxi, with Dalian in Liaoning, Yantai in Shandong and Qinhuangdao in Hebei being the most representative. Currently, the cherry-planting areas in Qinhuangdao cover 3,850 hectares, of which 2,000 hectares are in Shanhaiguan District, making it a famous cherry-producing area in China.

Cultivated since 1985, cherries have become a mainstay of Shanhaiguan District's economy, with cherry trees planted in both open-air and controlled environments. Currently, there are over 20 varieties, including Red Light, Summit, Zaodaguo, Sand King, Russian No.8 and Tieton, producing more than 30,000 tons of cherries that worth more than 500 million yuan annually.

Based on the existing tourism resources, a new agricultural complex integrating sightseeing and picking, leisure and vacation, catering and entertainment, and product processing has been established in Shanhaiguan District. Every year, 400,000 tourists are attracted to the place, generating a tourism revenue of nearly 60 million yuan. With the aid of the Internet, Shanhaiguan cherries have been sold outside of Hebei to Shanghai and Guangzhou, among others.

In recent years, the cherry industry in Shanhaiguan District has transformed from the traditional production-oriented type to a characteristic, large-scale and comprehensive modern type. In 2001, Shanhaiguan District was awarded the title of "Hometown of Chinese Cherries" by the State Forestry Administration of the People's Republic of China. In 2020, "Shanhaiguan Cherry" was recognized by China National Intellectual Property Administration as a Geographical Indication.

(By: Wang Meijuan and Qin Xuewu)

14．卢龙甘薯 Lulong Sweet Potato[1]

甘薯学名番薯，属旋花科甘薯属。番薯别称众多，常称甘薯、地瓜、红薯、白薯、山芋等。明清文献常作蕃苕、番葛、番储、番茹、番芋等。

（1）甘薯的引进与推广

番薯原产于美洲，明朝中叶后传入中国，有三条路线：一是从美洲传到菲律宾，再到福建；二是从美洲传到越南，再到广东；三是从美洲传到缅甸，再到云南。

《金薯传习录》载：明万历二十一年（1593）五月，福建商人陈振龙从菲律宾吕宋岛购得薯藤数尺，冒死将其带回故乡栽植。陈氏及五代后人赓续推广栽植甘薯，从福建到山东再到直隶。陈振龙被誉为"红薯之父"。

明代福建巡抚金学曾在《海外新传七则》介绍甘薯栽植方法，将其好处归为：高产、多用、易活。徐光启的《农政全书》称甘薯的优点、价值有"十三胜"，并指出："农人之家，不可一岁不种。"清乾隆时期更是开展了规模浩大的"劝种"活动。

从 1593 年甘薯引入中国，到清乾隆十年（1745）山东德州农民改善窖藏方法，彻底解决薯种越冬难题，历时 150 余年，甘薯栽植从长

---

[1] 感谢中国孤竹文化研究中心提供相关资料。
We are thankful to China Guzhu Culture Research Center for providing the information.

江以南推广到全国。

甘薯的栽植是中国粮食生产史上的一次革命，极大改变了中国人的饮食结构，也曾帮助国人度过饥饿年代。目前，中国的甘薯栽植面积和总产量均居世界首位。

卢龙粉丝（摄影：张京政）
Lulong vermicelli (Photographed by Zhang Jingzheng)

（2）甘薯的营养价值

甘薯含有淀粉、维生素、纤维素等营养成分，以及镁、磷、钙等矿物元素。

甘薯既是健康食品，也是祛病良药。《本草纲目》云，甘薯有"补虚乏，益气力，健脾胃，强肾阴"的功效。

（3）卢龙的甘薯栽植

《卢龙县志》载，清咸丰年间（1851—1861），蛤泊镇开始栽植甘薯；光绪二十九年（1903），木井乡一邸姓农家栽植甘薯，此后渐布全县。甘薯被誉为"铁杆庄稼"。

20世纪30年代末40年代初，卢龙县出现淀粉和粉条的加工生产。2007年，卢龙粉条传统加工技艺入选河北省级非物质文化遗产名录。

1954年，卢龙县始创"顿水顿火"回龙火炕育秧法。1971年，又在火炕加盖塑料薄膜，最终完善了"顿水顿火加盖塑料薄膜育秧法"[1]。北京科技电影制片厂曾摄制科教专题片。1972年，卢龙县技术人员曾赴安徽、山东、陕西、山西、天津、辽宁、吉林等地指导育秧。

---

1 甘薯育秧的第一茬需21天，从种薯上炕第一天起，每天浇一次水、烧一次火，温度在34—35°C；出苗前两天，停水停火两天，温度在26—27°C，使秧苗逐渐长成长壮；第二茬秧苗开始，每7天一茬苗，出苗前两天停水停火，其前后的温度控制，浇水、烧火的次数，与第一茬相同。

1990年，农民李秀祥成功培育新品种"卢选1号"，品质好、产量高、高淀粉，亩产2200公斤。2004年，该品系被审定为"冀审薯200001号"。

（4）卢龙的甘薯产业

甘薯产业是卢龙县第一主导产业，也是河北省重点龙头产业之一。目前，卢龙县甘薯栽植分淀粉薯、鲜食薯两种，面积15万亩，总产近6亿公斤。

卢龙县现有薯制品加工企业20余家，产品有精制淀粉、精制粉条、方便粉丝、粉皮、冷面、薯脯、薯片、薯酥、工业酒精等20余个品种，年产10万吨以上，年产值逾20亿元。卢龙粉丝已进入韩国、日本、美国、加拿大等20余个国家和地区。

1996年，卢龙县被命名为"中国甘薯之乡"。1999年，卢龙粉丝被评为"中国国际农业博览会名牌产品"。2004年8月，"卢龙粉丝"获得国家地理标志产品保护。2019年，"卢龙甘薯"区域公用品牌正式启用。

（作者：秦学武，王姝娟）

The sweet potato is a plant of the genus Ipomoea, family Convolvulaceae. It has many nicknames, such as *gan shu*, red potato and white potato. In Ming and Qing literature, it is often referred to as *fan fu*, *fan ge*, *fan chu*, *fan ru*, *fan yu*, etc.

(1) The Introduction and Popularization of Sweet Potatoes

The sweet potato, native to the Americas, was introduced to China in the latter half of the Ming Dynasty through three routes: the Americas–the Philippines–Fujian, the Americas–Vietnam–Guangdong, and the Americas–Myanmar–Yunnan.

According to *Records of Golden Potatoes*, in the 5th month of the 21st year of Wanli of Ming (1593), Chen Zhenlong, a Fujian businessman, bought some sweet potato vines in Luzon of the Philippines and risked his life to bring them back to his hometown. With the efforts of Chen and his descendants through five generations, the cultivation of sweet potatoes was popularized from Fujian to Shandong and to Hebei. Chen Zhenlong was known as the "Father of Sweet Potatoes".

Jin Xue, Governor of Fujian in the Ming Dynasty, recorded the cultivation methods of sweet potatoes in *Seven New Stories from Overseas*. He described the benefits of the plant as "high-yield, multipurpose and tough". Xu Guangqi's *Complete Book of Agricultural Affairs* sums up the advantages and values of sweet potato as "Thirteen Merits". It also notes: "a farming family must plant sweet potatoes every year." During the reign of Emperor Qianlong in the Qing Dynasty, a large-scale campaign of "persuading farmers to plant sweet potatoes" was carried out.

In the 10th year of Qianlong of the Qing Dynasty (1745), farmers in Dezhou, Shandong improved the cellar storage solutions, solving the difficult problem of getting the seeds safely through the winter. After over 150 years, the sweet potato had spread from the south of the Yangtze River all the way across China.

The cultivation of sweet potatoes is a revolution in the history of food production in China. It greatly changed the dietary structure of the Chinese people and helped them survived the famine years. Today, China's planting area and yield of sweet potatoes rank first in the world.

(2) The Nutritional Value of Sweet Potatoes

The sweet potato is rich in starch, vitamins, cellulose, etc., and it also contains minerals such as magnesium, phosphorus and calcium.

The sweet potato is both a healthy food and a cure for diseases. According to *Compendium of Materia Medica*, it has the medicinal properties of "reinforcing deficiency, replenishing *qi*, strengthening the spleen and stomach and tonifying the kidney *yin*".

Cultivation of Lulong sweet potatoes (Photographed by Gu Zhaoliang)

(3) The Cultivation of Lulong Sweet Potatoes

According to *Local Records of Lulong County*, in the years of Xianfeng of the Qing Dynasty (1851–1861), sweet potatoes started to be planted in Gebo Town. In the 29th year of Guangxu (1903), a farming family surnamed Di began to cultivate sweet potatoes in Mujing Village. Later, the cultivation of sweet potatoes was popularized in the county. Since then, the plant has been reputed as an "iron-like crop".

In the late 1930s and early 1940s, the natives of Lulong County began to extract sweet potato starch and produce Chinese vermicelli. In 2007, the traditional technique of Lulong vermicelli making was added to the Intangible Cultural Heritage List of Hebei Province.

In 1954, the natives of Lulong County invented the "Intermittent Watering and Heating on a Hot *Kang*" seedling raising method. In 1971, the method was improved by covering the hot *kang* with a plastic film and eventually became the "Intermittent Watering and Heating under a Plastic Film" seedling raising method.[1] A science documentary on this method was

---

[1] The first batch of sweet potato seedlings takes 21 days to grow. From the first day when seed potatoes are planted on the *kang*, watering and heating are done once a day, and the temperature is kept at 34–35℃. Two days before germination, watering and heating are stopped, and the temperature is kept at 26–27℃, so that the seedlings gradually grow strong. Starting from the second batch of seedlings, each batch takes 7 days to grow, and the temperature control, watering and heating before and after germination are executed the same as the first batch.

made by the Beijing Science Film Studio. In 1972, technicians in Lulong County went to Anhui, Shandong, Shaanxi, Shanxi, Tianjin, Liaoning and Jilin to guide local farmers on seedling raising.

In 1990, farmer Li Xiuxiang bred a new variety "Luxuan No.1" that boasted high quality, high yield and high starch content with an annual average yield of 2,200 kilograms per *mu*. In 2004, the variety was approved as "Jishenshu 200001".

(4) The Sweet Potato Industry in Lulong

The sweet potato industry is the mainstay industry of Lulong County and one of the key leading industries of Hebei Province. There are two types of Lulong sweet potatoes—one for starch extraction and the other for eating, and they are planted on an area of 150 thousand *mu* with a total annual yield of 600 million kilograms.

Currently, there are more than 20 sweet potato processing enterprises in Lulong County, offering more than 20 kinds of products, such as refined starch, refined vermicelli, instant vermicelli, vermicelli sheets, chilled noodles, preserved sweet potatoes, sweet potato chips, sweet potato crisps and industrial alcohol. The annual output is over 100 thousand tons, and the industry is worth more than 2 billion yuan. Lulong vermicelli is exported to more than 20 countries and regions, such as South Korea, Japan, the United

States and Canada.

In 1996, Lulong County was named "Hometown of Chinese Sweet Potatoes". In 1999, Lulong vermicelli was named a Famous Product at the China International Agricultural Exhibition. In August 2004, "Lulong Vermicelli" was listed as a Protected Geographical Indication Product of China. In 2019, "Lulong Sweet Potato" was officially launched as a regional public brand.

(By: Qin Xuewu and Wang Meijuan)

15. 昌黎葡萄酒 Changli Wine[1]

葡萄，古作蒲陶、蒲桃、蒲萄，为葡萄科葡萄属木质藤本植物，是常见水果，也可酿酒。葡萄原产于中亚，汉武帝时传入中国。

（1）历史渊源

昌黎县种植葡萄历史悠久，明朝中期就已种植鲜食葡萄，距今600余年。鲜食葡萄主栽品种为玫瑰香，还有牛奶、巨峰、龙眼等。昌黎葡萄沟，现有一株150余岁的葡萄树王。1930年7月，荷兰传教士文欣华来到昌黎县西山场村，教会村民酿造葡萄酒。

中国第一瓶干红（供图：碣石山片区开发管理委员会）

China's first dry red wine (Provided by Jieshi Region Development Management Committee)

（2）葡萄酒产区

昌黎地处北纬39°世界酿酒葡萄黄金种植带，是著名的葡萄与葡

---

[1] 感谢昌黎县碣石山片区开发管理委员会提供相关资料。

We are thankful to Changli County Jieshi Region Development Management Committee for providing the information.

萄酒产区，被誉为"东方的波尔多"。

1979年，昌黎从法国购入赤霞珠酒葡萄幼苗，建立中国第一个酿酒葡萄基地。现有酿酒葡萄基地10万亩，主栽品种为赤霞珠，还有马瑟兰、品丽珠、美乐、霞多丽等。

昌黎干红酒生产线（摄影：刘文军）
Production line for Changli dry red wine (Photographed by Liu Wenjun)

昌黎葡萄酒澄清透明、有光泽，具有纯正、浓郁的果香，口感纯正、细腻，酒体丰满、完整，回味绵长。昌黎开创了众多中国干红酒业的第一：1983年，生产中国第一瓶干红葡萄酒——北戴河牌赤霞珠干红葡萄酒；1988年，诞生中国第一家干红葡萄酒专营企业；2002年，获批中国第一个葡萄酒行业地理标志保护产品——昌黎葡萄酒；以及其他业内工艺第一。

（3）葡萄酒产业

昌黎产区现有葡萄酒生产企业65家，葡萄酒加工能力21万吨，拥有华夏长城、茅台、朗格斯、金士等知名葡萄酒品牌。产品远销法国、英国、美国、新加坡、中国香港等20多个国家和地区。20世纪80年代末至21世纪初，国内干红酒出口80%来自昌黎。

华夏酒窖（供图：碣石山片区开发管理委员会）
A wine cellar (Provided by Jieshi Region Development Management Committee)

第七章　产业文化　　　　Chapter VII Industrial Culture　　　　403

葡萄酒产业是昌黎的支柱产业，已形成覆盖全产业链的葡萄酒产业集群，年营收超 25 亿元。近年来，昌黎葡萄酒文化游日渐兴起，年接待游客 40 万人次。

（4）取得荣誉

1984 年，北戴河牌干红葡萄酒获得全国轻工业系统优秀新产品奖、轻工业部全国酒类质量大赛金杯奖；1989 年、1990 年、2004 年，长城干红葡萄酒分获法国第 29 届国际评酒会特别奖、第 14 届巴黎国际食品博览会金奖和第 5 届布鲁塞尔国际评酒会特别金奖；2015 年，晟杰至尊干红葡萄酒获第 21 届巴黎国际葡萄酒评比大赛金奖。

2000 年 8 月，昌黎被命名为"中国干红葡萄酒之乡""中国酿酒葡萄之乡"和"中国干红葡萄酒城"。2013 年，昌黎县葡萄酒产业园区被认定为国家农业产业化示范基地；2015 年，昌黎干红葡萄酒产业聚集区被认定为河北省现代农业园区。

（作者：秦学武，王妹娟）

A grape, known as "蒲陶", "蒲桃" or "蒲萄" in Chinese history, is the fruit of the woody vines of the genus Vitis, family Vitaceae. This common fruit, which can be used to produce wine, originated from Central Asia and was introduced to China during the reign of Emperor Wu of the Han Dynasty.

(1) The History

Changli County has a long history of cultivating table grapes, which can be traced back to the middle of the Ming Dynasty some 600 years ago. The main varieties of table grapes in Changli include Muscat, Milk, Kyoho and Longyan. In the Grape Valley, Changli, there is a grapevine over 150 years old. In July 1930, Wen Xinhua, a Dutch missionary, came to Xishanchang Village, Changli County and passed on to the villagers the technique of wine making.

(2) A Wine Region

Located in the Golden Planting Area of *Vitis Vinifera* at 39°N, Changli is a renowned grape and wine producing area. It enjoys a reputation for being the "Oriental Equivalent of Bordeaux".

In 1979, Changli government purchased the seedlings of Cabernet Sauvignon from France and established China's first wine grape base. The county now has 100,000 *mu* of wine grape bases, mainly cultivating Cabernet Sauvignon, as well as Marselan, Cabernet Franc, Merlot and Chardonnay.

The wine produced in Changli has a clean and bright color, a fruity fragrance, a genuine and delicate taste, a rich flavor and an elegant

葡萄架下（摄影：刘文军）
Under a grape trellis (Photographed by Liu Wenjun)

收集酒葡萄（摄影：田延光）
Collecting wine grapes (Photographed by Tian Yanguang)

lingering finish. Changli boasts many firsts in the dry red wine industry of China. For example, in 1983, the first bottle of dry red wine in China—Beidaihe Cabernet Sauvignon Dry Red Wine—was produced here; in 1988, China's first dry red wine franchise was established here; in 2002, Changli Wine was approved as the first Protected Geographical Indication Product of China in the wine industry.

(3) The Wine Industry

Changli's wine region is home to 65 wine enterprises with a production capacity of 210,000 tons. Among them are prestige brands such as Greatwall, Moutai, Longues Reges, and Kings. The products are exported to 20 countries and regions, including France, Britain, the United States, Singapore and China's Hong Kong. From the late 1980s to the early 2000s, 80% of the exported dry red wine came from Changli.

The wine industry is a mainstay of Changli's economy. A wine industry cluster covering the whole industrial chain worth 2.5 billion yuan has taken shape. With the rising of wine culture in recent years, Changli has become a tourist attraction receiving 400,000 visitors every year.

(4) Honors

In 1984, Beidaihe Dry Red Wine won the Excellent New Product Award of the National Light Industry System and the Gold Cup Award of the National Wine Quality Competition of the Ministry of Light Industry. In 1989, 1990 and 2004, Greatwall Dry Red Wine won the Special Award of the 29th International Wine Tasting Competition in France, the Gold Award of the 14th SIAL Paris and the Great Gold Medal of the 5th Concours Mondial de Bruxelles. In 2015, Shengjie Zhizun Dry Red Wine won the Gold Award of the 21st Vinalies Internationales Wine Competition.

In August 2000, Changli was named "Hometown of Chinese Dry Red Wine", "Hometown of Chinese Wine Grapes" and "Dry Red Wine City of China". In 2013, Changli County's Wine Industrial Park was recognized as a national agricultural industrialization demonstration base; in 2015, the Changli Dry Red Wine Industry Cluster was recognized as a Modern Agricultural Park of Hebei.

(By: Qin Xuewu and Wang Meijuan)

三、商业文化 III. Commerce

16. 呔商 Tai Merchant[1]

呔商，也作岱商。当年大批来自乐亭、滦州、滦南、昌黎等县的人到东北经商，他们讲昌黎方言，二声少、三声多，东北人称其为"老呔"。

老呔商帮始于清乾隆年间，止于社会主义改造时期，历时160余年。老呔商帮与张库帮、冀中帮，并称冀商三大帮派。

（1）代表人物

呔商从小本生意做起，慢慢在东北扎根。之后在长春、哈尔滨、沈阳、四平、大连等大城市兴商办厂开钱庄，足迹遍及东北。"九·一八"事变前，他们开办的商号、企业达1000余家，从业者有10万之众。民间有"东北三个省，无商不乐亭"的说法。刘新亭、张希孔、武百祥、赵汉臣、杨焕亭、王玉堂、母海岳、刘临阁等为呔商代表。

铁匠出身的刘新亭，首开乐亭人在东北经商之先河。刘家的"发字号""合字号"买卖遍及东北、华北和华南。民国时期，"益发合"成为东北地区民族金融企业的旗帜。时任中华民国总统黎元洪为刘家写就"京东第一家"匾额。

木匠出身的张希孔，在船厂（今吉林）经营小木匠铺。东北某"木帮"把大批积压木料赊给他，言定次年秋后付款。他等了四年仍不见"木帮"踪迹，才用这笔钱开设"万合木局"。他靠诚信起家，成为富甲一方的巨商。

武百祥从摆地摊到开小店，最后在哈尔滨创办产供销一条龙的"大同记"，高峰时营业额曾居哈尔滨之首，被誉为"北国商魂"。

---

[1] 韩建伟等:《呔商文化：冀东商业史上的一朵奇葩》,《保定学院学报》2014年01期。
Han Jianwei, etc.: "The Culture of Tai Merchants: A Wonderful Flower in the Business History of Jidong", *Journal of Baoding University*, 2014, Issue 01.

（2）呔商文化

一是"和为贵，信为本"。同行之间和谐共处，内部之间和衷共济。对待顾客重信守义，以质取胜。武百祥在经营大罗新寰球货店时，坚持"利公司、利顾客、利劳资、利同业"的"四利"经营原则，兼顾各方利益。他在东北商界首创"明码标价""言不二价"的文明经商之风，制定了"货真、价平、优待、快感"的店规。

二是选贤任能，严格管理。民国以后，呔商打破"用乡不用亲"[1]的商规，广揽人才。武百祥不惜重金从天津请来糕点名师，从江浙地区请来制衣能手，还延聘外国专家，使得"同记"商场人才济济。刘毅侯大胆启用孙秀三，执掌"益发合"30余年，将其从旧式商号发展成集商业、金融、工业于一体的现代化企业。二人被誉为"南孙北武"。

三是擅长谋略，敢为人先。清光绪末年，刘新亭抓住东北开禁放垦的商机，通过做农具生意，完成资本的原始积累。20世纪初，武百祥在哈尔滨开办百货商场——大罗新寰球货店，这在当时的上海也很少见。

四是回馈社会，造福乡梓。清光绪年间，刘新亭创办乐亭私立第一所学校"刘氏第一中学堂"，还创办了"亲仁小学""尚义女子中学"。民国时期，武百祥创办"赵滩小学"和"百善学校"[2]。王执中、刘临阁、杨逢春、母海岳等也创办了小学和中学。到新中国成立初期，呔商创办学校达30余所，为社会培养了数以万计的人才。在扶危济贫、赈济灾民和民族解放事业中，呔商也做出了突出贡献。

（作者：秦学武，王姝娟）

Tai merchants refer to a group of people in the past who went from Laoting, Luanzhou, Luannan and Changli to Northeast China and engaged in trade there. They spoke the Changli dialect which featured fewer rising

---

1 "用乡"，即非冀东人不用；"不用亲"，即本家商号不用亲属。

2 乐亭县何新庄村的百善学校建于1928年，为武百祥、赵婵堂共建，2014年复建，是唐山市仅存的呔商遗迹。

tones and more dipping tones, and the people in Northeast China called them "Lao Tai".

The Lao Tai merchant group lasted some 160 years from the years of Qianlong in the Qing Dynasty to China's socialist transformation period. Lao Tai, Zhang-Ku and Jizhong were the three major merchant groups of Hebei.

(1) Representatives

Tai merchants started with small businesses and gradually put down roots in Northeast China. Afterwards, they set up factories and money shops in big cities such as Changchun, Harbin, Shenyang, Siping and Dalian, and their traces could be found across Northeast China. Before the September 18 Incident, the shops and enterprises ran by Tai merchants numbered more than 1,000, with over 100,000 people participating in the businesses. There was a local saying, "All businessmen in the three northeastern provinces are from Laoting." Liu Xinting, Zhang Xikong, Wu Baixiang, Zhao Hanchen, Yang Huanting, Wang Yutang, Mu Haiyue and Liu Linge were representatives of Tai merchants.

Liu Xinting, a blacksmith-turned-merchant, was a pioneer of Laoting people doing business in Northeast China. Businesses under the names of "Fa Shop" and "He Shop" run by the Liu family spread across Northeast, North and South China. In the Republic of China era, "Yi Fa He" had become a flagship among domestic financial enterprises in Northeast China. Li Yuanhong, then president of the Republic of China, wrote the words meaning "best enterprise to the east of the Capital " for an inscribed board of the Liu family.

Zhang Xikong, a carpenter-turned-merchant, ran a small carpenter shop in Chuanchang (today's Jilin). Once, a timber dealer group in Northeast China sold him an excess inventory of timbers on credit and agreed that the payment could be made after the next autumn. Zhang Xikong waited for four years, but the timber dealer group didn't show up. He founded Wanhe Wood Company with the money. The honest man became a merchant with great wealth.

Wu Baixiang was renowned as the "Soul of Merchants in the North". He started as a peddler and then became the runner of a small shop. At last, he founded "Da Tong Ji", a shop in Harbin integrating production, supply and sales. At its peak, the shop had the highest turnover among all the shops in Harbin.

(2) Tai Merchant Culture

At the core of the Tai merchant culture is "harmony among the contemporaries and honest with the customers". When he ran the Daluo New Universe Department Store, Wu Baixiang held firm to his principles of "benefiting the company, the customers, the labor and capital and the industry" and accommodated the interests of all parties. His store followed a set of rules to ensure that "quality goods should be reasonably priced for the pleasant experience of customers". Thanks to his efforts, the trend of "clear pricing" and "honest trading" became prevalent in the business circles in Northeast China.

To attract talents and standardize the management, Tai merchants broke the rule of "using villagers and not using relatives"[1] in the Republic of China era. Wu Baixiang paid good money to employ famous pastry chefs from Tianjin, proficient tailors from Jiangsu and Zhejiang, and experts from other countries. As a result, his Tongji Shopping Mall teemed with professional talents. Liu Yihou boldly appointed Sun Xiusan to run the operations of "Yi Fa He". After some 30 years, Yi Fa He had evolved from

---

1 "Using villagers" means that only the natives of Jidong could be hired; "not using relatives" means that one's own relatives should not be hired in his shop.

an old-style business to a modernized enterprise combining commerce, finance and industry. The two people were known as "South Sun and North Wu".

Tai merchants were reputed to be innovative and extremely sharp of wit. In the last years of Guangxu of the Qing Dynasty, the government lifted the ban on land reclamation in Northeast China, and Liu Xinting took the opportunity to make his fortune by selling farm tools. In early 1900s, Wu Baixiang opened his Daluo New Universe Department Store in Harbin. At the time, department stores were rare even in Shanghai.

Tai merchants actively made efforts to contribute to the betterment of the community. In the years of Guangxu of Qing, Liu Xinting founded Liu's No.1 Middle School—the first private school in Laoting, as well as Qinren Primary School and Shangyi Girls' Middle School. In the Republic of China era, Wu Baixiang founded Zhaotan Primary School and Baishan School[1]. Wang Zhizhong, Liu Linge, Yang Fengchun and Mu Haiyue had founded primary and secondary schools, too. By the early years of the People's Republic of China, the 30-some schools founded by Tai merchants had nurtured tens of thousands of talents. Besides, Tai merchants had also made outstanding contributions in respect of poverty alleviation, disaster relief and national liberation.

(By: Qin Xuewu and Wang Meijuan)

---

1 The Baishan School in Hexinzhuang Village, Laoting County was founded in 1928 by Wu Baixiang and Zhao Chantang, and it was reestablished in 2014. It is the only remaining relic of Tai merchants in Tangshan.

第八章

时代文化

Chapter VIII Culture of the Times

一、民主革命 I. Democratic Revolutions

1. 辛亥滦州起义 Luanzhou Uprising of 1911[1]

滦州兵谏和滦州起义，是 1911 年武昌起义后以新军第二十镇革命官兵为主体，在直隶滦州发生的两个有重大影响的历史事件，沉重打击了清王朝的统治，有力支持了湖北及其他各省的资产阶级民主革命。辛亥滦州起义是滦州兵谏的继续和发展。

（1）滦州兵谏

1911 年 10 月，清政府为炫耀军威，决定在直隶永平府举行新军秋操（即军事演习）。武昌起义前，同盟会会员张绍曾、蓝天蔚、吴禄贞密谋利用率部参加秋操的机会，暗带子弹，相机起义。10 月 10 日武昌起义爆发，打乱了清政府的秋操部署，也极大鼓舞了滦州准备起义的新军官兵。清政府决定停止秋操，参操部队从滦州撤回，命令东路新军第二十镇官兵"暂住滦州，听候调度"。

10 月 27 日，新军第二十镇统制张绍曾发动本镇官兵在滦州举事，蓝天蔚等在奉天以电报上奏奏折和"十二条政纲"，要求清政府召开国会、制定宪法、赦免国事犯等，史称"滦州兵谏"。清政府为维护统治，解除张绍曾职务，削除兵权，把二十镇分散调开，化整为零，共襄义举的第六镇统制吴禄贞在石家庄被暗杀，滦州兵谏宣告失败。

（2）滦州起义

吴禄贞被刺杀，燕晋联军解体，张绍曾退隐天津，滦州兵谏失败，使革命遭受严重挫折。但参加革命的官兵愈挫愈勇。

参与滦州兵谏的二十镇各营管带王金铭、施从云、冯玉祥等人，密图在驻地滦州起义。天津共和会会长白雅雨几经坎坷亲赴滦州，会见王金铭、施从云等骨干，策划滦州起义。12 月 31 日，同盟会会员

---

[1] 赵润生，马亮宽：《直隶惊雷——辛亥革命在京津冀》，天津人民出版社 2011 年版。
Zhao Runsheng and Ma Liangkuan: *A Clap of Thunder—Revolution of 1911 in Beijing, Tianjin and Hebei*, Tianjin People's Publishing House, 2011.

王金铭、施从云、白雅雨率滦州新军宣布起义，响应南方革命。1912年1月3日，他们在滦州城举行大典，宣布成立"中华民国北方革命军政府"，并通电全国，推举王金铭为都督，施从云为总司令，冯玉祥为参谋总长，白雅雨为参谋长；1月4日，起义军发表檄文，声讨清政府，准备攻打京津。后因清政府的镇压，王金铭、施从云、白雅雨等人壮烈牺牲，大批革命志士被捕，起义失败。

滦州起义是辛亥革命的重要组成部分，是辛亥革命初期具有重大影响的一次起义，在整个民主革命进程中起着举足轻重的作用。国民政府1936年颁布的《国民政府令》云："辛亥光复，发轫于武昌，而滦州一役，实促其成。"

（作者：吴子国）

In the wake of the Wuchang Uprising of 1911, the Luanzhou Armed Remonstrance and Luanzhou Uprising broke out in Luanzhou, Zhili (Today's Hebei). With the officers and soldiers of the 20th Garrison of the New Army as the main forces, these two historical events carried profound implications. They caused severe disruption to the reign of the Qing Dynasty and gave strong support to the bourgeois-democratic revolution of Hubei and other provinces. The Luanzhou Uprising of 1911 was the continuation of the Luanzhou Armed Remonstrance.

(1) Luanzhou Armed Remonstrance

In October 1911, the Qing government, to show off their military power, decided to put on an autumn exercise (military drill) of the New Army in Yongping Prefecture, Zhili Province. Zhang Shaozeng, Lan Tianwei and Wu Luzhen, members of the Tongmenghui, tried to take this opportunity to engineer an uprising. They smuggled bullets into the autumn exercise site with their troops. On October 10, the Wuchang Uprising broke out, disrupting the autumn exercise of the Qing government and boosting the morale of the officers and soldiers of the New Army preparing to launch the uprising in Luanzhou. The Qing government decided to stop the autumn exercise and remove the participating troops from Luanzhou. Officers and soldiers of the 20th Garrison of the New Army in the east were ordered to "stay in Luanzhou and wait for dispatches".

On October 27, officers and soldiers in Luanzhou, under the leadership of Zhang Shaozeng, commander of the 20th Garrison of the New Army, rose up in arms. In Mukden, Lan Tianwei submitted a memorial and the Twelve Political Programs to the Qing government by telegraph, requesting the government to establish a parliament, frame a constitution and grant amnesty to the state criminals. The incident was known historically as the "Luanzhou Armed Remonstrance". In order to keep its reign, the Qing government removed the duty of Zhang Shaozeng and his command of the army. The 20th Garrison was dissolved and dispatched to different places. Wu Luzhen, commander of the 6th Garrison with generous contributions to the undertaking, was assassinated in Shijiazhuang. The Luanzhou Armed Remonstrance ended in failure.

(2) Luanzhou Uprising

After Wu Luzhen was assassinated, the Yan-Jin Allied Forces was broken up, and Zhang Shaozeng retreated to Tianjin. The failure of the Luanzhou Armed Remonstrance had inflicted serious damage on the democratic revolution, but it also made the revolutionary officers and soldiers stronger.

Wang Jinming, Shi Congyun and Feng Yuxiang, officers of the 20th Garrison participating in the Luanzhou Armed Remonstrance, planned an uprising in the barracks in Luanzhou. Bai Yayu, head of the Tianjin Republican Association, went to Luanzhou after many twists and turns. There, he met, among others, Wang Jinming and Shi Congyun, backbones of the association, and planned the Luanzhou Uprising with them. On December 31, an uprising was unleashed by the New Army following the leadership of Wang Jinming, Shi Congyun and Bai Yayu, members of the Tongmenghui, in response to the revolution in the south. On January 3, 1912, a ceremony was held in Luanzhou celebrating the establishment of Northern Revolutionary Military Government of the Republic of China, and a telegraph reporting the event was sent across the country. Wang Jinming, Shi Congyun, Feng Yuxiang and Bai Yayu were installed as Governor, Commander-in-chief, Chief of General Staff and Chief of Staff. On January 4, the insurrectionary army issued a call to arms against the Qing government and prepared for an attack against Beijing and Tianjin. The uprising was squelched by the governmental troops, and Wang Jinming, Shi Congyun and Bai Yayu heroically gave up their lives. A large number of revolutionaries were arrested, and the uprising ended in failure.

The Luanzhou Uprising was an important part of the Revolution of 1911. Occurring in the early stage of the Revolution, it meant a lot to the bourgeois-democratic revolution throughout the whole course. Here's what the National Government's Decree sent out by the Nanjing National Government in 1936 says, "The Revolution of 1911 started in Wuchang, and the Luanzhou Uprising helped deliver it."

(By: Wu Ziguo)

二、先驱足迹 II. Footprints of the Pioneers

2. 李大钊在五峰山 Li Dazhao in the Wufeng Mountain[1]

李大钊（1889—1927），河北省乐亭县大黑坨村人。他是坚定的

---

[1] 本词条的相关史实，除另有标注外，以杨琥著《李大钊年谱》（上、下册）（云南教育出版社，2021年12月版）为据。

Unless otherwise noted, relevant historical facts of this entry are based on Yang Hu's *Chronicles of Li Dazhao* (Vol.1 and Vol.2) (Yunnan Education Press, December 2021).

革命家，中国共产党的主要创始人之一；是勇立潮头的社会活动家，"五四"新文化运动的先驱；是深受北京大学等高校学生欢迎的教授；是战斗在时代一线的著名媒体人。

五峰山[1]位于河北省昌黎县城北5千米，属碣石山支脉。由紧密相连的五座山峰组成，东曰"望海峰"，东北曰"锦绣峰"，北曰"平斗峰"，西北曰"飞来峰"，西曰"挂月峰"。韩文公祠建在五峰山的半山腰处。

1907年至1924年，李大钊数次来到五峰山，或游览，或客居，或避难，这里留下了李大钊生活、战斗的足迹。如今，五峰山前矗立着李大钊全身汉白玉雕像和半身花岗岩雕像。1998年，五峰山被确定为省级爱国主义教育基地。2000年，李大钊革命活动旧址展陈室落成。

（1）1907年8月，首游五峰山

1907年8月，李大钊从永平府中学堂毕业，与三位同学到天津参加北洋法政专门学堂的入学考试。从天津返乐亭途中，素爱登山的李大钊在昌黎[2]下火车后游兴勃发，力主登碣石山，但恰逢雨天而作罢。在韩文公祠结识了守祠人刘克顺，小憩后，李大钊一行雨中畅游五峰山。其《游碣石山杂记》详载此事。从此，李大钊与五峰山结下不解之缘。其长女李星华曾说："昌黎五峰山，几乎成了父亲的第二故乡。"

（2）1913年9月，再游五峰山

1913年6月，李大钊从北洋法政专门学堂毕业。经孙洪伊介绍，进步党领袖汤化龙用党费资助李大钊等9名进步青年赴日留学，补助每人每年300元生活费。

9月初，李大钊与同学子默（郭须静）同往五峰山，客居约十日。期间，昌黎站五名铁路警察被日本驻军杀害，激起李大钊心中极大愤慨，立下誓言："所与倭奴不共戴天者，有如碣石。"[3]

---

[1] 此五峰山，实为"西五峰山"，居"东五峰山"之西。因其声名显赫，当地称其"五峰山"。

[2] 彼时，昌黎县与乐亭县同属直隶永平府。大黑坨村距昌黎县城仅80里。碣石山为永平府名山。

[3] 李大钊《游碣石山杂记》，发表于1913年11月1日《言治》第6期。

李大钊雕像（摄影：何志利）
Statue of Li Dazhao (Photographed by He Zhili)

（3）1917年5月，三游五峰山

1917年5月5日晚8时35分，李大钊从北京乘京奉（沈阳）线火车返回乐亭，探视病中的妻子。拂晓时，车过雷庄——辛亥滦州起义白亚雨等烈士就义地，心中感慨万千。6日晨抵达昌黎，乘骡车再游五峰山，并看望故友刘克顺[1]夫妇。7日离开昌黎返乐亭。6月22日，李大钊自乡返京。期间，李大钊的《旅行日记》于5月9日至11日发表在章士钊主编的《甲寅日刊》。

12月17日，章士钊向蔡元培推荐李大钊接任自己的北大图书馆主任。1918年1月中旬，李大钊正式就任。入职北大，对李大钊影响甚巨。他与当时中国思想界最前沿的陈独秀、胡适、钱玄同、周作人等朝夕相处，遂成新文化运动的倡导者之一。

他于1918年1月成为《新青年》杂志的轮值编辑，后主编《晨钟报》副刊。1918年6月30日，参与发起创建少年中国学会。11月底，在中央公园（今中山公园）演讲《庶民的胜利》。12月，与陈独秀共创《每周评论》。1919年1月，在《新青年》第5卷第5号上发

---

1 其长女李星华说："他同五峰山有这样深厚的感情，是同刘克顺一家分不开的，以后他每次来五峰山避居、过暑假，总是住在昌黎祠刘克顺的家里。"

韩文公祠（摄影：何志利）
Temple of Han Wengong (Photographed by He Zhili)

表《庶民的胜利》《布尔什维主义的胜利》。这两篇文章，深刻探讨了"一战"后，世界与中国的关系，以及中国的前途和出路。这两篇雄文揭开了新文化运动的新思潮，深刻影响了年轻一代知识分子的成长。

（4）1918年夏，小住五峰山

1918年暑假，已任北大图书馆主任的李大钊返乡，接妻儿来北京。《李大钊年谱》等著述无此次小住五峰山的直接记载。但从好友白坚武8月1日至19日的日记可见端倪。白多次接到李的信函，19日更是接到李创作的四首白话诗。

《山中即景》[1]：

其一：自然的美，美的自然。绝无人处，流水空山。

其二：人在白云中，云在青山外。云飞人自还，依旧青山在。

其三：一年一度果树红，一年一度果花落。借问今朝摘果人，忆否春雨梨花白。

《悲犬》[2]：

我初入山，犬狂吠门前。我既入山，犬摇尾乞怜。犬哉！犬哉！何前倨而后谦？

从诗中，可以看出李大钊在五峰山期间，身心愉悦。

（5）1919年7月至8月，客居五峰山

1919年7月20日，李大钊携待产的妻子和孩子返乡，21日到乐

---

1 《山中即景》的前两首发表在1918年9月15日的《新青年》第5卷第3号。

2 杜春和、耿来金整理：《白坚武日记》第1册，江苏古籍出版社1992年版。

亭。7月下旬至8月下旬，携10岁的长子李葆华赴五峰山短住。11月底，次女李炎华在乐亭出生。

是年，8月30日的《新生活》第2期和9月7日的《新生活》第3期，分两次发表李大钊的《五峰游记》。9月初，李大钊主编的《新青年》第6卷第5号"马克思研究专号"出版，《我的马克思主义观（上）》等9篇文章发表。《我的马克思主义观（下）》于11月在《新青年》第6卷第6号发表。李大钊的《我的马克思主义观》，全文近3万字。该文是中国人首次较为系统、完整地介绍马克思主义，在中国马克思主义传播史上具有重要作用和重大意义，标志着李大钊已转变为一名马克思主义者。学界普遍认为，李大钊7—8月客居五峰山期间完成了这篇经典文献的写作。

（6）1920年2月，冬游五峰山

1920年2月中旬，为避免陈独秀再次被捕入狱，李大钊护送陈独秀出京，经天津于2月14日抵上海。

二人分手后，李大钊去向哪里？相关文献并无其回昌黎五峰山的直接记载。当地学者推论：李大钊从天津乘火车回老家，在昌黎下车后去五峰山给刘克顺家拜早年[1]。3月11日，陈独秀给周作人的信中询问："2月29日来信已收到了。……守常兄久未来京，不知是何缘故？"显然，陈牵挂李的安全。9月下旬，李大钊致信周作人，告知陈独秀在沪的通信地址，特意指出："我那时亦跑到昌黎山中去了，所以未曾答你。今天接他的信，知道他已回沪，仍住渔阳里二号。"如此，二人分别致周作人的信，或可证明李大钊送别陈独秀后回昌黎五峰山的事实。

1920年7月，李大钊任北大政治学系教授兼史学系教授，讲授《唯物史观》《社会进化论》。此后又开设《现代政治》《史学思想史》《社会主义运动史》等课。他还兼任朝阳大学、北京高等师范学校、女子高等师范学校、中国大学等校教员，讲授《史学思想史》《社会

---

[1] 此年除夕为2月19日。

学》等课程。8月，赵世炎首提"北李南陈"。

（7）1922年夏，五峰山度假

1922年夏，李大钊利用暑假携全家在五峰山度假。

（8）1924年5月，五峰山避难

1924年5月下旬，为躲避北洋军政府的通缉，已是北方国共两党领导人的李大钊与长子李葆华到五峰山避难，住韩文公祠。

这是李大钊最后一次来到五峰山。在山中，李大钊接到妻子赵纫兰的书信，问李大钊可否请曾经的好友白坚武帮助撤销通缉令。李大钊表示拒绝并坚信："目前统治者的猖狂，只不过是一时的恐怖罢了。不用多久，红旗将会飘满北京城，看那时的中国，竟是谁家的天下！"

1927年4月28日，李大钊等20名革命者被军阀张作霖绞刑杀害。李大钊神色未变，从容就死，英年38岁。

（作者：秦学武，吴子国）

Li Dazhao (1889–1927), a native of Daheituo Village, Laoting County, Hebei Province, was a determined revolutionist and a main founder of the Communist Party of China. He was a social activist at the forefront of the democratic campaign, and a pioneer of the "May 4th" New Culture Movement. He was a professor well-received by the students of Peking University and other universities, and a media worker fighting at the forefront of the times.

The Wufeng Mountain[1], 5 kilometers north of Changli County, Hebei Province, is a branch range of the Jieshi Mountain. It consists of five connecting peaks—Wanghai Peak in the east, Jinxiu Peak in the northeast, Pingdou Peak in the north, Feilai Peak in the northwest, and Guayue Peak in the west. The Temple of Han Wengong is half-way down the Wufeng Mountain.

1　The Wufeng Mountain here is actually the West Wufeng Mountain to the west of the East Wufeng Mountain. As it is of more repute, the locals simply call it Wufeng Mountain.

From 1907 to 1924, Li Dazhao came several times to the Wufeng Mountain for visit, stay or refuge, and he left traces of his life and battle here. Today, a whole-length white marble statue and a half-length granite statue of Li Dazhao are standing in front of the Wufeng Mountain. In 1998, the Wufeng Mountain was designated as a Provincial Patriotism Education Base. In 2000, the Exhibition Room of the Former Site of Li Dazhao's Revolutionary Activities was built here.

(1) First Visit to the Wufeng Mountain in August 1907

When he graduated from Yongping Prefecture Middle School in August 1907, Li Dazhao took the entry test of Beiyang Legal and Political College in Tianjin with three fellow students. During the return from Tianjin to Laoting, they got off the train at Changli[1]. As an avid climber, Li Dazhao was feeling in the mood for climbing the Jieshi Mountain. However, as it was raining, the activity was out of the question. They went to the Temple of Han Wengong and met Liu Keshun, the temple keeper. After resting for a while, Li Dazhao and his companions visited the Wufeng Mountain in the rain. The event was recorded in "Miscellanies on Jieshi Mountain". Li had since been linked inextricably with the Wufeng Mountain. Li Xinghua, the eldest daughter of Li Dazhao, said, "Changli's Wufeng Mountain was almost the second hometown of my father."

(2) Second Visit to the Wufeng Mountain in September 1913

In June 1913, Li Dazhao graduated from Beiyang Legal and Political College. He was introduced by Sun Hongyi to Tang Hualong, leader of the Progressive Party. Tang provided Li and eight other progressive youths with subsidies of 300 silver yuan a year per person during their study in Japan.

---

1 At that time, both Changli County and Laoting County were administered by Yongping Prefecture. Daheituo Village was just 80 *li* away from Changli County. The Jieshi Mountain was a famous mountain in Yongping Prefecture.

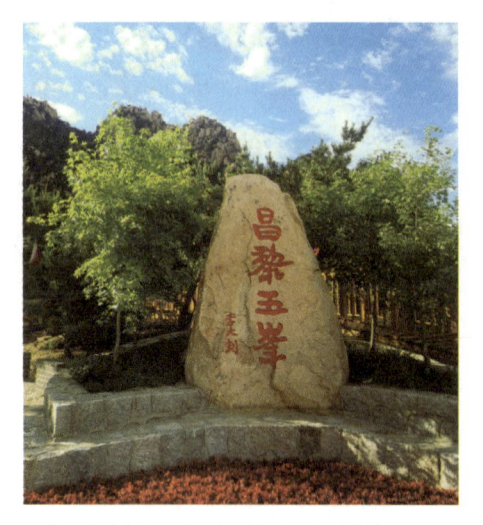

昌黎五峰（李大钊手迹）（摄影：何志利）
Wufeng Mountain in Changli (Handwritten by Li Dazhao) (Photographed by He Zhili)

In early September, Li Dazhao and his classmate Zi Mo (Guo Xujing) stayed in the Wufeng Mountain for a dozen days. During this time, five railway policemen at Changli Station were killed by the Japanese soldiers. This aroused Li Dazhao to indignation and he swore: "My enmity with the Japanese invaders is endless. My determination will remain rock-solid as the Jieshi Mountain." [1]

(3) Third Visit to the Wufeng Mountain in May 1917

At 08:35 pm on May 5, 1917, Li Dazhao travelled by train on the Peking–Mukedun Railway from Beijing to Laoting to see his sickened wife. At dawn, the train went past Leizhuang, where Bai Yayu and others sacrificed their lives in the Luanzhou Uprising of 1911, and Li Dazhao was overcome with emotion. When Li left the train at Changli in the morning of May 6, he travelled around the Wufeng Mountain again on a mule-drawn wagon. There, he looked up his old friend Liu Keshun[2] and Liu's wife. On May 7, he left Changli for Laoting. On June 22, Li Dazhao went back to Beijing. His "Travel Diaries" was published in *1914 Daily* edited by Zhang

---

1 Li Dazhao: "Miscellanies on Jieshi Mountain", published on November 1, 1913 in *On Governance*, Issue 6.

2 His eldest daughter Li Xinghua said, "He had an emotional attachment to the Wufeng Mountain, which was inseparable from Liu Keshun and his family. Since that time, when he stayed or spent summer in the Wufeng Mountain, he used to live in Liu Keshun's house in the Temple of Han Wengong."

Shizhao from May 9 to 11.

On December 17, Zhang Shizhao put Li Dazhao forward to Cai Yuanpei to succeed his post as Director of Peking University Library. In mid-January 1918, Li Dazhao officially took up the position. The experience at Peking University had a profound influence on Li's life. Working together with intellects at the forefront of the Chinese academic circles, such as Chen Duxiu, Hu Shi, Qian Xuantong and Zhou Zuoren, he became a proponent of the New Culture Movement.

In January 1918, Li Dazhao became the rotating editor of the magazine *New Youth*. Later, he became the Chief Editor of the supplement *Morning Bell*. On June 30, 1918, Li became the cofounder of the Chinese Youth Association. In late November, he delivered the speech "Victory of the Commoners" in the Central Park (today's Zhongshan Park). In December, he founded *Weekly Review* with Chen Duxiu. In January 1919, *New Youth* (Vol.5, No.5) carried "Victory of the Commoners" and "Victory of Bolshevism". The two articles took a close look at the relationship between China and the world in the post-WWI era and the course of China in future. They represented a new thought of the New Culture Movement and had profound implications for young intellectuals.

(4) A Short Stay in the Wufeng Mountain in the Summer of 1918

In the summer holiday of 1918, Li Dazhao, by the time Director of Peking University Library, brought his wife and children to Beijing. We couldn't read about this stay in the Wufeng Mountain in *Chronicles of Li Dazhao*, but the event was mentioned in the diaries of his friend Bai Jianwu from August 1 to 19. Bai received many letters from Li, and the one on August 19 consisted of four free verses in vernacular Chinese. They are as follows:

"Impromptu in the Mountain"[1]:

1. The beauty of nature requires no overstatement. In the out-of-the-way place, streams are trickling downhill.

2. A man is enshrouded in clouds, and clouds are beyond the mountain. When clouds roll away, the man and the mountain remain.

3. Once a year, fruit trees turn red. Once a year, blossoms fall on the ground. I'd like to ask the fruit picker: Can you remember the rain-soaked blooms?

"Poor Dog"[2]:

When I came to the mountain the first time, the house-dog barked at me. When I came to the mountain again, the dog wagged its tail. Alas, the dog! Why would you change your attitude?

We could tell by the poems that Li Dazhao had a pleasant stay in the Wufeng Mountain.

(5) Residing in the Wufeng Mountain from July to August 1919

On July 20, 1919, Li Dazhao returned home with his pregnant wife and children, and they arrived at Laoting on July 21. From late July to late August, he went staying in the Wufeng Mountain with Li Baohua, his son of 10 years old. In late November, his second daughter Li Yanhua was born in Laoting.

On August 30 and September 7, the magazine *New Life* (Issue 2 and 3) carried Li Dazhao's "Travel Notes of Wufeng Mountain". In early September, the "Special Issue on Marxist Studies" of *New Youth* (Vol.6, No.5) edited by Li Dazhao published his "My Marxist View (Part 1)" and

---

[1] The first two poems of "Impromptu in the Mountain" were published on September 15, 1918 in *New Youth*, Vol.3, No.3.

[2] Organized by Du Chunhe and Geng Laijin: *Bai Jianwu's Diaries*, Vol.1, Jiangsu Ancient Book Publishing House, 1992.

Wufeng Mountain in distance (Photographed by He Zhili)

eight other articles. In November, *New Youth* (Vol.6, No.6) published the 30,000-word "My Marxist View (Part 2)". It was the first time a Chinese people probed Marxism systematically and comprehensively. The article had been enormously important to the spreading of Marxism in China. It marked Li Dazhao's transformation to a Marxist. Scholars generally believed that "My Marxist View" was created during Li Dazhao's residence in the Wufeng Mountain from July to August.

(6) Winter Visit to the Wufeng Mountain in February 1920

In the middle of February 1920, Li Dazhao escorted Chen Duxiu out of Beijing to avoid the latter's being thrown back to prison. The two people arrived at Shanghai by way of Tianjin on February 14.

Where did Li Dazhao go after they said goodbye? There is no direct record of his returning to the Wufeng Mountain in any literature. According to the local scholars, there is a possibility that Li returned to his hometown from Tianjin by train. When he got off the train at Changli, Li might have gone to Liu Keshun's house in the Wufeng Mountain with greetings before the Spring Festival[1]. On March 11, Chen Duxiu sent a letter to Zhou Zuoren, which ran as follows: "I've received the letter on February 29...Li Dazhao has not arrived at Beijing. I wonder what has happened." Chen was evidently concerned with the safety of Li. In late September, Li Dazhao sent a letter to Zhou Zuoren, informing him of the address of Chen Duxiu in Shanghai. He said in the letter, "I didn't answer the letter because I had been to the mountain in Changli. Today, I have a letter from Chen in which he mentioned that he was back in Shanghai and still lived in No. 2, Yuyangli." The two letters to Zhou Zuoren might confirm that Li Dazhao had gone to the Wufeng Mountain after saying goodbye to Chen Duxiu.

In July 1920, Li Dazhao became the professor of Political Science Department and History Department of Peking University, and he lectured on Historical Materialism and Social Evolutionism. New courses such as Modern Politics, History of Historical Thought and History of Socialist Movement were offered later. He was also appointed as the instructor of Chaoyang University, Beijing Higher Normal University, Women's Normal University and University of China, lecturing on History of Historical Thought, Sociology, etc. In August, Zhao Shiyan first proposed the "North Li and South Chen".

(7) Having A Holiday in the Wufeng Mountain in the Summer of 1922

In the summer of 1922, Li Dazhao went on a holiday excursion with his family in the Wufeng Mountain.

(8) Seeking Refuge in the Wufeng Mountain in May 1924

In late May 1924, the Beiyang Military Government issued an arrest warrant for Li Dazhao. Li, then leader of the Kuomintang and the Communist Party of China in the north, sought refuge in the Wufeng

---

[1] The Spring Festival Eve of this year is on February 19.

Mountain with his eldest son Li Baohua. They lived in the Temple of Han Wengong.

It was the last time Li Dazhao went to the Wufeng Mountain. During his stay in the mountain, Li received a letter from his wife Zhao Renlan. Zhao asked if he needed to ask the help of Bai Jianwu to have the warrant quashed. Li Dazhao refused stubbornly and said confidently: "The rulers are behaving in an outrageous way, but the hard time will pass. Before long, the red flags will fly over Beijing. We'll be the masters of our own country again!"

On April 28, 1927, Li Dazhao and 19 other revolutionists were hanged by Warlord Zhang Zuolin. Li faced death with no change of expression. He was 38 years old when he died.

(By: Qin Xuewu and Wu Ziguo)

3. 王尽美在山海关铁工厂 Wang Jinmei in Shanhaiguan Ironworks

王尽美（1898—1925），原名王瑞俊，山东省诸城市人，中国共产党创始人之一。

1922年8月，王尽美奉李大钊的指示，来到京奉铁路的咽喉山海关，组织和开展京奉铁路工人运动。

为便于工作，王尽美化名刘瑞俊，在京奉铁路山海关铁工厂（原山海关桥梁厂的前身，现中铁山桥集团有限公司）当了一名学徒工。白天，他在工厂劳动。晚上，他到工友俱乐部开办的工人夜校上文化课，借此向工人宣讲革命道理，传播马克思列宁主义。

1922年9月，王尽美与杨宝昆在工人中秘密建立党小组。这是冀东地区第一个党组织，也是京奉铁路最早的党组织之一。

1922年10月4日，王尽美在山海关领导了一千余名工人参加的京奉铁路工人大罢工。10月12日，铁路局被迫答应了工人的全部要求。这是中国共产党领导的早期工人运动的成功范例，在中国工运史上留下浓重的一笔。

1923年1月，京奉铁路总工会成立，王尽美担任总工会秘书，后以山海关工友俱乐部为基础组建了"京奉铁路总工会山海关分会"。2月中旬，王尽美等人因敌人密报被临榆县警察署缉捕，后在数百名工人的强烈要求下获释。

1923年2月下旬，为保护他的安全，王尽美被党组织调回北京。此后，他转往山东淄博、青岛，并带病奔走于济南、北京、上海、广州等地开展工农运动。1925年8月19日，王尽美病逝于青岛。

（作者：吴子国，秦学武）

Wang Jinmei (1898–1925), his real name Wang Ruijun, was a native of Zhucheng City, Shandong Province. He was one of the founders of the Communist Party of China.

In August 1922, Wang Jinmei went to the Shanhai Pass, main artery of the Peking–Mukden Railway, in conformity with the instructions of Li Dazhao. There, he launched the Peking–Mukden Railway Workers' Movement.

For convenience, Wang Jinmei, under the alias of Liu Ruijin, apprenticed himself in the Peking–Mukden Railway Shanhaiguan Ironworks (predecessor to former Shanhaiguan Bridge Factory and present China Railway Shanhaiguan Bridge Group Co., Ltd.). He worked in the daytime in the factory and attended classes at the night school for workers established by the Workers' Club. He took this opportunity to publicize revolutionary thoughts and spread Marxism-Leninism.

In September 1922, Wang Jinmei and Yang Baokun secretly established a Party group among the workers. It was the first Party organization in Jidong and one of the earliest Party organizations along the Peking–Mukden Railway.

On October 4, 1922, more than 1,000 workers went on the Peking–Mukden Railway Workers' Strike under the leadership of Wang Jinmei. On

October 12, the Railway Bureau was forced to accept the demands of the workers. As a successful example of the early workers' movements led by the CPC, the Peking–Mukden Railway Workers' Strike shines out in the history of China's labor movement.

When the Federation of Peking–Mukden Railway Workers' Unions (FPMRWU) was founded in January 1923, Wang Jinmei served as the secretary. Afterwards, the FPMRWU Shanhaiguan Branch was founded by him based on the Shanhaiguan Workers' Club. In the middle of February, the intelligence was leaked, and Wang Jinmei and other people were arrested by the Linyu County Police Department. In the face of the violent protests of hundreds of workers, they were released.

In late February 1923, the Party organization sent Wang Jinmei back to Beijing to keep him safe. Afterwards, he went to Zibo and Qingdao of Shandong. In spite of his sickness, he travelled to Jinan, Beijing, Shanghai and Guangzhou where he launched workers' and peasants' movements. On August 19, 1925, Wang Jinmei died of illness in Qingdao.

(By: Wu Ziguo and Qin Xuewu)

三、救亡图存 III. Saving the Nation from Destruction

4. 长城抗战 Battles Against Japanese Aggression Along the Great Wall[1]

"九·一八"事变后，日军侵占中国东北。1932年3月1日，建立伪满洲国政权。此后，日本谋划侵略热河省并进行各种准备。

---

[1] 中国社会科学院近代史研究所中华民国史研究室编：《中华民国史》第八卷，中华书局2011年版。
Research Office of the History of the Republic of China, Institute of Modern History, CASS: *History of the Republic of China*, Vol.8, Zhong Hua Book Company, 2011.

1933年1月1日至3日，榆关（今山海关）保卫战失败，揭开长城抗战的序幕。

2月23日，3.5万日伪军分三路进攻热河，直指承德。至3月21日，除热西、丰宁外，热河沦陷，国民政府8万大军仓皇败走。

日军侵占热河后，大举进攻长城各口，以达到划长城为"国界"的目的。3月5日至5月25日，长城抗战在长城各口及平榆大道以北地区展开。

第一阶段：3月7日至26日，我军在古北口、冷口、喜峰口、罗文峪、界岭口、义院口等长城东段隘口与日军的争夺战，以喜峰口之战为最。

3月7日，长城各口战役首先在古北口打响，战斗持续到12日。

3月9日晚，第29军500名战士组成大刀队在喜峰口夜袭日军，砍杀毙敌百余人，仅30余人生还。10日至11日，29军与日军展开肉搏战，双方伤亡惨重。11日夜，29军的两个旅两次分别从潘家口和铁门关迂回袭击，日军死伤200余人。

喜峰口之战，是长城抗战以来的唯一胜利，极大提振了中国军民的士气和抗日热情。著名的《大刀进行曲》，就是以此为题材创作的。[1]

第二阶段：3月27日至5月2日，日军在长城东段南侧的滦东和南天门交替进攻。

3月27日，日军越过长城，向滦东[2]进攻。4月1日，占领石门寨。11日，突破冷口。17日，占领滦东。迫于国际压力，日军自4月21日逐次撤回长城。

4月20日起，我军与日军在南天门持续激战。26日，日军猛攻主阵地，我军因伤亡过大撤出。28日，敌我激战竟日，日军占领南天门。

南天门之战与古北口之战，是长城抗战中时间最长、战事最烈的战斗。第17军在古北口、南天门、石匣镇一线同日军顽强战斗，显

---

[1] 艾立起等：《抗日烽火中诞生的〈大刀进行曲〉》，《华北民兵》2003年8期。

[2] 滦东，指滦河以东地区，包括迁安大部、卢龙、昌黎、抚宁和秦榆地区。

示了中国军队的爱国热情和守土御侮的能力。

第三阶段：5月7日至25日，长城以南冀东的作战。

5月7日，日军在西起古北口、东至山海关的长城全线，向中国守军发起进攻。滦东再次沦陷。日军相继占领丰润、遵化、密云、滦县、玉田、平谷、蓟县、三河等县，兵临平津。25日，近3个月的长城战役结束。

长城抗战，是全面抗战前规模最大的一场民族自卫战，沉重打击了日本侵略者的嚣张气焰，阻滞了日军侵略华北的进程，展现了中国军民反抗侵略的力量和决心。国民政府"攘外必先安内"的政策，是长城抗战失败的根本原因。

5月31日，中方被迫接受日方既定条款，签订《塘沽协定》，事实上承认日本占领东北三省和热河，并把冀东22县置于日伪势力范围内。华北大门被打开。

（作者：秦学武，吴子国）

When the September 18 Incident broke out, the Japanese troops seized control of Northeast China. On March 1, 1932, the Manchukuo puppet regime was established. Afterwards, Japan conspired to invade Jehol Province and preparations were underway.

Between January 1 and 3, 1933, the Yuguan (today's Shanhaiguan) Defense Battle took place. Its failure was the prologue to the Battles against Japanese Aggression along the Great Wall.

On February 23, the 35,000-strong Japanese Puppet Army attacked Jehol by three routes right down to Chengde. On March 21, Jehol was breached aside from Rexi and Fengning. The 80,000-strong National Government Army was defeated and fled in disorder.

When Jehol was taken, the Japanese troops launched a major offensive against the Great Wall passes, in an attempt to make the Great Wall their self-imposed "national boundaries". From March 5 to May 25, the Battles against Japanese Aggression along the Great Wall were launched in the passes of the Great Wall and the area north of the Ping–Yu Avenue.

Stage 1: From March 7 to 26, Chinese troops and Japanese troops fought in the eastern passes of the Great Wall, such as Gubeikou, Lengkou, Xifengkou, Luowenyu, Jielingkou and Yiyuankou. The Xifengkou Battle was the fiercest.

March 7 saw the outbreak of the Battles against Japanese Aggression along the Great Wall in Gubeikou. The fighting lasted to March 12.

On the night of March 9, the Big Sword Team formed by 500 soldiers of the 29th Army attacked the Japanese troops. More than 100 Japanese were killed and there were only 30 Chinese soldiers who survived. From March 10 to 11, troops of the 29th Army were engaged in a hand-to-hand combat with Japanese troops with heavy casualties on both sides. On the night of March 11, two brigades of the 29th Army outflanked Japanese troops from Panjiakou and Tiemenguan, and more than 200 Japanese lay dead or injured.

The Xifengkou Battle, as the only victory since the outbreak of the Battles against Japanese Aggression along the Great Wall, boosted the morale and fighting enthusiasm of Chinese soldiers and civilians. It was the inspiration of the famous song "The Big Sword March".[1]

Stage 2: From March 27 to May 2, Japanese troops attacked Luandong and Nantianmen to the south of the east section of the Great Wall alternatively.

On March 27, Japanese troops went across the Great Wall and launched an offensive on Luandong[2]. On April 1, Shimenzhai was taken. Lengkou was breached on April 11 and Luandong was taken on 17. Under international pressure, the Japanese gradually pulled back to the Great Wall since April 21.

---

1 Ai Liqi, etc: "The Big Sword March Born in the War of Resistance against Japanese Aggression", *North China Militia*, 2003, Issue 8.

2 Luandong refers to the area to the east of the Luan River, including large parts of Qian'an, Lulong, Changli, Funing and Qinyu.

Starting from April 20, Chinese and Japanese troops were locked in a fierce battle in Nantianmen. On April 26, the Japanese stormed the battle position. With heavy casualties, Chinese troops made a retreat. After several days of fighting, Japanese troops took Nantianmen.

The Nantianmen Battle and the Gubeikou Battle were the fiercest battles with the longest duration in the Battles against Japanese Aggression along the Great Wall. The invasion of the Japanese troops in Gubeikou, Nantianmen and Shixiazhen was held up by the stout resistance of the 17th Army. The patriotic enthusiasm of the Chinese troops and their determination to defend the country were manifested.

Stage 3: The battle in Jidong to the south of the Great Wall from May 7 to 25.

On May 7, Japanese troops launched an offensive against Chinese troops defending the whole lines of the Great Wall from Gubeikou in the west to Shanhaiguan in the east. Luandong was breached again. The Japanese took Fengrun, Zunhua, Miyun, Luanxian, Yutian, Pinggu, Jixian and Sanhe counties, and the troops were massed outside Peiping (Beijing) and Tianjin. On May 25, the Battles against Japanese Aggression along the Great Wall, which lasted for nearly 3 months, ended.

The Battles against Japanese Aggression along the Great Wall were the largest self-defense war of China before the full-scale outbreak of the War of Resistance against Japanese Aggression. It dealt a heavy blow to the arrogance of the Japanese and hindered their invasion into North China. The battles demonstrated the resolve and resilience of the Chinese people in the face of invaders. However, the National Government pursued the policy of "Maintaining Internal Security before Resisting Foreign Aggression", which ultimately led to the failure of the battles.

On May 31, China signed the Tanggu Truce under duress and accepted all the conditions of Japan. It was an effective acknowledgement of Japan's occupation of Northeast China and Jehol. The 22 counties in Jidong were put under the control of the Japanese puppet forces. The door to North China was opened to the invaders.

(By: Qin Xuewu and Wu Ziguo)

5. 冀东抗战 Battles Against Japanese Aggression in Jidong

抗日战争时期，冀东包括唐山、秦皇岛各县及京东、津北一些县在内，共22个县。1933年，国民党军长城抗战失败，冀东沦陷。"七七事变"后，日军进攻中国的兵力和军用物资，大量经冀东运送。因此，冀东的战略位置对中日双方极为重要。

1937年8月，中共中央召开洛川会议，毛泽东明确提出："红军可出一部于敌后的冀东，以雾灵山为根据地进行游击战争。"10月起，以李运昌、胡锡奎为主要负责人的中共冀热边特别区委员会，通过冀东抗日统一战线组织，联系洪麟阁等抗日人士，广泛发动民众，准备举行武装起义。为策应起义，根据八路军总部指示，晋察冀军区邓华支队与第120师宋时轮支队合编为八路军第四纵队，于1938年5月31日从平西向冀东挺进。

经过一年来的发动和准备，冀东抗日暴动的条件已成熟。1938年6月末，冀东抗日联军成立，高志远为抗联总司令，李运昌、洪麟阁为副总司令。

1938年7月6日至7日，港北起义打响冀东抗日暴动第一枪。短短两个月，东起山海关，西到潮白河，北从雾灵山，南至渤海滨，大起义遍及20多个县，参加人数达20余万，组成了7万余人的冀东抗日联军和近3万人的其他抗日武装。起义军与八路军协同作战，收复迁安等9座县城，动摇了日伪统治。由于严重错估形势，8月中旬，四纵主要领导决定将主力全部撤到平西整训。部队在西撤途中遭敌人围追堵截，导致整个起义队伍和根据地损失百分之九十以上，在平西和冀东保留下来的抗联人员只有3000人，冀东抗战形势一落千丈。

在西撤受挫的危急时刻，李运昌等当机立断，率余部返回冀东。1939年3月，正式建立中共冀东地方委员会，恢复基层党组织。从1939年10月成立冀东第一个联合县——丰（润）滦（县）迁（安）联合县起，冀东进入联合县秘密开辟根据地的艰苦抗战时期。

冀东党和军区带领人民，在实战中汲取失败教训，不断探索开辟根据地的新模式，遵循机动灵活的战术，在运动战中歼灭敌人有生力量。在冀东形成了以鲁家峪、腰带山为中心和以盘山为中心的东西两大游击区。冀东八路军主力部队在地方武装配合下，成功进行打治安军、恢复基本区等战役，改变了敌我双方的态势和力量对比。据不完全统计，从"七七事变"到1945年抗战胜利，冀东几乎无日无战事，我军有3万多战士牺牲，数千名干部牺牲；诞生了洪麟阁、高志远、李运昌、包森、节振国、杨十三（杨裕民）、张百策（张强）、陈群、魏春波等抗日英雄；累计毙伤俘日军7万人。

孤悬敌后的冀东抗战主要是中共领导下开展的敌后游击战。在极端险恶的环境下，冀东八路军驰骋长城内外，血战千里无人区，几经起落，终于建成一个拥有560万人口的冀热辽根据地，建立起一支人数众多的武装力量，成为日寇咽喉地带强有力的抵抗力量。

（作者：吴子国）

During the War of Resistance against Japanese Aggression, Jidong consisted of 22 counties in Tangshan, Qinhuangdao, eastern Beijing and northern Tianjin. In 1933, the KMT army was defeated in the Battles against Japanese Aggression along the Great Wall, and Jidong fell into the enemy's hands. In the wake of the July 7 Incident of 1937, Japanese troops delivered men and supplies mainly through Jidong. The place was of strategic importance to both China and Japan.

In August 1937, Mao Zedong laid down a clear direction at the Luochuan Conference of the CPC Central Committee: "A force of the Red Army

记录战士生活的老照片（图源：国防部网）
Old photos recording soldiers' life in those days (Credit: http://www.mod.gov.cn/)

should infiltrate behind the enemy lines in Jidong. They should establish a base in the Wuling Mountain and wage a guerrilla war." In October, the CPC Jidong-Jehol Border Special Region Committee, of which Li Yunchang and Hu Xikui were the principal members, reached out to Hong Linge and other revolutionaries through the Jidong United Front against Japanese Aggression. They mobilized the masses on a large scale for an armed uprising. Under the directive of the Headquarters of the Eighth Route Army, the Deng Hua Detachment of the Shanxi-Chahar-Hebei Military Region and the Song Shilun Detachment of the 120th Division were consolidated into the Fourth Column of the Eighth Route Army. On May 31, 1938, they advanced from Pingxi towards Jidong.

After preparing and mobilizing for a year, the conditions for the Riot against Japanese Aggression in Jidong were right. In late June 1938, the Jidong Allied Forces against Japanese Aggression was established. Gao Zhiyuan was appointed as Commander-in-chief, and Li Yunchang and Honglin Linge were appointed as Deputy Commanders-in-chief.

With the outbreak of the Gangbei Uprising from July 6 to 7, 1938, the first shots were fired in the Riot against Japanese Aggression in Jidong. In a couple of months, 200,000 people in more than 20 counties ranging from Shanhaiguan in the east and Wuling Mountain in the north to Chaobai River in the west and Bohai Coast in the south participated in the uprising. They formed the 70,000-strong Jidong Allied Forces and the 30,000-member other armed forces to resist Japanese aggression. The rebellion fought with the Eighth Route Army to retake Qian'an and eight other counties. They shocked the foundation of the rule of Japanese puppet regime. In the middle of August, the leaders of the Fourth Column of the Eighth Route Army underestimated the situation and called for a full retreat of the main forces to Pingxi to rest and reorganize. On their way westward, the troops were ambushed by the enemy. More than 90% of troops and bases were lost. In Pingxi and Jidong, the Allied Forces against Japanese Aggression maintained only 3,000 soldiers. The Battles against Japanese Aggression in Jidong took a sudden turn for the worse.

Under the most dire of circumstances, Li Yunchang made a quick decision and beat a retreat to Jidong. In March 1939, the CPC Jidong Local Committee was established, and the grass-roots Party organizations were restored. In October 1939, Feng-Luan-Qian, the first united county in Jidong, was established. Since then, Jidong had entered upon a tough time of united counties secretly establishing bases.

Under the leadership of the Party and the military region, Jidong people learned lessons from the failures in battles. They explored new models of opening up bases, and crippled enemies through the flexible application of combat power. In Jidong, the East Guerrilla Zone, of which Lujiayu and Yaodaishan were the center, and the West Guerrilla Zone, of which Panshan was the center, were formed. In coordination with local armed forces, the main forces of the Eighth Route Army in Jidong defeated the Japanese puppet army and recovered the basic base area. The dynamic of the battle was radically changed. According to incomplete statistics, there were battles in Jidong nearly every day from the July 7 Incident of 1937 to the victory in the War of Resistance in 1945. More than 30,000 Chinese troops and thousands of cadres had died. Heroes of the resistance appeared in waves, such as Hong Linge, Gao Zhiyuan, Li Yunchang, Bao Sen, Jie Zhenguo, Yang Shisan (Yang Yumin), Zhang Baice (Zhang Qiang), Chen Qun and Wei Chunbo. More than 70,000 Japanese troops were killed, injured or captured.

Under the leadership of the CPC, the Chinese troops infiltrated behind the Japanese troops and launched a guerrilla war in Jidong. The Eighth Route Army moved back and forth across the Great Wall under extreme circumstances. They fought bloody battles in the vast no man's land. With great difficulty, the Jidong-Jehol-Liaoning Base against Japanese Aggression comprised of 5.6 million people was established. An armed force with huge numbers of soldiers was built up to ward off the attacks of Japanese troops in strategic points.

(By: Wu Ziguo)

四、设施遗址 IV. Memorial Facilities and Sites

6. 山海关八国联军营盘旧址 Barracks of the Eight-Power Allied Forces in Shanhaiguan[1]

山海关八国联军营盘旧址，位于秦皇岛市老龙头的西部和北部，是指八国联军侵华时期占领山海关的英、法、德、日、意、俄六国

---

[1] 冯颖:《山海关八国联军营盘旧址及其保护和利用》,《文物春秋》2010 年 03 期。
Feng Ying: "The Former Barracks of the Eight-Power Allied Forces in Shanhaiguan and Their Protection and Utilization", *Cultural Relics Annals*, 2010, Issue 03.

六国营盘旧址的老照片（供图：王进勤）
An old photo of six nations' barracks (Provided by Wang Jinqin)

所建的营盘及六国饭店。现存房屋 40 幢，建筑面积 12,309 平方米。2006 年 5 月，被公布为全国重点文物保护单位。

1900 年 8 月，八国联军侵占北京。1901 年 9 月 7 日，清政府与列强签订丧权辱国的《辛丑条约》，北京黄村至山海关铁路沿线 12 处被八国联军侵占。1902—1904 年，列强在山海关南部沿海一带建立军营，在山海关火车站南侧修建"六国饭店"，还修建了连接六国饭店至各国军营的马拉小铁路。直到第二次世界大战后，列强才全部撤出。

英国营盘在宁海城，面积最大，现存房屋 13 幢，水泥地桩上刻有英文"W↑D"、中文"英国地界"。海神庙一带的印度营盘，1914 年后为英军占用；法国营盘在小湾村北，分东北、西南两院，现存房屋 18 幢；德国营盘在石河口东，现存房屋 2 幢，一战后为英军占用；意大利营盘在小湾村南，分南北两院，现存南院房屋 6 幢；日本营盘位于肖庄村，现存的将军楼是 1933 年 1 月日军侵占山海关、发动"榆

英、法、德、意、日军军营旧址（摄影：王进勤）
British, French, German, Italian and Japanese barracks (Photographed by Wang Jinqin)

关事变"的指挥中心；俄国营盘有两处，一处在绥远城北侧，一处在东罗城东南，未建正式营房。

六国饭店，位于山海关区工人街，是八国联军的接待站和娱乐场所，现存一幢工字形两层楼房。

山海关八国联军营盘旧址，是中国现存规模最大、保存最完整的八国联军军营旧址，具有极为重要的历史价值，既是八国联军侵华的铁证，也是爱国主义教育的活教材。它们时刻警示国人："落后就要挨打！"

（作者：秦学武，吴子国）

Located to the west and north of Laolongtou, Qinhuangdao, the Barracks of the Eight-Power Allied Forces include the former barracks along with the Six Nations Hotel of Britain, France, Germany, Japan, Italy and Russia. During the Eight-Power Allied Forces' invasion of China, the six countries had occupied the Shanhai Pass (Shanhaiguan). There exist 40 buildings with a total floorage of 12,309 square meters. In May 2006, it was designated as a Major Historical and Cultural Site Protected at the National Level.

In August 1900, the Eight-Power Allied Forces seized control of Beijing. On September 7, 1901, the humiliating Xin Chou Treaty was made under duress. The Qing government ceded 12 places along the railway from Huangcun of Beijing to Shanhaiguan to the Eight-Power Allied Forces.

From 1902 to 1904, the Western powers set up barracks along the southern coastal area of the Shanhai Pass. They built the Six Nations Hotel to the south of the Shanhaiguan Railway Station with horse-drawn railway lines connecting the barracks and the hotel. After World War II, the Western powers withdrew.

Located in the Ninghai Fort, the British barrack covers the largest area. There exist 13 buildings, of which the cement pilings are engraved with English letters "W ↑ D" and "British Territory" in Chinese characters. In 1914, the British army took possession of the Indian barrack around the Temple of Sea God. Located in the north of Xiaowan Village, the French barrack is divided into northeast and southwest compounds. There exist 18 buildings. Located in the east of Shihekou, the German barrack was possessed by the British army after WWI. There exist 2 buildings. Located in the south of Xiaowan Village, the Italian barrack is divided into southern and northern compounds. There exist 6 buildings in the southern compound. The Japanese barrack is located in Xiaozhuang Village. The existent General Building was the Operations Command Center of Japanese troops when they invaded the Shanhai Pass in January 1933 and launched the Yuguan Incident. There are two Russian barrack areas, one in the north of Suiyuan Town, and the other in the southeast of Dongluo Town. No permanent building was built.

Located in the Worker Street, Shanhaiguan District, the Six Nations Hotel was the place of amusement for the Eight-Power Allied Forces where guests were received. There exists an H-shaped, two-story building.

The Barracks of the Eight-Power Allied Forces in Shanhaiguan are the largest, best-preserved barrack site of the Eight-Power Allied Forces that survives today. With important historical value, they are a concrete proof of the Eight-Power Allied Forces' invasion of China and a vivid example for patriotism education. They are an alarm call to warn the Chinese people: "When a nation falls behind, it will get beaten!"

(By: Qin Xuewu and Wu Ziguo)

7. 热河革命烈士纪念馆 Jehol Revolutionary Martyrs' Memorial Hall

热河革命烈士纪念馆位于承德市双桥区，占地8万平方米。2009年3月被国务院批准为全国重点烈士纪念建筑物保护单位，5月被中宣部评为全国爱国主义教育示范基地。2015年，被国务院公布为国家级抗战纪念设施、遗址。

1955年12月29日，热河省[1]一届人大三次会议决定修建热河革命烈士纪念馆。1956年动工，1964年竣工开放。原热河省政府主席李运昌题写馆名。

纪念馆依山就势、坐西朝东，主体建筑在一条中轴线上。九十八级台阶，寓意中国人民永远不忘"九·一八"国难。通过百米长的甬道，革命烈士纪念碑展现眼前，朱德总司令亲题"革命烈士永垂不朽"八个大字。纪念碑后面是三座陈列馆，萧克将军题写馆名。

纪念馆收集了数百万字的烈士资料和大量革命文物，保存了5000

---

[1] 1949年11月1日，热河省人民政府成立，下辖承德市、赤峰、围场、隆化、丰宁、滦平、平泉、青龙、兴隆、承德、朝阳、北票、建平、建昌、凌源、宁城、乌丹等16县，敖汉、喀喇沁、翁牛特、喀喇沁左翼等4旗。1956年1月，热河撤省。

多位烈士英名，包括陈镜湖、韩麟符、孙永勤、包森、姚铁民、刘桂五、董存瑞等，生动展现了1919—1955年间热河军民抵御外侮、追求解放的壮美篇章和英雄事迹。从金丹教起义、锛子沟人民抗洋拒官斗争，到热辽义勇军、抗日救国军的反侵略斗争，热河人民在中国革命史上写下光辉的一页。

孙永勤雕像（摄影：杨瑞华）
Statue of Sun Yongqin (Photographed by Yang Ruihua)

（1）孙永勤

1933年12月11日，兴隆县农民孙永勤成立民众军，发动黄花川农民抗日大暴动。1934年5月，孙永勤接受共产党的建议，将民众军改为抗日救国军。这支军队与日伪军作战200余次，攻克敌据点100多个，歼敌5000余人，威震长城内外。1935年5月24日，抗日救国军在遵化茅山一带与日伪军激战两昼夜，孙永勤壮烈牺牲。中共中央《八一宣言》称赞孙永勤是为国捐躯的民族英雄。

（2）包森

原名赵宝森，陕西蒲城人。1932年2月，加入中国共产党。曾领导农民游击活动。1937年秋，到晋察冀抗日根据地工作；1938年6月，八路军四纵挺进冀东，包森任四纵支队长。1940年6月，冀东军分区成立，包森任副司令兼十三团团长，率部以盘山为中心，在蓟县、平谷、密云、遵化等地开展抗日斗争，为发展冀东抗日根据地作出重要贡献。1942年2月17日，在遵化县野狐山与日军激战。在观察敌情时，包森被狙击手击中，壮烈牺牲。

（3）董存瑞

河北怀来人。1945年7月，参加八路军。1947年3月，加入中国共产党。1948年5月，第十一纵队奉命攻打隆化。24日，董存瑞被选为六连爆破组组长。25日下午3时半，在解放隆化战斗中，董存瑞同志用身体当支架手托炸药包，炸毁了国民党军队在隆化中学最后据守的桥型暗堡，壮烈牺牲，为部队打开前进的道路。1948年6月8日，董存瑞被部队党委授予"战斗英雄""模范共产党员"称号。1950年9月，董存瑞被追授全国战斗英雄。

（作者：吴子国，秦学武）

董存瑞雕像（摄影：杨瑞华）
Statue of Dong Cunrui (Photographed by Yang Ruihua)

Located in Shuangqiao District, Chengde City, the Jehol Revolutionary Martyrs' Memorial Hall covers an area of 80,000 square meters. In March 2009, it was approved by the State Council as a major martyrs' memorial building protected at the national level. In May, it was designated by the Publicity Department of the Communist Party of China as a National Demonstration Base for Patriotism Education. In 2015, it was designated by the State Council as a National Memorial Facility and Site of the War of Resistance against Japanese Aggression.

On December 29, 1955, it was decided at the Third Session of the First People's Congress of Jehol Province[1] that the Jehol Revolutionary Martyrs' Memorial Hall should be built. The construction lasted from 1956 to 1964. Li Yunchang, former Chairman of Jehol Provincial Government, wrote the

---

[1] On November 1, 1949, Jehol Provincial People's Government was founded. It governed Chengdu City; Chifeng, Weichang, Longhua, Fengning, Luanping, Pingquan, Qinglong, Xinglong, Chengde, Chaoyang, Beipiao, Jianping, Jianchang, Lingyuan, Ningcheng and Wudan counties; and Aohan, Kharchin, Ongniud and Harqin Left Wing banners. In January 1956, Jehol Province was abolished.

name of the hall.

The memorial hall sits on a hillside and faces the east. The main buildings are located on a central axis. The 98-step stairway is a constant reminder for the Chinese people to remember the September 18 Incident. Walking through the 100-meter-long path, the Monument to Revolutionary Martyrs, with "Revolutionary Martyrs Are Immortal" written in Chinese characters by Commander-in-chief Zhu De, lies before our eyes. The monument is backed by three exhibition halls, the names of which were written by General Xiao Ke.

The memorial hall houses martyrs' information with a total of millions of characters and a large number of revolutionary relics. It keeps a record of more than 5,000 martyrs' names, including Chen Jinghu, Han Linfu, Sun Yongqin, Bao Sen, Yao Tiemin, Liu Guiwu and Dong Cunrui. The splendid deeds of Jehol people's defending against foreign invaders to liberate the country between 1919 and 1955 are vividly manifested. Those deeds, such as the Jindan Taoist Uprising, Huazigou People's Struggle against Foreign Religions and Corrupted Officials, and the anti-aggression battles by the Jehol-Liaoning Army of Volunteers and the National Salvation Army, were a glorious chapter in China's revolutionary history.

(1) Sun Yongqin

On December 11, 1933, Sun Yongqin, a peasant in Xinglong County, established the Mass Army and launched the Peasants' Riot against Japanese Aggression in Huanghuachuan. In May 1934, Sun, on the advice of the CPC, changed his army to the National Salvation Army against Japanese Aggression. In more than 200 battles with the Japanese puppet army, this army captured more than 100 strongholds and killed over 5,000 enemy troops. Its fame reached beyond the Great Wall. On May 24, 1935, the National Salvation Army and the Japanese puppet army were locked in a fierce battle in Maoshan, Zunhua. After two days and nights, Sun Yongqin heroically gave up his life. In the August 1 Declaration, the CPC Central Committee praised him as a hero defending the country at the sacrifice of his own life.

(2) Bao Sen

Bao Sen, his real name Zhao Baosen, was a native of Pucheng, Shaanxi. In February 1932, he joined the Communist Party of China and led peasants to conduct guerrilla warfare afterwards. In the autumn of 1937, he was transferred to the Shanxi-Chahar-Hebei Base Areas against Japanese Aggression. In June 1938, the Fourth Column of the Eighth Route Army, under the leadership of Bao Sen, advanced towards Jidong. In June 1940, the Jidong Military Sub-command was established, and Bao Sen was assigned as Deputy Commander of the Sub-command and Commander of the Thirteenth Regiment. With Panshan at the center, he led his troops in the War of Resistance against Japanese Aggression in Jixian, Pinggu, Miyun and Zunhua, contributing to the development of the Jidong Base Areas against Japanese Aggression. On February 17, 1942, the Thirteenth Regiment was engaged in a fierce battle with Japanese troops in the Yehu Mountain, Zunhua County. When observing enemy activities, Bao Sen was shot by a sniper and heroically gave up his life.

(3) Dong Cunrui

Dong Cunrui was a native of Huailai, Hebei. In July 1945, he joined the Eighth Route Army. In March 1947, he joined the CPC. In May 1948, the Eleventh Column of the Eighth Route Army was ordered to attack Longhua. On May 24, Dong Cunrui was selected as the commander of the blasting team of the Sixth Company. At half past five in the afternoon of May 25, during the battle to liberate Longhua, Dong Cunrui held an explosive package over his head, and the explosive destroyed the bridge-type bunker in Longhua Middle School where the KMT troops were holding their

革命烈士纪念碑（摄影：杨瑞华）
Monument to the Revolutionary Martyrs (Photographed by Yang Ruihua)

ground. Dong gave up his life to eliminate the obstacle for the troops to advance. On June 8, 1948, the army awarded Dong Cunrui the titles "Combat Hero" and "Model Communist Party Member". In September 1950, he was posthumously confirmed as a National Combat Hero.

(By: Wu Ziguo and Qin Xuewu)

8. 冀东烈士陵园 Jidong Martyrs' Cemetery

冀东烈士陵园位于唐山市路南区。1989年，被国务院批准为全国重点烈士纪念建筑物保护单位。2015年，入选国家国防教育示范基地，被国务院公布为国家级抗战纪念设施、遗址。先后被国家民政部、河北省、唐山市命名为爱国主义教育基地。

1955年，河北省人民政府批准建设冀东烈士陵园，1958年清明节落成并开放。1976年唐山大地震，陵园被震毁，复建工程于1986年竣工。聂荣臻元帅为冀东烈士陵园题名。

冀东烈士陵园占地7.5万平方米，系中轴对称布局。主体建筑有古典牌楼式大门、烈士纪念塔、烈士纪念馆和烈士墓区。每年接待社会各界谒陵群众数十万人次。

烈士纪念塔通体由汉白玉砌成，巍峨挺拔。塔高34.5米，塔身四面镌刻着老一辈无产阶级革命家朱德、林伯渠、彭德怀、萧克的题词。20位冀东革命英烈的铜像矗立在纪念塔至纪念馆小广场的两侧。

包森用过的望远镜（供图：冀东烈士陵园）
Binoculars used by Bao Sen (Provided by Jidong Martyrs' Cemetery)

冀东烈士纪念馆由序厅、陈列馆组成，共8个展厅，建筑面积2149平方米，馆名由萧克将军题写。馆内基本陈列为"冀东革命烈士斗争业绩展"。全园有在册烈士238名，包括

节振国夺获的日军战刀（供图：冀东烈士陵园）
Japanese saber captured by Jie Zhenguo (Provided by Jidong Martyrs' Cemetery)

早期工人运动领袖邓培、早期革命家于方舟、华北抗日联军人民第一支队司令员王平陆、冀东军分区副司令员包森、国际主义战士周文彬、抗日民族英雄节振国和民族女英雄王册等。

烈士墓区位于冀东烈士陵园北端，共166座，安葬着178位烈士。

冀东烈士陵园收藏文物1030件，包括安体诚与周恩来等在日本京都的合影照片[1]、华北人民抗日联军第一支队关防印、冀东抗日联军袖标、节振国夺获的日军战刀、包森用过的望远镜[2]等17件国家一级文物。

（作者：秦学武，吴子国）

1　安体诚（1896—1927），字存斋，河北丰润人。该照片拍摄于1919年4月6日。1958年冀东烈士陵园落成，作为安体诚烈士遗物入藏。这是中国青年爱国知识分子在五四运动前夕革命活动的重要物证，也是国内首次发现周恩来（字翔宇）在日本的早期照片。

2　1939年冀东抗日武装缴获的日军战利品，由司令员李运昌使用。1940年初，副司令员包森开辟盘山抗日根据地，李运昌将其赠给包森。

Monument to the Martyrs (Provided by Jidong Martyrs' Cemetery)

Jidong Martyrs' Cemetery is located in Lunan District, Tangshan. In 1989, it was approved by the State Council as a major martyrs' memorial building protected at the national level. In 2015, it was named a National Defense Education Demonstration Base and designated by the State Council as a National Memorial Facility and Site of the War of Resistance against Japanese Aggression. It was named a Patriotism Education Base by the Ministry of Civil Affairs of the People's Republic of China, the People's Government of Hebei Province, and the Tangshan Municipal People's Government.

In 1955, the People's Government of Hebei Province gave an approval for the construction of Jidong Martyrs' Cemetery. It was completed in 1958 and opened to the public on the Tomb Sweeping Day. The cemetery was destroyed in the Tangshan Earthquake in 1976, and the reconstruction program finished in 1986. The name of the cemetery was written by Marshal Nie Rongzhen.

Jidong Martyrs' Cemetery covers an area of 75,000 square meters in an axisymmetric arrangement. The main buildings include a classical archway

安东烈士陵园）
安体诚，1919年4月6日摄于日本京都（供图：冀东烈士陵园）
Photo of An Ticheng, taken on April 6, 1919 in Kyoto, Japan (Provided by Jidong Martyrs' Cemetery)

entrance, the Monument to the Martyrs, the Martyrs' Memorial Hall, and the Martyrs' Tombs. There are hundreds of thousands of visitors annually.

The marble Monument to the Martyrs is 34.5 meters high, with characters written by four proletarian revolutionaries of the older generation—Zhu De, Lin Boqu, Peng Dehuai and Xiao Ke—engraved on the four sides. Lining both sides of the path from the monument to the small square in front of the memorial hall are the bronze statues of 20 revolutionary martyrs of Jidong.

Jidong Martyrs' Memorial Hall comprises an introductory hall and several exhibition halls, totalling eight sub-halls with a floor area of 2,149 square meters. The name of the hall was written by General Xiao Ke. The hall displays the deeds of Jidong revolutionary martyrs. 238 martyrs are listed and documented, including Deng Pei, a leader of early workers' movements; Yu Fangzhou, an early revolutionist; Wang Pinglu, Commander of the First Detachment of the North China People's Allied Forces against Japanese Aggression; Bao Sen, Deputy Commander of Jidong Military Sub-command; Zhou Wenbin, an international communist soldier; Jie Zhenguo, a national hero against Japanese aggression; and Wang Ce, a national heroin.

The bodies of 178 martyrs lie buried in 166 tombs in the northern end of the cemetery.

Jidong Martyrs' Cemetery holds 1,030 cultural relics, including 17 national first-class cultural relics, such as the photo of An Ticheng and Zhou Enlai in Kyoto of Japan[1], the seal of the First Detachment of the North China People's Allied Forces against Japanese Aggression, the armband of the Jidong Allied Forces against Japanese Aggression, the Japanese saber captured by Jie Zhenguo, and the binoculars[2] used by Bao Sen.

(By: Qin Xuewu and Wu Ziguo)

五、时代精神 V. Spirits of the Times

9. 唐山抗震精神 Tangshan Earthquake Relief Spirit

1976 年 7 月 28 日 3 时 42 分，河北省唐山、丰南一带发生 7.8 级强烈地震，地震持续约 12 秒。这座百万人口的工业重镇瞬间夷为废墟，242,419 人（含京津地区）殒命瓦砾，164,581 人重伤，7218 户全家震亡，直接经济损失 54 亿元。唐山大地震被视为"20 世纪全球十大灾难之一"。

地震发生后，党中央和国务院急电全国火速救援，10 余万解放军和 5 万名医护人员、干部民工星夜驰援。在全国军民支援下，70 万多

---

1 An Ticheng (1896–1927), styled Cunzhai, was a native of Fengrun, Hebei. The photo was taken on April 6, 1919. In 1958, Jidong Martyrs' Cemetery was completed and the photo was housed there as the relic of martyr An Ticheng. This is an important material evidence of the revolutionary activities of Chinese young patriotic intellectuals before the May 4th Movement. It is also the first photo of Zhou Enlai (styled Xiangyu) on his early days in Japan discovered in China.

2 An equipment of the Japanese troops captured by the Jidong Armed Forces against Japanese Aggression in 1939 for Commander Li Yunchang. Early in 1940, Deputy Commander Bao Sen established the Panshan Base against Japanese Aggression, and Li Yunchang gave the binoculars to Bao as a gift.

伤员得到及时救治，16万多伤残人得到照顾，4千余名孤儿健康成长。截至1986年底，共投入灾后重建资金43亿元，完成建筑面积1800万平方千米，唐山人告别"砖头压油毡"的简易房，完成十年重建的艰巨任务。

历经30年的重建、振兴和快速发展，这座英雄城市涅槃重生。震后的建筑物均达到了8度设防，使唐山成为"世界上最安全的城市"。1990年获联合国"人居荣誉奖"，2004年获"迪拜国际改善居住环境最佳范例奖"。

唐山抗震纪念碑（供图：唐山抗震纪念馆）
Tangshan Earthquake Monument (Provided by Tangshan Earthquake Memorial Hall)

今日唐山，已发展成为渤海湾北岸的现代化名城，中心城区308平方千米，市区人口251万。2021年，完成地区生产总值8230.6亿元，连续十二年排名河北省首位。先后被评为国家园林城市、全国文明城市和国家森林城市。

2016年7月，习近平总书记在唐山调研考察时指出："在同地震灾害斗争的过程中，唐山人民铸就了'公而忘私、患难与共、百折不挠、勇往直前'的抗震精神。这是中华民族精神的重要体现。"唐山抗震精神，是全国军民在抗震斗争中用鲜血、生命和艰苦卓绝的斗争，共同铸就的民族之魂。

为缅怀逝者、旌表英烈、感召后人，唐山市1986年建成唐山抗震纪念碑和唐山抗震纪念馆，2009年建成唐山地震遗址纪念公园。2006年，唐山大地震遗址被公布为全国重点文物保护单位。

（作者：吴子国，秦学武）

At 15: 42 on July 28, 1976, an earthquake of magnitude 7.8 struck the region around Tangshan and Fengnan of Hebei. The earthquake continued for about 12 seconds. In an instant, the industrial powerhouse of over a million people was turned into ruins, causing a direct economic loss of 5.4 billion yuan. 242,419 people (including those in Beijing and Tianjin) died in the quake, 164,581 people were seriously injured, and 7,218 families were totally destroyed. The Tangshan Earthquake was ranked among the Top 10 Major Disasters of the World in the 20th Century.

唐山机车车辆厂地震遗址（供图：唐山抗震纪念馆）
Earthquake site of Tangshan Locomotive and Rolling Stock Works (Provided by Tangshan Earthquake Memorial Hall)

After the earthquake, the Party's Central Committee and the State Council sent emergency calls across the country. 100,000 PLA soldiers, 50,000 health workers, and many cadres and common workers travelled as fast as they could to Tangshan. With the support of the whole country, more than 700,000 wounded people were promptly treated, more than 160,000 disabled people were properly looked after, and more than 4,000 orphans grew up healthily. By the end of 1986, 4.3 billion yuan were invested for the post-earthquake recovery, and buildings with a total floor area of 18 million square meters were erected. The city was restored after ten years, and its people put an end to the temporary accommodation of "bricks and linoleum".

After 30 years of reconstruction, revitalization and fast development, the heroic city was reborn. The new architectures could withstand an

唐山地震遗址公园（纪念墙）（供图：唐山市政府办公厅）
Tangshan Earthquake Site Park (Memorial Wall) (Provided by the General Office of the Tangshan Municipal People's Government)

8-magnitude earthquake, and Tangshan ranked among "the safest cities in the world". In 1990, Tangshan won the UN-Habitat Scroll of Honor Award; in 2004, the city won the Dubai International Award for Best Practices to Improve the Living Environment.

Today's Tangshan has become a well-known modern city facing the Bohai Bay in the south. Its central urban area covers 308 square kilometers, and it has an urban population of 2.51 million people. In 2021, the GDP of the city reached 823.06 billion yuan, ranking No.1 for the 12th year in a row in Hebei Province. Tangshan was named a National Garden City, National Civilized City and National Forest City.

On the visit to Tangshan in July 2016, Xi Jinping, General Secretary of the CPC Central Committee, noted: "In the struggle against the earthquake, Tangshan people have fostered the spirit featuring 'selflessness, comradeship, dauntlessness and the will to forge ahead'. It embodies the spirit of the Chinese nation." The Tangshan Earthquake Relief Spirit represents the soul of the Chinese nation born out of blood, life and hard struggle of the army and the people of the whole country.

To honor the memory of those innocents who were lost during the earthquake and the people giving up their lives for saving the citizens, the Tangshan government built the Tangshan Earthquake Monument and the Tangshan Earthquake Memorial Hall in 1986, and the Tangshan Earthquake Site Memorial Park in 2009. In 2006, the Tangshan Earthquake Site was designated as a Major Historical and Cultural Site Protected at the National Level.

(By: Wu Ziguo and Qin Xuewu)

10. 塞罕坝精神 Saihanba Spirit

塞罕坝机械林场是河北省林业和草原局直属大型国有林场。林场地处河北省最北部、内蒙古高原浑善达克沙地南缘，属森林 - 草原交错带，海拔 1010—1939.9 米，年均气温零下 1.3℃，年均积雪 7 个月，年均无霜期 64 天，年均降水量 479 毫米，总经营面积 140 万亩。

塞罕坝是蒙古语，意为"美丽的高岭"。历史上的塞罕坝，曾经水草丰沛、森林茂密、禽兽繁集，是辽金时期"千里松林"、清代"木兰围场"的重要组成。由于过度采伐，土地日渐贫瘠，20 世纪 50 年代，这里已成为风沙肆虐的沙源地。

1962 年 9 月，原国家林业部建立塞罕坝机械林场，369 名来自全国 18 个省区市、平均年龄不到 24 岁的创业者豪迈地开启了高原沙地造林的伟大征程。他们无惧高海拔、高寒、风沙、少雨等极端环境，战胜物资匮乏、交通闭塞等极端困难，三代人接续奋斗，成功营造了 112 万亩人工林海，构筑了"为首都阻沙源、

当年机械造林现场（供图：吴雪银）
Mechanical afforestation in those days (Provided by Wu Xueyin)

为辽津涵水源"的绿色生态屏障。

1993年5月，原国家林业部批准建立塞罕坝国家森林公园。2002年，公园被评为国家AAAA级景区。2007年5月，塞罕坝被国务院批准为国家级自然保护区。主要树种有落叶松、樟子松、云杉、白桦等，栖息着陆生野生脊椎动物256种、鱼类13种、昆虫548种、植物625种。

2017年8月，习近平总书记作出重要指示："55年来，河北塞罕坝林场的建设者们听从党的召唤，在'黄沙遮天日，飞鸟无栖树'的

桦木沟金秋（摄影：王怀强）
Huamu Dale in autumn (Photographed by Wang Huaiqiang)

桃山湖日出（摄影：王怀强）
Taoshan Lake at sunrise (Photographed by Wang Huaiqiang)

荒漠沙地上艰苦奋斗、甘于奉献，创造了荒原变林海的人间奇迹，用实际行动诠释了绿水青山就是金山银山的理念，铸就了牢记使命、艰苦创业、绿色发展的塞罕坝精神。"

2017年12月5日，联合国环境规划署将环保最高荣誉"地球卫士奖"授予塞罕坝林场建设者。2021年9月，塞罕坝机械林场荣获联合国防治荒漠化领域最高荣誉"土地生命奖"，成为全球生态文明建设的生动范例。

2021年2月25日，塞罕坝机械林场获得"全国脱贫攻坚楷模"荣誉称号。

（作者：吴子国，秦学武）

The Saihanba Mechanical Forest Farm is a large state-owned forest farm affiliated with the Forestry and Grassland Bureau of Hebei Province. Located in the northernmost part of Hebei Province and the southern edge of the Hunshandak Sandland of Inner Mongolia, the forest farm lies in a forest-

军马场（摄影：王怀强）
Military horse ranch (Photographed by Wang Huaiqiang)

steppe ecotone at the altitude of 1,010–1,939.9 meters and has an average annual temperature of −1.3 ℃. The land is covered by snow for seven months a year, and the average frost-free period is 64 days. The annual rainfall is 479 mm. The total operating area is 1.4 million *mu*.

Saihanba means "beautiful mountains" in Mongolian. Historically, the place once had lush forests and wetlands, providing habitats for many birds and beasts. In the Liao and Jin dynasties and the Qing Dynasty, it was an important part of the "Thousand-*li* Pine Forest" and the "Mulan Enclosure". Due to excessive logging, the land gradually became barren. In the 1950s, it had become a source of sandstorms.

In September 1962, the former Forestry Department established the Saihanba Mechanical Forest Farm. 369 pioneers from 18 provinces, autonomous regions and municipalities in China, with an average age of under 24, enthusiastically started a great adventure of afforestation on sandy land on the plateau. They had no fear of the extreme conditions such as high altitude, coldness, sandstorm and dryness, and overcame the difficulties such as supply shortages and poor transportation. An

1.12-million-*mu* artificial forest was established as a result of the efforts of three generations. It became an ecological barrier "stopping the sand from entering Beijing and storing water for Liaoning and Tianjin".

In May 1993, the former Forestry Department gave an approval for the establishment of Saihanba National Forest Park. In 2002, the park was named a National AAAA Level Tourist Attraction. In May 2007, Saihanba was designated by the State Council as a National Nature Reserve. The main tree species in the park include *Larix gmelinii*, *Pinus sylvestris* var. *mongolica* Litv., *Picea asperata* and *Betula platyphylla*, and the park is home to 256 species of wild terrestrial vertebrates, 13 species of fish, 548 species of insects and 625 species of plants.

In August 2017, Xi Jinping, General Secretary of the CPC Central Committee, gave an important speech: "Over the past 55 years, the establishers of Hebei Saihanba Forest Farm followed the call of the Party. In a desert where 'the sun is obscured by yellow sands, and birds have no trees to perch on', they dedicated their lives to turn it into a forest. With practical actions, they embodied what 'lucid waters and lush mountains are invaluable assets' means. They kept their mission in mind, made strenuous efforts and pursued green development. This is the true Saihanba Spirit indeed."

On December 5, 2017, the United Nations Environment Programme gave the Champions of the Earth award, the UN's highest environmental honor, to the Saihanba Afforestation Community. In September 2021, the Saihanba Forest Farm won the UNCCD Land for Life Award, the UN's highest honor for combating desertification. The forest farm has become a vivid example of global ecological conservation.

On February 25, 2021, the Saihanba Mechanical Forest Farm was honored with the title of National Model for Poverty Alleviation.

(By: Wu Ziguo and Qin Xuewu)

第九章

生态文明

Chapter IX Ecological Civilization

一、水利工程 I. Water Conservancy Projects

1. 引滦工程 Luan River Diversion Project

引滦工程是滦河流域集城市生活用水、工业供水、农业灌溉、发电、防洪、水环境保护于一体的综合性大型水利工程群，包括引滦枢纽工程、引滦入津工程、引滦入唐工程、桃林口水库和引青济秦工程。

进入 20 世纪 70 年代，海河流域水资源日益紧缺，京津唐地区迫切需要解决供水问题，而滦河水资源尚有较大潜力，大规模开发滦河势在必行。根据 1973 年 4 月水电部《关于推迟张坊水库，加快进行引滦工程和统一规划京津供水问题的报告》，潘家口水库、大黑汀水库，于 1985 年、1986 年相继建成；引滦入津工程（即引滦工程北线）、引滦入唐工程（即引滦工程南线），于 1983 年、1984 年先后通水。引滦工程南北线总长 286 千米，是当时中国规模最大的跨流域引水工程。

引滦工程使潘家口、大黑汀、桃林口、于桥、邱庄、陡河六座水库连通。潘家口水库居最上游，水库容量最大，是调蓄引滦工程水量的关键。

通过引滦工程及相关河道，潘家口、大黑汀、于桥三座水库可向天津市供水，潘家口、大黑汀、邱庄、陡河四座水库可向唐山市供水，桃林口水库可向秦皇岛市供水，同时，作为天津、唐山、秦皇岛三市重要引水源地，潘家口、大黑汀、桃林口三水库均可向唐山、秦皇岛的滦河下游进行农业供水。

（作者：秦学武）

The Luan River Diversion Project is a comprehensive, large-scale water conservancy project group in the Luan River basin integrating urban domestic water supply, industrial water supply, agricultural irrigation, power generation, flood control and water environment protection. It consists of Luan River Diversion Multipurpose Project, Luan–Tianjin Water Diversion Project, Luan–Tangshan Water Diversion Project, Taolinkou

Reservoir Project and Qinglong-Qinhuangdao Water Diversion Project.

As the water shortage in the Haihe River basin became increasingly serious in the 1970s, how to ensure water supplies of Beijing, Tianjin and Tangshan became a pressing question. Since the Luan River had so much unrealized potential, it was imperative to develop its water resources on a large scale. In April 1973, the Ministry of Water and Power delivered the "Report on Delaying the Construction of Zhangfang Reservoir, Speeding up the Luan River Diversion Project and Solving the Water Supply Problems of Beijing and Tianjin under a Unified Program". According to the report, the Panjiakou Reservoir and the Daheiting Reservoir should be built in 1985 and 1986; the Luan–Tianjin Water Diversion Project (Luan River Diversion Project's North Route), and the Luan–Tangshan Water Diversion Project (Luan River Diversion Project's South Route) would begin to supply water in 1983 and 1984. Running 286 kilometers from south to north, it was the largest interbasin water diversion project in China of that time.

The Luan River Diversion Project connects Panjiakou, Daheiting, Taolinkou, Yuqiao, Qiuzhuang and Douhe reservoirs. The Panjiakou Reservoir in the upstream, with the largest capacity for water storage, is key to regulating the amount of water stored and diverted.

Thanks to the Luan River Diversion Project and the relevant river courses, the water supply of Tianjin has been ensured by Panjiakou, Daheiting and Yuqiao reservoirs, the water supply of Tangshan by Panjiakou, Daheiting, Qiuzhuang and Douhe reservoirs, and the water supply of Qinghuangdao by Taolinkou Reservoir. Meanwhile, as the important water sources of Tianjin, Tangshan and Qinhuangdao, Panjiakou, Daheiting and Taolinkou reservoirs can also supply water to the crops in the lower reaches of the Luan River in Tangshan and Qinhuangdao.

(By: Qin Xuewu)

2. 引滦枢纽工程 Luan River Diversion Multipurpose Project

引滦枢纽工程坐落在河北省迁西县境内的滦河干流上，由潘家口水库、大黑汀水库和引滦枢纽闸组成。它与引滦入津工程、引滦入唐工程，是20世纪80年代建成的大型跨流域调水工程。1983年，引滦工程管理局成立，隶属于水利部海河水利委员会，负责潘家口水库、大黑汀水库和引滦枢纽闸的维护、管理和运行。

（1）潘家口水库

潘家口水库是华北地区最大的水库之一，是开发滦河水资源的控制性工程，以向天津、唐山两市供水为主，兼顾发电、防洪，为多年调节水库。它与引滦工程保障了京津唐地区的供水安全，是华北地区带有全局性的战略工程。

潘家口水库工程包括水库大坝、下池枢纽、两座副坝和坝后式电站，分两期施工：一期工程1975年10月开工，1980年开始蓄水，1983年引滦入津工程建成通水；二期工程1984年夏动工，1985年基本竣工并投入运行，1988年7月通过国家验收。

潘家口水库流域面积3.37万平方千米，总库容29.3亿立方米。主坝全长1039米，最大坝高107.5米，最大泄洪能力43,300立方米/秒。防洪标准为千年一遇。

滦河来水量年内分布不均，年际变化悬殊。潘家口水库多年年均水量19.5亿立方米，除补充下游农业用水外，向天津市供水10亿立方米，向唐山市供水3亿立方米。

40年来，潘家口水库防洪减灾效益显著。截至2020年8月，先后调蓄1000立方米/秒以上的洪水12次，2000立方米/秒以上的洪水9次。1994年7月，滦河流域发生有水文记录第二位的洪水，入库洪峰达9870立方米/秒。水库为下游连续错峰8小时，防洪减灾效益达17亿元。

依托潘家口水库建成的蟠龙湖是国家级水利风景区，湖区面积约

潘家口水库（摄影：王爱军）
Panjiakou Reservoir (Photographed by Wang Aijun)

150平方千米，号称"北国江南"。湖区呈狭长形，地跨迁西、承德、兴隆、宽城四县。

（2）大黑汀水库

大黑汀水库位于潘家口水库主坝下游30千米的滦河干流上，包括宽缝式砼拦河坝一座、坝后式水电站两座、110千伏高压开关站一座。1982年开工，1986年建成使用。

大黑汀水库为年调节水库，流域面积1400平方千米，库容3.37亿立方米。主坝长1354.5米，最大坝高52.8米，最大泄洪能力60,750立方米/秒。防洪标准为百年一遇。

大黑汀水库的作用是承接上游潘家口水库的调节水量，提高水位，为跨流域引水创造条件，同时拦蓄潘家口、大黑汀区间来水，为唐山市、天津市及滦河下游工农业及城市用水提供水源，并利用输水进行发电。

（3）引滦枢纽闸

引滦枢纽闸位于大黑汀水库渠首，左侧闸为入唐闸，右侧闸为入津闸，控制引水流量160立方米/秒。

（作者：秦学武）

大黑汀水库（摄影：王爱军）
Daheiting Reservoir (Photographed by Wang Aijun)

Located on the main stream of the Luan River in Qianxi County, Hebei Province, the Luan River Diversion Multipurpose Project consists of Panjiakou Reservoir, Daheiting Reservoir and Luan Water Diversion Hub. This project, the Luan–Tianjin Water Diversion Project, and the Luan–Tangshan Water Diversion Project are three large scale interbasin water diversion projects completed in the 1980s. In 1983, the Luan River Diversion Project Management Bureau was established. Affiliated with the Haihe River Water Conservancy Commission, MWR, it is responsible for the maintenance, management and operation of Panjiakou Reservoir, Daheiting Reservoir and Luan Water Diversion Hub.

(1) Panjiakou Reservoir

As one of the largest reservoirs in North China, the Panjiakou Reservoir is key to develop the water resources of the Luan River. While also useful for flood control and power generation, the primary purpose of this overyear regulation reservoir is to provide water for Tianjin and Tangshan. As a strategic project in North China with overall importance, it, together with the whole Luan River Diversion Project, ensures the water supply security of the Beijing-Tianjin-Tangshan region.

The Panjiakou Reservoir project includes a main dam, a lower reservoir dam, two auxiliary dams, and a hydropower station at dam toe. There were two stages of construction. The first stage commenced in October 1975, and water storage began in 1980. In 1983, the Luan–Tianjin Water Diversion Project was completed, and the water supply began. The second stage commenced in the summer of 1984. It was completed and put into operation in 1985. In July 1988, the project passed the national inspection.

The Panjiakou Reservoir has a drainage area of 33,700 square kilometers, and its total storage capacity is 2.93 billion cubic meters. The main dam is 1,039 meters long and 107.5 meters high, and it has a maximum flood discharge capacity of 43,300 m^3/s. The dam is expected to withstand 1,000-year floods.

The water flow of the Luan River is uneven and shows great annual variation. The Panjiakou Reservoir, with an average annual capacity of 1.95 billion cubic meters, serves to irrigate the crops in the lower reaches while providing 1 billion cubic meters of water to Tianjin and 300 million cubic meters of water to Tangshan every year.

Over the past 40-some years, the Panjiakou Reservoir has proved effective in flood control and disaster alleviation. As of August 2020, it had controlled 12 floods of more than 1,000 m^3/s and 9 floods of more than 2,000 m^3/s. In July 1994, the Luan River basin encountered the second largest recorded flood with a peak flow of 9,870 m^3/s. The reservoir continuously shifted the peak for 8 hours for the lower reaches, reducing 1.7 billion yuan of losses.

The Panlong Lake in the Panjiakou Reservoir, with an area of 150 square kilometers, is a National Water Park and has a reputation as "Jiangnan in the North". The long, narrow lake spans Qianxi, Chengde, Xinglong and Kuancheng counties.

(2) Daheiting Reservoir

Located on the mainstem of the Luan River 30 kilometers down the main dam of the Panjiakou Reservoir, the Daheiting Reservoir consists of a concrete dam across the river, two hydropower stations at dam toe, and a 110 kV high-voltage switchyard. The construction lasted from 1982 to 1986.

As an annual regulation reservoir, Daheiting covers an area of 1,400 square kilometers with a storage capacity of 337 million cubic meters. The main dam is 1,354.5 meters long and 52.8 meters high, and it has a maximum flood discharge capacity of 60,750 m^3/s. The dam is expected to withstand 100-year floods.

The Daheiting Reservoir serves to store the regulated water from the Panjiakou Reservoir in the upper reaches and raise the water level, thus creating conditions for interbasin water diversion. By retaining water between Panjiakou and Daheiting, it also serves to irrigate the crops in the lower reaches of the Luan River, ensure the water supply of Tangshan and Tianjin, and generate electricity from hydropower.

(3) Luan Water Diversion Hub

The Luan Water Diversion Hub is situated at the head of Daheiting's diversion channel, with Tangshan Sluice on the left and Tianjin Sluice on the right. Its maximum diversion flow is 160 m^3/s.

(By: Qin Xuewu)

3. 引滦入津工程 Luan–Tianjin Water Diversion Project

引滦入津工程，是将河北省境内的滦河水引入天津市的集工业、农业和城市供水、防洪、发电为一体的综合性大型水利工程。这是新中国成立后首个跨流域调水工程，也是国家"六五"时期重点建设项目。1984年，引滦入津工程被评为国家优质工程，荣获金质奖。

引滦入津工程由取水、输水、蓄水、净水、配水等工程组成。潘

引滦枢纽闸（摄影：王爱军）
Luan Water Diversion Hub (Photographed by Wang Aijun)

家口水库为水源地，经大黑汀水库抬高水位，起点为引水枢纽右侧闸（即入津闸），经12.4千米引水隧洞穿越滦河与海河分水岭，沿黎河进入天津市蓟州区于桥水库，经水库反调节，下泄设计流量为100立方米/秒，再经宝坻区至宜兴埠泵站，前后经三次提升一次加压送水，分两路进入天津市：一路由明渠入北运河、海河，另一路由暗渠、暗管入天津自来水厂。工程年输水量10亿立方米，最大输水能力60—100立方米/秒，引水线全长234千米，包括隧道、明渠、倒虹吸涵洞、泵站、水库、水闸、变电站、桥梁和水处理厂等215项设施。

20世纪70年代末80年代初，天津所在的海河流域遭遇严重水荒，天津市的城市工业用水和生活用水严重不足。1981年8月，党中央、国务院决定兴建引滦入津工程。

1982年5月11日，引滦入津工程正式开工，高峰时参建人员达17万人。穿越燕山山脉的12.4千米长引水隧洞，是引滦入津的控制性工程。铁道兵第8师和天津驻军198师起到了决定性作用。经过14个月的奋战，隧洞开挖和衬砌任务提前1年多完成。引滦入津工程原定3年工期，实际仅用时16个月。工程总投资11.34亿元。

1983年8月15日，引滦入津工程全线试通水，历时9个昼夜。1983年9月5日8时，潘家口、大黑汀水库和引滦枢纽闸依次提起，工程正式向天津供水。9月11日，甘甜清澈的滦河水流进千家万户，津城百姓彻底告别苦咸水。这一天也成为引滦通水纪念日。

为修建潘家口、大黑汀水库，河北省宽城、迁西、遵化三县的3.07万人迁居他乡，1.91万间房屋、3.34万亩土地被淹没，工程沿线

470　　　　　　　　　　　　　　　　　　　　冀东文化关键词

群众做出巨大的牺牲。

40年来，引滦入津工程取得了显著的经济效益、社会效益和生态效益，为天津全面建设现代化大都市提供了坚实保障。截至2021年，引滦入津工程累计向天津供水260多亿立方米，与南水北调工程共同构成天津市双水源保障格局。

引滦入津工程具有历史意义，是津冀人民心中的宝贵财富。工程建设中，22名战士献出了宝贵的生命。广大建设者用实际行动创造了永不褪色的"引滦精神"：为民造福的伟大思想，顽强拼搏的革命斗志，严肃认真的科学态度，勇于创新的进取精神，团结协作的高尚风格，雷厉风行的工作作风。迁西县、天津市分别树立了引滦入津工程纪念碑。

（作者：王杰彦，秦学武）

The Luan–Tianjin Water Diversion Project is a comprehensive, large-scale water conservancy project integrating industrial, agricultural and urban water supply, flood control and power generation. It is the first interbasin water diversion project after the founding of the People's Republic of China and a key construction project of China during the 6th Five-Year Plan period (1981–1985). In 1984, the Luan–Tianjin Water Diversion Project was granted the honor of National Quality Engineering Award (Gold Award).

The Luan–Tianjin Water Diversion Project consists of water intake, transmission, storage, purification and distribution. The water flows from the Panjiakou Reservoir into the Daheiting Reservoir, and its level is raised by the latter. Starting from the right sluice (Tianjin Sluice) of the Luan Water Diversion Hub, the water flows past the watershed between the Luan River and the Haihe River through a 12.4-kilometer-long intake tunnel. Then it flows along the Lihe River into the re-regulating Yuqiao Reservoir in Jizhou District, Tianjin, with a designed discharge capacity of 100 m^3/s.

At last, the water runs through Baodi District to the Yixingbu Pump Station. After three liftings and one pressurization, the water is delivered to the urban areas of Tianjin through two channels, one being the open channel to the North Canal and the Haihe River, and the other being the closed channel to the Tianjin Water Works. With a maximum water delivery capacity of 60–100 m^3/s and a diversion line of 234 kilometers long, the project can channel 1 billion cubic meters of water annually. There are 215 facilities along the diversion route, including tunnels, open channels, inverted siphon culverts, pump stations, reservoirs, sluices, electrical substations, bridges and water treatment plants.

In the late 1970s and early 1980s, the Haihe River basin suffered from serious water shortage, with insufficient water for both industrial and domestic purposes in Tianjin. In August 1981, it was decided by the CPC Central Committee and the State Council to start the Luan–Tianjin Water Diversion Project.

On May 11, 1982, construction of the Luan–Tianjin Water Diversion Project commenced. At its peak, there were 170,000 workers participating in construction. The 12.4-kilometer-long headrace tunnel running through the Yan Mountains is key to the project. After 14 months of strenuous efforts with the Railway Corps 8th Division and the Tianjin Garrison 198th Division playing a decisive role, the excavation and lining works were completed more than a year ahead of schedule. The Luan–Tianjin Water Diversion Project, which was scheduled for completion in three years, was completed within just 16 months. The total investment was 1.134 billion yuan.

On August 15, 1983, the trial operation began for the whole Luan–Tianjin Water Diversion Project, which lasted for 9 days and nights. At 8:00 on September 5, 1983, the Panjiakou Reservoir, the Daheiting Reservoir, and the Luan Water Diversion Hub were opened, starting to supply water to

Tianjin. On September 11, which has since been designated as a memorial day, the fresh water of the Luan River reached the households in Tianjin, and the citizens no longer needed to drink bitter water.

During the construction of Panjiakou and Daheiting reservoirs, 30,700 people moved out of Kuancheng, Qianxi and Zunhua counties in Hebei Province, and 19,100 houses and 33,400 *mu* of land were flooded. Their sacrifices for the project were tremendous.

Over the past 40 years, the Luan–Tianjin Water Diversion Project has yielded remarkable social, economic and ecological benefits, providing a solid underpinning for developing Tianjin into a modern city. By 2021, the Luan–Tianjin Water Diversion Project had supplied over 26 billion cubic meters of water to Tianjin. The Luan–Tianjin Water Diversion Project and the South-to-North Water Diversion Project together guarantee the water supply of Tianjin.

With profound historical significance, the Luan–Tianjin Water Diversion Project is an invaluable asset in the minds of Tianjin and Jidong people. 22 soldiers gave their lives for its construction. A vast number of builders demonstrated the everlasting "Luan Water Diversion Spirit" with their practical actions. It embodies the idea of benefiting people, the can-do spirit, the earnest and scientific mind, the innovative and creative style, the solidary and noble attitude, and the decisive action. Monuments commemorating the Luan–Tianjin Water Diversion Project have been erected in Qianxi and Tianjin.

(By: Wang Jieyan and Qin Xuewu)

4. 引滦入唐工程 Luan–Tangshan Water Diversion Project

引滦入唐工程是引滦入津工程后又一项跨流域大型调水工程，是国家重点建设项目。工程由引滦入还（还乡河）、邱庄水库、引还入陡（陡河）、陡河水库四大工程组成。

唐山市是华北工业重镇，工业用水居高不下。为缓解唐山市水资源短缺，保障工农业用水和居民生活用水，国家决定修建引滦入唐工程。工程于1978年底开工，1981年缓建，1982年复工，1984年12月26日竣工通水，1985年正式投入运行。工程共开挖石方200余万立方米，浇筑混凝土54万立方米，各种砌石18万余立方米，总投资4.29亿元。时任国务院副总理万里、李鹏等领导人出席了1984年的通水典礼。

引滦入唐工程起点为大黑汀水库引水枢纽的左侧闸（即入唐闸），跨流域输入蓟运河支流还乡河，经邱庄水库调节后，进入引还入陡渠道，最终进入陡河水库，将水输入滦河下游和唐山市区。全程经7条隧洞，6条埋管，16段明渠，2座渡槽，以及水电站、桥闸涵等多项设施，全长52千米，每年输水5—8亿立方米。

截至2020年8月，引滦工程管理局向唐山市和滦河下游分别供水58.18亿立方米、174.82亿立方米。引滦入唐工程缓解了唐山地区水资源供需矛盾，为经济社会发展提供了坚实的水安全保障，取得了巨大的经济效益、社会效益和生态效益。

（作者：王杰彦）

The Luan–Tangshan Water Diversion Project is another interbasin water diversion project following the Luan–Tianjin Water Diversion Project. It is a national key construction project consisting of Luan–Huanxiang Water Diversion Route, Qiuzhuang Reservoir, Huanxiang–Douhe Water Diversion Route and Douhe Reservoir.

Tangshan is an industrial powerhouse in North China consuming large amounts of industrial water. To help alleviate the shortage of water in Tangshan for industrial, agricultural and domestic purposes, China decided to launch the Luan–Tangshan Water Diversion Project. The construction began in the end of 1978. It was suspended in 1981 and resumed in 1982.

On December 26, 1984, the project was completed and water supply began. In 1985, it was officially put into operation. During the construction period, over 2 million cubic meters of rock was excavated, 540,000 cubic meters of concrete was poured, and 180,000 cubic meters of stone blocks were laid. The total investment for the project was 429 million yuan. In 1984, Wan Li and Li Peng, then Vice Premiers of the State Council, attended the water supply ceremony.

The Luan–Tangshan Water Diversion Project starts from the left sluice (Tangshan Sluice) of the Luan Water Diversion Hub. The water then feeds into the Huanxiang River, a tributary of the Ji Canal in another basin. It is regulated by the Qiuzhuang Reservoir before entering the diversion channel from the Huanxiang River to the Douhe River. Finally, it enters the Douhe Reservoir and is supplied to the lower reaches of the Luan River and the urban area of Tangshan. Running for 52 kilometers, the project has a lot of facilities along the route, including 7 tunnels, 6 buried pipes, 16 open channels, 2 aqueducts, a hydropower station, and many bridges, sluices and culverts. Its annual water delivery capacity is 500–800 million cubic meters.

By August 2020, the Luan River Diversion Project Management Bureau has supplied 5.818 and 17.482 billion cubic meters of water to Tangshan and the lower reaches of the Luan River respectively. The Luan–Tangshan Water Diversion Project helps alleviate the shortage of water resources in the Tangshan area, provides solid safeguards for its social and economic development, and yields tremendous economic, social and ecological benefits.

(By: Wang Jieyan)

5. 引青济秦工程 Qinglong–Qinhuangdao Water Diversion Project

引青济秦工程是通过引青龙河水来解决秦皇岛城市供水，兼顾农业用水而兴建的大型跨流域引水工程。

1989 年，秦皇岛市域 1—8 月降水量仅 350 毫米，遭遇到五十年一遇的严重干旱，石河水库蓄水量仅为 2100 万立方米，地上、地下可供水量总共约 3200 万立方米，同期需水量为 4682 万立方米，可用水资源缺口巨大。为解燃眉之急，秦皇岛市政府决定实施引青济秦工程。

工程总投资近 4 亿元。一期工程 1989 年 10 月开工，以洋河水库为界分西线工程和东线工程。西线工程从青龙河桃林口小坝至洋河水库，全长 29.35 千米；东线工程从洋河水库取水至秦皇岛市区，全长 37.41 千米。1991 年 6 月竣工。

随着秦皇岛城市发展，用水量逐年增加。1999 年，石河水库蓄水量 2600 万立方米，可供城市水量约 2000 万立方米，加上柳江和枣园水源地合计供水量 2370 万立方米，剩余 8230 万立方米均由引青济秦工程供水，但一期东线工程年引水量仅 6300 万立方米。为此，秦皇岛市于 2000 年实施了东线一期扩建工程，2006 年 10 月至 2007 年 4 月实施了东西线对接暨东线二期扩建工程。近年来，引青济秦工程相继完成了洋河水库除险加固、西线改造等项目，使工程的功能进一步完善，保障供水能力进一步提高。

引青济秦工程不仅缓解了秦皇岛市的用水压力，还创造了"艰苦创业、无私奉献、团结协作、顽强拼搏"的引青精神。在新的时代征程中，引青精神必将为把秦皇岛建设成一流国际旅游城市注入不竭动力。

（作者：王杰彦）

The Qinglong–Qinhuangdao Water Diversion Project is a large-scale interbasin water diversion project. It diverts water from the Qinglong River to ensure the water supply of Qinhuangdao for both domestic and agricultural purposes.

In 1989, Qinhuangdao received a precipitation of only 350 mm from January to August, experiencing the worst drought in the past 50 years. The water reserve of the Shihe Reservoir was only 21 million cubic meters, and the aboveground and underground water supply totalled only 32 million cubic meters. By contrast, water demand in the corresponding period was 46.82 million cubic meters. There was a huge shortage of available water resources. To relieve the city of water shortage, Qinhuangdao Municipal Government decided to launch the Qinglong–Qinhuangdao Water Diversion Project.

The total investment for the project was nearly 400 million yuan. The first stage commenced in October 1989, with the Yanghe Reservoir serving as the boundary between the west route and the east route. The west route of 29.35 kilometers long runs from the Taolinkou Dam on the Qinglong River to the Yanghe Reservoir. The east route of 37.41 kilometers long delivers water from the Yanghe Reservoir to the urban area of Qinhuangdao. The project was completed in June 1991.

As the city developed, Qinhuangdao's water consumption increased every year. In 1999, the Shihe Reservoir's storage was 26 million cubic meters, with about 20 million cubic meters available for the urban area. Together with the Liujiang River and the Zaoyuan Water Source, the total water supply was 23.7 million cubic meters. As for the remaining 82.3 million cubic meters of water needed, the east route of the Qinglong–Qinhuangdao Water Diversion Project could only supply 63 million cubic meters. Therefore, the Qinhuangdao government implemented the first-state expansion project of the east route in 2000, then connected the east and west routes and implemented the second-stage expansion project of the east route from October 2006 to April 2007. In recent years, the Yanghe Reservoir was reinforced to eliminate danger, and the west route was revamped. The functions of the Qinglong–Qinhuangdao Water Diversion Project have been further improved to better ensure water supply.

The Qinglong–Qinhuangdao Water Diversion Project helps alleviate the shortage of water resources in Tangshan. It also embodies the Qinglong Diversion Spirit of "hard struggle, dedication, solidarity and tenacity". In the new era, the Qinglong Diversion Spirit will inject inexhaustible impetus into Qinhuangdao in its endeavor to become a first-class international tourism city.

(By: Wang Jieyan)

6. 桃林口水库 Taolinkou Reservoir

桃林口水库位于河北省青龙满族自治县二道河村的青龙河上，是一座以城市供水、农业灌溉为主，兼水力发电等功能的大型水利枢纽工程，是"八五"国家重点工程建设项目。

桃林口水库工程于1992年11月开工，1998年12月竣工，2000年8月通过水利部的工程验收。总投资180434万元。坝体为碾压混凝土重力坝，最大坝长500.7米，最大坝高74.5米。防洪标准为千年一遇。

水库流域面积5060平方千米，淹没范围涉及青龙县的8个乡36个行政村103个自然村，淹没耕地4.27万亩，迁移人口4万人。

水库总库容8.59亿立方米，每年可为秦皇岛市供水1.75亿立方米，为卢龙县供水0.07亿立方米，其余供滦河中下游农业灌溉用水，可灌溉面积120万亩。水库电站装机容量2万千瓦，设计年发电量6280万千瓦·时，实际年发电量1124万千瓦·时。

青龙湖国家湿地公园（摄影：张雪松）
Qinglong Lake National Wetland Park (Photographed by Zhang Xuesong)

桃林口水库是秦皇岛、唐山两市的重要水源地，通过引青济秦工程跨流域在洋河水库反调节后向秦皇岛市供水，为其发展提供水安全保证；通过与潘家口、大黑汀水库联合调度，向唐山市的滦河下游灌区供水，使其水资源配置更为优化。

桃林口水库建成后，周边生态环境大幅改善。依托桃林口水库创建的河北青龙湖国家湿地公园，总面积8400公顷。2016年，国家林业局批准青龙湖国家湿地公园试点工作。公园对于维护区域生态安全、保护和恢复湿地生态环境、保障生物多样性具有重要作用。

（作者：王杰彦）

Located on the Qinglong River in Erdaohe Village, Qinglong Manchu Autonomous County, Hebei Province, the Taolinkou Reservoir is a large-scale water conservancy project integrating urban domestic water supply, agricultural irrigation and hydro-electric engineering. It was a key construction project of China during the 8th Five-Year Plan period (1991–1995).

The construction of Taolinkou Reservoir began in November 1992 and was completed in December 1998. In August 2000, the project passed the national inspection of the Ministry of Water Resources of the People's Republic of China. The total investment was 1.80434 billion yuan. The

桃林口水库（摄影：于文江）
Taolinkou Reservoir (Photographed by Yu Wenjiang)

dam is a roller compacted concrete gravity dam, with a maximum length of 500.7 meters and a maximum height of 74.5 meters. It is expected to withstand 1,000-year floods.

The reservoir has a drainage area of 5,060 square kilometers. During its construction, 103 natural villages in 36 administrative villages in 8 townships of Qinglong County, with an arable land of 42,700 *mu*, were flooded, and 40,000 people were relocated.

The total storage capacity of the reservoir is 859 million cubic meters. The annual water deliveries to Qinhuangdao City and Lulong County are 175 million and 7 million cubic meters respectively, and the rest of the water is used for agricultural irrigation in the middle and lower reaches of the Luan River, covering an irrigated area of 1.2 million *mu*. The installed capacity of its hydropower station is 20,000 kW, the designed annual power generation is 62.8 million kW·h, and the actual annual power generation is 11.24 million kW·h.

The Taolinkou Reservoir is an important water source of Qinhuangdao and Tangshan. As a part of the Qinglong–Qinhuangdao Water Diversion

Project, it supplies water to Qinhuangdao by interbasin water diversion through the re-regulating Yanghe Reservoir, so as to ensure its water security. Combined with the Panjiakou and Daheiting reservoirs, it supplies water to the irrigated area in the lower reaches of the Luan River in Tangshan, so as to optimize the allocation of its water resources.

After the Taolinkou Reservoir was built, the ecological environment in the surroundings was improved substantially. Located in the Taolinkou Reservoir, Hebei Qinglong Lake National Wetland Park covers an area of 8,400 hectares. Under the approval of the National Forestry Administration of the People's Republic of China, the pilot project of Qinglong Lake National Wetland Park began in 2016. The park plays an important role in ensuring ecological security, protecting and restoring ecological environment, and maintaining biodiversity of the local region.

(By: Wang Jieyan)

7. "一渠百库"工程 "One Channel and One Hundred Reservoirs" Project

"一渠百库"是河北省卢龙县最大的水利工程。"一渠"，即引青（青龙河）渠，全长67.5千米。沿引青渠两侧，分布着大小百余座水库湖泊，被誉为"银河下凡"。

卢龙县地处浅山丘陵区，十年九旱。农业生产条件差，粮食产量低，农民生活贫困。干旱缺水严重制约着卢龙的经济社会发展。从20世纪50年代末开始，卢龙县政府先后掀起四次水利建设高潮，建成了以"一渠百库"为骨架的农田水利格局。

第一次水利建设高潮开始于1969年11月，经过7年施工，建成121座小型水库和181座塘坝，配套渠道164.3千米；第二次水利建设高潮开始于1976年底，历时4年，修建了引青灌渠工程，1980年5月1日竣工通水；第三次水利建设高潮开始于1989年10月，在修

修建"一渠百库"（供图：卢龙县文化馆）
Constructing the "One Channel and One Hundred Reservoirs" (Provided by Lulong County Cultural Center)

建引青济秦工程过程中，卢龙县负责修建四条分干渠；第四次水利建设高潮出现在 1999 年，卢龙县开展节水改造和续建配套工程，对引青渠等水利工程进行修缮，最终形成了"一渠百库"工程的总体架构。

"一渠百库"工程，有力促进了卢龙县农业的增产增收，保障了工业生产和生活用水的需求，极大改善了当地的生态环境。2016 年，卢龙一渠百库获批国家级湿地公园，这是全国唯一以人工渠道为特色的国家湿地公园试点。

在长达五十年的接力治水过程中，卢龙县历届政府以功成不必在我的信念，自力更生，艰苦奋斗，团结协作，无私奉献，建成了"一渠百库"工程并使用至今。

（作者：王杰彦）

The "One Channel and One Hundred Reservoirs" Project is the largest water conservancy project of Lulong County, Hebei Province. "One Channel" refers to the 67.5-kilometer-long Qinglong River Diversion Channel. On both sides of the channel, there are more than 100 reservoirs and lakes, which are praised as the "Milky Way Coming to Earth".

Located in a hilly area, Lulong County had been plagued by drought. With bad agricultural conditions, the land here yielded poorly and farmers lived in poverty. Drought and water shortage had seriously restricted the economic and social development of the place. Since the late 1950s, Lulong County had started four upsurges in water conservancy construction, and the pattern of irrigation and water conservancy featuring "One Channel and One Hundred Reservoirs" was formed.

The first upsurge began in November 1969. The construction work lasted seven years, during which period 121 small reservoirs and 181 hilly reservoirs, together with 164.3 kilometers of channels, were built. The second upsurge began in the end of 1976. The construction work lasted four years, during which period the Qinglong River Diversion Channel project was completed. On May 1, 1980, the water supply began. The third upsurge began in October 1989. During the construction of the Qinglong–Qinhuangdao Water Diversion Project, four sub-main channels were built in Lulong County. The fourth upsurge began in 1999. Lulong County carried out water-saving reconstruction, continued to build supporting facilities, and renovated the Qinglong River Diversion Channel and other water conservancy works. At last, the overall pattern of the project featuring "One Channel and One Hundred Reservoirs" was formed.

造福一方百姓（供图：卢龙县文化馆）
Channel for the benefit of people (Provided by Lulong County Cultural Center)

Thanks to the "One Channel and One Hundred Reservoirs" Project, the agricultural yield in Lulong County is greatly increased, industrial and urban domestic water supplies are ensured, and the ecological environment has improved significantly. In 2016, the "One Channel and One Hundred Reservoirs" in Lulong was approved as a National Wetland Park. It is the only such pilot project featuring artificial channels.

For 50 years, successive leaders of Lulong County, guided by the vision of never claiming credit, have been working in relays in water conservancy. With self-reliance, hard struggle, solidarity and selflessness, they completed the "One Channel and One Hundred Reservoirs" that are still being used today.

(By: Wang Jieyan)

二、生态修复 II. Ecological Restoration

8. 开滦国家矿山公园 Kailuan National Mine Park

开滦国家矿山公园位于唐山市路南区，是一座集工业遗迹保护、煤炭文化、近代工业文明展示于一体的大型主题公园。2005年，被国土资源部批准为全国首批国家级矿山公园。

开滦国家矿山公园建设在环境治理后的开滦煤矿废弃矿址上，2007年底筹建，2008年10月建成预展，2009年10月对社会开放。

开滦国家矿山公园，一方面在弃采区发展文化创意产业，将矿山原有部分建筑进行创新设计，重点恢复反映百年开滦历史文化的矿业遗迹；另一方面对塌陷区进行生态修复，扩大园区绿化和水体面积，以体现现代矿业的生态、环保、节能理念。

开滦国家矿山公园由矿业文化博览区、"国保"遗址观光区、时尚文化休闲区三大板块组成，包括开滦博物馆主馆、井下探秘游、中国第一佳矿1878、电力纪元1906、蒸汽机车观光园、中国铁路源头博物馆等一系列展馆和景区，形成了"一园六馆"的布局，展现了中国近代工业的发展和变迁。

核心景点开滦博物馆，展陈面积3000多平方米，展线长600余米。展陈以"黑色长河"为主题，展示了煤的生成过程、悠久的采煤史以及开滦煤矿的发展历程；陈列着中国存世最早的股票——开平矿务局老股票、唐胥铁路的铁轨、"开平矿权骗占案"跨国诉讼《笔录》等藏品、史料。展品丰富翔实，令人遍览百年工业遗迹、感受矿业文化的独特魅力。

开滦国家矿山公园不仅展示开滦煤矿的"黑色魅力"，还弘扬百年老矿的红色基因，如"开滦煤矿工人大罢工"、开滦人"特别能战斗"精神等。

开滦国家矿山公园凸显生态与文化的有机融合，集科普休闲和研学旅游于一体，具有独特的文化魅力和品牌价值。2010年12月，被评为国家AAAA级旅游景区。

（作者：王杰彦）

Located in Lunan District, Tangshan, the Kailuan National Mine Park is a large theme park integrating industrial relics protection, coal culture and modern industrial civilization. In 2005, it was listed among the first batch

开滦国家矿山公园（供图：唐山市政府办公厅）
Kailuan National Mine Park (Provided by the General Office of the Tangshan Municipal People's Government)

of National Mine Parks under the approval of the Ministry of Land and Resources of the People's Republic of China.

The Kailuan National Mine Park was built on the former site of Kailuan Coal Mine abandoned after environmental treatment. It was planned in the end of 2007, completed in October 2008, and opened to the public in October 2009.

Cultural and creative industries have been developed in the abandoned mining area inside the park. Some old buildings have been revamped with innovative ideas to bring to life the century-old mining heritage of the Kailuan Coal Mine. On the other hand, the collapsed area has been restored to expand the green and water area of the park, showcasing the concepts of eco-friendly development, environmental protection and energy saving of modern mining industry.

The Kailuan National Mine Park consists of Mining Culture Exhibition Area, "Major Historical and Cultural Site Protected at the National Level" Area, and Fashion and Cultural Leisure Area. There are many exhibition halls and scenic spots, including Main Hall of the Kailuan Museum,

Underground Exploration Tour, China's Best Mine 1878, Electric Power Era 1906, Steam Locomotive Sightseeing Park, and China Railway's Birth Museum. The layout features "One Park and Six Halls", showing the development and change of China's modern industry.

The Kailuan Museum, located at the center of the park, has an exhibition area of more than 3,000 square meters and an exhibition line of over 600 meters. The theme of the exhibition is "A Black River", which shows us the formation of coal, the long mining history, and the development of Kailuan Coal Mine. The museum displays the oldest stock in China—stock of Kaiping Mining Bureau, the track of Tangshan-Xugezhuang Railway, and the records of the transnational Kaiping Mining Right Infringement Case. The items on display are rich and informative, providing a valuable glimpse of the industrial relics over the past century and the unique charm of mining culture.

The Kailuan National Mine Park displays the "Black Charm" of Kailuan Coal Mine. From Kailuan Coal Mine workers' strike and their "combat-ready" spirit, we can see that the revolutionary spirit has been inherited like blood and genes.

The Kailuan National Mine Park blends ecology and culture. As a place for popular science, leisure, research and tourism, the park has its own cultural enchantment and brand value. In December 2010, it was named a National AAAA Level Tourist Attraction.

(By: Wang Jieyan)

9. 唐山南湖公园 Tangshan South Lake Park

唐山南湖公园全称唐山南湖城市中央生态公园，位于河北省唐山市中心南部670米处，面积近28平方千米。2005年被建设部批准为国家城市湿地公园，2009年被评为国家AAAA级景区，是2016年唐山世界园艺博览会的核心会址。

南湖公园原为开滦煤矿的采空塌陷区，这里曾是垃圾成山、污水横流、杂草丛生的城市废弃地，生态环境遭到破坏，严重影响了城市形象和人居环境。1996年南湖公园开始建设，2005年初具规模，2009年4月29日建成开园。

经过十几年治理，南湖公园已变成绿树成荫、环境友好的城市湿地公园，人工植被与天然植被相呼应，共有植物79科211属327种；为鸟类生存提供了舒适环境，共有鸟类13目33科82种，其中国家Ⅱ级重点保护鸟类7种。公园保留了煤矿、井架等工业元素与历史记忆，周边市民的生活环境得到改善，是城市棕地改造的代表。

南湖公园现有南北两个园区，北园以大型的自然山水景观为主，兼顾服务于市民的休闲娱乐功能；南园以生态保护和生态恢复功能为主。现有小南湖公园、南湖国家城市湿地公园、地震遗址公园、南湖运动绿地、国家体育休闲基地、南湖紫天鹅庄、凤凰台公园、植物园等大小公园，融自然生态、历史文化和现代文化于一体。

南湖公园是中国首个城市采煤塌陷区进行景观再生的案例，先后获2002年度中国人居环境范例奖，2004年迪拜国际改善居住环境最佳范例奖，2009年联合国人居署HBA·中国范例卓越贡献最佳奖，成为维护城市生态安全、保护和修复城市生态系统的典范。

（作者：王杰彦）

The Tangshan South Lake Park, its full name Tangshan South Lake Central Ecological Park, is 670 meters south of the center of Tangshan and covers an area of nearly 28 square kilometers. In 2005, it was named a National Urban Wetland Park by the Ministry of Construction of the People's Republic of China. In 2009, it was named a National AAAA Level Tourist Attraction. It was the main venue of 2016 Tangshan International Horticultural Expo .

Once a subsidence area of Kailuan Coal Mine, the South Lake Park had

Tangshan South Lake Park (Provided by the General Office of the Tangshan Municipal People's Government)

been an abandon land in Tangshan. It was piled up with waste, drenched in dirty water, and overgrown with wild grass. The ecological damage severely affected the image and living environment of the city. In 1996, the construction of the South Lake Park commenced. In 2005, the park began to take shape. On April 29, 2009, it was completed and opened.

After a dozen years, the South Lake Park has transformed into a tree-shaded, environmentally friendly urban wetland park, with the artificial vegetation echoing with the natural vegetation. There are 327 species of plants of 211 genera of 79 families, making the park a comfortable habitat for birds under 82 species of 33 families of 13 orders, of which 7 species are National Grade II Key Protected Birds. The park keeps the historical and industrial elements such as the coal mine and the headframe, and enhances the living environment of people in the neighborhood. It is a representative of brownfield transformation in the city.

The South Lake Park is divided into the north and south park areas. The north park area features large natural landscape while providing leisure sports facilities for the citizens, and the south park area is mainly oriented toward ecological protection and restoration. There are large and small subareas, such as Small South Lake Park, South Lake National Urban Wetland Park, Earthquake Site Park, South Lake Grassy Sports Field, National Sports and Leisure Base, South Lake Purple Swan Villa, Phoenix Terrace Park and Botanical Garden, integrating natural environment, historic culture and modern culture.

The South Lake Park is China's first case of landscape regeneration in an urban coal mining subsidence area. It won the 2002 China Habitat Environment Example Prize, the 2004 Dubai International Award for Best Practices to Improve the Living Environment, and the 2009 UN Habitat Business Award for Sustainable Urbanization (Special Contribution for Practice in China). The park has become a model of urban ecological security and urban ecosystem protection and restoration.

(By: Wang Jieyan)

三、地质公园 III. Geopark

10. 柳江国家地质公园 Liujiang National Geopark[1]

柳江国家地质公园位于河北省秦皇岛市，包括柳江盆地、北戴河、山海关国家级旅游区和昌黎黄金海岸国家级自然保护区、海滨国家森林公园、长寿山国家森林公园及祖山自然保护区，面积650平方千米。2002年2月，被国土资源部批准为国家地质公园。

---

[1] 齐童，乔晓红：《柳江国家地质公园地质遗迹评价》，2010年《中国地质学会旅游地学与地质公园研究分会第25届年会暨张家界世界地质公园建设与旅游发展战略研讨会论文集》。
Qi Tong and Qiao Xiaohong: "Geological Relics Evaluation of Liujiang National Geopark", 2010, *Proceedings of the 25*th *Annual Conference of Geological Society of China's Tourism Geoscience and Geopark Research Branch and the Seminar on Zhangjiajie Global Geopark's Construction and Tourism Development Strategies.*

柳江国家地质公园以柳江盆地的古生物化石、地层遗迹、岩溶地貌、花岗岩地貌为特色，被称为华北地台地质演化的教科书，是我国现代地质学的发祥地之一，人称地质学家的摇篮。柳江盆地是其核心部分，位于秦皇岛市区北 12 千米，有 240 平方千米，包含典型层型剖面、生物化石组合带地层剖面、岩性岩相建造剖面及典型地质构造剖面和构造形迹等地质遗迹，面积小而丰富，极具科学研究价值。

柳江国家地质公园大体分两部分：地质遗迹保护区和外围旅游景观区，以地质遗迹资源丰富、景观类型多样而闻名。柳江盆地是地质遗迹保护区的核心。1999 年河北省政府批准建立柳江盆地地质遗迹省级自然保护区，2005 年经国务院批准晋升为国家级自然保护区。

地质遗迹保护区，包括 9 个一级保护区：张岩子 - 东部落地层剖面区，沙河寨地层剖面区，东部落 - 潮水峪 - 半壁店地层剖面区，亮甲山地层剖面区，石门寨西 - 瓦家山地层剖面区，黑山窑 - 大洼山地层剖面区，鸡冠山地堑构造区，吴庄背斜构造区，沙锅店保护区；2 个二级保护区：山羊寨哺乳动物化石点，沙河寨地层剖面点。

外围旅游景观区包括地质地貌景观区、人文历史景观区及山水风光景区。

地质地貌景观区主要有流水地貌、岩溶地貌、冰冻地貌、花岗岩地貌、海蚀地貌等类型，以燕山期花岗岩风化地貌为主要特色，如祖山、长寿山、角山、燕塞湖等景区。

人文历史景观包括董家口长城、板厂峪长城砖窑遗址群、九门口长城、花场峪、苇子峪长城、傍水崖古战场、旱门关长城等，体现自然与人文景观的完美结合。

山水风光景观区包括北戴河景区、山海关景区、黄金海岸景区等。

2009 年，柳江盆地地质遗迹国家级自然保护区建成了集教学实习、科学研究、科普展示于一体的地学博览园。2018 年，柳江国家地质公园被教育部评为"全国中小学生研学实践教育基地"。

（作者：王杰彦）

Located in Qinhuangdao, Hebei Province, the Liujiang National Geopark consists of Liujiang Basin, Beidaihe, Shanhaiguan National Tourist Attraction, Changli Gold Coast National Nature Reserve, Coastal National Forest Park, Changshou Mountain National Forest Park, and Zushan Mountain Nature Reserve. It covers an area of 650 square kilometers. In February 2022, it was designated by the Ministry of Land and Resources of the People's Republic of China as a National Geopark.

The Liujiang National Geopark features the paleontological fossils, stratigraphic remains, karst landforms and granite landforms in the Liujiang Basin, thus being called a textbook on the geological evolution of North China Platform. As a birthplace of China's modern geology, it has become known as the cradle of geologists. The Liujiang Basin at its center is located 12 kilometers north of Qinhuangdao urban area. Covering an area of 240 square kilometers, it consists of geological relics such as typical stratotype sections, biostratigraphic assemblage zone sections, lithology and lithofacies sections, and typical geological structural sections and structural features. Though relatively small, the area boasts a rich variety of geological features and great scientific research value.

The Liujiang National Geopark can be broadly divided into two parts: geological relics protection area and peripheral tourist scenic area. It is famed for its abundant geological relics and diversified landscapes. The Liujiang Basin is the core of the geological relics protection area. In 1999, the People's Government of Hebei Province gave an approval for the establishment of Liujiang Basin Geological Relics Provincial Nature Reserve. In 2005, it was upgraded to a National Nature Reserve with the approval of the State Council.

The geological relics protection area includes nine Grade I protection areas and two Grade II protection areas. The nine Grade I protection areas are Zhangyanzi-Dongbuluo Stratigraphic Section Area, Shahezhai Stratigraphic Section Area, Dongbuluo-Chaoshuiyu-Banbidian Stratigraphic Section Area, Liangjiashan Stratigraphic Section Area, Shimenzhaixi-Wajiashan Stratigraphic Section Area, Heishanjiao-Dawashan Stratigraphic Section Area, Jiguanshan Graben Structure Area, Wuzhuang Anticline Structure Area and Shaguodian Protection Area. The two Grade II protection areas are Shanyangzhai Mammalian Fossil Site and Shahezhai Stratigraphic Section Spot.

The peripheral tourist scenic area includes geological and geomorphic landscapes, cultural and historical spots and scenic landscapes.

The geological and geomorphic landscapes include fluvial landforms, karst landforms, frozen landforms, granite landforms and sea erosion landforms, with weathered granite landforms of the Yanshanian Period being the main characteristic. There are Zushan Mountain, Changshou Mountain, Jiaoshan Mountain and Yansai Lake.

The cultural and historical spots include Dongjiakou Great Wall, Heritage Site of Banchangyu Kilns, Jiumenkou Great Wall, Huachangyu Village, Weiziyu Great Wall, Bangshuiya Ancient Battlefield and Hanmenguan Great Wall, presenting a perfect combination of natural and human landscapes.

The scenic landscapes include Beidaihe Scenic Area, Shanhaiguan Scenic Area and Gold Coast Scenic Area.

In 2009, a geoscience exhibition park integrating teaching practice, scientific research and science popularization was built in the Liujiang Basin Geological Relics National Nature Reserve. In 2018, the Liujiang National Geopark was designated by the Ministry of Education as a National Research and Practice Education Base for Primary and Secondary School Students.

(By: Wang Jieyan)

后记 Postscript

　　河北省古属冀州，简称冀。从行政地理讲，今之冀东通常是指河北省东北部的唐山、承德、秦皇岛三市。从历史地理讲，冀东所指范围则有所不同。

　　1928年6月28日，南京国民政府将直隶省更名为河北省，撤销京兆地方，所辖20县划归河北省。1935年，华北五省自治，通州、怀柔、顺义、昌平、密云、平谷、三河、香河、宝坻、宁河、蓟县、玉田、丰润、滦县、遵化、迁安、卢龙、昌黎、乐亭、抚宁、临榆、兴隆等县统称为冀东22县。1938年，冀东抗日大暴动，席卷滦县、昌黎、乐亭、迁安、遵化、丰润、玉田、蓟县、平谷、三河、卢龙、抚宁、密云、通县、顺义、香河、宝坻、宁河、武清、兴隆、青龙等21县。

　　新中国成立后，1952年撤销察哈尔省，察南、察北两个专区划归河北省。1956年撤销热河省，大部分辖区划归河北省。之后，原属河北省的部分县转隶北京、天津。1956年至1958年，河北省的昌平、通县、顺义、大兴、良乡、房山、密云、怀柔、平谷、延庆等县划归北京市。1973年，河北省的蓟县、宝坻、武清、静海、宁河等县划归天津市。遂形成河北省现在的辖区规模。

　　可见，20世纪上半叶的冀东曾涵盖今天北京市的通州、怀柔、顺义、昌平、密云、平谷等区，天津市的宁河、宝坻、蓟州、武清等区，廊坊市的香河、大厂、三河等县市，以及唐山市全境、秦皇岛市全境和承德市兴隆县、宽城县。从文化赓续看，冀东所指区域在20世纪呈现出北扩东移的历史进程。

冀东地区历史悠久、文化底蕴深厚，如何通过130余条关键词，文图并茂、由点及面地构建起冀东文化的整体样貌，在学术上无疑具有探索性；同时，撰写这样一部学科领域众多且兼具专业性和通俗性的文化著述，也深具挑战性。这种挑战不仅关涉体系框架是否科学、关键词是否权威、内容表述是否专业，还要克服新冠疫情带来的诸多限制以及资料收集的庞杂性、图片征集的复杂性等困难。很多问题看似简单，但在内容细节的真实、专业表述的精准、外文翻译的得体等方面，都要以严肃、谦谨的态度去处理。

本书是冀东文化团队集体智慧的结晶。选题立项和内容大纲通过了冀东文化研究中心学术委员会的专家论证。根据专家和业界的意见，团队对内容大纲进行了修改完善。秦学武、吴子国、王杰彦、李文钢、赵桂华、王芳、王妹娟、罗学锋、王海军参加了文稿的写作。秦学武负责文稿的统筹、修改和定稿工作。秦学武和吴子国负责图片的征集工作。

本书在前期调研和图片征集过程中得到了唐承秦三市的相关部门及各界人士的大力支持和无私帮助。特别感谢来自秦皇岛市政协、旅游和文化广电局、昌黎县、青龙满族自治县、卢龙县、抚宁区、山海关区、唐山市政府办公厅、退役军人事务局、教育局、丰润区、滦州市、迁西县、玉田县、乐亭县、滦南县、迁安市，承德市教育局、检察院、宽城满族自治县、丰宁满族自治县、围场满族蒙古族自治县、平泉市、隆化县、滦平县，保定市定兴县，以及河北科技大学、河北农业大学、唐山师范学院、唐山市评剧团、秦皇岛日报社、承德博物馆、冀东烈士陵园、热河革命烈士纪念馆、秦皇岛市摄影家协会、中国孤竹文化研究中心、滦河文化研究会、昌黎文化研究会等单位的领导、专家和广大朋友。名单恕不一一列出。

本书在编写过程中还得到了河北省教育厅科技处、河北科技师范学院的有关领导、专家的鼎力支持。外语教学与研究出版社的领导和编辑对本书的出版和学术外译也给予了全方位支持，在此一并深表谢忱！

弘扬冀东文化，讲好中国故事的冀东篇章，是我们的共同追求。但撰写这样一部领域众多、时空跨度大、体例出新的著述，我们深感力有不逮。尽管我们组建了多学科的写作团队，并且得益于专家和业界的无私帮助，但仍心怀忐忑，恳请各界朋友批评指正！

秦学武

Hebei Province, Ji for short, was administered by Jizhou Prefecture in ancient times. In terms of administrative geography, today's Jidong (Eastern Hebei) generally refers to Tangshan, Chengde and Qinhuangdao cities in the northeast of Hebei Province. In terms of historical geography, the scope of Jidong is different.

On June 28, 1928, the Nanjing National Government of the Republic of China renamed Zhili Province to Hebei Province. Jingzhao Region was abolished and its 20 counties were put under the governance of Hebei Province. In 1935, the five provinces in North China achieved autonomy. Tongzhou, Huairou, Shunyi, Changping, Miyun, Pinggu, Sanhe, Xianghe, Baodi, Ninghe, Jixian, Yutian, Fengrun, Luanxian, Zunhua, Qian'an, Lulong, Changli, Laoting, Funing, Linyu and Xinglong were known collectively as the 22 counties in Jidong. In 1938, the Riot against Japanese Aggression in Jidong swept through Luanxian, Changli, Laoting, Qian'an, Zunhua, Fengrun, Yutian, Jixian, Pinggu, Sanhe, Lulong, Funing, Miyun, Tongxian (Tongzhou), Shunyi, Xianghe, Baodi, Ninghe, Wuqing, Xinglong and Qinglong counties.

After the founding of the People's Republic of China, Chahar Province was abolished in 1952 and Cha'nan and Chabei special regions were put under the governance of Hebei Province. In 1956, Jehol Province was abolished and most parts of it were put under the governance of Hebei Province. Afterwards, some parts of Hebei Province were put under the governance of Beijing and Tianjin. From 1956 to 1958, Changping, Tongxian, Shunyi, Daxing, Liangxiang, Fangshan, Miyun, Huairou, Pinggu and Yanqing counties were put under the governance of Beijing. In 1973, Jixian, Baodi, Wuqing, Jinghai and Ninghe counties were put under the governance of Tianjin. Thus, the present area administered by Hebei Province was formed.

As we can see, in the first half of the 20th century, besides entire Tangshan, entire Qinhuangdao, and Xinglong and Kuancheng of today's Chengde, Jidong also covered Tongzhou, Huairou, Shunyi, Changping, Miyun and Pinggu, among others, of today's Beijing; Ninghe, Baodi, Jizhou and Wuqing, among others, of today's Tianjin; and Xianghe, Dachang and Sanhe, among others, of today's Langfang. From the perspective of cultural evolvement, the area of Jidong had gone through a northern expansion and eastern shift in the 20th century.

The Jidong area has a long history and profound cultural foundation. To give an overall picture of its culture is quite an academic challenge. We seek to illustrate in microcosm what the place is like with some 130 key concepts that combine texts and vivid pictures. This requires expertise in various disciplines and efforts to make the book clear and understandable. The challenge first came from the requirements for a rational framework, authoritative key concepts and professional presentation. Then there was the outbreak of the COVID-19 pandemic that had disrupted our life, as well as the difficulty in data collection and photo solicitation. Many things looked easy, but in fact we had gone through great pains to check up on the details, the technical terms and the translation. A serious and prudent attitude was required in the process.

This book is the crystallization of wisdom of the Jidong Culture Team. The subject and the contents were approved by experts of the Academic

Committee of the Eastern Hebei Culture Research Center. According to their opinions and after consultation with colleagues, the contents and outlines were further revised. Qin Xuewu, Wu Ziguo, Wang Jieyan, Li Wengang, Zhao Guihua, Wang Fang, Wang Meijuan, Luo Xuefeng and Wang Haijun were engaged in the writing. Qin Xuewu was in charge of the planning, revision and finalization of the draft; Qin Xuewu and Wu Ziguo were in charge of photo solicitation.

In early-stage investigation and photo solicitation, we had gotten an enormous amount of support and help from relevant authorities and personages of all circles of Tangshan, Chengde and Qinhuangdao. We particularly appreciate the CPPCC Municipal Committee of Qinhuangdao, Qinhuangdao Tourism and Cultural Broadcasting Bureau, governments of Changli County, Qinglong Manchu Autonomous County, Lulong County, Funing District and Shanhaiguan District, General Office of the Tangshan Municipal People's Government, Tangshan Municipal Bureau of Veterans Affairs, Tangshan City Education Bureau, governments of Fengrun District, Luanzhou City, Qianxi County, Yutian County, Laoting County, Luannan County and Qian'an City, Chengde City Education Bureau, the People's Procuratorate of Chengde City, governments of Kuancheng Manchu Autonomous County, Fengning Manchu Autonomous County, Weichang Manchu and Mongolian Autonomous County, Pingquan City, Longhua County and Luanping County, the government of Dingxing County of Baoding City, Hebei University of Science and Technology, Hebei Agricultural University, Tangshan Normal University, Tangshan Pingju Opera Troupe, *Qinhuangdao Daily*, Chengde Museum, Jidong Martyrs' Cemetery, Jehol Revolutionary Martyrs' Memorial Hall, Qinhuangdao Photographers Association, China Guzhu Culture Research Center, Luan Culture Research Association, and Changli Culture Research Association.

There is no enumerating the names of leaders, experts and friends involved.

In the writing process, we engaged the support of leaders and experts of Hebei Education Department Science and Technology Division and Hebei Normal University of Science and Technology. The leaders and editors of Foreign Language Teaching and Research Press have given their full support to the editing, translation and foreign publicity of the book. My sincere appreciation to them!

Popularizing Jidong culture—a chapter in the narrative of China, is our shared goal. We have put together a multi-discipline team and gotten help from experts and colleagues, but it still leaves a great deal to be desired, given the wide range of topics, the large span of time and space, and the novelty of the subject. We are utterly humble before the task, and shall be glad if you oblige us with your valuable comments!

Qin Xuewu